THERAPEUTIC CHEF

RECIPES TO PREVENT CANCER, HEART DISEASE AND DIABETES

BY

KRISTIN DOYLE, RN, CNC

THIS BOOK IS DEDICATED TO ALL THE ORGANIC FARMERS.

Author: Kristin Doyle
Illustrations and Cover Design: Abbie Johnson
Editor: Julie Bauer
Copy Editing and Composition: Maggie Brubaker

First Printing, November 2009
Second Printing, May 2010, revised

Printed by CreateSpace

ISBN 978-0-615-32849-2

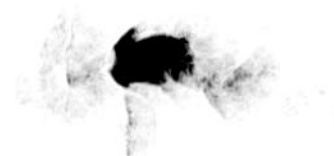

This book is not intended to replace medical advice, diagnosis or treatment. Please talk to your doctor or health care provider before making major changes to your diet or exercise program, especially if you're receiving treatment or taking medications for any illness or disease. For example, if you have Type 2 diabetes and begin eating only healthy foods your need for medication may be reduced. Work with your doctor to safely taper your medications as your diet changes. Also, some herbs/herbal remedies may interfere with certain medications. Always check with your doctor or health care provider first before adding new foods or herbs to the diet.

ACKNOWLEDGMENTS

I owe a tremendous amount of thanks to the following people who helped make this book a reality. To Radha Vignola, teacher and activist who shed light on the importance of a plant-based diet; Kathy Cummins, for her guidance, inspiration and wisdom on the healing benefits of food; and Becky Dienner, for her spunky and positive attitude, delectable kitchen skills and for completing the daunting task of reviewing my recipes and organizing my files.

To Deb Lewis - who can put together the most beautiful and delicious meal you'll ever eat - for carefully reviewing each recipe and adding bling where it belonged. To Herbalist Cara Saunders, for writing the incredible Herbal Remedies section of this book; Abbie Johnson, for providing the adorable illustrations, cover and logo design; Lisa Steffek, for her careful editing; Jennifer Carino, my acupuncturist and friend who was there to heal me when I became stressed or overworked; and Krista, Susanne, Laura, Matty, Jolene and Aaron for always being there to sample my recipes and provide feedback and new recipe ideas.

To Julie Bauer, for giving me the voice I always wanted and for helping with the research; Dr. Lisa Leit, for her positive motivation and spiritual guidance; Maggie Brubaker, the organizer and layout designer with an eye so detailed and clever that this book would not have been possible without her; and to Glenn, for being my rock and keeping me true.

TABLE OF CONTENTS

"The doctor of the future will give no medicine, but will interest his patient in the care of the human frame - in diet and in the cause and prevention of disease."

~ Thomas Edison

Introduction

American consumers and employers will spend over two trillion dollars this year on health insurance, pharmaceutical drugs and medical bills, yet we will remain mentally and physically among the unhealthiest people on earth. Forty-eight percent of U.S. men and 38 percent of women can look forward to getting cancer. Eight percent of our children suffer from serious food allergies, 17 percent are diagnosed with learning or behavioral problems, and a third of low-income preschool kids are already overweight or obese. Heart disease, diabetes, mental illness, cancer and obesity are spiraling out of control among all sectors of the population. (www.consumersassociation.org.)

Sickness isn't an accident, it's the result.

Most chronic health problems are not directly genetic or inherited. They are caused by the consumption of highly processed, nutritionally-deficient foods and our sedentary lifestyles. Seventy percent of U.S. deaths are related to diet, particularly saturated animal fats and processed foods. Approximately one third of young people today are expected to develop diabetes, a completely avoidable illness.

Processed, refined foods make up 82 to 92 percent of the food we buy in the U.S. We eat more sugar, fat and meat than ever before. But instead of focusing on what we ingest, how it affects us, and getting to the root of the problems, we have been unsuccessfully treating diet related symptoms with cholesterol lowering drugs, blood sugar medications, anti-inflammatory drugs, antidepressants, antacids, pain killers and sleeping pills. I do agree that sometimes there is a need for pharmaceuticals but most of the time we will fare better if we aim to prevent illness by eating right. Put an end to the vicious cycle of masking a poor diet with Band-Aid pharmaceuticals by eating whole plant foods.

Chronic ill health can be prevented and reversed through exercise and a healthy diet. Research clearly shows that changing how we live is a much more powerful intervention for preventing heart disease, cancer and diabetes than any medication or risky surgical procedure. The recipes in this book are full of ingredients that will restore the body's natural ability to heal itself, lower cholesterol and blood pressure, stabilize blood sugar and brain chemicals, alleviate pain and reduce inflammation naturally.

Your body is your temple. Honor it and it will honor you. It is for you, and your desire to be healthy, that I write this book.

There is no magic recipe for everyone's health. As snowflakes are individually unique, so are we. Your best course is to listen to your body and notice how it feels. Take it slow. Introduce one new food at a time. Talk to your doctor about any changes you make to your diet and exercise plan.

Bottom line - the American diet is too high in fat, sugar and animal protein. And it's too low in fiber, whole grains and fruits and vegetables. It's time for a change. Inside, you'll learn about the smart plant foods - the cruciferous and the colorful - that provide antioxidants to help fight disease and illness. You'll learn about beans, whole grains and healthy fats and why you need these foods to maintain good health.

Make each bite count. Why spend money on foods with little nutrition and cause health problems when you can eat something that prevents illness and tastes great? Buy foods in their natural state. Choose whole plant foods over animal foods. This is not a trendy diet. This is how many long-life cultures around the planet have been eating for thousands of years. Accept no refined sugar, processed soy, trans-fats, and excessive amounts of animal protein, cholesterol and fat. It's time to take our health back into our own hands. It is possible and it is worth it. As you try new foods, and give them a chance to work their magic, your body will tell you what it likes. As you increase your intake of whole grains, vegetables and legumes, you'll easily reject refined grains, fried potatoes with ketchup and hotdogs. When you are ready, develop your own meal plan by remembering these simple rules:

- Build your meal around the whole grain. Seek out gluten-free whole grains most of the time (or all of the time if you suffer from a wheat or gluten intolerance). Gluten is a protein in wheat, rye and barley and sometimes oats.

- Eat at least seven servings of vegetables and fruit each day, some raw, some lightly cooked.

- Get your protein from plants (beans, lentils, split peas, nuts, seeds, whole grains). If you eat 100 percent plant foods, include a daily vitamin B12 supplement.

- Eliminate all dairy products. Eat beans and greens for healthy bones.

- Avoid the unhealthy fats (saturated animal fats, trans-fats and refined vegetable oils). Include a healthy fat at each meal but don't overdo it (avocados, olives, nuts and seeds).

- Avoid refined sugars (especially high fructose corn syrup), trans-fats and all processed fake foods. Eat real foods.

Changing your diet to the recipes in the book will drastically reduce your risk for heart disease, cancer and diabetes. This same way of eating will help you maintain a healthy weight and benefit the environment.

HOW TO USE THIS BOOK

The idea is that if you follow the recipes in this book you will have a decreased risk of developing the illnesses of our current low-nutrient, fast-paced food culture. Eating a healthy diet consisting of whole grains, plant sources of protein, lots of colorful vegetables and fruit, and small amounts of healthy fat, while avoiding refined sugars, processed foods and animal foods is the general concept of this book. It is this way of eating that provides your body with the most antioxidants, fiber and health promoting foods. Each ingredient used in the recipes was chosen for its therapeutic value. All of the recipes in this book were developed to be used to help prevent cancer, heart disease and diabetes. Some recipes are more targeted than others to a particular ailment, such as arthritis or cancer, so refer to the index for those specific recipes.

Some recipes feature a 'powerfood,' or healing ingredient. These are signified by a picture of a spoon, with the featured ingredient on the spoon, and the medicinal properties of this ingredient explained at the top of the recipe in the shaded box. Also, don't be intimidated if you aren't familiar with some of the foods used in this book. See page 456 for tips and a list of easy recipes so you can start eating healthy right away.

The icons in the recipe section depict helpful nutrition information and kitchen tips to make your therapeutic cooking experience more complete. Here are the icons and their meanings:

Shopping Basket - shopping instructions and optional ingredient suggestions

Pot - additional cooking and preparation tips

Bowl - serving suggestions

Cup - serving suggestions for beverages

Fridge - storage tips

Spoon with Apple - therapeutic and nutritional information

Medical Symbol - health and allergy information

Star with Heart - general tips and information

Lightbulb - idea

GF Gluten-Free Symbol

The Whole Plant Food Diet

Your Body Will Thank You

If you weren't serious about good health, you wouldn't be reading this book. A diet of whole plant foods will lower your risk of heart disease, cancer, diabetes and a host of other illnesses common to the Western world. If you are over 50, it could mean your latter years are active, energetic and pain-free.

Once a whole food is plucked off the tree or pulled out of the ground it begins to lose nutrients, so the fresher the better. Plant foods should be purchased in the same form as they were grown, not sliced, diced, preserved or otherwise processed. The least amount of processing - or cooking - a food undergoes, the more nutritional value it retains.

Plant foods - whole grains, nuts, seeds, peas and beans (legumes), fruits and vegetables - contain all the nutrients your body needs except for vitamin B12. This you will need to take as a supplement if you eat only plant foods.

You do not need meat for protein. Nor do you need milk, cheese or eggs. When you depend on these foods for protein or calcium, you eat less plant food, causing deficiencies. Many health issues begin with nutritional deficiencies that start with an inadequate diet.

Plant Foods for Protein

The first thing to realize is that the average American eats more protein than needed. More is NOT better. Consuming excessive meat protein puts a strain on the kidneys and can lead to bone loss, due to the acid-forming properties of most animal foods.

Protein yields approximately four calories per gram. The recommended level of protein intake for the general population is only 10 to 12 percent of the total calorie intake in a day, unless you are pregnant or a body builder. Most non-athletes do well with 0.36 grams of protein per pound of body weight. Using this guideline, a 165-pound woman has a protein requirement of 59 grams per day.

Instead of high cholesterol, artery-clogging saturated fats from animal foods, think beans, whole grains, and nuts and seeds for protein. It is no longer believed that vegetarians have to combine a certain bean with a certain grain to make a complete protein. We are learning new things about nutrition all the time and we now know that if you eat a variety of beans, nuts and seeds, whole grains, fruits and vegetables each day you will get all the amino acids, vitamins and minerals you need to stay healthy, while avoiding harmful cholesterol and saturated fats.

One cup of cooked black beans contains approximately 15 grams of protein, two tablespoons of hemp seeds contain 5 grams of protein and in one cup of cooked millet there are 6 grams of protein. All plant food contains a little protein. An avocado contains four grams of protein and even a fresh peach has half a gram. (*Nutrition Almanac*, fourth edition)

Ancestry can be important to your food choices. If you have African American, Asian, Native American, Aztec or Mayan ancestry, it's important to eat plant foods. The metabolism of indigenous people from Africa, North and South America are not suited to diets of processed food and meat. Their ancestors ate meat infrequently, and subsisted mainly on grains, berries and seeds. They are particularly susceptible to diabetes and obesity when eating the typical high-fat Western diet.

Quinoa (pronounced Keen-wah) is a complete protein food I highly recommend for people of indigenous ancestry or anyone sensitive to wheat or gluten. Once considered "the gold of the Incas", it is a seed from the Andes that cooks and looks like a grain so I will include it in a list of whole grains. It contains all nine essential amino acids and, when cooked, has a fluffy, creamy, slightly crunchy texture and somewhat nutty flavor. Quinoa is available in your local health food stores throughout the year.

It is easy to get all the protein you need by eating a diet of whole plant foods. If you've tried it in the past without success try again, this time with confidence. Follow the 'whole food' principle or you won't feel the benefits. Potatoes, in the form of french fries, and processed soy 'meats' don't count as whole plant foods and won't improve your health. You must be picky about the quality of your food and always choose nutrient dense ingredients. This may mean more time in the kitchen and shopping more at farmer's markets, but you're worth it!

Soy Protein

Switching from an animal based diet to a plant based diet is definitely the best thing you can do for your health, the health of the farmer, the animals and the planet. But switching to a diet of processed soy foods is not recommended. Many people make the mistake of buying highly processed vegetarian foods made to look like animal foods thinking it must be healthy. However, not all vegetarian foods are made from whole plants. Many are made from plant parts, processed soy and chemicals. A few examples would be tofu corn dogs, sliced soy meats, certain soy veggie burgers and most of the soy cheeses. Please avoid these processed foods.

Soybean-derived foods became popular after studies in Asia revealed that they help reduce the risk of certain cancers and heart disease.

Food manufacturers in the U.S. had a field day with this, adding extremely processed soy (not the same foods as in the research studies) to many packaged foods. The truth is, not all soy is created equal.

Food companies are taking genetically modified soybeans and processing them into unhealthy forms of soy, such as soy protein isolate and textured vegetable protein. These refined soy ingredients are never organic and should not be consumed. Commit this to memory: **Soybean ingredients to avoid** are soy protein isolate, textured vegetable protein, textured soy protein, monosodium glutamate (MSG), soybean oil, hydrogenated soybean oil, hydrolyzed vegetable protein, soy protein powder and soy protein concentrate. These are common ingredients in many packaged foods, such as cereals, breads, snack bars, protein bars and protein powders. You will find these unhealthy ingredients on the labels. However, if you adhere to a whole food, no processed diet, you will have no labels to read.

Most soybeans grown in the U.S. are genetically modified, which is unhealthy for our bodies, the soil and the planet. When you purchase soy products, buy organic. Organic foods cannot be genetically modified.

The healthy soy foods are those made from organic, whole soybeans that have been fermented. Unfermented soybeans contain phytic acid, which interferes with the body's ability to absorb calcium, magnesium and zinc. Once a whole soybean is fermented, the best qualities step forward and the negative effects of the phytic acid are diminished. Fermented soy has amino acids, essential fatty acids and antioxidants not found in processed soy. Foods made from whole, fermented soybeans include miso, tempeh and natto. And remember, always purchase organic soy.

The salty taste and buttery texture of miso, a fermented soybean paste originating in Japan, is becoming increasingly popular in the West as a versatile condiment to flavor soups, dressings and sauces. Add at the end of cooking once the heat has been turned off. Do not boil miso or the beneficial bacteria will be destroyed. Miso should be kept refrigerated.

Tempeh has more protein than hamburger, but none of the bad cholesterol, saturated fats, and cancer promoting IGF-1 found in meat. Cook your tempeh for 15 minutes before using in a recipe. It's a great substitute for meat since it has a similar texture and takes on the flavor of the sauce in a dish. Like meat, it can be cubed, ground, seared, baked, marinated, etc. Meat protein is heavy and sometimes difficult to digest. It requires high amounts of stomach acid, which diminish with age. Fermented soybeans, such as tempeh, are highly recommended for the older crowd as it digests easily (as long as you cook it properly).

Natto, also made from fermented, whole soybeans, is a popular protein food in Japan. Although you won't find any recipes using natto in this book, if you see natto - be brave and try it. You may love it!

Somewhere in the middle are edamame, soy milk and tofu. I don't think these foods are bad for you, but they should be eaten in moderation. This is because these soy foods have not been fermented and research indicates that it is the fermented soy that is nutritionally superior. Plus, soy milk and tofu are in the same category as white bread or white rice. They have been refined, meaning some of the parts have been removed. They are also harder to digest and include nutrient-blocking phytic acid.

It's not the end of the world if you are at a restaurant and order the vegetable tofu stir fry. Tofu contains protein and sometimes calcium, so it does have redeeming qualities. If your choice is between a steak and tofu, tofu is the better option. If you are choosing between tempeh and tofu, tempeh is the better option. Foods containing soy protein isolate or the other extremely processed soy foods mentioned above should never be an option.

If you have an allergy to soy please be aware that many packaged and processed foods contain hidden soy. TVP (textured vegetable protein), TSP (textured soy protein), vegetable oil, mono and diglycerides, MSG and lecithin are some examples. For recipes in this book that call for tamari or shoyu soy sauce you can substitute unrefined sea salt or Himalayan salt, to taste. Soy-free miso is also available.

Dairy Products are Not Good Sources of Calcium - or Food

Dairy consumption in the United States is among the highest in the world, and yet osteoporosis and fracture rates are also among the highest. U.S. food consumers may be the last to know what researchers have known for years - that dairy products do not promote bone health in growing children and young adults.

According to an article in the March 2005 issue of the medical journal Pediatrics, an analysis of 58 published studies found no relationship between dairy intake and bone health, or even that milk is a good source of calcium. The authors recommend that to build strong bones and healthy bodies, children need exercise, sunshine, and a diet rich in fruits and vegetables to help them maintain a healthy body weight.

If you depend on dairy products for calcium, be aware that milk products from animals actually cause calcium to be drawn from our bones. What you might gain, you end up losing because animal foods are acid-forming and to compensate, the body pulls calcium from the bones to neutralize the blood pH. Once the calcium has done its job, it is excreted in the urine. Fruits and vegetables, in general, have an alkalizing effect on our system. It takes 5-7 cups of raw fruit or vegetables to balance the acidity in one turkey and cheese sandwich.

Dairy products contain harmful cholesterol and saturated fats, and are hard to digest for many people. Stomachaches, diarrhea, gas and constipation after consuming dairy products are symptoms of lactose intolerance, a lack of the digestive enzymes needed to digest them. This problem is common in the aforementioned indigenous populations and in Asians. Dairy was not common in Asian diets until western foods invaded the East. Now we are seeing obesity and higher rates of diabetes, cancer and heart disease due to this introduction of processed food and larger amounts of animal products.

Dairy products are linked to cancer, diabetes and autoimmune diseases. A factor in animal protein, IGF-1 (insulin-like growth factor), is associated with breast, prostate and ovarian cancers because it promotes the growth of cancer cells. Researchers found a specific dairy protein that causes an autoimmune reaction leading to Type I, or childhood-onset diabetes. Dairy contains proteins difficult for the body to digest and assimilate; causing a sensitivity that can lead to autoimmune disorders. Added to that is the mucous-forming characteristics of dairy that can exacerbate allergies and sinus problems. Many people have told me that after eliminating all dairy products from their diet they no longer needed to take their allergy medication. Even if you aren't 'allergic' to dairy, consuming it can exacerbate allergy symptoms to pollen, dust, mold and pet dander. Stop eating dairy products and you'll feel better on many levels.

Plant Foods for Calcium

Instead of dairy, depend on plant foods for everything you need for strong bones and teeth and a calm nervous system. There are plant foods that contain equal or greater than the calcium content of dairy products. One cup of Swiss chard has 51 milligrams of calcium and raw broccoli has 42 milligrams of calcium. (Nutrition Almanac, fourth edition)

Osteoporosis is lowest in South African countries where people eat more leafy vegetables and less dairy products. Other foods with calcium include green leafy vegetables, peas, chickpeas, Brazil nuts, sunflower seeds, seaweed and walnuts.

Another advantage of plant foods for calcium is that they also include the minerals that work with calcium: potassium and magnesium. Foods high in these nutrients are sunflower seeds, soybeans (fermented), almonds, Brazil nuts, pistachios and pecans. These nutrients are also important to muscle function, most especially the heart.

If you miss your milk, there are many non-dairy milks to choose from. Try unsweetened almond milk or hemp milk. Use it in your whole grain cereal or in any recipe that calls for milk. Try to avoid the commercially prepared non-dairy milks made with sugar. Look for unsweetened versions or follow the recipes in this book to make your own nut or seed milks.

To keep the health benefits of calcium, avoid things that deplete it: excess sodium, caffeine, smoking and animal protein (including milk). Vitamin D is also important to strong bones, and works with calcium to keep it there. You get vitamin D from morning sun or supplements. Weight bearing exercise also strengthens the bones. For healthy bones, it is important to focus on all of these factors.

Probiotics - Natural Digestive Help

Your body contains good and bad bacteria. When all bacteria are killed by antibiotics, the bad guys can proliferate while the good guys are still down for the count. Harmful, or disease-causing, bacteria have Latin names like pseudomonas, aeruginosa, proteus, staphylococcus, clostridia and veillonellae.

Found in supplemental formulas and fermented, or cultured, food, are the body's disease-killing good-guy bacteria, Lactobacilli, Eubacteria and Bifidobacteria. Lactobacilli can inhibit the growth of harmful bacteria, stimulate immune function and aid in digestion, and Eubacteria can inhibit the growth of harmful bacteria. Bifidobacteria can reduce blood ammonia levels, lower cholesterol levels, regulate the immune system, produce vitamins, especially the B vitamin/folic acid group, restore normal intestinal flora during antibiotic therapy, and inhibit the growth of disease-causing germs. (Journal of Nutrition, v. 125)

In recent years, there has been a growing awareness of the medicinal use of beneficial bacteria, termed "probiotics" (from the Greek, "for life"). The medicinal use of beneficial bacteria is not new. In ancient times, the Roman historian, Pliny, recommended fermented beverages containing probiotics to treat gastrointestinal infections. The health benefits of food bacteria depend on the action of live microorganisms, especially lactic acid bacteria, which usually must be refrigerated.

t with active cultures is one way to eat your probiotics. But most yogurt contains ϲeners and artificial ingredients that interfere with the beneficial bacteria, rendering them useless. Plus, yogurt made from an animals' milk (cow, goat, sheep) still contains cholesterol and saturated fat.

Thankfully yogurt isn't the only source of probiotics. Other fermented foods and beverages that contain helpful bacteria are miso, rejuvelac, kombucha, and raw sauerkraut or kimchi (the refrigerated kind).

Supplemental probiotics can be used for a temporary bout of food poisoning or digestive distress (acid reflux, bloating, cramping, Irritable Bowel Syndrome), and supports absorption and assimilation of nutrients in the digestive tract. Probiotics, whether from food or supplements, are essential to keeping your immune system strong and for overall good health. If you don't have a regular source in your diet (miso, raw kimchi or sauerkraut, kombucha, rejuvelac) then take a broad-spectrum probiotic capsule regularly (containing many different species, not just acidophilus). Buy the capsules at a health food store and take as directed. Look for supplements that are dairy-free, and must be refrigerated. Learn to make your own raw kimchi (see in recipes), coconut yogurt or rejuvelac and begin experiencing the benefits of a healthy digestive tract.

While we're at it, digestive distress can be caused by eating too much food at once, eating too fast, too much high-fat food and a lack of hydrochloric - or stomach - acid. Too little stomach acid results in the same symptoms as too much: bloating and pain. This is because there isn't enough acid to fully break down your food, especially if you've eaten meat, and it ferments in the stomach and intestines. Say no to antacids, say yes to cultured food and raw plants that naturally contain enzymes.

Those who do not masticate, nature castigates. The digestive system is a superb orchestra of reactions, begun the moment you put food into your mouth. At the same time saliva is produced to help you chew, enzymes are being released in your mouth, your stomach is producing acid to break down the food, and your liver and pancreas are producing bile and digestive enzymes so the intestines can draw water and nutrients from it, delivering them to your tissues, blood and cells. When you eat too fast and chew too little, the stomach doesn't have enough time to prepare itself and may not have adequate stomach acid to break down the large chunks of food you just swallowed. Raw plant foods also help here. They require more chewing than a soft hamburger and contain essential enzymes to break down food.

Plant Enzymes = Life

All raw plants contain enzymes - living proteins necessary to digest food and for every chemical reaction that takes place in the human body. They are the workers that build our body from proteins, carbohydrates and fats, just as construction workers build our homes.

Their names are protease, amylase, lipase, cellulase and disaccharidases. Protease digests protein, amylase digests carbohydrates, disaccharides digest sugars, lipase digests fats and cellulase digests fiber.

Plant enzymes work in the mouth and stomach where they predigest food and spare the pancreas. The pancreas doesn't have to work as hard and predigested food is less likely to cause allergic reactions - not to mention indigestion.

Every raw food contains exactly the right quantities and types of enzymes necessary to digest that particular food. For example, fruits high in carbohydrates - such as apples - contain high amounts of amylase. Fruits high in fat - such as avocadoes - contain high amounts of lipase.

Although enzymes are present in all raw foods, they lose their viability when cooked or processed. Temperatures greater than 117° F kill enzymes. Even steaming vegetables kills enzymes, as does irradiating or microwaving them. Freezing, however, does not affect them. There are many recipes in this book that use both raw and cooked ingredients. Always include raw foods in each meal, whether it is in the form of a salad with raw vegetables or a piece of fresh fruit.

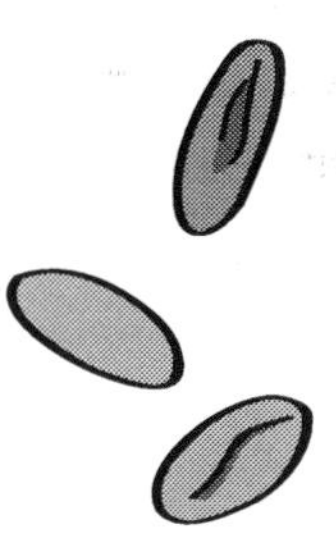

The Truth About Carbs and Fiber

Just as enzymes are necessary for digestive health so, too, are carbohydrates - the good kind that is.

Carbohydrates are important for energy and digestive health. Your liver breaks them down into glucose (blood sugar) and your body uses glucose for energy.

They are called simple or complex, depending on how fast your body digests and absorbs the sugar. Simple carbohydrates include fruits, dairy products, honey and table sugar. Complex carbohydrates include whole grain breads and cereals, starchy vegetables and legumes (beans and peas). Fiber, soluble and insoluble, is also a form of a complex carbohydrate. Fiber is not able to be converted into glucose but still plays an essential role in maintaining health. Soluble fiber absorbs fats and cholesterol in the body. Insoluble fiber helps provide bulk to the stool and promotes regular bowel movements.

You can judge how healthy a carbohydrate food is by looking at the amount of fiber it contains. The more fiber, the more slowly it will be digested, the more nutrient-dense the food will be, and the better it is for your heart, digestion, cholesterol and overall health. Every plant food has fiber. Animal products have no fiber. A lack of fiber increases your risk for cancers of the colon. It also puts you at a high risk for constipation, ulcerative colitis, diverticulitis and other bowel disorders. Unfortunately, the high protein diets were often dangerously low in fiber.

Aim to get about 40 grams of fiber per day from food, not supplements. Fiber powders or supplements are for emergencies only. They do not include the nutrients, enzymes and moisture present in whole foods. Their concentration of fiber can cause bowel blockage and the body can become dependent on them. You will get all the fiber you need if you eliminate foods that are void of fiber (all animal foods, white flour and refined foods) and replace them with beans, nuts and seeds, whole grains and fresh fruits and vegetables. Fiber helps reduce bad cholesterol, keeps blood sugar levels stable, removes toxins and waste from the body, and helps maintain a healthy digestive tract. If you stick to the new food groups; whole grains, beans and other legumes, fruits and vegetables, and nuts and seeds you won't need a fiber supplement.

If you take my advice and increase your intake of fiber, you may initially experience increased bowel movements. Fiber is nature's "rotor rooter." The longer you've been eating processed junk food, the more gunk is probably caked onto the walls of your digestive tract. It will take time for the fiber to do its job and, in the meantime, you may experience some discomfort. Take it slow; gradually increase your fiber intake and drink more water.

Whole Grains are the Key to Good Health

The best carbohydrates are whole grains. Most people don't eat enough, in part because "carbs" recently had a bad reputation. People wanting to lose weight were once told to avoid carbs. The truth is, eating too much of anything will make you gain weight. Yes, avoid the processed and refined carbs (white rice, white flour foods, sugar, etc.) but never avoid the good carbs, especially the whole grains. The fiber in whole grains helps reduce cholesterol, improves digestive health and reduces the kind of cravings that lead to poor eating habits. Plus whole grains contain protein, and vitamins and minerals such as iron and chromium. The good carbohydrates from whole grains are the preferred fuel for our brains. The fad diets of the past underestimated the value of whole grains and look where it got us.

What exactly are whole grains? Whole grains include the bran, the germ, and the endosperm. Whole grains contain B vitamins, iron, magnesium, selenium and fiber. Examples include brown rice, millet, and whole wheat berries.

Whole grains have a low Glycemic Index (GI) rating. This means they are converted slowly into blood glucose, and do not cause sudden rises. By contrast, refined carbs, especially white flour foods, typically have high-GI values that are associated with blood sugar problems and insulin disorders. Without fiber, the calories in refined carbohydrates hit our systems in a flood instead of a trickle. We get a burst of energy (the "sugar high") and then a letdown that makes us crave more calories (the sugar low). We can't burn all the calories so they are stored as fat, and the yo-yo effect of the blood sugar highs and lows creates metabolic problems. Insulin has a hard time doing its job when it is faced with a flood of sugar and fat.

When whole grains are processed into refined grains, the bran and the germ - and the nutrients they offer - are lost. Bread is fortified to add back some of the nutrients, but it will never be as beneficial as its whole food.

At best, bread is processed grains. At worst, it is additive-packed fattening filler, so negative in nutrition that the vitamins and minerals have to be put back in (enriched). Some bread is made with whole wheat flour, which is better than refined flour, but if you buy bread, make sure it has a very short ingredient list. And always avoid all breads and bread products with partially hydrogenated oils, preservatives and high fructose corn syrup.

Choose sprouted whole grain bread if you're going to buy bread. All of the vital nutrients stored within a whole grain are released when sprouted. Sprouting also activates the enzymes necessary to digest it, while retaining all of the grain's fiber. Sprouted grains are rich in protein and vitamins with the proteins and carbohydrates more easily assimilated by the body. A few bread companies use sprouted grains to make bread, pasta, tortillas and cereal. Look for these at your health food store.

Think outside the bread box. Instead of uncertain bread, buy and cook actual whole grains. Plan your meal around your favorite whole grain, such as brown rice or millet. Then add beans, vegetables and a simple sauce using my recipes. This is the best way of maximizing nutrition from a beneficial carbohydrate. Whole grains to look for: amaranth, barley, brown rice, red rice, wild rice, millet, oats, quinoa, teff, buckwheat, and 100 percent whole wheat, bulgur wheat, cracked wheat, kamut, spelt and rye.

Some grains are not tolerated well by certain people. Those who are allergic or sensitive to gluten, a protein in wheat, rye and barley, and sometimes in oats, should avoid these and instead choose gluten-free grains: amaranth, millet, buckwheat, quinoa, brown rice, wild rice, red rice, black rice, teff, and breads, cereal, pastas and tortillas made from these grains. Many feel their digestion and energy levels improve when they remove wheat and gluten foods from their diet. Read labels and beware of foods that are made of wheat, such as spelt, kamut, semolina, coucous, durum, einkorn, emmer and matzah. If you aren't sure, ask. People allergic to gluten can develop celiac disease. For more on gluten foods to avoid, read up on this affliction.

Beans

If you avoid beans because they give you gas, take heart. Gas, caused by a sugar in beans, is easily preventable. First, make sure you cook them properly. Soak dried beans for up to eight hours before cooking, then drain the beans and use the soak water for your house plants. Cook the beans in fresh, filtered water for the required amount of time and don't add any salt, lemon juice or tomatoes until they are cooked through and soft.

Add kombu seaweed to your beans to aid in digestion. You can find it at your health food store or Asian market. Add a five-inch strip of kombu to every pot of beans. Seaweed is a powerful detoxifier and is full of essential minerals. Learn to love all types of seaweed for their cleansing and impressive mineral content, but only kombu helps with the beans. Lentils and split peas may be easier to digest than other dried beans. They don't require soaking and they take much less time to cook. Try these legumes as a healthy way to get low-fat protein and lots of fiber.

Sweeteners

Please don't use artificial sweeteners such as Splenda or Nutrasweet (aspartame), even if you have diabetes because they are unnatural and have been linked to depression and imbalances in the nervous system. Plus, since they are made from chemicals they don't fit into the S.L.O.W. plant-foods model (seasonal, local, organic and whole). Opt for natural sweeteners like fruit, and then use small amounts of unrefined stevia, date syrup or yacon syrup if necessary. These foods will not raise your blood sugar levels so they are safe to use even for people with diabetes. Many foods are delicious naturally, especially when fresh, so give them a chance.

Liquid Refreshment

Drink fresh, filtered water - half your body weight in ounces. If you weigh 100 pounds, you need at least 50 ounces of water per day. If you weigh 150 pounds, then you should drink 75 ounces of water per day, and if you weigh 200 pounds, drink 100 ounces of water per day, and try to avoid the buying plastic water bottles because they are wasteful and the water may contain harmful toxins from the plastic.

Green tea is high in antioxidants and has only a small amount of caffeine. Drink one to two cups per day, but not in the evening if you are sensitive to caffeine.

Hot lemon water is best first thing in the morning, on an empty stomach. Heat two cups of water until hot, and then add the juice from half a lemon. Drink and wait half an hour before eating. Follow up with a high fiber breakfast. The hot lemon water will help flush out the gallbladder, alkalize your body, and prepare your digestive system for food.

Drink ginger, mint or chamomile tea after meals to help digest food. I like chamomile tea before bed to help me sleep.

Recommendations: What *NOT* to Eat

No more cow's milk. It is meant for cows, not humans. Instead, use unsweetened almond, hemp seed, rice, soy or oat milks.

No more refined grains such as white rice. Avoid bleached or enriched wheat flour, semolina or durum flour. Switch to whole grains, such as brown rice, quinoa, millet, buckwheat, etc.

No more white bread. Switch to breads, tortillas and buns made from sprouted whole grains. However, bread should not be your main source for grains. Purchase, cook and eat actual whole grains (brown rice, millet, quinoa, etc.).

No more sugary cereals. Buy only whole grain cereals with more than five grams of fiber and less than five grams of sugar per serving. Look for alternatives to wheat and gluten.

No more soda or drink mixes. Use freshly-squeezed whole lemons for lemonade and add date syrup or stevia for sweetness. Drink predominately water or herbal teas (hot or cold). Eat whole fruit instead of drinking juice (to get more fiber and nutrients).

Cut down on coffee. The acid it contains is detrimental to health, and the caffeine can pull calcium from your bones. If you can't live without it, buy organic coffee and don't drink more than one cup a day.

No processed chocolate. Chocolate is also acidic, but more than that, the chemicals added to its basic ingredient, cocoa, renders it unhealthy. Organic dark chocolate is a better choice than processed milk chocolate, but it still contains sugar. Instead, try unprocessed raw cacao powder and raw cacao nibs in recipes. This natural form of chocolate is not sweet but full of nutrition. You'll see these ingredients in some of the recipes in this book.

No more fast food. Instead, try healthy snack bars, fruit, or hummus and carrots for food on the go.

No more burgers from animal products or from processed soy. Use my recipes for bean and grain burgers.

No more low fiber foods. These are refined foods such as white bread, white flour, white rice, processed cereals, pastries, junk food, sodas, candy, juice, etc. No more no fiber foods. These are animal products of all kinds including chicken and fish, butter, eggs, cheese, milk, yogurt and whey.

No more processed foods - anything that is not in its whole, natural form.

No more processed soy products. These include TVP, TSP, soy protein isolate, soybean oil, hydrolyzed vegetable protein, soy protein powder, mono-diglycerides and MSG.

No more trans-fats. These are hydrogenated or partially hydrogenated oils.

No more artificial sweeteners, artificial colors, preservatives and additives.

No more fried foods.

No more sugar, including high fructose corn syrup, corn syrup, turbinado sugar, evaporated cane juice, honey, sucanat, brown sugar, etc.

I know some of this sounds direct and possibly harsh but I write this way because your health is important. And prevention is the best medicine. The old saying "everything in moderation" was too lenient and following the advice in my book may at first seem too hard. But eating for good health can still be really tasty and fun. Just give it a try.

Incorporating These New Ideas

Don't be overwhelmed when considering how to begin. Start with simple changes such as exchanging white rice or pasta for whole grain rice or pasta. Explore the organic produce section of your local health food store for colorful vegetables. Visit your local farmer's market for the freshest seasonal ingredients and foods, harvested at their peak of nutritional value.

Give yourself three weeks for your taste buds to adjust to new foods, especially if you're accustomed to the sweet and saltiness of processed foods. It may be hard at first, but soon you will feel healthier and happy you took the plunge. By following these guidelines, you will not only prevent illness and feel better, but you will be making a difference in the health of the planet.

Good health begins with digestion. Chew each mouthful of food 50 times to produce enough digestive enzymes to properly digest your food.

It's important to get exercise. Walk 10,000 steps a day and add strength training a couple of times a week.

Sunlight is important for getting your vitamin D. Vitamin D helps boost the immune system. If you can't get 15 minutes of morning sun every other day then you'll need to take a vitamin D supplement.

Vitamin B12

There is a supplement that you may need to take in the form of a pill or capsule if you are strictly eating plant foods and that is vitamin B12. Naturally found in bacteria in soil, this vitamin gets into our food supply through animal foods. If you eliminate all animal foods you may be lacking in this vitamin. Luckily, our need for this vitamin is very small, about 2.5 micrograms per day.

A deficiency of vitamin B12 can result in fatigue and apathy, bone loss, problems with balance and reflexes, abnormal gait, nervous system damage, tingling in hands or feet, tinnitus, eye disorders and migraine headaches. Adding nutritional yeast to your diet (one tablespoon per day, sprinkled on food after cooking) may give you some vitamin B12, although content diminishes with exposure to air and light. Look for foods fortified with B12, such as whole grain cereals and some non-dairy milks, or take a quality B12 supplement (in hydroxocobalamin form) from a health food store daily. This is extremely important!

Regarding the use of supplements other than vitamin B12 and vitamin D, I advocate getting nutrients from food rather than pills. Instead of an antioxidant supplement, eat a variety or organic whole grains, beans, nuts, seeds, fruits and vegetables. Instead of buying expensive pomegranate juice eat a fresh pomegranate. Most multivitamins are hard to absorb, have little benefit to the body, and end up excreted in the urine. Instead of flushing your money, use it to buy organic, whole foods. You'll see a much better return on your investment.

ALWAYS CHOOSE WHOLE, NATURAL, UNPROCESSED CARBS OVER REFINED CARBS.

Good Carbs = Not altered from its natural state. Food is complete, not processed, refined or broken down and put back together again. Nothing added or taken away. Examples: whole fruits and veggies with skin on, beans, brown rice, quinoa, or other whole grains .

Refined carbs = Those that have been changed from the natural state, stripped of fiber and nutrients. Examples: white rice, white flour, white tortillas, white bread, sweets and sodas.

Make Simple Changes

- Eat steel cut oats, rolled oats or oat berries instead of instant oatmeal
- Eat brown rice instead of white rice
- Eat sprouted whole grain tortillas instead of white flour tortillas
- Eat whole grain pasta or gluten-free pasta instead of white pasta
- Make quinoa or millet at least once a week for a protein packed grain
- Get a rice cooker to easily cook all of your whole grains
- Make stews using beans and/or lentils for a hearty protein full of cleansing fiber
- Make or buy baked goods with whole grain flours and natural sweeteners
- Discover new restaurants that feature whole grains as their staple. Look for vegetarian or macrobiotic restaurants that serve whole grains such as brown rice or quinoa.
- Shop at health food stores and farmer's markets
- Search bulk aisles for whole grains, beans, lentils, nuts and seeds
- Join a CSA (Community Supported Agriculture) and get local, seasonal, organic produce delivered to your home.

Frequently Asked Questions

Q: I've heard salt is bad for you. Should I stop eating it?

Salt is not a seasoning you have to avoid - not if you use high quality salt, such as unrefined sea salt or Himalayan mountain salt (beware: not all sea salt is unrefined). Unrefined salt contains essential minerals (up to 84). Regular table salt has been stripped of minerals, bleached, and heated to over 1,000 degrees F. This process not only alters the taste, but removes the valuable minerals that naturally accompany sodium chloride. Just as whole plant foods contain all nutrients essential to the body, so, too, does natural salt. Have you noticed how much better water with minerals tastes? Unrefined salt also tastes better. In addition, without these beneficial minerals, refined table salt causes water retention and high blood pressure, among other health problems.

If you are concerned that you may not be getting enough iodine when you switch from iodized table salt to Himalayan salt you can increase the amount of iodine-rich foods in your diet such as kelp, beets, radish, parsley and oatmeal. For more information on iodine and thyroid conditions please consult a Naturopathic doctor.

Processed and fast foods use refined salt - way too much of it. If you cook at home you can control the salt being used, but don't overdo it - even with the good stuff! Use just enough salt to bring out the flavors and add depth to the dish. If you omit salt completely certain foods may taste flat. You may notice that some of my dessert recipes call for salt. This is because adding a touch of salt will make the dessert taste sweeter and richer without having to add more sweetener or fat. You can always adjust the recipes to suit your needs, adding more or less salt as you see fit.

Q: What are the bad fats?

Not all fats are created equal. The bad fats are trans-fats and saturated fats from animal foods. The typical American diet is about 40 percent fat, and most of it is the bad fat. For optimal health, avoid the bad fats completely and instead choose the good fats from foods such as avocado, olives, nuts and seeds. Keep your fat intake low, between 10 to 20 percent of your total calories. A high fat diet is related to type 2 diabetes, heart disease, cancer and obesity.

Trans-fats, or partially hydrogenated oils, are oils altered chemically by processors to make food creamy or solid at room temperature and increase the product's shelf life. Examples of foods that typically contain trans-fats are margarines and shortenings made from hydrogenated plant oils, and most processed foods (cookies, crackers, chips, candy, bread, commercial frostings, fast foods, etc.). Research shows that trans-fats not only increase bad cholesterol, but decrease good cholesterol. Avoid animal fats and trans-fats at all costs to maintain a healthy heart and body. If a food ingredient list contains the words "partially hydrogenated oil" - don't buy it. Make this a rule.

Saturated fats are solid at room temperature. They are found in meats, fish and dairy products. These are associated with high cholesterol, heart disease and clogged arteries leading to strokes and circulation problems.

Some plant foods contain saturated fat, such as coconut, cacao and palm oils. They do not have the same detrimental effect on our health but, as with all fats, they contain nine calories per gram, which is more than double that of a carbohydrate or protein

Be conscious of how much fat is in your foods and look for ways to reduce it. Avoid fried foods and creamy dishes. For recipes that call for using oil to sauté your vegetables try using the "water sauté" method to reduce the fat content. Do this by substituting water or vegetable broth to sauté your ingredients instead of oil.

Q: Is fat necessary in the diet?

We need dietary fat to absorb the fat-soluble vitamins: A, D, E and K. It is also necessary for a healthy nervous system. Two-thirds of your brain is composed of specialized fats that protect the nerves and brain from degeneration. Neurons - brain cells that communicate with each other - are covered with a layer of fatty acid molecules. When you digest fat in food, your brain incorporates fatty acids into its cell membranes.

Stick with the fats recommended in this book and don't overdo it, even with the good fats. Your daily healthy fat intake should be in the form of a handful of nuts and seeds, a few slices of avocado, and small amounts of the oils used in the recipes in this book.

Q: What are fatty acids?

To build brain cells and nourish the nervous system, you need fatty acids. Two kinds of fatty acids are considered "essential", which means you must get them from the food you eat. Your body cannot manufacture them.

The first is alpha-linolenic acid, the foundation of the "omega-3" family of essential fatty acids (EFAs). The second essential fatty acid you need is linoleic acid (LA), the foundation of the "omega-6" family of fatty acids. Another fatty acid is oleic acid, the main component of olive oil, as well almonds, pecans, macadamias, peanuts and avocados.

One of the biggest problems surrounding essential fatty acids is that we are consuming not enough omega 3 and too much omega 6. If we eat factory farmed animal products (fed corn and soybeans instead of their natural diet of grass) and processed foods made with cheap oils (corn, soybean, safflower and sunflower) we end up having an unhealthy ratio of omega 3 to omega 6. The body needs a ratio of 1 to 4 (omega 3 to omega 6). Currently, the average western diet has a ratio of 1 to 10, or even as bad as 1 to 30. Having too much omega 6 fats in the diet has been associated with an increased risk for heart attack, stroke, arthritis, osteoporosis and depression. The right balance of these fats helps nourish the brain, eyes, heart, kidneys, adrenal glands, hair, skin and joints, relieve depression, lower blood pressure, support immune function, nervous system, reproduction, fertility, circulatory health and maintain a healthy metabolism. So avoid packaged and processed foods (typically too high in omega 6) and stick to more whole plant foods so you know exactly what you are eating.

Whole foods - grains, beans, nut and seeds, fruits and vegetables naturally give you what you need in all the right amounts. When you eat these regularly, you will be consuming a healthy amount of fatty acids, to help keep your cholesterol and blood pressure levels in check, reduce inflammation, and your risk of cancer, diabetes and heart disease.

Q: Should I include fish or eggs in my diet to get the essential fatty acid omega 3?

You need not buy expensive wild salmon or take fish oil capsules. Fish contain this polyunsaturated fat because they eat plankton that feed on algae, the original source of omega 3. Eating fish and fish oil is unwise because they contain mercury and other toxins, cholesterol, saturated fat and IGF-1.

Like algae, plants, nuts and seeds are wise choices for getting your daily dose of omega 3. One tablespoon of freshly-ground flax or chia seeds sprinkled on your morning oatmeal will provide you with 1.75 grams of omega 3 (the recommended daily allowance is one to two grams of omega 3 fat per day). Once flax seeds are ground they begin to go rancid, so grind fresh each time. Whole flax seeds can be stored in the freezer for up to two months.

One quarter cup of raw walnuts has about two grams of omega 3. Cauliflower, cabbage, soybeans, kale, collard greens and Brussels sprouts also contain healthy amounts of omega 3.

Eggs marked as being high in omega 3 means that the chickens were fed flax seeds. The eggs may contain some omega 3, but it is much healthier and efficient to get your omega 3 from the original source, which is always from a plant. When you eat flax seeds, you don't consume the unwanted cholesterol, saturated fats and IGF-1 found in chicken eggs.

Q: What oils should I buy?

Natural, unrefined oil contains all the nutrients of the nuts and seeds it was taken from. Always buy unrefined, organic and cold-pressed oils. My favorites are olive oil, sesame oil, macadamia nut oil, coconut oil and tea seed oil. I also like flax seed and hemp seed oils, but never cook with these last two because heat will destroy the beneficial properties. Flax seed and hemp seed oils are found in the refrigerated section of your health food store and should be kept cold. They can be used to make salad dressings, spreads and smoothies - anything that won't be heated.

Since good oil contains highly nutritious organic matter and can go rancid, buy it in small quantities (because you won't be using much of it either) and keep it in the refrigerator. Buy oil in dark glass bottles so light can't further degrade it.

Q: What are the bad oils?

The reason the oils on supermarket shelves are clear and flavorless is because there is nothing left to taste. Vegetable oils are refined to remove impurities (nutritive elements) to give it a higher smoke point and keep it from spoiling. These refined oils may undergo a deodorizing, bleaching and cleaning process as well, in effect "killing" the vital nature of the seed it came from. As if this weren't bad enough, hexane, a petroleum product, may have been used to extract the oil from the plant. Any nutrients left are killed by heat (cooking), sunlight and ultraviolet light (like the overheads in stores). You might as well use refined vegetable oil as a household lubricant for all the good it does your body. Please avoid processed foods because they likely contain these unhealthy oils.

There is a reason fried foods are so bad for you. Not only are they fattening but the fat is toxic! University of Minnesota researchers discovered that when unsaturated vegetable oils are heated at frying temperature (365 F), a highly toxic compound forms in the oil. In soybean oil, specifically, three toxic compounds formed. Please avoid all fried foods.

When oil is called for in this book please be sure that you are using organic, unrefined, cold-pressed oils. High heat is not necessary for any of the recipes in the book, and should not be used because it will damage the nutrition of the oils. Keep your heat to medium and if you ever see the oil start to smoke in the pan - stop, wait for it to cool, clean the pan and start again, at a lower temperature.

Q: Will I get enough iron if I leave off eating meat?

If you stay on a plant food diet made up of whole foods, not processed foods, you will get enough iron. Dark green leafy vegetables (spinach, Swiss chard, turnip greens, beet greens, etc.), beans, lentils and peas, whole grains, blackstrap molasses, parsley, seaweeds, nuts and seeds all contain iron. However, you will need to take an extra step to ensure you absorb this essential mineral since plant sources of iron are not as easily absorbed as the iron in animal meat. To increase the absorbability of iron, include a food source of vitamin C, such as a citrus fruit, kiwi, broccoli, tomatoes or cabbage with every meal. A squeeze of lemon juice over your vegetables can achieve this goal.

Just as important is to avoid anything that inhibits the full absorption of iron. Tannins found in coffee, tea and colas decrease iron absorption. Studies show that iron deficiency is no more common in vegans than in the general population. If you eat only plant foods you will need to supplement with vitamin B12 but you should not need an iron supplement.

Q: What about sweeteners?

All of the recipes in this book use sweeteners that have a low glycemic index. Whole fruit or fruit puree, date syrup, organic, raw agave nectar, brown rice syrup, yacon syrup and stevia are sweeteners that may be used even if you have diabetes. These foods are absorbed more steadily into the bloodstream and will not cause blood sugar levels to spike and then fall like honey, maple syrup and sugar will. If you have high triglyceride levels (which you shouldn't if you stick to eating the "Therapeutic Chef" way) then you should limit the amount of agave nectar to two tablespoons a day, because consuming more than that may further elevate triglyceride levels. As always, try to enjoy foods in their natural state without having to sweeten them. But if you do, choose from these healthier sweeteners and use only small amounts of these low-glycemic options. And remember to avoid high fructose corn syrup at all costs.

Q: So I don't need to drink milk?

That's right. Think about it. We are humans and we have been trying to drink the milk from another mammal. Cow's milk is meant for cows. Infants need mother's milk until they are weaned, then no milk of any kind is necessary in a healthy diet. For calcium always choose beans and greens, such as black beans, lentils, kale, bok choy and collard greens. Getting exercise, sunlight and reducing sodium and caffeine intake is important for healthy bones too. If you need to use a milk-like substance in a recipe or on your morning cereal try the recipes in this book or look for an unsweetened non-dairy milk such as almond milk or hemp seed milk at the grocery store. For thicker cream-like products, try making cashew cream (see pg. 92, 195).

> *"Nothing will benefit human health and increase chances for survival of life on earth as much as the evolution to a vegetarian diet."*
>
> *~ Albert Einstein*

Eating for a
Greener Planet &
a Healthier Body

When you look at the facts and consider the logic, it's not hard to see why a plant-based diet is the best choice - for us and our earth. Common sense - and much research - tells us that if, as a society, we embrace diets comprised of sustainable, renewable plants instead of environmentally detrimental meat, not only will the earth thank us, but we will live longer, better.

Plant food supplies the human body with fiber and essential nutrients - nutrients so potent that individually they increase resistance to diseases such as cancer, help the body shed fat and restore health when imbalances occur.

Beneficial fiber, antioxidants and phytochemicals that protect us from degenerative diseases, aging and chemical toxins are only found in plant foods. Harmful cholesterol is only found in animal foods.

The number one cause of death in the U.S. is from heart disease. If you eliminate harmful cholesterol and saturated fats from animal products and switch to a diet consisting of whole, plant foods (vegetables, whole grains, beans, fruits, nuts and seeds) you substantially reduce your risk of heart disease and stroke, not to mention most of the illnesses and diseases of Western society. Many, many specific fruits and vegetables have been found in studies to be medicinal in their very nature. "Eat fruits and vegetables" has become the health mantra of our time.

In the meantime, the earth is plagued with deforestation and overgrazing attributed to our love of meat. Instead of growing vital vegetation that supplies the soil - and humans - with nutrients, acres upon acres are cleared to sustain cattle or grow crops used to feed them and other supermarket meat. Nothing could be less logical or more inefficient than growing grains to feed animals so they can be eaten.

The U.S.'s insatiable appetite for beef literally takes food out of the mouths of the world's children. It takes 16 pounds of grain to produce 1 pound of meat! Instead of growing grain to feed to animals we could feed the world by feeding the grain directly to people. One hundred acres of land are needed to produce beef for 20 people but will produce enough wheat to feed 240 people. We waste so much to gain so little. If Americans ate less meat, world hunger could be a thing of the past.

The world's ecosystems would also benefit. As our appetite for beef increases, the world's rainforests are being cut down to make room for more. According to the Rainforest Action Network, 55 square feet of tropical rainforest, an area the size of a small kitchen, are destroyed for the production of every fast-food hamburger made from rainforest beef. Amazon rainforests are paying the price as the demand for beef around the world increases. A three-year study by

Greenpeace showed that Western demand for beef and leather and an increase in cattle ranching is leading to intensified deforestation in the Amazon. The organization estimates that between 2007 and 2008, three million acres of the Brazilian Amazon have been destroyed. The cattle business is expanding rapidly in the Amazon, and now poses the biggest threat to 80 percent of the forest that still stands (*Guardian News and Media Limited*, May 31, 2009). With the loss of rainforest for cattle grazing we are seeing even more detrimental changes to our climate because trees have the important job of absorbing harmful carbon dioxide and giving off oxygen.

In 2006, the United Nations Food and Agriculture Organization found that the meat industry was responsible for 18 percent of greenhouse gas emissions that cause global warming, more than cars, planes and all other forms of transport combined. Animal agriculture is the **leading** source of methane and nitrous oxide emissions, which - combined with carbon dioxide - causes the vast majority of global warming. Eating one pound of meat emits the same amount of greenhouse gasses as driving an SUV 40 miles. TIME magazine agrees, saying, "It's true that giving up that average 176 pounds of meat a year is one of the greenest lifestyle changes you can make as an individual."

In this nation of frequent droughts, cattle production alone consumes 50 percent of all water used in the United States. Researchers suggest that eliminating one beef meal a week will, on average, save more than 40,000 gallons of water, 70 tons of grain, and reduce 300 pounds of greenhouse gas emissions each year (*Warrior for a Healthy Planet* by James Faber).

The following important points demonstrate the devastating effect of the world's appetite for beef (*The Food Revolution* by John Robbins, Conari Press, 2000):

- It takes 16 pounds of grain to make one pound of beef.
- It takes 24 gallons of water to produce one pound of potatoes. It takes 5,214 gallons of water to produce one pound of beef.
- Three times more fossil fuels are needed to produce a meat-centered diet vs. a meat-free diet.
- Percentage of U.S. topsoil loss directly related to livestock raising: 85.
- Number of acres of U.S. forest cleared for cropland to produce a meat-centered diet: 260 million.
- Amount of meat imported to U.S. annually from Central and South America: 300 million pounds
- Percentage of Central American children under the age of five who are undernourished: 75
- Current rate of species extinction due to destruction of tropical rainforests for meat grazing and other uses: 1,000 per year
- Percentage of corn grown in the U.S. eaten by people: 20
- Percentage of corn grown in the U.S. eaten by livestock: 80
- Percentage of oats grown in the U.S. eaten by livestock: 95
- Percentage of protein wasted by cycling grain through livestock: 90

- Percentage of U.S. farmland devoted to beef production: 56
- Number of people worldwide who died as a result of malnutrition in 2000: 20 million
- Number of people who could be adequately fed using land freed if Americans reduced their intake of meat by 10 percent: 100 million

Our Diets are Killing Us

The Surgeon General's Report on Nutrition and Health found that nearly 70 percent of all diseases in the U.S. are diet-related. At the same time, less than one-third of American adults meet the recommendation to consume five or more servings of fruits and vegetables per day, according to the U.S. Departments of Agriculture and Health and Human Services.

The most convincing arguments for a plant-only diet are the detrimental effects of meat and dairy products on human health.

Animals are routinely fed antibiotics and steroids to induce growth and retard disease. As they graze, they pick up herbicides and pesticides, which accumulate in their muscles, fat and milk. Chickens and their eggs are affected, as is pork. Chemicals concentrate in fat, so the skin and fatty parts of an animal are the most contaminated. This is also true for fish and shellfish as toxins, most especially mercury, in polluted streams and oceans get stored in their fat. Even some canned tuna has been shown to contain mercury.

The residues of as many as 500 to 600 toxic chemicals may be present in this country's meat supply, according to the Food and Drug Administration. But this could be the tip of the iceberg, because only 60 residues are monitored by the Government.

According to the United States Department of Agriculture (USDA), 75 percent of all carcinogens and toxins in the human body get there through animal products.

Eggs contain whatever the chicken has been fed. Chicken feed may contain the same preservatives and hormones found in other animal feed. One of the causes of hormonal imbalances in humans and animals can be attributed to synthetic hormones used in food processing industries throughout the world.

Synthetic estrogens (female hormones) may be used in chicken feed. Since most chickens raised for our supermarkets are female hens, synthetic estrogens are added to feed so they will develop more quickly. Synthetic male hormones are either injected into beef cattle, or put in their feed for the same reason.

Eggs laid from even free range chickens have been found to contain toxic chemicals, when they are grazing in a pasture high in herbicides and pesticides.

Add to that, plastic packaging containing chemicals are used which are found to infect food.

"Food packaging is a large but underestimated source of chemical food contamination", said Jane Muncke, a Swiss environmental toxicologist who conducted a review of 104 scientific studies (*Science of the Total Environment*, August 2009).

The number of chemicals capable of interfering with hormones and permitted in packaging in the United States and the European Union is at least 50. The best known are bisphenol A (BPA), which mimics estrogen and blocks the production of testosterone. It is used to make polycarbonate, and phthalates, which are added to plastic to make it more flexible.

The hormones in these plasticizers have been found in the blood of humans, and while the health effects are still largely unknown, they are suspected to influence early puberty in girls and are carcinogenic. Plus, plastic is made from petroleum, a non-renewable resource.

Plastic is forever. Unlike many discarded materials, plastic does not biodegrade; instead it "photodegrades." Instead of breaking down, it breaks up, as sunlight cracks it into smaller and smaller sized pieces. Even molecules of plastic are too tough for anything - including bacteria - to break them down.

In the northeast Pacific Ocean - between San Francisco and the Hawaiian Islands - there exists a huge stew of floating garbage estimated to be twice the size of Texas. Known as the Great Pacific Garbage Patch, oceanographers estimate it weighs some 3.5 million tons and consists of 80 percent plastics. It is believed that this "patch" has been growing for the past 50 years, ever since plastics first entered the consumer market and began making their way into our oceans.

Tiny fragments of plastic act as sponges for persistent organic pollutants such as DDT and PCBs - oily toxins that don't dissolve in water. Plastic pieces can accumulate up to one million times the level of these poisons.

The Algalita Marine Research Foundation in Long Beach, headed by Captain Charles Moore, has been monitoring the Garbage Patch for ten years. In 2007, they found 10 pounds of microscopic plastic to one pound of plankton. More plastic than plankton means marine organisms are feeding on poison, passing it through the food chain.

Researchers looking at the stomach contents of dead albatrosses have found disposable cigarette lighters, bottle caps, syringes, fishing line, buttons, toys, balloons, pens and toothbrushes. Piles of bones and feathers on remote islands and atolls reveal albatross carcasses full of plastic pieces ingested by the regal birds that subsequently died of dehydration and starvation. Worse yet, albatross chicks are fed plastic, regurgitated from the stomachs of their parents. It was reported in a 2006 *LA Times* article that of the 500,000 albatross chicks born on the Midway Atoll each year, about 200,000 die, mostly from dehydration or starvation. Turtles and marine animals mistake floating plastic bags and plastic wrap for jellyfish and other food sources, causing them to choke to death.

Plant foods are sometimes wrapped or shipped in plastic for sale, which is one of the many reasons I advocate eating foods that don't come in packages; whole fruits and vegetables grown seasonably and purchased as close to the farm as possible. If you cannot purchase your fruits, vegetables and herbs from a farmer, grow them yourself. Avoid packaged foods and fast foods. When storing food at home, use glass or stainless steel containers instead of plastic to avoid further contamination. Remember to take your reusable bags with you when shopping and help save the landfills and the oceans. Little changes do make a difference!

Genetically-Modified Foods

If it smells like a peach, tastes like a peach, looks like a peach, is it a peach? Not if it's a genetically-engineered peach.

Because genetically-engineered food has been genetically altered, it is called a genetically modified organism, or GMO. Genes from different organisms - even animals - are imbedded into a plant's genetic code, modifying it to make it more pest resistant or drought tolerant.

Material from organisms that have never been part of the human food supply are being used to change the fundamental nature of the food. These creations are now being patented and released into the environment, and without long-term testing no one knows if these foods are safe.

Up to 45 percent of U.S. corn is genetically engineered, as is 85 percent of soybeans, according to the Center for Food Safety. The Center estimates that 70-75 percent of processed foods on supermarket shelves - from soda to soup, crackers to condiments - contain genetically engineered ingredients.

While consumers fight to have genetically engineered foods labeled, the best we can do to protect ourselves is avoid processed food, know where our plant food comes from and buy organic. Organic produce cannot be grown from genetically modified seeds. When shopping at the supermarket read your labels and look for 100% organic food.

Besides knowing that you will be avoiding risky GM foods, it is worth it to seek out organic food for many reasons. Organic food is good for the environment, good for us and good for the farmers. Organic farmers don't use harmful pesticides, antibiotics or hormones that contaminate our food, air and drinking water. A report by the French Agency for Food Safety found that organic plant foods are more nutrient dense, have higher levels of minerals and contain more antioxidants such as phenols (known to protect against cancers, heart disease and many other health problems) (*Food Magazine*, September 3, 2009). Grow your own organic produce, join a CSA (Community Supported Agriculture), or shop at your local organic farmer's market or health food store.

The Therapeutic
Chef Kitchen

The road to healthy eating starts with your kitchen. The first step is getting rid of foods that aren't good for you. The next step is stocking your kitchen with the right foods. Begin with a trash can and end with a shopping list.

Throw away all refined and processed foods including any food that contains white flour, enriched flour, partially hydrogenated oils (trans-fats), high fructose corn syrup, corn syrup, preservatives, artificial flavors, food colorings, or chemicals of any kind, especially artificial sweeteners. Commit this list to memory and be strict on avoiding these ingredients.

Stock your pantry with whole grains such as brown rice, quinoa, millet, buckwheat, whole grain pastas (spelt, brown rice, quinoa), and sprouted whole grain breads and tortillas. Focus on the gluten-free grains as much as possible, and save yourself time by making grains in a rice cooker. Purchase dried beans, split peas and lentils for healthy protein. Use organic canned beans (I like Eden brand) when you're in a hurry.

Buy organic foods as much as possible to reduce the consumption of toxic pesticides and herbicides. Grow whatever food you can even if it's just herbs and sprouts. Shop at local, organic farmer's markets or join a CSA (Community Supported Agriculture) for affordable fresh, seasonal, local produce. Shop at a health food store to stock up on the rest of your grocery needs. To find a CSA or Farmer's Market in your area, visit: www.localharvest.org.

Throw away all white and brown sugar, even sugar-in-the-raw and sucanat.

Replace processed sugar with date syrup, brown rice syrup, **raw, organic** agave nectar, yacon syrup, stevia, rapadura and molasses to sweeten foods and baked goods. All of these, with the exception of rapadura and molasses, are safe sweeteners even for people with diabetes because they don't cause an increase in blood sugar level. Molasses is high in iron and B vitamins.

Throw away your white iodized table salt.

Replace table salt with mineral-rich **unrefined** sea salt, Himalayan salt or seaweed flakes (dulse, nori, kelp). Miso can be used to salt food. Buy mellow, white or sweet miso.

Throw away dairy products made from cow's milk (or other animal milk). This is a priority.

Replace cow's milk with unsweetened almond milk, hemp seed milk, rice milk or soy milk. Use in the same way you would cow's milk. If you like yogurt, experiment with making your own from nuts and seeds, or even young coconuts. This is a much healthier option. You'll have to give up cheese too (I know, this may be difficult for some of you). And don't be tempted to buy cheeses made from processed soy and other unnatural ingredients because they are just as unhealthy for us as the dairy cheese. Refer to the recipes in this book for cheese spreads and sauces made from beans, nuts and seeds. And remember that the best way to get calcium is through beans and greens.

Throw away butter, lard, shortening and refined vegetable oils.

Stock your kitchen pantry with small bottles of organic, first cold-pressed olive oil, macadamia nut oil or unrefined sesame oil to use in moderation. Keep flax seed oil in the refrigerator.

Throw away all aluminum cookware and non-stick pans. Toxins can be released when they get old and scratched.

Keep or obtain stainless steel, ceramic, titanium or glass cookware.

Reduce your need for plastic wrap and aluminum foil. Wrap individual pieces of leftover lasagna, polenta pie or burritos in unbleached parchment paper and reheat in an oven. Also use unbleached parchment paper to line baking pans instead of oiling them.

Throw away plastic or aluminum cooking and serving utensils.

Use stainless steel or wooden cooking and serving utensils.

Dispose of (recycle) all plastic containers, bowls, cups and bottles. The toxic chemicals used to make plastic may leach out of the food containers and bottles into your food or beverage, and may be linked to cancer and fertility problems. Plus, plastic containers, especially plastic water bottles are wasteful and a burden to the environment.

Replace plastic with glass, ceramic or stainless steel food storage containers, bowls, cups and bottles. Carry with you reusable stainless steel travel mugs and water bottles to cut down on disposable cups and bottles.

Get rid of your microwave. Using it to cook, heat or defrost foods and even water destroys the vitamin and mineral content of the food and has been linked to cancer and digestive problems, among many other illnesses. This is important. If you are going to buy healthy foods, take one more important step. Ensure that the nutrients remain intact by eating the foods in their raw state or by cooking foods lightly on the stovetop through steaming, water sautéing, or baking at lower temperatures. Microwaving food is not a healthy option. Really.

Use a filter system for your water. Drink and cook with only purified, filtered water. Chlorine in our water leaches vital nutrients from our bodies. It's also a good idea to buy a water filter that attaches to your shower head to avoid inhaling chlorine vapors while you shower.

HEALTHY EATING ON A BUDGET

You don't have to spend a fortune to be healthy! Buying dried beans and whole grains are very inexpensive and contain loads of nutrition. Pound for pound you save money by using beans for protein than if you ate meat or cheese as your protein source. Plus you save money by eating whole plant foods over processed foods and animal products because you will be healthier, which means less trips to the doctor, less medications and less missed work. In the long run it pays to eat healthy.

The Therapeutic Chef Principles of Healthy Meals

When you plan a meal, make whole grains the entree and work around them. Learn to cook and appreciate them. Many grains can be cooked together in a rice cooker or crock pot. Shorter cooking grains such as amaranth, teff, buckwheat, quinoa and millet can be cooked together. Longer cooking grains such as hulled barley, spelt, kamut, brown rice, wild rice, hato mugi, and wheat berries can be cooked together. Once you have the grains cooked, half the meal is ready. From here, all you have to do is prepare your vegetables.

Plan for about half your plate to be vegetables. Eat them raw by chopping, slicing or grating and adding to dishes, or lightly cook them to help preserve nutrition content by steaming, baking, or using the water-sauté method. This method is described below as a substitute for cooking with oil.

If you want to add a quick protein to the meal have tempeh, lentils, seitan, or organic canned beans on hand. Keep protein to about 10 to 12 percent of calories. Lentils are ideal for a quick, high protein, high fiber, low-fat, easy-to-cook dish. They don't require soaking, like most other dried beans or legumes, and they only take 20 minutes to cook. Just rinse well and simmer in three parts water to one part lentils. Add more liquid or broth to make soup. I usually start cooking lentils as soon as I think of making dinner, and while they are simmering I chop the vegetables and add them to the lentils during the last five minutes, then make a quick sauce or dressing. It all comes together in 30 minutes and I've only used one pot, one cutting board, the rice cooker and a small bowl and whisk (for the dressing or sauce). Not bad for a meal that is complete and tasty, not to mention much cheaper than ordering out from a restaurant. Plus, you will have made enough for lunch the next day, perhaps in the form of a burrito. Your body will thank you for taking a few extra minutes each night to prepare simple, healthy meals - so will your wallet and the planet!

Have a few good sauces up your sleeve so that a delicious dinner can come together without much planning or time. Keep basic ingredients on hand (lemon, ginger, garlic, miso, tahini, cashews, fresh herbs, etc.) so you can whip up a sauce in no time.

Have healthy snacks on hand for when hunger strikes... raw or sprouted organic nuts, seeds, fresh or dried fruit, sprouted whole grain tortillas, sliced vegetables and hummus.

Choose foods in a rainbow of colors to ensure you are getting all the different vitamins and minerals. Carrots and sweet potatoes are high in beta-carotene, green leafy vegetables are high in calcium and magnesium and tomatoes are high in lycopene. The more colors you have on your plate at each meal the more vitamins, minerals, antioxidants and phytochemicals you will ingest.

Include a cruciferous vegetable (or several) at each meal. These include kale, cabbage, broccoli, cauliflower, radish, collard greens, turnips, rutabaga, Brussels sprouts, spinach, arugula, Swiss chard and bok choy. Many of these contain calcium and powerful antioxidants that help fight illness and disease, including cancer.

Use miso to season foods such as soups, or use to make a sauce, gravy or dressing. It is made from whole, fermented soybeans and is a source of protein and probiotics. To use place about one tablespoon in a small bowl and add about one tablespoon of water or broth and whisk together to make a 'slurry.' Add this to any dish for richness, flavor and nutrition. Remember to always add miso at the end of cooking. Never boil miso. The process destroys its enzymes and beneficial bacteria. Soy-free miso is available as well.

Keep added fats to a minimum. Don't drown foods in oils or creamy sauces. Although you need healthy fat (nuts, seeds, olives, avocado) as a part of each meal don't over do it.

If using a little bit of oil in a pan never cook above medium heat. This means no fried foods. High temperature cooking destroys the beneficial properties of unrefined oils and turns the oil into a rancid and toxic fat. If you see your oil start to smoke in the pan, throw it out and start again. Tea seed oil, coconut oil and macadamia nut oil can be used for slightly higher heat cooking and baking, but still no frying. And remember, flax seed and hemp seed oils can't take heat of any kind. Use these fragile oils in salad dressings or smoothies.

HEALTHY COOKING TIPS

Buy a good quality knife. It makes chopping vegetables more fun, less labor intensive and safer.

To reduce fat use the 'water sauté' method as much as possible. This is where you 'sauté' your onions or vegetables in water instead of oil. If the pan starts to get dry when 'sautéing' just add a little more water to prevent sticking to the pan and proceed with recipe.

How will you include an omega 3 essential fatty acid in your meal if you are avoiding fish? One easy way is to offer fresh fruits and vegetables at every meal, because they naturally contain this EFA. If you want extra omega 3, buy WHOLE flax seeds or chia seeds, and grind them, one tablespoon at a time, in a clean coffee grinder. Do not purchase already-ground seeds because they start to go rancid immediately after grinding. Use freshly ground seeds to garnish whole grains, beans and salads. Use flax seed oil in salad dressings and smoothies. Do not heat the seeds or flax seed oil or the beneficial properties of the oil will be lost and potentially converted into a harmful fatty acid.

Garlic and onions contain allicin, a powerful anti-cancer nutrient. Onions must be chopped, sliced or diced to activate the allicin. Garlic needs to be crushed or pressed. A garlic press is perfect for this job. After onions are chopped or sliced, and the garlic is pressed or crushed, they should rest on the cutting board for at least ten minutes if you plan to cook with them. This step is not necessary if the dish will not be heated. You will notice the garlic takes on a wonderful flavor when you take this step to activate the cancer-fighting allicin.

Reheat your leftovers using the stovetop, oven or toaster oven, never the microwave. To reheat rice and beans or braised vegetables, place 1-2 tablespoons of water in the bottom of a pan. Add your leftovers, cover, and reheat on the stovetop over medium to medium-low heat. Check after a few minutes and add another tablespoon or two of water to prevent sticking. Heat until warmed to your desired temperature. Other foods like a burrito or slice of lasagna can be warmed by wrapping in parchment paper and placing in a 300 F oven for 15-20 minutes, or until heated through.

Cleaning vegetables is important, even if you buy organic. To clean foods like broccoli, leeks and green leafy vegetables, fill a large bowl with cold water. Chop the produce and add it to the bowl. Swish it around with your hand and let it rest. Sand, dirt and other debris will sink to the bottom. Carefully lift the vegetables out of the bowl leaving the water and grit. Place vegetables in a strainer, rinse and let drain.

To clean foods such as carrots, burdock and apples buy organic, scrub, rinse and proceed with recipe. If the produce is not organic you should peel or wash it with a vegetable wash solution, then rinse thoroughly. Be sure to eat the skin or peel of organic fruits and vegetables whenever possible. Some of the most nutritious components of the plant are contained in or just beneath the skin.

To clean whole grains, beans and lentils, pour the amount needed onto a large white plate or baking dish and sort through, looking for stones. If you skip this step you may end up biting down on a small stone during dinner. Place the grains/beans in a bowl and fill with cold water. Swish the grains/beans around, then let settle. You will notice debris floating on top of the water. Pour the water and debris off and repeat until the water is clear (usually 2-3 times). Strain, and proceed with recipe.

Keep oils, nuts, seeds, nut butters, flours, and miso refrigerated to keep from going rancid.

The Plant-Based Macrobiotic Diet

Taking the whole plant food diet one step further will bring you to a Macrobiotic diet. This principle of eating promises you a longer, healthier life - 'macro' for long and 'biotic' for life.

The Macrobiotic Diet is based on maintaining your body in a state of harmony by eating foods that cleanse and strengthen, and which are low-fat, non mucous forming and alkaline, at the same time living an active lifestyle in balance with nature.

A strict macrobiotic diet can take years to master since it includes not only the food but how it is prepared and cooked. You can incorporate key macrobiotic principles into your lifestyle by following the points below. As you become familiar with the new whole plant foods diet you will want to incorporate more of the macrobiotic lifestyle. Start by learning the basics:

Eat SLOW foods - Seasonal, Local, Organic and Whole.

Buy fresh and prepare simply.

No fried foods, and nothing processed, stripped or changed from its whole form.

No chemicals, colorants or preservatives.

Avoid packaged and canned foods as much as possible.

Avoid animal products, including all meat, eggs, cheese and milk.

No white sugar or honey. If you must use a sweetener use only small amounts of fruit puree, brown rice syrup, date syrup, yacon syrup, barley malt syrup or stevia.

Limit tropical fruits, carbonated beverages, caffeine and strong alcoholic beverages.

Make whole grains the core of each meal. Examples are brown rice, whole oats, barley, millet, quinoa, amaranth, buckwheat and teff. Soak whole grains for up to 24 hours before cooking (see pg 254).

Make vegetables (raw, fermented and cooked) the second part of each meal. Include dark green leafy vegetables, cruciferous vegetables (cabbage, collard greens, broccoli, etc.), parsley, burdock, carrots, squashes and scallions. Include small amounts of sea vegetables each day in soups, salads, and bean and grain dishes. Limit potatoes, tomatoes, eggplant, peppers, spinach, beets and zucchini, which may aggravate body inflammation.

Include beans, miso soup, some nuts and seeds, and herbals teas.

In moderation, include vegetable oils such as organic first cold-pressed olive oil, unrefined sesame oil and flax seed oil. Nuts such as raw almonds, pecans, walnuts, pumpkin seeds, sesame seeds, hemp seeds and sunflower seeds are acceptable. Local, seasonal fruits are acceptable in moderation. It is always recommended to eat more vegetables than fruit.

Chew food well, at least 50 times per bite, to release digestive enzymes, absorb nutrients, and neutralize the acidity of food.

Nutritionally exceptional foods include green tea, kukicha/bancha twig tea, medicinal mushrooms (maitake, reishi, and shiitakes), raw sauerkraut or kimchi and umeboshi plums.

When the body is acidic disease can grow. All body functions, including mood and emotion, are adversely affected. By adhering to the principles of the macrobiotic diet the body moves into a state of harmony and balance. Diseases cannot flourish in a balanced, alkaline body. Positive results will be felt immediately.

The Final Step on Your Road to Health - Detox Your Home

Avoid cleaning and beauty products that contain toxic chemicals. Properly dispose of all toxic cleaners, laundry detergents and toiletries. Switch to natural cleaners, soaps, beauty products and air fresheners.

Make your own household cleaners with white vinegar, borax and organic soap. Find a recipe online and get cleaning. Most health food stores sell environmentally safe products.

Buy recycled paper products as much as possible, and bring your own bags when you go shopping. Avoid plastic grocery bags. Reduce, Reuse, Recycle.

This may seem expensive at first, but in the long run the environment will be healthier, and so will you!

THE NEW FOOD PYRAMID: WHOLE PLANT FOODS

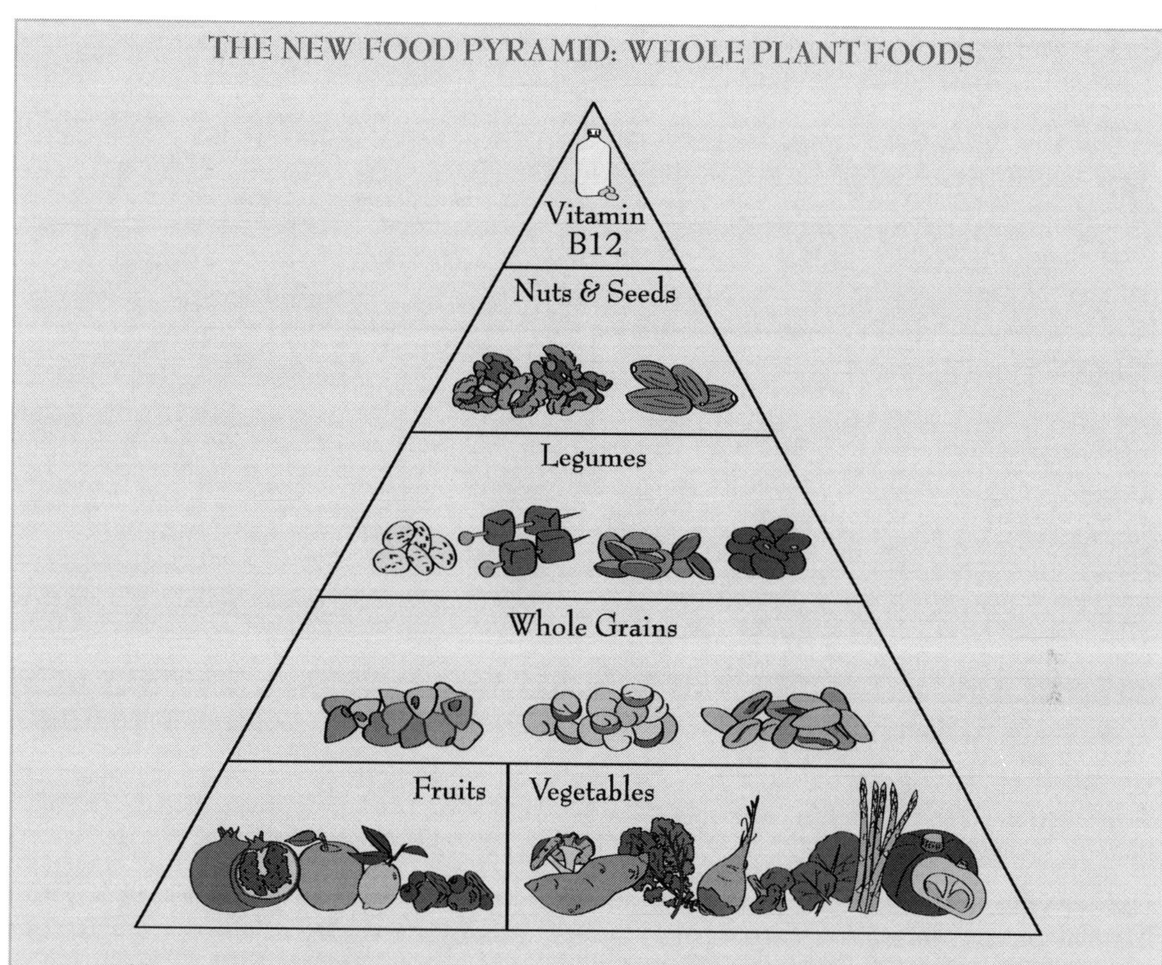

- Vegetables – think colorful, especially green (four or more servings per day)
  One cup of raw crunchy vegetables or two cups of raw leafy vegetables = one serving

- Fruit (three or more servings per day)
  Juice is not a serving unless you make your own and eat the pulp
  One medium piece of fruit = one serving

- Whole grains (five or more servings per day)
  Half a cup of cooked grains = one serving

- Beans and other legumes, including tempeh (two or more servings per day)
  Half a cup of cooked legumes/beans = one serving

- Nuts and Seeds (two servings per day)
  A handful of nuts and/or seeds = one serving
  One tablespoon of flax seeds or flax seed oil = one serving

- Vitamin B12 (one supplement per day)

PANTRY LIST

Produce

Buy Organic. All fruits and vegetables are good to eat. Here are my favorites:

Arugula
Asparagus
Bananas
Berries (Organic only! Buy frozen if necessary.)
Bok choy, baby bok choy
Broccoli
Burdock root
Carrots
Cauliflower
Celery
Daikon
Garlic
Ginger (Buy young ginger if possible. Always buy organic.)
Granny smith apples and other apples
Green and red cabbage
Kale, chard, collard greens (for calcium!)
Lemons (1/2 lemon per day)
Mixed salad greens
New potatoes or yukon gold potatoes
Onions (all kinds)
Oranges
Red grapes (organic only)
Rutabaga
Shiitake mushrooms
Yams and sweet potatoes

Whole Grains

Can be prepared in your rice cooker.

*Brown rice, red rice, black rice (short grain or long grain) - but no white rice
*Wild rice
*Bulgur wheat
*Whole wheat couscous
*Barley (hulled is better than pearled)
*Quinoa
*Amaranth
*Teff
*Millet
*Buckwheat
*Rolled oats
*Steel cut oats
Cornmeal or polenta (organic only)
Whole wheat flour, whole wheat pastry flour, unbleached flour
Brown rice flour
Barley flour, kamut flour and spelt flour
Buckwheat flour
Cold breakfast cereals that are high in fiber (at least 5-10 gms per serving) and low in fat and sugar (less than 5 gms of fat and less than 5 gms of sugar per serving)
Whole wheat or other whole grain/sprouted pastas

Dried Beans, Lentils and Peas

All are good, but here are some favorites:

Pinto beans

Black beans
Garbanzo beans/chickpeas
Lentils (All kinds. Lentils do not need to be soaked overnight!)
Split peas (yellow or green)
Mung beans (whole or split)
Adzuki beans (a.k.a. azuki, aduki beans)

Frozen Foods

Frozen bananas (place ripe bananas in a bag and freeze), then use in baking or smoothies

Frozen berries (Always buy organic berries please!)

Frozen peas, broccoli, mixed vegetables, beans, spinach, corn (organic corn only)

Frozen veggie burgers (not with TVP or soy protein, but instead made from whole grains, brown rice, and vegetables) I like Amy's Organics – "California Burger."

Nuts, Seeds, Dried Fruit

Almond butter (use to replace peanut butter)

Tahini (sesame butter)

Raw or roasted almonds, raw walnuts, raw pecans, raw pumpkin seeds, tan sesame seeds (not white), sunflower seeds, whole flax seeds, chia seeds, hemp seeds
(Store nuts and seeds in freezer or refrigerator.)

Goji berries (use to replace raisins, add to trail mix, oatmeal, salads, grains)

Dried apricots, figs, dates, mangoes, apples, berries (buy organic or no sulfur added)

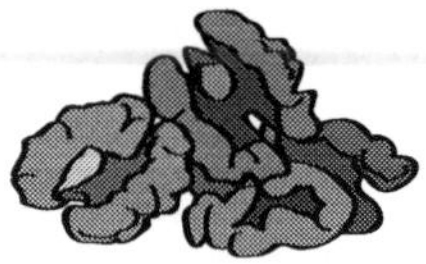

Raw cacao nibs (to add to smoothies, trail mix, baking, etc.)

Breads, Crackers and Snack Foods

Whole grain bread (may be frozen)

Whole wheat/whole grain pita bread

Sprouted grain bread and tortillas (I like "Ezekiel Food for Life" brand.)

Baked tortilla chips (organic corn only)

Whole grain pretzels (Newman's makes spelt pretzels)

"Mary's Gone Crackers" whole grain crackers

Popcorn (organic) for air-popping (no microwaving)

Meat Substitute Foods (protein)

Beans and Lentils of all kinds (canned or dried)

Nut butters and nuts and seeds

Veggie burgers (from whole grains, beans and vegetables, not TVP or soy protein isolate)

Tempeh (must cook this before using in recipes for at least 15 minutes)

Sprouted Tofu (on occasion)

Seitan (wheat gluten)

Prepared beans (organic and vegan chili, bean soups, baked beans, lentil soup)

Condiments and Seasonings

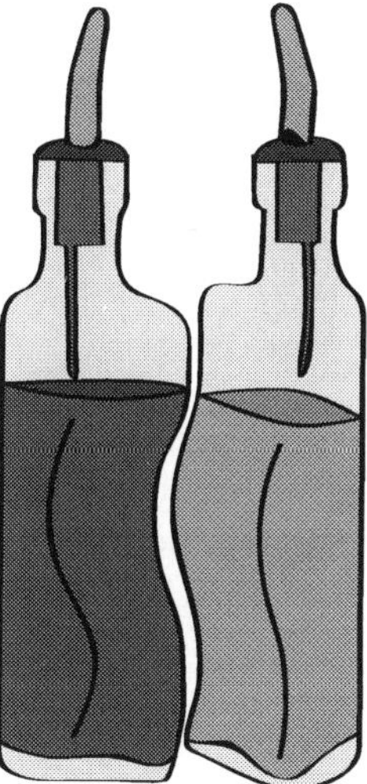

Herbs and spices (organic is best to avoid radiation)
Unrefined sea salt and Himalayan salt
Organic soy sauce, shoyu, or tamari (wheat-free)
Apple cider vinegar (only buy organic, unfiltered and unpasteurized)
Brown rice vinegar
Umeboshi plum vinegar
Vegetable broth (to replace chicken or beef stocks)
Cocoa powder or Raw Cacao powder
Raw Agave nectar (to use instead of honey or maple syrup - must be raw and organic, don't use more than 2 TBS per day)
Brown rice syrup and Date syrup (to use instead of honey/maple syrup)
Spreadable fruit preserves (no added sugars or artificial sweeteners)
Organic, unsweetened applesauce
Pumpkin puree, unsweetened
Flax seed and Hemp seed oils (to use in salad dressings, do not heat or cook with these oils)
Olive oil (organic, first cold pressing only)
Unrefined Sesame oil (organic)
Coconut, Macadamia and Tea Seed oils (for higher heat cooking, but no frying, of course!)
Mustard, any kind you like
Ketchup (organic only)
Miso (mellow, white or sweet miso) buy refrigerated, non-pasteurized
Tomato products (paste, diced, crushed, sauce, etc.), glass jars recommended over canned
Roasted red peppers
Salsa
Nutritional yeast (not brewers yeast or baking yeast) - use 1 TBS a day to sprinkle on popcorn, and pasta for a nutty flavor. It contains some vitamin B12 and other B vitamins
Kombu seaweed strips (use to cook beans to improve digestion of beans)
Nori seaweed (to make brown rice-veggie sushi, or to sprinkle on savory foods)
Wakame and arame (to make seaweed salad)
Dulse and kelp flakes (to use like salt): detoxifies and has healthy iodine
Green powders (spirulina, wheat grass, chlorella, etc.) to add to smoothies or water
Probiotic capsule (in refrigerated section at health food store, buy broad spectrum, non-dairy)

Beverages

Non-dairy milks (unsweetened almond, rice, soy, or hemp milks)
Teas (green, chamomile, ginger, herbal chai, un-smoked yerba mate and herbal coffee substitutes)

EQUIPMENT LIST

Stainless steel travel mugs (no plastic, no more one time paper coffee cups)
Stainless steel water bottles (to replace plastic water bottle)
Stainless steel or glass food storage containers
Re-useable shopping bags (keep in your car or purse)
Small whisk
Large whisk
Knives
Microplane grater (for ginger, citrus zest, nutmeg)
Mortar and pestle
Suribachi bowl (for making gomasio)
Vegetable peeler
Mesh strainer, large and small
Steamer basket, stainless steel or a bamboo steamer
Stainless steel saucepans, heavy bottomed with lids
Stainless steel large soup pot, heavy bottomed, with lid
Stainless steel or glass mixing bowls, various sizes, especially large (for washing greens)
Cutting boards, wooden or bamboo, use different boards for garlic, fruit, veg, etc.
Coffee grinder, for grinding flax seeds, chia seeds, spices, herbs, amaranth
(Clean the coffee grinder by adding an uncooked grain, like brown rice to the coffee grinder and grinding. Then discard the grain and wipe clean with a damp towel.)
Vegetable scrubber/brush, natural fibers
Garlic press (Always press your garlic. This activates a cancer-fighting compound.)
Blender, glass jar not plastic
Food processor
Rubber spatulas, small, large
Baking sheets, preferably with rims
Baking pans (stainless steel, glass or ceramic)
Stainless steel cooling racks and at least one rack with a small grid pattern to use when roasting tomatoes, etc.
Medical gloves (for working with hot peppers)
Garden gloves (for handling nettles)
Slotted spoon, stainless steel, not plastic
Unbleached parchment paper
Unbleached parchment paper muffin liners, regular and mini
Muffin pan, regular and mini
Baking dishes, glass or ceramic, various sizes
Pie dish, glass or ceramic
Spring-form pans, various sizes

Roasting pans, glass or ceramic
Mason jars, all sizes up to 1 gallon
Tongs, stainless steel or wooden
Kitchen scissors (for food, not household use)
Bamboo sushi mat
Chopsticks
Wooden spoons
Unbleached cheesecloth
Nut milk bags
Rice cooker (for making brown rice, porridge, congee, quinoa, millet, barley, oats, etc.)
Flame tamer
Potato masher, stainless steel
Hand held blender, stainless steel
Kitchen scale, digital is nice
Measuring cups and spoons
Large glass measuring cup (for measuring hot liquids)
Grater (for grating carrots, beets, etc.)
Timer

GLUTEN-FREE DIETS

Many people are quickly realizing that they feel better on a wheat-free or gluten-free diet. Energy improves, allergies disappear and weight comes off. An allergy to wheat is one of the more common food allergies, especially in children. Symptoms include hives, difficulty breathing, nausea, redness and irritation of the mouth and throat, itchy eyes, fatigue, nasal congestion, stomachache, diarrhea and indigestion.

Celiac disease is a more serious condition where the small intestines become inflamed and damaged when a person eats any food containing gluten. Gluten is the protein found in certain cereal type grains including wheat, kamut, spelt, barley, rye, triticale and sometimes oats. Although oats themselves are gluten-free they contain a protein similar to gluten and are often contaminated by other gluten containing grains during processing so it is best to also avoid oats if you have celiac disease.

Whether or not you suffer from a gluten or wheat allergy it is wise to seek out the gluten-free grains as often as possible to decrease your risk of developing symptoms in the future. Wheat is not the only grain out there, but lately it has been dominating our food supply in an unhealthy abundance. Gluten-free grains, seeds and starches include, amaranth, arrowroot, buckwheat, chickpea, millet, quinoa, sorghum, potatoes, rice, teff, corn, tapioca (cassava), sweet potatoes, taro, seeds, beans and nuts. When buying any packaged food, including soy sauce, salad dressings, seasonings, gravy, certain miso, nutritional yeast, vanilla extract and even vitamin supplements, check the manufacturers label to make sure the product is wheat-free and gluten-free. There are many recipes in this cookbook that are wheat-free. But not all wheat-free recipes will necessarily be gluten-free. Gluten-free recipes are indicated in this book with the gluten-free symbol (right), but keep in mind if you have celiac disease and you are using any packaged food (such as those listed above) that it must be clearly labeled gluten-free. Convert additional recipes to gluten-free by omitting foods such as shoyu soy sauce, barley miso, oats and other gluten containing ingredients and substituting tamari, brown rice miso and quinoa. Once you get the hang of it you can turn most meals into gluten-free without even thinking about it.

Please see the Gluten-Free Index on pg. 462.

SEVEN DAY MEAL PLAN FOR GOOD HEALTH

Day 1

Hot Lemon Water Tonic: Always have a large glass of warm or hot water with ½ of a lemon squeezed into it every morning on an empty stomach to help liver release toxins. Follow with a high fiber meal (anything listed below) to escort toxins out of body.

Breakfast

Smoothie with a banana, fresh or frozen berries, 1 TBS of hemp seeds or freshly ground flax or chia seeds, unsweetened almond milk, green powder ("Berry Greens or Vita-Mineral Greens), ice.

Green tea with or after breakfast.

Lunch

Quinoa tabouleh with garbanzo beans, lemon, parsley, tomatoes, cucumbers and carrot.

Lots of water or herbal teas throughout the day.

Dinner

Baked squash halves stuffed with whole grains (wild rice, quinoa and millet), apple, walnuts, and vegetables.
Side of steamed kale.

Before bed: chamomile tea to aid digestion and rest.

Day 2
Hot Lemon Water Tonic (see day 1)

Breakfast
Sprouted grain toast with almond butter and banana.

Green tea with and/or after breakfast.

Lunch
Burrito with black beans, brown rice, vegetables, salsa and avocado on sprouted whole grain tortilla (see pg. 325).

Lots of water or herbal teas throughout the day.

Dinner
Mushroom barley stew with mixed green salad sprinkled with hemp seeds or walnuts and fresh lemon juice (see pg. 134).

Before bed: chamomile tea to aid digestion and rest.

Day 3
Hot Lemon Water Tonic

Breakfast
Steel cut oats with fresh fruit or goji berries, unsweetened non-dairy milk, and freshly ground flax seeds or chia seeds (see pg. 378).

Green tea with and/or after breakfast.

Lunch
Cajun black-eyed peas and brown rice with steamed sweet potato and collard greens (see pg. 292)

Lots of water or herbal teas throughout the day.

Dinner
Miso soup, brown rice, steamed vegetables and pressed kale and seaweed salad (see pg. 104 and 230).

Before bed: chamomile tea to aid digestion and rest.

Day 4
Hot Lemon Water Tonic

Breakfast
Tempeh sausage patties with a side of steamed vegetables (including something green), salsa and some avocado with sprouted whole grain toast (see pg. 410).

Green tea with and/or after breakfast.

Lunch
Split pea soup with yams with a side of millet or buckwheat and cabbage slaw (see pg. 125 and 214).

Lots of water or herbal teas throughout the day.

Dinner
Whole grain pasta with lentil-marinara and vegetable sauce. Sprinkle with nutritional yeast instead of parmesan cheese. Serve with a mixed green salad and healthy dressing (see pg. 341).

Before bed: chamomile tea to aid digestion and rest.

Day 5
Hot Lemon Water Tonic

Breakfast
Quinoa or Amaranth porridge with fresh fruit, 1 TBS raw walnuts, and unsweetened almond milk (see pg. 378).

Green tea with and/or after breakfast.

Lunch
Hummus wrap with shredded vegetables, broccoli sprouts and salsa on a sprouted whole grain tortilla.

Lots of water or herbal teas throughout the day.

Dinner
Stir fry vegetables with adzuki beans served over brown rice, sprinkled with dulse seaweed flakes and 1 TBS hemp seeds or walnuts.

Before bed: chamomile tea to aid digestion and rest.

Day 6
Hot Lemon Water Tonic

Breakfast
Fruit salad with chopped raw pecans or walnuts (include apples and berries) with fresh chopped mint leaves.

Green tea with and/or after breakfast.

Lunch
Bean chili over quinoa and a side of steamed broccoli and kale. Top with avocado slices (see pg. 301).

Lots of water or herbal teas throughout the day.

Dinner
Homemade veggie burger with all the fixings (broccoli sprouts, tomato, red onion, red leaf lettuce, avocado and mustard, but skip the mayo and cheese). Serve on a whole grain bun with baked sweet potato fries and mixed green salad (see pg. 333).

Before bed: chamomile tea to aid digestion and rest.

Day 7
Hot Lemon Water Tonic

Breakfast
Black beans over sprouted whole grain toast with salsa and avocado.

Green tea with and/or after breakfast.

Lunch
Lentil vegetable soup with wild rice and broccoli seaweed salad (see pg. 131 and 206).

Lots of water or herbal teas throughout the day.

Dinner
Tempeh with teriyaki, pesto or Bar B-Q sauce, over brown rice and steamed or raw mixed vegetables (all colors, especially green).

Before bed: chamomile tea to aid digestion and rest.

Snacks

It's best to eat small meals every 3-4 hours. Here are some snack ideas to include in between meals…

- Eat a piece of fruit in between meals and before and after exercising for energy and nutrients.
- Almond butter on sprouted whole grain bread or with whole grain crackers or with sliced apple, banana and celery.
- Make a trail mix with raw walnuts, pumpkin seeds, pecans, sunflower seeds and almonds. Add goji berries and organic dried apricots. Each just a handful.
- "Mary's Gone Crackers" dipped into hummus or other bean dip.
- Raw vegetable sticks with hummus.
- Air-popped popcorn sprinkled with flax seed oil, nutritional yeast and dulse seaweed flakes (see pg. 364).
- A square or two of Dark Chocolate is Ok now and then.
- Lara bars or other 5-ingredient or less snack bar. Read your labels.
- Baked chickpea snacks (see pg. 367).
- Mixed bean salad over quinoa.
- Whole grain pasta salad with mixed beans, chopped vegetables, and healthy dressing.
- Quesadilla with mashed beans, sweet potatoes, garlic, mixed vegetables, and served with salsa.
- Pizza on whole grain pita bread with marinara or hummus sauce, broccoli, spinach, red peppers and sprinkled with chopped walnuts and nutritional yeast.
- Baked tortilla chip nachos with pinto or black beans, steamed vegetables, salsa and avocado slices.

"He who does not know food, how can he understand the diseases of man?"

~ Hippocrates, The Father of Medicine (460-377 B.C.)

Food Remedies for Illness Prevention

Food is powerful medicine. Just as certain ingredients, such as garlic, can help fight illness so too can the wrong foods contribute to disease. Follow the Therapeutic Chef Guidelines for Preventing Cancer, Heart Disease and Diabetes (see pg. 444) for general rules on how to stay healthy. For more specific remedies using food to help prevent or reverse a condition refer to the information below and the Index section of the book for the particular recipes.

Also see the 'Herbal Remedies' chapter for information on how herbs can help prevent or reverse an illness or ailment.

Arthritis: The best thing to do for arthritis is to prevent it. Once arthritis is full blown it may be difficult to reverse without adhering to a very strict diet plan. To prevent arthritis avoid trigger foods: animal meat and dairy products, corn, wheat, gluten, coffee, chocolate, soda, alcohol, fried foods, refined salt, and nightshade vegetables (tomatoes, potatoes, eggplant, peppers and zucchini). Include foods that help reduce inflammation: Seaweed, leafy green vegetables, flax seed oil, ginger, parsley, cherries, cabbage, and turmeric. Drink plenty of water. Many recipes in the book may be easily converted to anti-inflammation recipes by removing any gluten foods or nightshade vegetables from the ingredients. See 'Arthritis' in the Index section for specific helpful recipes.

Immune System: Without a strong immune system our health deteriorates quickly. Chronic fatigue, frequent colds, candida, lupus, fibromyalgia and cancer are just a few indicators that our immune system is not operating at full potential. Things that depress our immune system include stress, poor rest, repeated exposure to allergy-causing foods or chemicals, toxins in our environment, fried foods, processed foods, sugar, alcohol, drugs (including over-the-counter, prescription and recreational), and a diet low in nutrient dense plant foods. To maintain a healthy immune system you should get plenty of rest, drink lots of clean water, eat organic, whole plant foods and have a positive outlook on life. See 'Immune System' in the Index section for recipes to give your immune system an extra boost.

Cancer: Many different things can cause cancer. Toxins, chemicals, radiation, smoking and poor diet all contribute to cancer risk. It is important to keep our immune system strong and to lead a happy life full of fresh air, exercise, healthy foods and a loving support system. Keep fat in the diet low. Avoid animal foods and processed foods. Eat organic, whole plant foods. Avoid sugar and artificial sweeteners. Drink lots of water and herbal teas. Eat seven servings of vegetables and fruit each day (1 cup of raw crunchy vegetables or 2 cups of leafy vegetables = 1 serving. 1 medium piece of fruit = 1 serving). A high intake of vegetables and fruits will keep your immune system strong and help defend against toxins. Plus vegetables and most fruits are alkaline. Cancer cannot grow when the body is alkaline. The cruciferous vegetables (broccoli, cabbage, kale, etc.) are particularly beneficial in the prevention of cancer, as are onions and garlic. Many, many recipes in the book can be used to help prevent cancer, however, see 'Cancer' in the Index section for a list of recipes that are extra helpful for preventing cancer.

Heart Disease: Stress, smoking, poor diet and a sedentary lifestyle all contribute to heart disease and high blood pressure. Meat and dairy are full of saturated fat and cholesterol, which block arteries, leading to heart disease. Removing all animal foods and replacing with beans and greens (for protein and calcium) is a very important step in preventing and reversing heart disease. Also, include more whole grains and avoid sugar, salty foods (especially refined salt), fried foods and all trans-fats. Exercise, meditate, eat whole plant foods and drink plenty of clean water and herbal teas. Include garlic, ginger, beets, cherries, goji berries, seaweed, tempeh and other legumes, whole grains, walnuts, flax seeds, hemp seeds, bananas and dark green leafy vegetables. Almost every recipe in the book is heart friendly, however, for the most heart healthy recipes see 'Heart Disease' in the Index section.

Cholesterol: There are two types of cholesterol: HDL and LDL. We need both kinds but we need them to be in a healthy ratio. Too much of the bad cholesterol in our blood (LDL) puts us at an increased risk for heart disease. LDL levels become raised when we eat saturated fats from animal foods and from trans-fats and sugary foods. You must remove these foods from your diet. If you see the words 'partially hydrogenated oil' or 'trans-fat' on a label don't buy it. This is a rule not just to maintain healthy cholesterol levels but also to maintain overall good health. If you switch to a diet of whole plant foods, rich in antioxidants and fiber, and you get daily exercise you should be able to maintain healthy cholesterol levels. Certain foods are particularly helpful in reducing bad cholesterol and increasing the good cholesterol. Examples include: oats, flax seeds, chia seeds, hemp seeds, lemon, ginger, green tea, dandelion, and turmeric. None of the recipes in this book have ingredients that will raise your bad cholesterol. In fact, most of the recipes were designed to promote healthy cholesterol levels. There are a few that stand out as being exceptionally helpful. See 'Cholesterol' in the Index section for these recipes.

Diabetes: New research indicates that a low-fat diet rich in whole plant foods is the key to preventing Type 2 diabetes. When blood sugar levels are continually out of normal range you have an increased risk for developing heart disease, kidney disease, nerve damage, poor vision and poor circulation. Refined carbohydrates (white flour, soda, cookies, etc.) and fatty foods (meat, dairy, fried foods) need to be replaced with whole grains, whole fruits, vegetables, beans and **small** amounts of healthy fat (nuts, seeds, avocado, olives). Yes- you may eat **unrefined** carbohydrates such as brown rice and fruit if you have diabetes but it is important that you work with your doctor to taper your blood sugar medication accordingly. All of the recipes in this book use ingredients that are safe for people with diabetes. See 'Diabetes' in the Index section for a list of recipes that are especially helpful in maintaining stable blood sugar levels.

Cleansing/Detox: We all need a little help in the cleansing department. Our liver regularly filters the blood, processing toxins. However, with our fast food culture and an increasing exposure to environmental toxins it is hard for our liver to keep up with the amount of toxins entering the body through our food, water, air and skin. Signs that your liver is not functioning efficiently: allergies, chronic fatigue, weight gain, poor digestion, abnormal bowel function, nausea, headaches, bad breath, body odor, mood swings, depression, and immune disorders. Things we can do to nourish the liver: eat clean foods, organic and unprocessed. Drink clean water, use non-toxic cleaners and skin care products, and get exercise in clean air. Eat more plant foods, especially green vegetables like dandelion, seaweed, artichokes, beets, lemons, berries and burdock. Make sure you get plenty of fiber from whole grains, beans and fresh fruits and vegetables each day (30-40 grams, not from supplements) to help expel toxins out of the body, and drink plenty of water and herbal teas. Avoid the foods that are harmful to the liver including alcohol, drugs (over-the-counter, prescription and recreational), caffeine, dairy products, excess fat, sugar and processed and refined foods. See 'Cleansing/Detox' in the Index section for a list of recipes that are particularly cleansing and nourishing to the liver.

Digestion: If you have to take medication for acid reflux, indigestion or irritable bowel syndrome that's a clear sign that the body is not happy with what you're putting into it. Instead of masking symptoms with pills why not discover what foods and food combinations are triggering this reaction. Many times it's from eating too many processed foods, or from not having enough probiotics in your digestive tract to help digest food. Our bodies were not designed to be able to digest the chemical laden foods of our culture so it makes sense that many people suffer from heartburn and other digestive complaints. So start by eating real food, avoiding processed food and take a high quality broad-spectrum probiotic capsule daily to see if that helps. Next, pay attention to how food makes you feel. Many people have trouble digesting dairy products and other animal protein. Refined foods and heavy fats are also hard to digest. Mild to severe allergies to wheat and gluten are on the rise due to their dominance in processed foods. Removing wheat and gluten foods from the diet and using other grains such as brown rice, buckwheat, quinoa and millet can certainly help on many levels. If this does not relieve your symptoms you'll need to do an 'elimination diet' to determine what foods are causing you trouble (research this on the web for specific instructions). You will need to read labels carefully but it is absolutely worth trying. Also, keep meals simple and eat slowly. As we age we produce less and less digestive enzymes. Eating a little bit of raw foods at each meal will provide you with enzymes necessary for digestion. However, some people have trouble digesting certain raw vegetables such as cauliflower, so eat other raw foods instead. It's also very important to chew your food well if you desire healthy digestion. The rule is to chew 50 times per mouthful of food. Food should be like liquid by the time you swallow it. This ensures that enough enzymes are released in your mouth to help break down and digest the food. For quick relief from sour stomach, acid reflux and indigestion try adding 1 tsp of organic, unfiltered, raw apple cider vinegar to a cup of water. For heartburn add 1-2 TBS pure aloe vera juice to a cup of water. Umeboshi plums are also helpful for heartburn and other digestive complaints. Eat one plum or 1 tsp plum paste to relieve symptoms. See 'Digestion' in the Index section for a list of recipes that are helpful in aiding digestion.

Herbal Medicine for First Aid & Common Illnesses

By Cara Saunders

Taking care of yourself and your family with natural remedies can be empowering and inspiring. Using plants as your medicine can give you a connection to nature, something we all need for holistic well-being. You only need to learn about the properties of a few herbs to be prepared to heal a wide variety of common injuries and ailments.

Herbal Medicine Basics

The information given here is intended to be an introduction to the use of herbs to take care of your health. If you are new to herbal medicine, it may be best to seek a consultation from an herbalist to help you decide on the best herbs for your optimum health. Pay attention to how the herbs affect you personally since they can affect each person differently. A remedy that helps one person may make symptoms worse for someone else. Sometimes herbs work by increasing the symptoms to push toward a change. For example, an herbal remedy for a fever can make you hotter so you start sweating and the fever breaks. But if a change doesn't happen and the problem persists or gets worse, listen to your body and stop taking the herbs. Try a different remedy or ask an herbalist for advice.

Before you begin using herbal medicines, there are some concepts and principles to be aware of. It is important to know the source of the herbs that you plan to use. Good quality herbs are grown in a clean environment and harvested during the season and time of day when the medicine of the plant is at its peak. The herbs are then processed while fresh or carefully dried. Some commercially available herbs have been over-harvested from the wild and as more natural habitats for herbs are destroyed by development, some medicine plants have become threatened or endangered. Herbalists, coordinated by United Plant Savers, are monitoring medicinal plant populations and a current list of "at-risk" herbs can be found at www.unitedplantsavers.org. More extensive information about herbal medicine can also be found here. When you buy herbal medicine products, make sure the herbs were organically grown or sustainably wildcrafted from a clean natural area.

If you want to harvest herbs yourself, have the plant identified correctly before using it for herbal medicine. Use a good resource book specific to your area that teaches how to identify plants, or learn directly from a botanist or an herbalist. Besides knowing that you have the right herb, you also need to know that the plant has been grown in an area not treated with chemicals or inundated with pollution. Do not harvest herbs for medicine if they are growing by railroads or highways. Unfortunately, you can do more harm than good if you ingest herbs that have absorbed toxic chemicals from the soil or air.

Herbal Tinctures, Glycerites, Salves, and Teas

Tinctures are made using alcohol to extract and preserve the herbal medicine of a plant. Since tinctures are concentrated, the recommended doses are usually small, listed in number of drops. The drops are put in your mouth under your tongue and are absorbed through the bloodstream. It may be helpful to watch yourself in a mirror so you can see how many drops go into your mouth. Tincture drops can also be added to water or hot water and drank as tea. When a tincture is added to hot water, the alcohol evaporates, but the medicine stays in the water.

Tinctures, such as Elderberry or Catnip, can be used by children, starting with ¼ of the adult dose. Pregnant women need to check with their health care provider because many herbs should not be used during pregnancy. Some herbs may not be appropriate to give directly to an infant, but giving tinctures to a nursing mom can pass the herbs to the baby through the milk. Likewise, a nursing mother needs to be sure any herbs she takes are safe for her baby. Anyone taking pharmaceutical drugs should be sure there is no risk of herb/drug interactions. You don't want to take an herb to lower blood pressure at the same time as a pharmaceutical to lower blood pressure without telling your doctor. Herbal sedatives, such as California Poppy Tincture, should not be mixed with similar pharmaceuticals.

Glycerites are liquid herbal medicines that are made by extracting herbs in vegetable glycerine instead of alcohol. Herbal glycerites are good for children, seniors, or alcohol-sensitive adults. Glycerites are taken internally - the sweet taste making it a pleasure to put the drops directly in your mouth. Glycerites are half as strong as tinctures, so the recommended doses are double that of tinctures. Glycerites should be used within a year since glycerine does not preserve as well as alcohol.

Salves are herb infused oils thickened to make an ointment. Salves are herbal medicines applied topically and absorbed through the skin or gums. Apply salves with clean hands. You can reapply as often as needed. Salves will melt in heat and should be stored in a cool place, out of direct sunlight.

Tea used for herbal medicine should be brewed much stronger than tea for a tasty drink. Leaves and flowers should steep in boiled water for one hour before being strained. Roots or bark needs to be simmered for one hour before straining. A medicinal dose of tea is usually ¼ cup to 1 cup. Any brewed tea that is not used immediately can be refrigerated for up to two days.

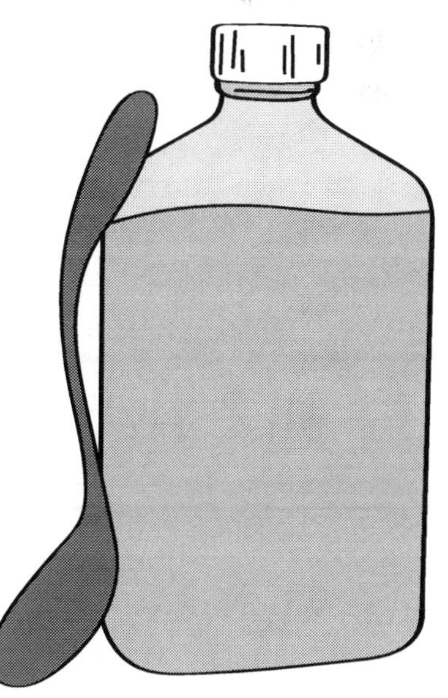

Ailments and Herbal Remedies

Allergies

Symptoms of allergies can include itchy/watery eyes, runny/stuffy nose, dry/itchy throat, hives or other skin rash, upset stomach, or other individual reactions. Digestion, lungs and skin can all be affected depending on the cause of the allergy. When your body needs to process toxins or something difficult to digest - that is the job of the liver. Bitter herbs are liver cleansers. A good liver cleansing herb is Dandelion Root Tincture or Dandelion Root Glycerite (Taraxacum officinale). Another effective bitter herb for allergies is Goldenrod. Goldenrod Tincture (Solidago canadensis) is specific for hay fever and cat allergies, but it is also boosts the immune system. Goldenrod Tincture strengthens your immune system so that your body does not overreact to something in the environment that is not really a big threat. You can describe itchy, watery eyes and a runny nose as an "overreaction" to pollen in the air. Yerba Santa Tincture (Eriodycton californicum) also provides respiratory relief for sinus congestion and runny nose. Yerba Santa strengthens the lungs and the respiratory system. Yerba Santa is an expectorant and is very soothing to a cough. Dandelion Root, Goldenrod and Yerba Santa tinctures can be used together to combat allergies. Sometimes an allergic reaction can occur as a result of stress. If allergy symptoms are due to nerves, include the herbs listed under Anxiety.

Anemia

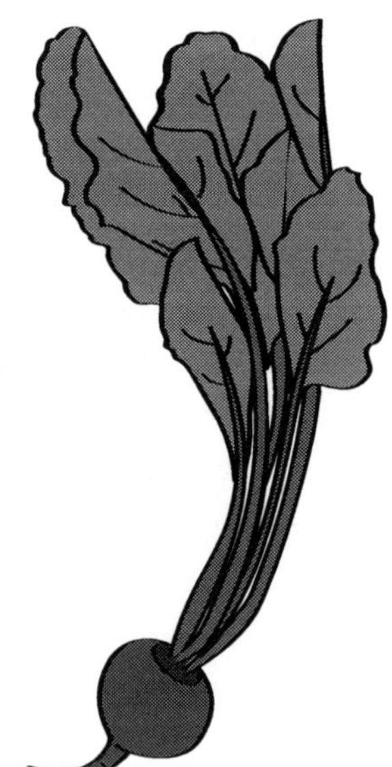

Anemia is a condition in which your blood is depleted and does not have enough iron. When you are low on iron, your body can be slow to heal. The treatment of iron deficiency requires the intake of iron and vitamin C because in order for our bodies to break down and assimilate iron, stomach acid is needed. Many foods rich in vitamin C and iron are used in the recipes in this book (carrots, beets, almonds, walnuts, leafy greens, red kidney beans). Yellow Dock Roots, Dandelion Roots, and Chickweed are herbs that are high in iron and aid in the absorption of iron. You can put doses of Yellow Dock Root Tincture (Rumex Crispus), Dandelion Root Tincture, and Chickweed Tincture (Stellaria media) into a cup of juice (orange, pineapple, or grapefruit) for a dose of natural iron and vitamin C. Elderberry Tincture or Elderberry Glycerite (Sambucus canadensis) is high in vitamin C and iron. You can also use Oregon Grape Root Tincture (Mahonia nervosa) because it releases the iron that is stored in your liver.

Anxiety

California Poppy Tincture (Eschscholzia californica) should be carried with you in case of an emergency. California Poppy does not contain opium like its well-known plant cousin, but it is a sedative and a pain killer. California Poppy is calming, and is used to quiet nervousness and anxiety. It can be used to soothe the tension of a first aid situation or to help chill out a stressful lifestyle. Although California Poppy Tincture is effective for relieving anxiety, some people find it too sedating to take during the day. Blue Vervain Tincture (Verbena hastata) is used to relieve anxiety and it is not sedating. Blue Vervain calms the nerves and quiets the mind. It can be used by people who worry and think too much. Some use Blue Vervain Tincture during the day and California Poppy Tincture in the evening or before sleeping. St. John's Wort Tincture (Hypericum perforatum) is helpful for people who are frustrated, nervously agitated, overwhelmed, anxious or depressed. When you hold a leaf of St. John's Wort up to the sky you will see many tiny pin-prick holes through each leaf. These holes symbolize the action of St. John's Tincture as the light breaking through dark emotions and restoring the ability to trust your instincts. Lemon Balm Tincture or Lemon Balm Glycerite (Melissa officinalis) is used for calming a nervous stomach, an anxious heart and trouble sleeping.

Arthritis

Chickweed Tincture is good for arthritis. Chickweed is a common weed and can be grown in a garden or planter. The leaves are eaten fresh or added to salads. Chickweed is cooling, lubricating and acts as an anti-inflammatory. It also helps the kidneys regulate water. Taking a tea or tincture of Horsetail (Equisetum arvense) improves arthritis (more detail in the section on Bones). A topical remedy for arthritis is Arnica Salve (Arnica latifolia). Many feel relief when they rub Arnica Salve into arthritic joints. You can reapply the salve as often as needed, but do not use on a cut or open sore because Arnica absorbed internally can be toxic. Turmeric Root is an herbal remedy for arthritis. Cooking with turmeric is beneficial, but when you need a more concentrated dose a few times a day, Turmeric Root Tincture (Curcuma longa) is more convenient. Turmeric detoxifies and cleanses the blood and reduces joint inflammation.

Bee Stings and Insect Bites

Some insect bites and bee stings can be very painful. There are several remedies that can quickly ease the pain, itching and swelling. Plantain Salve (Plantago lanceolata.) is used as a drawing agent to pull the poison out of the skin. You can also use fresh plantain leaves, but you actually need to chew up the leaves in your mouth. The enzymes in your saliva break down the leaves and make its healing medicine available. Simply pick some fresh plantain leaves, chew a few times and then press the wet leaves onto the bite or sting. Once you know this herbal trick, it's fun to teach it to your friends. If you don't have plantain growing in a convenient location year round, it is good to have Plantain Salve on hand for the unexpected mosquito bite, spider bite or bee sting. Plantain Salve can be applied regularly until the itching stops, the swelling goes down, and the skin has healed. If the pain persists or the person who got stung or bit needs to calm down, California Poppy Tincture is a natural pain reliever and relaxant (do not use right before driving). Staying calm is important because overreacting can cause the blood to pump faster and spread the poison. If someone is allergic to bee stings, these herbal remedies are no replacement for epinephrine (epi-pen). Speed the healing of a bite or sting by taking Elderberry Tincture or Elderberry Glycerite to boost your immune system and help your body fight the poison.

Bleeding

Yarrow is a good herb to have on hand for bleeding. Yarrow leaves can be applied to a cut, a bleeding wound, or a nosebleed to clot the blood and speed healing. If you grow Yarrow in your garden, you will always have this important remedy easily at home. Yarrow grows in a wide variety of environments, but if you don't have fresh Yarrow on hand, I recommend having Yarrow Salve (Achellia millefolium) in your first aid kit. You can reapply Yarrow Salve as often as needed. Be sure to keep wounds clean to prevent infection. You can also try an herb you probably have in your kitchen – Cayenne Powder (Capsicum annuum). Be brave and sprinkle Cayenne powder onto your cut. Surprisingly, it does not sting. Cayenne stops the bleeding quickly.

Bones

To build strong bones and fight osteoporosis, make a cup of Horsetail Tea or Tincture a part of your daily routine. Horsetail is naturally high in minerals such as silica. Horsetail also strengthens and rebuilds cartilage.

Burns and Sunburn

While trying out these new recipes and spending time in the kitchen, be prepared for what to do if you burn your skin. St. John's Wort Salve is a natural burn remedy. St. John's Wort taken internally is well known as an antidepressant but when applied topically to a burn, it draws heat out and heals the skin. St. John's Wort also heals nerve damage, which can be caused by burning yourself repeatedly in the same place. That makes St. John's Wort Salve a great remedy for chefs and mechanics, or anyone who cooks or works with tools. St. John's Wort is also used to heal sunburn. Another natural burn remedy is Aloe (Aloe vera). If you have an aloe plant growing in your house, break off a fresh leaf. Slice the leaf down the side and open it to reveal the slimy gel. Scoop out the cooling gel and apply it to the burn.

Bruises

It is important to heal bruises soon after they occur. A bruise is stagnant blood and stagnant blood can be a potential cancer site. No need to worry. Yarrow Salve applied to bruises, even old bruises, will quickly help to break up the stagnant blood of a bruise and heal the damaged tissues. Arnica Salve can be massaged into bruises as long as the skin is not cut or broken open. Arnica is great when you are banged up and have sore muscles. (See details in the section on Muscle Injury.) If the topical treatment isn't enough, Calendula Tincture (Calendula officinalis) can be taken internally to heal old wounds, move stagnant blood and remove bruises.

Blisters

If your skin has been rubbed raw or if a blister has formed, reach for Yarrow Salve. Apply Yarrow Salve then cover the area with a bandage to prevent further rubbing. If the blister opens, continue applying Yarrow Salve until the skin is completely healed.

Cancer

For preventing cancer, regular cleansing of the body systems can prevent a build up of carcinogens. (See section on herbs to Detoxify.) For treating cancer, since each situation and person is unique, consultation with an herbalist and strong social support is important. An herbalist can help get to the root of the spiritual, emotional, and physical causes of cancer and create an action plan for changes that need to be made. Some herbs are too stimulating and should not be used with cancer. Remedies an herbalist might suggest are Red Clover Tincture (Trifolium pretense), Shiitake Mushroom (Lentinula edodes) Tincture, and Turmeric Root Tincture, but they are not necessarily appropriate for all individuals and circumstances. Red Clover Tincture is used when the goal is to wall off cancerous tissue, creating a cyst around the cancer that separates it from the rest of the body. The cancer is not cured, but it is not able to spread. Shiitake Mushroom Tincture concentrates and preserves the medicinal qualities of shiitake mushrooms. Scientific research has shown that shiitake mushrooms boost the immune system, accelerate degeneration of tumor cells, and inhibit abnormal cell growth. Turmeric Root Tincture has been shown to reduce tumors and inflammation. In some cases, Violets are used to reduce cysts, tumors, breast cancer or skin cancer. Violet Salve (Viola odorata) can be applied topically at the site of the cancer.

Candida, Yeast Infection, Thrush, Fungus on Skin

Candida is a yeast that normally lives peacefully in our bodies, but colonies can grow out of control when we are under stress or if the immune system has been suppressed from long term use of antibiotics. Colonies of Candida can live in the vagina, intestines, nipples, and arm folds. A Candida overgrowth that causes flaky red skin and white patches in the throat, mouth or on the tongue is called thrush. Candida overgrowth can be indicated by a white vaginal discharge and itching in the vagina or anus. Shepherd's Purse Tincture (Capsella versa) is a remedy for thrush. Calendula Tincture is an anti-fungal remedy for yeast in the intestines. Oregon Grape Root Tincture helps bring your intestines back into balance. Chaparral Tincture (Larrea divaricata), Fireweed Tincture (Epilobium angustifolium), and Horsetail Tincture are balancing herbs that help push Candida back to normal levels. Chaparral Tincture is anti-fungal and helpful when the immune system and liver are overwhelmed with toxins. Fireweed is an anti-inflammatory and reduces heat. Horsetail Tincture is a good astringent, changing your body's environment so the yeast cannot flourish. The body's environment that allows yeast to overgrow is the same environment that grows fungus. Athlete's foot, toenail fungus, and "jungle rot" are related problems. For these topical conditions, the tinctures can be applied to the skin and also taken internally.

Colds, Flu, Virus, Bacteria (fever, sinus infection, sore throat)

We are the most susceptible to colds and flu when we are under stress, overworked, run-down, and our immune system is not functioning at its best. For a quick recovery, it is important to get lots of sleep, since your body heals while it is resting. (See section on herbs for Sleep.) Elderberry Tincture or Elderberry Glycerite is an herb to think of as soon as you feel the first signs of a cold or flu. Many times, if you take Elderberry right away, you can fight off a virus before it causes a cold or the flu. Elderberry boosts your immune system and can be used regularly as a preventative. It is naturally anti-viral, high in bioflavonoids, vitamin C, beta-carotene, iron and potassium. Another way to build a strong immune system is with Shiitake Mushroom Tincture. It's great to eat your medicine by cooking with shiitake mushrooms, but if you want to give extra strength to your immune system, you can take Shiitake Mushroom Tincture three times a day or add the tincture to your food or tea. Echinacea Root Tincture (Echinacea purpurea) stimulates the immune system and increases the production of white blood cells, improving the body's ability to fight infection. A quality Echinacea Root Tincture is made from fresh roots that are at least four years old and gives your mouth a tingling sensation.

A fever is your body's way of raising the temperature to make an inhospitable environment for viruses and bacteria. But when the fever is no longer serving this purpose, you want to break it and start sweating. A good way to do this is by taking a hot shower or bath, then bundling up in warm clothes and blankets and drinking a cup of hot Elderberry Tea or Yarrow Tea (Achillea millefolium). You can simply put the tincture drops into hot water, or if you have Elderberries or Yarrow leaves and flowers you can brew fresh tea. This will cause you to start sweating and the fever will go down. For sinus or chest congestion, sore throat, and cough, you will be happy to know about the holy herb Yerba Santa. Yerba Santa Tincture is a strong lung tonic that will help you breathe easier. It is an expectorant, but is also effective for a dry cough. Yerba Santa is an anti-bacterial and is a wonderful remedy for sinus infections. If the sore throat is severe, it is possibly Strep throat, caused by the bacteria Streptococcus. In this case, you should reach for a strong antibiotic herb such as Oregon Grape Root Tincture. With acute symptoms, you can take a dose of Oregon Grape Root Tincture every couple hours. A sore throat is not the only symptom that can indicate a bacterial infection. Other symptoms may include fever, earache, yellow or green mucus, painful urination, diarrhea, nausea or vomiting. If you suspect that your symptoms are caused by a bacterial infection, Oregon Grape Root Tincture may be just the remedy you need. Calendula Tincture builds up the immune system and is indicated when symptoms include swollen glands. Calendula can also be helpful for bacterial infections that stay in the body due to poor lymphatic drainage. Red Clover Tincture is also good at moving the lymph and relieving swollen glands.

Detoxify

Today, pollution and chemicals are so abundant that even people who eat mostly organic food can benefit from herbs that remove toxins from the body. Get in the routine of using herbs to cleanse the body twice a year, in the spring and fall, or whenever is convenient for you. I recommend taking the detox herbs for a month, or 28 days in a row. Dandelion Root is the first herb I think of for cleansing. It is a bitter tasting remedy that cleanses the liver and gallbladder, allowing these organs to work more efficiently. Dandelion Root Tincture or Dandelion Root Glycerite improves digestion and is a mild laxative. Chickweed Tincture is an important remedy for cleansing the body. Chickweed decongests the lymph system and clears out stagnant water held in the body by flushing it through the kidneys. Another wonderful herb for detoxifying the body is Chaparral. Chaparral Tincture, made from the leaves and flowers of this desert herb, has an intensely bitter taste, but one that is worth trying when you need to remove toxins from your body. Anyone who has been exposed to chemicals, taken medical drugs, used recreational drugs, smoked tobacco, or regularly consumed alcohol or caffeine may have a compromised lymph system, immune system and liver. Toxins can accumulate in any of our pathways of elimination lungs, skin, kidneys, colon or menstruation – and symptoms of toxicity can appear in any of these pathways. We are lucky to have Chaparral Tincture to help our bodies remove accumulated toxins and return our body systems back to peak performance. Red Clover Tincture is another great herb for detox because it removes impurities from the blood. St. John's Wort Tincture affects the nerves and liver and also cleanses toxins from the blood. When the body is loaded down with toxins, depression and anxiety can result. Lightening the load of toxins in the body can bring clarity to the mind and peace to the emotions. During a detox, eat healthy food using recipes from this book, so that you are not adding more toxins from junk food. Remember to drink a lot of water and eat foods rich in fiber since water and fiber help remove waste from the body.

Diabetes

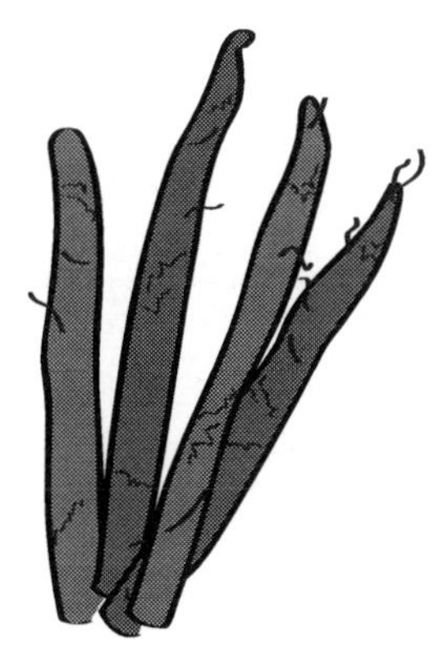

A diet high in processed foods and a lifestyle that lacks exercise can lead to poor sugar management by the body as well as insulin resistance. Insulin Resistance can lead to type 2 diabetes, high blood pressure, heart attack, stroke, and can be a factor in the initiation or growth of cancers. Exercise, especially muscle building, is key to preventing insulin resistance. Getting enough rest and adequate sleep at night are also very important. In addition to diet, exercise and sleep, there are herbs that can help. Shiitake Mushroom Tincture has been shown to lower blood sugar levels. Burdock Root Tincture (Articum lappa) and Chaparral Tincture can help stabilize blood sugar levels by stimulating the digestion and metabolism of fats and oils. When the body is able to digest fats, it is not as heavily reliant on sugars and carbohydrates. Yellow Dock Root Tincture reduces stress on the pancreas by sedating the appetite, digestion and metabolism.

Digestion

Good digestion is a key to good health. Without proper digestion, essential nutrients are not assimilated. Properly chewing your food is the first step to good digestion. You should chew 40-50 times per mouthful of food. The food should be liquid by the time you are ready to swallow. This ensures that enough of the enzyme amylase is released in your saliva to start the break down of starches or carbohydrates. Consuming more raw foods (fruits and vegetables, sprouted nuts, seeds, legumes and grains) is a good idea since they are naturally abundant in digestive enzymes. The older we get, the harder it is for the body to produce enzymes, leading to poor digestion and other health problems. You can take supplemental digestive enzymes if it is not always possible to consume food in its raw state. Taking a non-dairy, broad spectrum probiotic capsule from a health food store can do wonders to help digestive problems. In addition, Oregon Grape Root Tincture is our herbal ally when it comes to maintaining a healthy digestive system and helping us get the most nutrition out of the foods we eat. Many people are surprised to learn that Oregon Grape Root is a remedy for both constipation and diarrhea, seemingly opposite problems. This is because Oregon Grape Root works by balancing the intestines, stomach and liver. It is also effective for relieving indigestion or acid reflux. Oregon Grape Root is antibacterial and anti-amoebic, so it is used for travelers' dysentery and food poisoning, which may cause nausea and vomiting. Unlike conventional antibiotics, Oregon Grape Root does not destroy the beneficial bacteria that live in our gut and aid digestion. I have heard many people say that they like to take Oregon Grape Root Tincture daily as a preventative while traveling. Even at home, Oregon Grape Root can be used to stimulate digestion, especially protein and fats, and improve nutrition. Another great herb for digestion is Yellow Dock Root. Use Yellow Dock Root Tincture to speed up digestion when food sits in the stomach or colon too long. Diarrhea or constipation may be symptoms of this problem, and reasons to use Yellow Dock Root Tincture. Dandelion Root Tincture or Glycerite can help tone the muscles that move food through the digestive tract. Dandelion Root is a gentle laxative that promotes healthy digestion and elimination.

Energy

California Spikenard is a giant herb that grows in creek water and has stars of blue-black berries. California Spikenard Berries are used to relieve stress and fatigue. California Spikenard Berry Tincture (Aralia californica) eases the physical symptoms of stress and lightens emotions. It works quickly to provide a mood shift when emotions are running high. It gives energy when stress has left you feeling run down. California Spikenard Berry Tincture is a great herb to have around if you are having mood swings, feeling over emotional, or stressed out. Blue Vervain Tincture is also useful if you are feeling low on energy. Blue Vervain balances your body's hormones and fluids. (Read more on Blue Vervain in the sections on Anxiety and Sleep.) Fatigue can cause dehydration. Drink water early in the day so you don't get dehydrated and tired in the afternoon. Add fresh-squeezed lemon or lime juice. If you are tired from being active in the summer heat, an herbal ice tea may be just the thing to cool you down and give you more energy. Use herbs like peppermint, basil flowers, catnip, lemon balm and nettles. To make an electrolyte drink, add sea salt to your herbal ice tea. Resist the temptation for stimulants with caffeine since caffeine upsets the normal electrolyte balance. If low energy is a regular problem, you may need to boost your immune system. Use herbs such as Elderberry, Yerba Santa, Echinacea, and shiitake mushrooms that are described in the section on Colds, Flu, Virus, Bacteria.

Heart Health (blood pressure, circulation, blood thinners, cholesterol)

A healthy heart requires a healthy cardiovascular system, with good circulation and little pressure on the heart. Blood pressure is affected by the elasticity of veins and arteries. The less elastic blood vessels are, the more resistant they will be to blood flow, which leads to higher blood pressure. Yarrow Tincture increases the elasticity of blood vessels and lowers blood pressure. Yarrow thins the blood and improves circulation. Salt increases blood pressure by constricting blood vessels. Shiitake mushrooms remove excess salt from the body and lowers blood pressure. Since fluid retention raises blood pressure, herbs that strengthens the kidneys are beneficial to heart health. Dandelion Root Tincture and Chickweed Tincture are safe and effective diuretics that can be used to flush out extra fluid and lower blood pressure. Red Clover Tincture is used to thin the blood because Red Clover contains natural coumarins. High blood pressure can also be caused by stress, anxiety and mental tension. California Poppy, Blue Vervain, or California Spikenard (see Anxiety and Energy) can help you relax and re-energize from stress, alleviating the strain on your heart. The body uses cholesterol to line the arteries as a reaction to inflammation. Cholesterol soothes irritated tissue in the arteries, but too much can block the arteries and stress the heart. Studies show that Shiitake Mushroom Tincture lowers cholesterol. Hawthorn Berries contain bioflavonoids and fruit acids that are cooling to heat and irritation. Hawthorn Berry Tincture (Crataegus sp.) prevents your body from needing to line the arteries with cholesterol, thus lowering cholesterol. Hawthorn Berry Tincture is a tonic herb that strengthens the heart and can be used as a preventative by people with a family history of heart disease. Hawthorn Berry Tincture works slowly over months and years as you take a dose a few times each day.

Infection

Oregon Grape Root Tincture is an herbal antibiotic that can be used to prevent and treat infections. When treating an open wound, take Oregon Grape Root Tincture internally and apply Plantain Salve topically, directly on the wound. Both herbs act as an antibiotic. Plantain is a drawing agent that can draw out pus and heal wounds. Staph infections can be treated with Oregon Grape Root Tincture, taken internally and/or applied topically. Use a cotton ball to wipe the affected area with the tincture. We know that Oregon Grape Root Tincture is good for intestinal infections, but also remember to use Oregon Grape Root Tincture when you have symptoms of a bacterial infection - headache, fever, aches, or sore throat (see section on herbs for Colds, Flu).

Menopause

Blue Vervain Tincture is an excellent remedy for hot flashes and night sweats. It works by regulating hormones, cleansing the liver and balancing body temperature. Red Clover Tincture is also useful during menopause because of its cooling, moistening and cleansing effects. Red Clover has natural plant estrogens (phyto-estrogens), which are chemically similar to the estrogen our bodies make, but they do not cause excessive growth. The plant estrogen from Red Clover binds to the body's estrogen receptor sites to prevent our body's estrogen from causing problems. Cleansing herbs, such as Dandelion Root Tincture, and other mentioned in the Detoxify section, are beneficial during menopause.

Menstruation

To set your menstrual cycle to a "normal" 28 day cycle, use Yarrow Tincture. High estrogen levels during the second half of the cycle can cause buildup of the uterine lining, uterine fibroids and excessive bleeding with heavy cramping. Yarrow Tincture eases a heavy menstrual blood flow and shortens a long menstrual cycle. Dark and clotted menstrual blood can be a sign that the uterine muscles are weak and are having trouble expelling the uterine lining. Weak uterine muscles can lead to fibroids. Shepherd's Purse Tincture is a remedy for fibroids. It strengthens the uterus and quickly stops excessive bleeding. Extra estrogen means the liver has to work harder. Yarrow Tincture, Calendula Tincture, Dandelion Root Tincture and Blue Vervain Tincture help the liver break down extra hormones. These four herbs are also good for bringing on a late period and easing PMS symptoms such as mood swings and food cravings. Heavy bleeding and a long menstrual cycle can cause anemia. Use Yellow Dock Root Tincture and other herbs mentioned in the section on Anemia. Sometimes low estrogen is the problem. Low estrogen can cause a cycle where the bleeding starts slowly with spotting and extends a long time. Low estrogen can decrease vaginal lubrication. Easter Lily Tincture (Lilium longiflorum) nourishes the ovaries and builds fluids. It is also a remedy for cysts in the breasts or ovaries. Feverfew Tincture (Tanacetum parthenium) is a remedy for menstrual cramps, blood congestion and headaches. Some of the above remedies need to be used for three cycles before symptoms are completely resolved. In the meantime, California Poppy Tincture works quickly as a pain killer and antispasmodic to relieve cramps.

Muscle Injury

Arnica is an herb you won't forget once you have used it to heal sore muscles or relieve joint pain. Arnica salve is massaged into muscle injuries, sore muscles, sprains, strains, torn ligaments and pulled muscles. It is anti-inflammatory and can be used to reduce pain, redness and skin swelling. Joint pain and arthritis pain are relieved by Arnica. It is also a remedy for bruises when the skin is not cut or bleeding. You don't want to use arnica on broken skin because in large doses it can be toxic. Arnica salve applied to unbroken skin, or homeopathic arnica taken internally are safe ways to take the herb.

Nerve Injury

St. John's Wort applied topically as a salve or massage oil is amazing in its ability to heal nerves. St. John's Wort Salve can be applied topically to nerve injuries, nerve damage or nerve pain. The salve can be massaged into the skin at the location of the pain or along the spine where the nerves connect. You can even put St. John's Wort Salve in your mouth. Apply it to gums to soothe the nerve pain of a toothache.

Prostate Health

Prostatitis is inflammation of the prostate gland due to infection. A common symptom is pain during urination. Take Oregon Grape Root Tincture or Echinacea Tincture for their antibacterial properties. Yarrow Tincture reduces irritation of the prostate. Benign Prostate Hypertrophy (BPH) is swelling of the prostate gland, which can interfere with the flow of urine. The main symptom is frequent, slow, or painful urination, especially at night. Yarrow Tincture can help soothe the prostate, especially since Yarrow improves circulation. The herbs described in the Detoxify section are useful here because accumulated toxins from plastics or growth hormones can cause BPH. Red Clover Tincture helps detoxify, and it also helps reduce swelling of glands. Fireweed Tincture reduces inflammation and prostate irritation.

Skin

Plantain is so useful for first aid that it is also known as "Soldiers' Weed." Plantain Salve is antibacterial, making it a good remedy for any scratch or scrape to prevent infection and heal the skin. If a wound has gotten infected, it can be used to draw out pus and counter the bacteria. Plantain Salve is such a good drawing agent that it can be used to draw out slivers, splinters, thorns, dirt, glass, or anything else stuck in the skin. Apply Plantain Salve and wait with a pair of tweezers to withdraw the material as it emerges. It soothes any type of skin rash, calms the itch and irritation, reduces redness, and combats any bacteria that may try to live in an open wound. Apply Plantain Salve to skin bothered by eczema, poison oak, poison ivy, acne or hives. While Plantain Salve is working topically, it is also beneficial to use herbs internally that reduce heat and irritation. Stimulate your internal defenses with Dandelion Root Tincture, which cleanses the liver and gallbladder. Chickweed Tincture taken internally cools inflamed tissues. Chickweed improves the functioning of body systems that affect the skin, such as lymph and digestion. Red Clover Tincture is an excellent remedy to take internally for skin issues. Red Clover clears impurities from the blood that would otherwise try to exit from the skin and cause a rash, eczema, or hives.

Sleep

A good night's sleep is crucial to your health. If you have trouble falling asleep or staying asleep through the night, reach for California Poppy Tincture. You can take one dose an hour before you want to sleep and another when you are ready for bed. Keep California Poppy Tincture by your bed so if needed you can take a third dose when you wake up in the night. Since California Poppy is also a pain killer, it will help if pain is keeping you awake. Many have used California Poppy while traveling overseas and need to adjust to a new time zone. Take California Poppy to help you sleep and with jetlag. When traveling or at home, sometimes we can't sleep because the mind is so busy thinking. Thinking over everything ten times or worrying over little details is not helpful, especially if it is happening at night while you should be sleeping. Blue Vervain Tincture quiets the mind, and allows you to rest and sleep. Blue Vervain also helps women during menopause when insomnia becomes a common symptom. Wild Lettuce Tincture (Lactuca scariola), is a deeply sedative remedy that relaxes tight muscles. Wild Lettuce is the remedy of choice when there is a pattern of negative thinking. If you notice that each train of thought ends with a negative outcome, instead of staying awake, reach for Wild Lettuce Tincture and enjoy a good night's sleep. Lemon Balm Tincture or Lemon Balm Glycerite calms the nervous system and helps you sleep when anxiety or nervousness is keeping you awake. More than one herbal sleep remedy can be taken at the same time to help end your sleepless nights.

Toothache

A toothache should not be ignored since it can be a sign of a serious problem. If you are on your way to the dentist and can't stand the pain of the toothache, take some California Poppy Tincture. If the toothache involves nerve pain, apply St. John's Wort Salve to the gums in the affected area. Plantain Salve is used to draw an imbedded tooth out of the gums, which can be necessary for wisdom or baby teeth. This use of plantain was discovered while using plantain in the mouth for an infection. Not only did plantain draw out the infection, but it also pulled the tooth up to where it needed to be. If there is an infection in your mouth, apply Plantain Salve and take Oregon Grape Root Tincture on your way to the dentist.

Weight Loss

If you are not at the ideal place of only eating recipes out of this cookbook, getting some exercise every day, and living a stress-free lifestyle, then you might have some extra weight you would prefer to live without. Chickweed Tincture helps with weight loss and is very nourishing. It improves metabolism by balancing the liver and the endocrine system, and is a healthy way to rid your body of excess fat and water. If your body is not good at breaking down the fats you eat, Chaparral Tincture can help by cooling and stimulating the liver. Stress and a poor diet can be a real strain on your liver. Chaparral Tincture can help bring you back into balance.

Where to Get Your Herbs

The herbs described here, and many others, can be ordered from Bear Wallow Herbs. Seven of the herbs discussed here are available from Bear Wallow Herbs in one package, the Herbal Medicine First Aid Kit. It is good to have the kit on hand when traveling or at home, so that you have natural remedies handy for emergencies or common illnesses. The kit comes with direction cards that list each ailment alphabetically so that you can quickly find what you need.

Bear Wallow Herbs uses only organic grape alcohol to make tinctures. All Bear Wallow Herbs salves are made with fresh herbs, organic extra-virgin olive oil, and natural beeswax. All herbs grown for Bear Wallow Herbs are organic and harvested using sustainable principles. Plus each product is infused with healing intentions.

Bear Wallow Herbs
Cara Saunders, Herbalist
PO Box 803
Mount Shasta, CA 96067
(530) 462-4784
cara@bearwallowherbs.com
www.bearwallowherbs.com

NOTES ON HERBAL REMEDIES

Now you are ready to learn simple ways you can use herbal medicine for healing yourself and your friends and family. If a problem persists or gets worse, seek additional advice from your herbalist or health care practitioner. The symptoms described here are ones we don't want to live with for long, and a signal that something is wrong, so start taking herbs now and the symptoms should disappear in a few days. Even after the symptoms subside, continue taking the herbs for a few weeks to prevent a reoccurrence. Be sure to practice good hygiene to prevent spreading.

- Bear Wallow Herbs lists a range of doses on each tincture label. Since each person and situation is unique, the dose varies. Each individual should use the lowest effective dose and repeat that dose as needed. If you are using the herb for prevention or for changing a long term chronic issue, take the tinctures three times a day. For acute symptoms that come on suddenly, take another dose every hour.

- If you move into symptoms such as fever, congestion, cough, sore throat and nausea, continue taking immune boosting herbs every couple of hours and drink lots of water.

- Take a dose of Oregon Grape Root Tincture or Yellow Dock Root Tincture right before eating to stimulate digestion. If experiencing diarrhea, vomiting or constipation, take another dose every 20 minutes. When the symptoms are relieved, for the next couple days, take a dose three times a day to continue healing your digestive tract.

- In addition to the topical remedies for muscle and nerve injuries, also take California Poppy Tincture internally as a pain killer. California Poppy relieves pain but it is also sedative, so it should only be used when you don't have to drive or be attentive to work.

- California Poppy Tincture and Wild Lettuce Tincture are physical sedatives. Don't use large doses before driving or when you need to be alert and attentive. Some people can use small doses of these herbs during the day to ease anxiety and negative thinking. Each person needs to find the right dose for the situation.

Beverages

We need to drink plenty of fluids each day to stay hydrated, ideally clean water and herbal teas. A hydrated body is able to flush out toxins more efficiently, and will help to increase energy and reduce pain in stiff joints. All systems run more smoothly when you are properly hydrated including circulation, digestion, nutrient absorption, elimination and regulation of body temperature. Chronic dehydration leaves the cells of the body weak and vulnerable to disease. To calculate how much water you need each day take your body weight in pounds and divide it in half. This gives you the number in ounces that you need to drink each day. For example, if you weigh 150 pounds you should drink 75 ounces of water each day. If you drink coffee and other caffeinated beverages, and/or alcoholic beverages you will need to drink even more water because these cause the body to lose water. The beverage recipes in this book provide you with beneficial nutrients and alternatives to common unhealthy beverages. Drinking herbal teas is a delicious way to add more vitamins and minerals into the diet. Smoothies are an easy way to get your daily requirement of fruits and vegetables.

A Word on Coffee

One week there's a study out that states coffee is full of antioxidants and can help with weight loss. The next week there's a study out that says coffee is related to anemia and osteoporosis. What to do?!? My suggestion is this... if you drink coffee make sure it's fair trade and organic (better for you, the environment and better for the workers). Only drink 1 cup a day. Drinking too much coffee can leach calcium from your bones, leading to an increased risk for osteoporosis. Also, coffee makes us dehydrated so for every cup of joe drink two cups of water to replenish fluids. And lastly, be mindful of what you're putting into your coffee. Artificial creamers, sweeteners and milk are probably worse for you than the coffee. Decaf coffee is ok if you are looking to decrease caffeine intake (good idea if you have trouble sleeping or have osteoporosis) but be sure to buy decaf coffee that says "Naturally Decaffeinated" or "Swiss Water Process."

Here Are Some Alternative Options for Your Morning Beverage

- Grain coffee (made from barley and other grains)
- Green Tea
- Homemade nut or seed milk instead of cow's milk or creamer
- Stevia, date syrup, agave nectar, brown rice syrup or yacon syrup to sweeten, but use small amounts

What About Kombucha?

This popular fermented vinegar-like tea that has been around for hundreds, if not thousands of years...Why is it not in the book? Don't I like kombucha? Sure I do, I even make my own. The thing is, it's a tricky thing to describe and write about. If you've never had it before, then you should try a store bought brand first to see if it's something you want to invest in making at home. It's not that it's hard to make or very time consuming once you've got it down, but there are many little details and instructions for the first timer, so I thought I would save that recipe for another time. But, by all means, try some kombucha, see how it makes you feel and if you like it, investigate how to make your own.

A few of the reported benefits of drinking kombucha: alkalizes the body, restores balance, aids digestion, increases energy, balances blood sugar levels, decreases appetite, increases immune system strength and creates healthy skin, hair and nails. It contains beneficial probiotics, antioxidants, enzymes, B vitamins and amino acids; yet it is very low in calories and sugar.

Milks

At the end of this chapter there are several recipes for non-dairy milks. These healthy beverages can be used on your morning cereal or in any recipe that calls for cow's milk in a 1:1 ratio. It is not necessary to drink cow's milk or consume dairy products to get your calcium. Instead consume beans and greens with most meals to get your calcium and other bone strengthening nutrients, and drink water and herbal teas to stay hydrated.

GF

TURMERIC TEA

SERVES 1

Turmeric has amazing healing properties! It has been used to help fight cancer, arthritis and joint pain, and is full of antioxidants. It reduces inflammation in the body, clears skin of acne, is important for healthy bones, helps to regulate cholesterol and helps to maintain stable blood sugar levels. Learn ways to get turmeric into your diet (curry powder has turmeric!!!).

1 cup water
¼ tsp ground turmeric
½ cup unsweetened hemp seed, almond or rice milk
yacon syrup to sweeten, if desired

Bring water to a boil in a medium saucepan. Reduce to a simmer and add the turmeric, whisking well to combine. Cover and let simmer for about 10 minutes, stirring occasionally. Stir in the milk and let simmer just another minute to heat through. Remove from heat and add sweetener if desired. If it is too strong, dilute with water.

Drink this tea at the first sign of a cold.

ANOTHER GREAT TURMERIC TEA

SERVES 1-2

This tea is more of an everyday tea because its flavor is more appealing due to the ginger and lemon. This tea has cleansing properties.

2 cups water
½ tsp ground turmeric
½ tsp ground ginger
½ lemon, juiced
sweetener of choice (date syrup, agave, stevia, yacon syrup, molasses)

Bring water to a boil in a medium saucepan. Reduce heat and whisk in the turmeric and ginger. Cover and let simmer for 10 minutes. Pour into mugs and add fresh lemon juice and sweetener to meet your taste buds.

ASTRAGALUS IMMUN-I-TEA

GF

SERVES 2

Astragalus is a Chinese root that is usually sold dried in the herbal department of health food stores or at most Chinese grocery stores. It looks like a white tongue depressor. Astragalus is beneficial for boosting the immune system. Astragalus is also good for replenishing the body after chemotherapy or radiation. It is strengthening, energizing and revitalizing. It is has anti-inflammation and anti-bacterial properties, and can help restore the liver.

2 oz. (by weight) dried astragalus root
3 cups water
2 cups water

Place the astragalus root and 3 cups of water in a medium pot. Cover and bring to a boil. Reduce heat to low and let simmer, covered, for one hour. Strain liquid into a cup or other heatproof vessel (no plastic). Return the pot and the boiled astragalus to the stove. Add another 2 cups of water, cover and bring to a boil. Reduce to low and let it simmer again, this time for 30 minutes. This is to extract as much as you can from the root. After 30 minutes, strain the liquid into a cup. Combine the liquid from the first batch with the liquid from the second batch. Drink this tea 15 minutes before meals.

Optional Ingredients: add a small handful of one, some, or all of the following ingredients plus more water as needed for super immuni-tea: dried shiitake mushrooms, licorice root, pau d'arco, dried nettles, rooibos tea, dried peppermint, goji berries, Chinese dates, poria locos, grated ginger, dried burdock root, oatstraw, and/or kombu seaweed. Reishi mushrooms may also be used. This mushroom has super immune boosting properties. To use, cut off a small piece from a dried reishi mushroom and soak until soft. Then boil with the astragalus. Warning: Reishi has a strong, bitter flavor! You'll need to add fresh lemon juice or stevia to the tea after it has boiled to mask the bitter reishi.

Drink this tea during fall and winter months to help prevent the flu and colds. However, do NOT drink this tea if you feel like you are coming down with a cold, a fever or the flu. If these symptoms are already present drinking astragalus tea may exacerbate your symptoms. Use for prevention only.

EVERYDAY HOT LEMON TONIC

SERVES 1

It's important to hydrate first thing in the morning with plenty of water being it has probably been hours since you last had something to drink. Drink this every morning on an empty stomach. It helps the gallbladder and liver finish their job of dealing with fats and toxins. It also stimulates sluggish bowels and helps energize the system and makes you feel clean and balanced. Just make sure you wait half an hour after drinking this tonic to have your breakfast. And, as always, make sure it's a healthy, high fiber breakfast full of fruits and whole grains.

2 cups of hot water
½ a medium lemon

Squeeze half a lemon into 2 cups of hot water and drink! Simple, easy and refreshing.

HAPPY TUMMY TEA

SERVES 4

Many people suffer from poor digestion especially those who eat processed and refined foods, which wreak havoc on the digestive system. These ingredients aid in the digestion of foods.

1 tsp fennel seeds
1 tsp licorice root, dried
1 tsp lemon peel
1-inch cinnamon stick
1 TBS rose hips
2 tsp fresh ginger root, minced
1 tsp peppermint leaves
1 tsp dried lemon grass (may substitute 1 TBS fresh lemon grass, inner bulb, chopped)
1 TBS chamomile flowers, dried

Take the fennel seeds, licorice root, lemon peel, cinnamon stick, rose hips, and ginger and place in a non-aluminum pot with 4 cups of water. Simmer, covered over low heat for 40 minutes. Turn off heat and add the peppermint leaves, lemon grass and chamomile flowers and steep, covered, for 5 minutes. Strain and serve after meals to help increase digestion.

CHAI TEA

SERVES 1

Chai is perfect for drinking after meals because it can help with digestion. This particular recipe is also great for warming you to the bone on a cold winter's day.

Spice Mixture

Mix equal parts, about 1 TBS each: ***ground*** *ginger, star anise, cloves, nutmeg, cinnamon and cardamom. Then add a* ***dash*** *of cayenne or some freshly ground black pepper to the mix and stir to combine. Store this in a spice container away from heat and light. Use with the recipe below whenever you desire fresh chai.*

For Each Serving You Will Need

1 cup of water
½ cup milk (almond, soy, rice)
1-2 tsp sweetener of choice (date syrup, agave, brown rice syrup, yacon syrup, stevia)
¼ tsp spice mixture
1 rooibos tea bag (may substitute green tea bag)

Place milk and water in a pan and bring to a boil. Let boil for a few seconds then turn off heat and add the sweetener, spices and tea. Cover and let steep for 5 minutes. Strain into a mug and sip, adding more milk or sweetener if desired.

NETTLE TEA

SERVES 2

Nettles are great for combating anemia, eczema, allergies, diarrhea and arthritis and can help balance blood sugar levels. It is also used as a diuretic and to help protect the lungs.

2 cups water
1 handful of fresh nettles, rinsed or 2 tsp dried nettles
1 lemon

Bring water to a boil. Place fresh nettles in a pot (or place dried nettles into a tea ball) and pour boiling water over them, making sure they are covered with water. Steep, covered for 10 minutes. Strain into cups. Season with fresh lemon juice and enjoy.

Use gloves or tongs when handling fresh nettles - no need to remove the leaves from the stems.

(GF) LEMON VERBENA-MINT TEA

SERVES 2-4

Lemon verbena and mint are useful as digestive aids.

Fresh mint leaves, about 20 leaves, stems discarded
Fresh lemon verbena leaves, about 15, stems discarded
2 cups water
1 orange
1 lemon
sweetener of choice (I like stevia or yacon syrup)
sparkling water, optional

Boil 2 cups of water. Place the mint and lemon verbena leaves in a glass jar or ceramic tea pot (something that can take the heat!). Pour the hot water over the leaves and cover. Let steep for 5 minutes. Strain and add juice from half the orange and half the lemon. Taste and add sweetener if desired.

Serve hot or add sparkling water and ice to serve chilled.

(GF) COLD PREVENTION TEA

Make a batch of this once or twice a week to stay immune to colds.

1 TBS alfalfa
1 TBS horsetail
1 TBS lemon balm
1 TBS nettles
1 TBS red clover
1 TBS rose hips

Mix the dried herbs together in a bowl. Figure out how much tea you want to make. I suggest making a liter at a time. In that case, boil one liter of water, then take 3 TBS of the herb mixture and place in a pan. Pour the boiling water over the herbs, cover and let steep for 15 minutes or up to several hours. Strain and drink, reheating if desired.

Use dried herbs for this recipe. Store remaining herbs in a dark glass jar away from heat, sunlight and moisture.

HIBISCUS TEA

SERVES 1

(GF)

High in vitamin C, this pretty flower makes a tasty tea!

1 cup water
1-2 tsp dried, ground hibiscus
lemon to taste
sweetener, to taste, (date syrup, agave nectar, brown rice syrup, yacon syrup or stevia)

Bring water to a boil in a pan. Add hibiscus, cover and let steep 5-10 minutes. Strain, add a squeeze of lemon and a dash of sweetener.

ROSE HIP TEA AND ROSE HIP LEMONADE

(GF)

Rose hips are the fruit of the rose bush. They are high in vitamin C and bioflavonoids. Rose hips are associated with helping to cure the common cold and boost the immune system. They can also be helpful in the prevention of heart disease, cancer and urinary infections.

To make tea, boil 1 liter (or 4 cups) of water. Place 2-3 TBS rose hips in a large glass mason jar or ceramic tea pot (something that can take the heat!). Pour the boiling water over the rose hips and cover. Let steep for 15-20 minutes. Strain into a cup and sip (you can just keep the rose hips in your jar if you want).

To make lemonade, add freshly squeezed lemon juice and your choice of sweetener (I use 4-6 lemons for every liter of rose hip tea. Then I like to add a dash of stevia powder, date syrup or agave nectar, until sweetness level is reached).

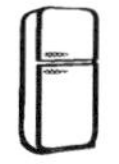

Save the rose hips after you make the tea and put them into soups or stews, because they are edible and add a unique tangy flavor to foods. Plus, you'll get additional vitamins that may not have been fully extracted during the tea making process.

UME-SHOYU-KUDZU TEA: THE MACROBIOTIC "CURE ALL"

SERVES 1

This classic macrobiotic remedy is used to help treat colds and the flu, and to help relieve fatigue, headaches, hangovers, diarrhea and digestive problems. The umeboshi plum has a powerful alkalizing effect on the body. If you aren't feeling perfect try drinking this and see if it helps!

1 ½ TBS ground kudzu * *(see note)*
2 cups twig tea, cooled (may substitute water)
1 tsp umeboshi paste (may substitute ½ umeboshi plum, chopped, pit removed)
1 tsp shoyu soy sauce
½ tsp freshly squeezed ginger juice * *(see note)*

Place the kudzu in 1 cup cold tea and whisk until dissolved. Add the umeboshi, shoyu and ginger juice. Pour into a saucepan and bring to a boil. Stir constantly and simmer for 1 minute. Pour into a large mug and whisk in the other cup of twig tea.

Kudzu root powder may sometimes need to be finely ground before using in a recipe. Do this with a mortar and pestle or in a clean coffee grinder.

To make fresh ginger juice grate fresh ginger on a microplane placed over a bowl. Pick up the grated ginger and squeeze the pulp, releasing the juice and collect in the bowl. Measure juice and proceed with recipe. Pulp can then be used in a smoothie for extra fiber and a little zing!

Drink warm or hot.

(GF) ROOIBOS (A.K.A. RED TEA)

From South Africa, contains no caffeine and is sweet in flavor. It is high in antioxidants and helpful in cancer prevention.

Brew tea and drink daily or use in recipes where a little sweetness would be nice.

GREEN TEA

GF

Polyphenol (an antioxidant) is a compound in green tea that has been shown to inhibit the growth of cancer cells. Research also indicates that drinking green tea may lower cholesterol and improve immune system functioning. It is also beneficial in aiding weight loss, and preventing cancer, rheumatoid arthritis, cardiovascular disease and infection.

Follow brewing instructions to prevent over-steeping of tea, which makes green tea bitter.

Drink 1-2 cups of green tea per day.

Green tea does contain some caffeine but not nearly as much as coffee. Drink earlier in the day if your are sensitive to caffeine.

MATCHA

GF

Matcha is a green tea powder made from the whole green tea leaf. When you drink matcha you ingest the green tea leaf, not just the brewed water. Green tea leaves contain antioxidants and chlorophyll which are beneficial in fighting disease, aging, and helpful in removing toxins from the body. One glass of matcha is the equivalent of drinking 10 glasses of regular green tea in terms of antioxidants and chlorophyll!

To make matcha, bring water to a boil then let cool for 10 minutes. Place 1 tsp of matcha powder into a small bowl and whisk with a couple tablespoons of cool water to make a paste. Then whisk the paste with 1 cup of hot water to make a tea. Add your favorite non-dairy milk, sweetener or lemon, if desired. I like matcha tea plain or with a dash of unsweetened almond milk.

There are special whisks, made from bamboo, designed for making matcha. I highly recommend getting one of these.

GF YERBA MATE

Native to South America, this relative of the holly bush is a wonderful alternative to coffee. It contains a compound similar to caffeine and has been traditionally used to treat fatigue, appetite control and a weakened immune system. It gives you a boost in energy but without the 'jitters' sometimes associated with coffee. This tea is full of heart-healthy compounds and antioxidants.

Please buy **unsmoked** yerba mate because the health properties are lost during the smoking process.

GF ROSEMARY-GINGER-LEMONADE WITH BERRIES AND MINT

MAKES ABOUT 5 CUPS

Rosemary helps stimulate the immune system, increase circulation, decrease inflammation, and improve digestion, memory and concentration.

8 medium rosemary sprigs
2 TBS grated ginger
5-6 large lemons, juiced
½ tsp stevia powder
2 TBS freshly minced mint leaves
2 TBS goji berries, rinsed

Place rosemary sprigs in a saucepan with the grated ginger. Add 2 cups of filtered water. Cover and bring to a boil. Turn off heat and let steep for 15 minutes.

Meanwhile add the lemon juice to a 1 quart/liter glass jar (something that can take the heat; a mason jar works well). Add 2 cups of cold water to the jar. Next, carefully pour the rosemary-ginger tea through a strainer into the glass jar, then add the stevia powder and shake to dissolve. Taste and adjust if needed. You may want more stevia (go slowly though) or you may want more lemon or water. Chill and serve garnished with some fresh mint and floating goji berries in each glass.

BARLEY LEMONADE
MAKES 2 QTS.

This elixir is a diuretic, fights colds, aids digestion, and is helpful in reducing inflammation.

1 cup hulled barley, rinsed (not pearled barley)
2 qts. water (8 cups)
2 lemons, zested and juiced
¼ cup raw local honey (not a vegan ingredient, so use yacon syrup if you are vegan)
mint leaves, optional

Place the barley and water in a heavy bottomed pot, bring to a boil, reduce heat and simmer over medium-low heat, covered, for 40 minutes. Let cool to room temperature, strain liquid and pour into a serving pitcher. Add the zest and juice of 2 lemons, the honey and some minced mint leaves.

After straining off the liquid to make this beverage you will have a couple of cups of cooked barley. Use this barley in soups or as a side dish instead of rice.

Serve over ice or sip it as is.

Please use a local, raw honey. If it doesn't say raw, it probably isn't. Cooked honey has no medicinal properties and may actually be harmful to your health.

SPA WATER
MAKES 1 LITER

This simple beverage is so invigorating and refreshing that you'll think you're at the spa! Perfect drink for a hot summer day.

1 medium cucumber, peeled and sliced
1 lemon, sliced
4-8 mint leaves
1 liter fresh, filter water

Slice the cucumber and lemon and place in a pitcher with the mint leaves. Pour 1 liter of fresh, filtered water into the pitcher, cover and place in the refrigerator until ready to serve. I like to make this in the morning and drink it throughout the day. It is unbelievably refreshing! If you drink all the water in less than one day you can add another liter of water and place back in the refrigerator. Discard the cucumber, lemon and mint pieces after 24 hours.

POMEGRANATE FIZZ

SERVES 2

Pomegranates are popular for their antioxidant power. Studies have shown that consuming pomegranate seeds or fresh juice helps improve cardiovascular health and prostate health.

½ cup fresh pomegranate juice from 2-3 whole pomegranates (see note)*
¼ cup orange juice
1 ½ cups sparkling water, chilled
a squeeze of fresh lemon juice
10-15 pomegranate seeds, optional, for garnish

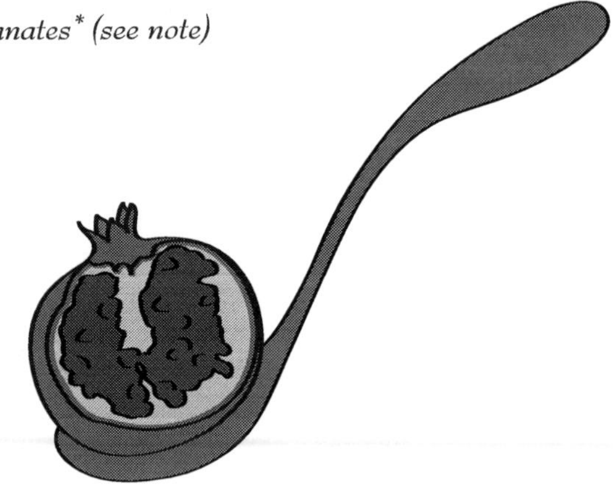

Pour the juices into a pitcher then add the sparkling water. Add a squeeze of lemon juice and stir gently. Pour into glasses and garnish with a few pomegranate seeds. Enjoy!

How to open a pomegranate: Wearing an apron or clothes you don't mind staining, cut the pomegranate into wedges. Then fill up a medium bowl with cold water and place one of the pomegranate wedges into the water. Use your fingers to release the seeds (arils) from the white membrane. The edible seeds will sink to the bottom and the tasteless white membranes will float to the top. Repeat with each wedge, then skim off the white membranes from the top of the water and discard. Drain off the water and you are left with the pomegranate seeds. Use these delightful, juicy seeds to garnish any dish, add to salads or grain dishes, or process the seeds through a sieve to make pomegranate juice.

CLEANSING GINGER ALE (GF)

SERVES 4

Ginger is very helpful in aiding in digestion, relieving nausea, improving circulation, reducing inflammation and supporting the liver. The ginger, red raspberry, sassafras and sarsaparilla all help cleanse your liver and blood. Who doesn't need that?

3 cups water
2 tsp grated fresh ginger * *(see note)*
1 tsp red raspberry leaf * *(see note)*
1 tsp sassafras root * *(see note)*
1 tsp sarsaparilla root * *(see note)*
stevia, to sweeten
1 cup sparkling mineral water, chilled
lemon slices, for garnish

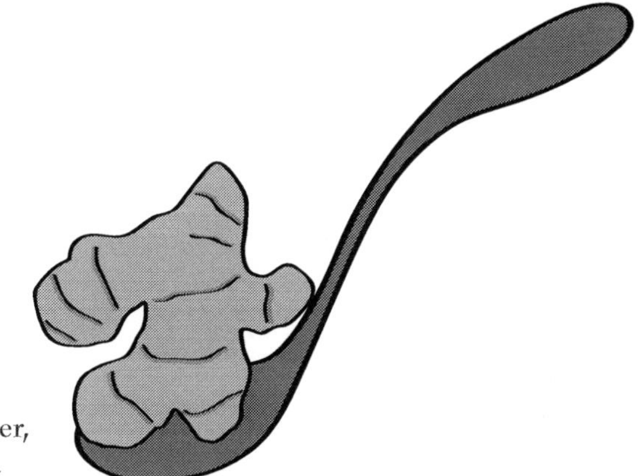

Bring the 3 cups of water to a boil. Add the ginger, red raspberry leaf, sassafras and sarsaparilla root. Let simmer, covered, for 30 minutes. Strain and let cool completely in the refrigerator. Add stevia to sweeten to your liking, then add the sparkling mineral water just before serving. Garnish with lemon slices and serve.

Buy the dried red raspberry leaf, sassafras root and sarsaparilla at your health food store.

APPLE CIDER VINEGAR WATER

Used daily by Hippocrates as a health tonic and by American soldiers to combat indigestion and pneumonia on the battle field. This fermented cure-all is said to prevent joint pain and stiffness from arthritis, aid in digestion, balance good bacteria in the digestive tract, stabilize blood sugar levels, increase energy, improve skin, aid in weight loss, improve cholesterol and blood pressure and help thin blood.

To use: add 2 tsp of apple cider vinegar to 1 cup of water and drink slowly with or between meals.

Make sure to always purchase raw, unpasteurized, organic and unfiltered apple cider vinegar. This is important!

GF

ALMOND MILK
MAKES ABOUT 2-3 CUPS

1 cup raw almonds (see note)*
3 cups filtered water
1 date, pitted, optional (may substitute 1 TBS agave nectar, brown rice syrup or yacon syrup)
dash of Himalayan salt, optional

Soak almonds overnight or up to 24 hours in enough filtered water to cover by 2-inches in a cool, dark place, or in the refrigerator. Drain and rinse almonds, discarding soak water. Place almonds in a blender with 3 cups fresh filtered water. Add the date if you want a sweeter milk. Add a dash of salt to bring out more sweetness, if desired. Blend until very smooth. Then pour into a large strainer lined with two layers of cheesecloth, on top of a bowl, and let drain. Use large pieces of cheesecloth so you can pick it up and squeeze the milk out into the bowl. This is sometimes a little messy. Once strained, store nut milk in refrigerator for 4-5 days. Some separation may occur so shake before using.

If you plan on making nut milks often then it's worth investing in a nut milk bag.

Soaking the almonds overnight or up to 24 hours makes the almonds easier to digest and easier to blend. If you don't have time to soak you can still soften them by boiling them in plenty of water for 3 minutes. Drain, let cool and add to blender with 3 cups fresh filtered water and proceed as indicated.

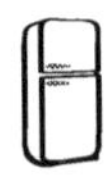

Save almond pulp to use in raw cracker recipes, as a filler for veggie burgers, or use in raw crust recipes and other baked goods. I keep leftover almond pulp stored in my freezer for up to 2 months.

COOKED OAT MILK

MAKES ABOUT 5 CUPS

1 cup rolled oats
5 cups filtered water
1 tsp vanilla extract, optional
1 banana, ripe

Combine rolled oats and water in a saucepan, bring to a boil, cover and simmer over low heat for 30 minutes, stirring often to prevent sticking. Let rest, covered for about an hour. Strain off liquid (oat milk) into a glass bowl, discarding any remaining oats (or use as your morning cereal). Place oat milk in a blender with the vanilla and banana and blend until smooth. Store oat milk in the refrigerator and use within 4 days. Shake before serving.

SOAKED OAT MILK

MAKES ABOUT 4 CUPS

1 cup rolled oats
4 cups water
a dash of vanilla extract, optional
sweetener of choice, optional

Soak the rolled oats in a large bowl with the 4 cups water for 6 hours or overnight. If soaking longer place in a cool dark spot, or in the refrigerator. After soaking, place oats in the blender and blend until smooth, adding more water gradually through the top of the blender until desired thickness is reached. Add optional vanilla or sweetener and blend again. Let mixture rest in the refrigerator for 1 hour, then stain through a fine mesh strainer or through two layers of cheesecloth placed in a strainer and over a large bowl. Pick up cheesecloth and squeeze out the liquid into the bowl. Discard the remaining oats.

Store oat milk in the refrigerator for up to 5 days.

CASHEW MILK

MAKES 5-8 CUPS

1 cup cashews
filtered water
unrefined sea salt or Himalayan salt, optional
vanilla, and sweetener, optional

Soak cashews in plenty of water overnight or up to 24 hours, in a cool, dark spot (could place in refrigerator). Drain, discarding water, and place cashews in a blender with 1 cup of fresh filtered water. Blend until smooth then slowly add more water while blending until desired thickness is reached (use less water for making cashew cream, more water for cashew milk). Add optional ingredients and blend again. Strain if desired, or just shake before each use (that's what I do). Consume within 4 days.

If you don't have time to soak the cashews, then boil them for 3 minutes in enough water to cover. Drain, rinse and drain again, then place in a blender with 1 cup of water and proceed as indicated below.

HEMP SEED MILK

MAKES ABOUT 5 CUPS

3 ½ cups water
1 cup hemp seeds (shelled)
1 pitted date, (may substitute ½ a banana,ripe)
a dash of Himalayan salt, optional

Add 1 cup of the water and 1 cup of hemp seeds to a blender and blend until smooth. Then add the rest of the water, the sweetener, and salt (if using) and blend again until smooth. Keep refrigerated for up to 5 days. Shake well before using.

You could soak your hemp seeds in the water for 4 hours before blending. This will make blending easier. You can use the soak water for blending.

SUNFLOWER SEED AND HEMP SEED MILK (GF)

MAKES ABOUT 4-5 CUPS

Soak ½ cup each of sunflower and hemp seeds for 4-6 hours in enough filtered water to cover by an inch. Add seeds and soak water to a blender with an additional 2-3 cups of pure water (depending on how thick or thin you like the milk). Blend with 1 TBS agave nectar, brown rice syrup or 1 pitted date and a dash of salt. Add a dash of cinnamon and vanilla if desired. Blend until smooth. Strain through two layers of unbleached cheesecloth or through a mesh nut milk bag. If you like it really thick, you don't have to strain it. Keep refrigerated. Shake before using.

This milk will last 3-5 days in the refrigerator.

BROWN RICE MILK (GF)

MAKES ABOUT 4 CUPS

1 cup brown rice * *(see note)*
3 cups water
2 cups water
a dash of unrefined sea salt or Himalayan salt, optional
1-2 pitted dates, optional (may substitute sweetener of choice)
1 tsp vanilla extract, optional

Bring the first 3 cups water to a boil in a medium saucepan. Add the brown rice, return to a boil, reduce heat, and simmer for 45 minutes. Once cooked and cooled, add the rice to a blender with another 2 cups water and blend until very smooth. Add optional ingredients if desired and blend again. Add a little more water if necessary to make it thinner. You don't have to strain this milk, just shake well before using. This will keep for about 3 days in a glass container in the refrigerator.

If you have time you can soak the rice overnight or up to 24 hours in 3 cups of fresh water in the refrigerator. Then cook the rice in the soak water for 30 minutes, let cool, then blend with the 2 cups of water and optional ingredients until smooth. Soaking grains makes them alkaline, easier to digest, and reduces cooking time.

You can strain this milk through a nut milk bag if you desire a thinner milk. You may want to add a little less water to the blender so it's not too thin after straining.

CHOCOLATE MILK
MAKES ABOUT 2 CUPS

Even better than what I remember drinking at the school cafeteria in second grade. If your bananas are really ripe, you won't need to add any other sweeteners. A few ice cubes can also be added if you like it colder.

1 cup non-dairy milk (almond, cashew, hemp, rice, oat, etc.)
1 medium banana, ripe
a dash of unrefined sea salt or Himalayan salt
1 TBS unsweetened cocoa powder (may substitute carob powder or raw cacao powder)
1 TBS almond butter, optional, if you like it thick and nutty
a small bit of sweetener of choice optional (pitted date, agave nectar, brown rice syrup, yacon syrup, barley malt syrup, stevia, or molasses)
ice, optional

Blend all ingredients except sweetener and ice in a blender until smooth and creamy. Taste for sweetness and add if needed, along with the ice, if using.

GF

HOLIDAY CASHEW-BANANA "NOG"
SERVES 2-4

1 cup cashews (see note)*
1 ripe banana
1 tsp. vanilla extract
¼ tsp cinnamon
⅛ tsp each ground ginger, nutmeg and clove
⅛ tsp unrefined sea salt or Himalayan salt
a dash of turmeric (just a dash!)
1 cup water
1 cup ice
sweetener of choice, if needed (stevia, dates, agave nectar, or brown rice syrup)

Recipe continues on next page...

Place cashews in a bowl and cover with enough filtered water to cover by 2-inches. Soak overnight or up to 24 hours in a cool, dark place. Drain and discard the soak water. Add the drained cashews to a blender with the banana, vanilla, spices, salt, turmeric and 1 cup of fresh water. Blend until cashews are almost smooth, then add the ice and blend again until creamy, adding more water or sweetener if needed until desired thickness and sweetness is reached. Serve immediately, or refrigerate and serve within 2 days, shaking well before serving.

Soaking the cashews makes them alkaline and easier to digest, plus it softens them so the recipe will be creamy. If you don't have time to soak the cashews you can still soften them by boiling them in enough water to cover for 3 minutes. Drain and discard water, rinse and drain again, then proceed with recipe.

ORANGE DREAM SHAKE

SERVES 2-4

2 large oranges, peeled and chopped, seeds discarded (see note)*
1 cup unsweetened almond milk (may substitute soy or rice milk)
½ cup ice
½ of a ripe banana
1 pitted date, chopped (to make it sweeter, if desired)

Place all ingredients except the date in a blender and blend until creamy and frothy. Taste for sweetness and add the chopped, pitted date, if desired, and blend again to combine.

Try also with mango, instead of the orange!

(GF)

VEG-BERRY SHAKE

SERVES 2

This is a great way to get your vegetables for breakfast or as a snack. Honest, you won't even know they're there!

1 cup chopped broccoli, chopped (may substitute 3 large kale leaves)
½ carrot, scrubbed and chopped
1 cup non-dairy milk (may substitute water)
1 cup frozen berries
1 TBS goji berries, rinsed
1 tsp grated ginger
ice, if desired

Blend until smooth, adding ice if desired, and enjoy!

(GF)

FRUITY GREEN SMOOTHIE

SERVES 2

1 orange, peeled and chopped, seeds discarded
1 banana, peeled and chopped
1 cup chopped green apple (don't have to peel if it's organic)
1 cup red grapes
1-2 cups of chopped kale (may substitute chard, broccoli, collard greens, etc.)
1 tsp grated ginger
dash of cinnamon
water or unsweetened hemp milk (may substitute almond, rice or soy milk)
ice, as needed

Blend all ingredients until smooth, adding liquid and ice as needed.

COCONUT ALMOND SHAKE (GF)

SERVES 3

1 young coconut
½ cup raw almonds, soaked in water in the fridge for up to 24 hours, then drained
4 pitted dates, soaked for 1-4 hours, or until soft, then drained
½ tsp vanilla extract
1 TBS green powder (mix of spirulina, wheat grass, barley grass, etc.)
2 TBS goji berries, rinsed
2 tsp minced fresh ginger
1 TBS raw cacao nibs, to taste (may substitute raw cacao powder)

Cut open coconut and pour coconut water through a strainer. Place coconut water in a blender. Scoop out coconut meat and place in the blender. Combine remaining ingredients in a blender and blend until smooth.

If the coconut water and meat have a purple-ish color then discard. The meat should be white and the water should be clear.

CHOCOLATE ALMOND BUTTER SHAKE

SERVES 2 (MAKES ABOUT 2 ½ CUPS)

1 cup unsweetened almond milk
2 TBS cocoa powder (may substitute raw cacao powder)
2 TBS raw almond butter
2 small ripe bananas
1 cup ice
1 pinch of unrefined sea salt or Himalayan salt (see note)*
1 TBS sweetener (agave nectar, brown rice syrup, yacon syrup, or 1 pitted date)

Place the almond milk, cocoa powder, almond butter, bananas, ice, and salt in a blender and blend until smooth. Taste and add the sweetener, if necessary, then blend again.

The salt helps to heighten the sweetness, the chocolate and the almond butter taste.

MA-CACAO SHAKE

SERVES 2-3

Maca is a root vegetable that grows near the Andes mountains of Peru. It is known as a Super food that can help rebuild weak immune systems, increase energy and endurance, and balance and stabilize all body systems. It is used to improve memory, combat fatigue, anemia, depression, enhance fertility, balance hormones, and increase libido. Add 1-2 TBS to any smoothie or shake to increase nutritional value.

⅓ cup raw cacao nibs (see note)*
3 cups water (may substitute coconut water or non-dairy milk)
2 TBS maca powder
⅛ -¼ tsp unrefined sea salt or Himalayan salt (start with ⅛ tsp)
2 pitted dates (see note)*
1 TBS nut butter, optional (I like raw almond butter or just use 1 TBS hemp seeds)
ice, as needed

Place the cacao nibs in a blender and blend until finely ground. Add about ½ cup of the water, the maca powder, salt, dates and optional nut butter. Blend until smooth, then add the rest of the water and blend until well combined. Add ice if desired and blend again until frothy.

You may substitute 2 TBS cocoa powder, carob powder or raw cacao powder for the cacao nibs. Just add it with the maca powder and proceed.

You can substitute one ripe banana in place of the dates.

You can strain through a fine mesh strainer if your blender did not completely pulverize the cacao nibs, or just drink as is.

Soups

IMMUNE BOOSTING BROTH

MAKES 1 LITER

The Reishi mushroom is prized for its medicinal properties, including the ability to boost the immune system. It is used to help treat AIDS, allergies, arthritis, cancer, hepatitis, high blood pressure, autoimmune disease and many other illnesses. It has a strong, bitter taste, which can be masked by adding miso, lemon or sweetener after cooking.

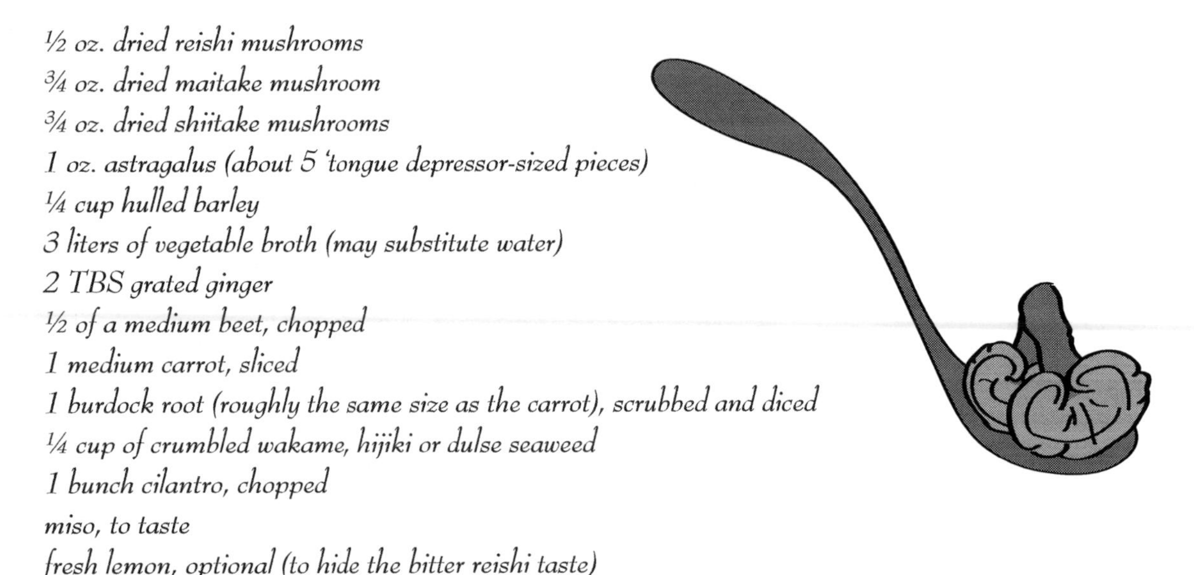

½ oz. dried reishi mushrooms
¾ oz. dried maitake mushroom
¾ oz. dried shiitake mushrooms
1 oz. astragalus (about 5 'tongue depressor-sized pieces)
¼ cup hulled barley
3 liters of vegetable broth (may substitute water)
2 TBS grated ginger
½ of a medium beet, chopped
1 medium carrot, sliced
1 burdock root (roughly the same size as the carrot), scrubbed and diced
¼ cup of crumbled wakame, hijiki or dulse seaweed
1 bunch cilantro, chopped
miso, to taste
fresh lemon, optional (to hide the bitter reishi taste)

Rinse the dried mushrooms, astragalus and barley then place in a large pot. Cover with the broth. Over low heat simmer, covered, for 1-2 hours. Add the ginger, beet, carrot, burdock, and seaweed and simmer another 30 minutes. Strain broth into another pot and add the cilantro and miso, to taste. Add fresh squeezed lemon juice, if necessary.

If you can't find all of the ingredients, that's Ok. Just make it with what you have.

Freeze remaining broth in small containers (for easy thawing) for up to 3 months.

Drink 1-2 cups of broth daily as a tea or use to make soup to keep your immune system strong.

As always, please don't use aluminum or anything plastic when making this healing broth. A ceramic pot is preferred, although stainless steel will do.

As with all herbs and supplements, always check with your doctor or health care provider first to be sure that the herbs won't interfere with your current condition or medication.

SIMPLE RICE CONGEE (JOOK)

SERVES 6

This rice porridge is considered to be therapeutic for the unwell and for infants because it is very easy to digest. Almost every country in Asia has its own version, using different grains, water amounts and condiments. Find one you like or here's a pretty basic recipe.

9 cups water
1 cup brown rice, rinsed and drained
1 ½ tsp unrefined sea salt or Himalayan salt
1 tbs grated ginger
miso slurry, minced green onions, and/or minced cilantro, for serving

Combine the water, rice, salt and ginger in a large heavy bottomed pot. Bring to a boil over medium-high heat, then cover, reduce to low and cook for at least 1 ½ hours or up to 6 hours, stirring occasionally. You want the grains to be broken down and creamy. Serve warm, garnished with a drizzle of miso slurry, onions and cilantro.

PUMPKIN RICE CONGEE (GF)

SERVES 6

This is yummy for breakfast!

9 cups water
¾ cup brown rice, rinsed
2 cups chopped pumpkin or any winter squash
dash of unrefined sea salt or Himalayan salt, optional

Bring water and rice to boil in a large, heavy bottomed pot (or in a rice cooker with a congee/porridge setting). Reduce heat to low and cover. Cook 2-3 hours, stirring occasionally, until you have a smooth porridge. Add the chopped pumpkin and dash of salt, cover and simmer another hour, or until desired texture is reached (I like it really creamy). Mash the pumpkin with a potato masher for a smoother consistency. You can add more water if you like it thinner. Then serve for breakfast, topped with fruit or for lunch and dinner, topped with green onions and cilantro.

Use a flame tamer to prevent burning if you don't have a heavy bottomed pot.

IMMUNITY CONGEE

SERVES 4-6

Astragalus strengthens the immune system and protects against colds and flu.
This congee is helpful for improving energy.

½ cup brown rice, rinsed and drained
6 cups water
1 astragalus root (the size of a tongue depressor)
2 tsp of dried hijiki seaweed
pinch of unrefined sea salt or Himalayan salt, optional
½ cup sliced dried shiitake mushrooms,
soaked in 1 ½ cups hot water for 20 minutes
1 medium carrot, scrubbed and diced
1 burdock root, same size as the carrot, scrubbed and diced
1 TBS grated ginger
3 garlic cloves, pressed
1 TBS goji berries
3 green onions, sliced
nori or dulse seaweed flakes

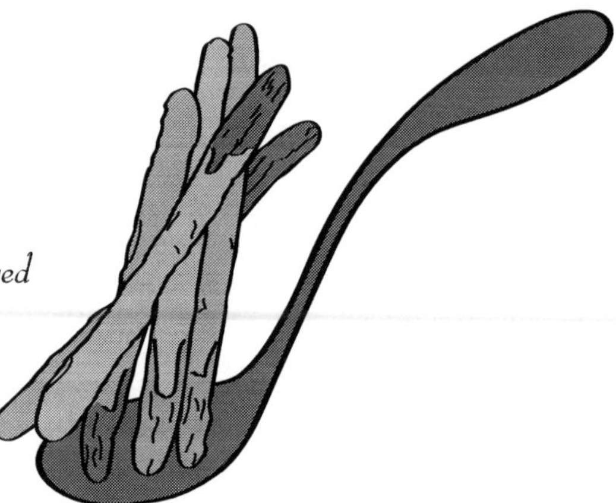

Put the brown rice, water, astragalus, hijiki and a pinch of salt in a large, heavy bottomed pot or crock pot/slow cooker. Bring to a boil, cover and reduce heat to low. Let the rice cook for about 2 hours, checking every hour to make sure it's not sticking to the bottom. The more you cook the rice the more strengthening properties the congee will have. Add the rehydrated mushrooms and the soaking water, the carrots, burdock, ginger, garlic and goji berries to the rice and let simmer for another 2 hours. Finally, remove the astragalus and add the green onions and stir to combine. Serve into soup bowls, garnished with nori or dulse flakes.

Eat this to prevent sickness before or after surgery or recovery from injury or illness. This is not to be eaten if you begin to feel signs and symptoms of the flu or sickness. Astragalus is for prevention only and may worsen symptoms if eaten when you're already sick.

KITCHARI

SERVES 6-8

A balanced, nourishing recipe that is easy to digest and helpful in cleansing. It is used in Ayurvedic cooking as part of a fast to rid the body of toxins, while giving strength and vitality to the body.

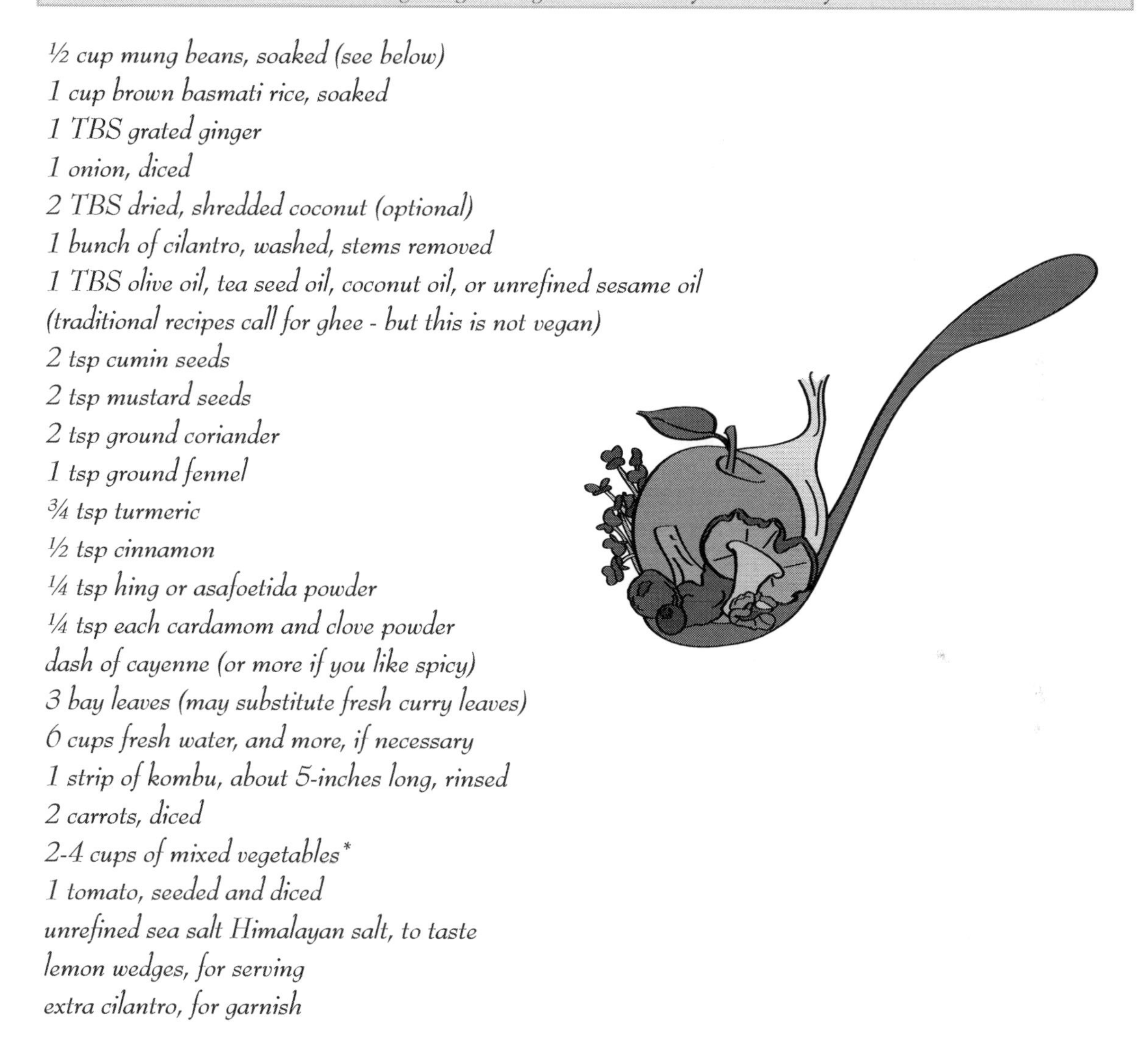

½ cup mung beans, soaked (see below)
1 cup brown basmati rice, soaked
1 TBS grated ginger
1 onion, diced
2 TBS dried, shredded coconut (optional)
1 bunch of cilantro, washed, stems removed
1 TBS olive oil, tea seed oil, coconut oil, or unrefined sesame oil
(traditional recipes call for ghee - but this is not vegan)
2 tsp cumin seeds
2 tsp mustard seeds
2 tsp ground coriander
1 tsp ground fennel
¾ tsp turmeric
½ tsp cinnamon
¼ tsp hing or asafoetida powder
¼ tsp each cardamom and clove powder
dash of cayenne (or more if you like spicy)
3 bay leaves (may substitute fresh curry leaves)
6 cups fresh water, and more, if necessary
1 strip of kombu, about 5-inches long, rinsed
2 carrots, diced
*2-4 cups of mixed vegetables**
1 tomato, seeded and diced
unrefined sea salt Himalayan salt, to taste
lemon wedges, for serving
extra cilantro, for garnish

**beet and their greens, chard, yellow squash, cauliflower, rutabaga, radish, turnip, sweet potato or yam, zucchini, asparagus, dandelion, nettles, daikon, shiitakes, burdock, collards, broccoli, etc.*

Recipe continues on next page...

KITCHARI...

Carefully pick over the beans and rice to remove any stones. Soak beans in 3 cups of water for 4-8 hours. Soak the rice separately in 3 cups of water for any amount of time (up to 24 hours) in a cool dark place. Drain and discard the soaking water from the beans and rice. Place the ginger, onion, coconut, cilantro and ½ cup fresh water in a blender and blend until smooth. In a large soup pot, heat oil over medium heat and lightly brown the cumin seeds and mustard seeds for 30 seconds. Add the coriander, fennel, turmeric, cinnamon, hing, cardamom, cloves, cayenne and bay leaves and stir for another 30 seconds. Do not let the spices burn. Stir in the drained beans and rice. Stir well to coat then add the coconut-cilantro mixture, 6 cups of fresh water and the kombu. Bring to a boil, cover, reduce heat to a simmer and cook for 30 minutes. Then add the vegetables (save leafy greens until very end) and cook another 10-15 minutes over low heat. Once vegetables, beans and rice are all tender remove the bay leaves and stir in the chopped tomatoes, leafy greens (if using) and the salt. Cook another 5 minutes, uncovered. Taste for salt. Serve with fresh lemon slices and chopped cilantro.

You can add more water at any point if you don't like it so thick. At end of cooking, remove kombu and chop into small pieces and add back to kitchari - if it didn't naturally break apart into tiny pieces.

You could try a mini cleanse by drinking only water and eating only kitchari for 3 days. Always check with your doctor before starting a cleanse!

HEARTY MISO-VEGETABLE SOUP WITH SESAME BROWN RICE

SERVES 6-8

I could eat miso soup and brown rice everyday and there's nothing wrong with that. This version here is hearty and complete. Miso contains beneficial bacteria, or probiotics, but they can be destroyed when the miso is boiled so always add miso at the end of cooking, once the heat is turned off. I buy mellow, sweet or white miso because it is less salty.

Rice

2 cups of short grain brown rice
3 ½ cups filtered water
1 5-inch piece of kombu seaweed, or any mild tasting seaweed you like, rinsed
2 TBS sesame seeds, toasted lightly (stirring in a dry pan over very low heat)

Recipe continues on next page...

HEARTY MISO-VEGETABLE SOUP WITH SESAME BROWN RICE...

Soup

1 small onion, diced
1 cup of sliced fresh shiitake mushrooms, stems discarded
1 6-inch piece of burdock root, scrubbed well, then diced small
1 TBS grated ginger
2-3 garlic cloves, pressed
1 TBS unrefined sesame oil, optional
1 TBS tamari or shoyu soy sauce, optional
4-6 cups filtered water
¼ cup crumbled dry wakame seaweed (pulse in a food processor if necessary)
1 small red beet, scrubbed well, diced small
1 cup of peeled and diced butternut squash (½-inch dice)
4 large kale leaves, cleaned, chopped into 1-inch pieces, stems discarded
1 3-inch piece daikon radish, scrubbed and cut into ¼-inch thick half moons
1 small head of broccoli, chopped into bite sized florets
1 cup of cooked adzuki beans (could substitute green peas)
2-3 TBS mellow white miso paste, whisked with 2 TBS water to make a slurry
½ avocado, sliced, optional
3 green onions, minced
1 small bunch of cilantro, cleaned well and minced

To make the rice, place the rice in a bowl and cover with lots of cold water and swoosh around with a wooden spoon. Let rice settle to the bottom of the bowl then pour off the water and anything that was floating on top of the water. Repeat until water runs clear. Then let drain well through a fine mesh strainer. Place rice and 3 ½ cups filtered water in a pan with the seaweed. Bring to a boil, cover and reduce to very low and let simmer for 40 minutes. Turn off the heat but do not lift the lid. Let sit for another 10 minutes before lifting lid. Add the toasted sesame seeds just before serving.

To make the soup, place the onions, shiitakes, burdock, ginger and garlic in a large pot with the sesame oil and tamari (if using, otherwise just add ¼ cup water to prevent sticking). Heat over medium heat for 5 minutes being careful not to burn the garlic. Now add the water (start with 4 cups and add more water if needed), seaweed, beets and butternut squash. Let simmer for 5 minutes. Next add the kale and daikon and simmer another 5 minutes. Then add the broccoli and simmer for 1 minute. Finally add the cooked beans and stir to combine. Turn off the heat and add the miso slurry. Stir to incorporate then taste for salt. Add a little more water and/or miso slurry if desired. Just remember not to boil the soup once the miso has been added or the beneficial bacteria will be destroyed. Now serve the soup in a bowl topped with avocado slices, green onions and cilantro, with a side of sesame brown rice.

GF

NETTLE SOUP

SERVES 4-6

SUPER nutritious, SUPER simple, and SUPER delicious. Use Nettles, sorrel, purslane or a combination of these. See directions for how to handle fresh nettles on pg. 252. If using purslane discard tough stems when separating leaves from stem.

1 large bunch of fresh nettles, about 1 pound
4 cups water (may substitute vegetavle broth)
6 garlic cloves, pressed
½ tsp unrefined sea salt or Himalayan salt
3 TBS olive oil
1 lemon, zest and juice
1 cup cooked white beans, optional (see note)*

Use tongs or gloves when handling uncooked nettles to avoid being stung. Bring 4 cups of filtered water to a boil in a large soup pot. Meanwhile, trim away the large, tough stems of the nettle with kitchen shears and discard. Place nettle leaves and tender stems in a pot of boiling water. Let simmer partially covered for 3-5 minutes or until tender but still bright green. Turn off heat. Do not drain.

Meanwhile, place garlic in a mortar and pestle with salt and mash to a paste. Then add to a small, heavy bottomed pan with olive oil over very low heat. Heat gently for 15 minutes to infuse the oil with the garlic, taking great care not to burn the garlic or let it turn brown (you could place a flame tamer under your pot to help prevent it from burning). Add the garlic oil, lemon zest, lemon juice to the pot with the nettles and water. Once cooled, purée with a hand held blender or in batches in a blender (no hot foods and plastic!). Add more lemon, oil, garlic or salt if desired.

Add 1 cup of cooked white beans before puréeing if you desire a heartier, creamy soup. I like to reserve a few white beans to put in the soup after puréeing for a little texture.

If the garlic turns brown or the oil starts to smoke, the heat is too high. Discard garlic and oil and start again over very low heat, stirring often. You may want to add more olive oil for a richer soup, but as always, use an oil that says organic and first, cold press.

Sip warm soup on cold days to help rejuvenate your system.

POTATO SOUP WITH NETTLES AND SORREL

SERVES 6

1 TBS olive oil
2 leeks, chopped, cleaned well in a bowl of cold water
4 garlic cloves, pressed
2 medium Yukon gold potatoes, scrubbed and cubed
4 cups vegetable broth
2 cups chopped nettles, hard stems discarded (use scissors, gloves and tongs)
2 cups chopped sorrel leaves, center stem discarded
salt and pepper, to taste (use unrefined sea salt or Himalayan salt)
2 TBS minced chives, for garnish
3 TBS nutritional yeast, optional

Scoop the chopped leeks out of the bowl of cold water with a slotted spoon, leaving any sand in the bottom of the bowl. Place the oil, leeks and garlic in a heavy bottomed soup pot and heat over medium heat for 5 minutes, stirring often. Be careful not to let the garlic burn. Add the potatoes and broth and bring to a boil. Cover, reduce heat and let simmer for 15 minutes or until potatoes are tender. Add the chopped nettles and simmer another 2 minutes. Turn off heat and stir in the chopped sorrel. Add salt and pepper to taste. Use a hand held immersion blender and blend soup until desired creaminess is achieved. Serve garnished with chives and nutritional yeast.

Sometimes I blend about ½ of the soup and combine with the rest, which I leave chunky, using scissors if necessary to chop up any nettles that are too long.

If you don't have a hand held stainless steel immersion blender you can also pour some of the soup into a glass blender and blend until creamy (never fill blender more than ⅔ full, and make sure the lid is secure so you don't end up covered in hot soup).

Don't use a plastic blender if food is hot because some of the plastic may leach into your food.

GF

DANDELION DANDY-LIVER SOUP

SERVES 6-8

Dandelion is SUPER nutrient dense so please find ways to enjoy it. It can help prevent or cure liver diseases; help to purify the blood, gallbladder and kidneys; and help cleanse the body. The leaves are high in beta-carotene and vitamin C, plus iron and many other minerals. Great for treating anemia, reducing bad cholesterol, and clearing skin. Dandelion is best in the spring. Other times of the year it may be too bitter tasting for first-timers. If so, give it another try in April, or add more lemon to your dish.

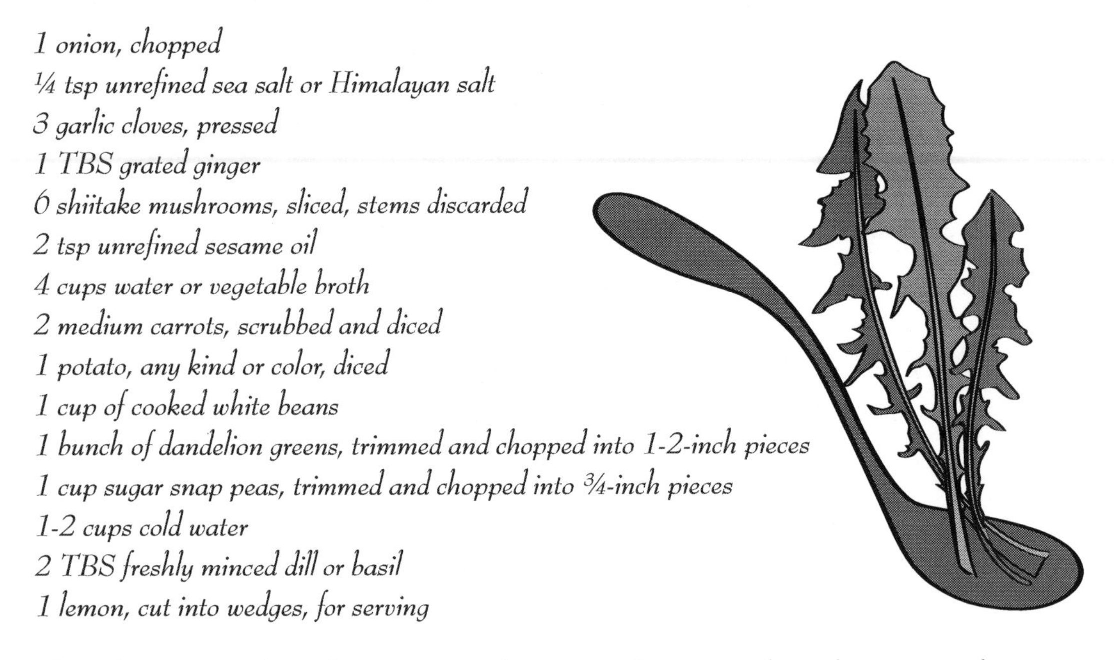

1 onion, chopped
¼ tsp unrefined sea salt or Himalayan salt
3 garlic cloves, pressed
1 TBS grated ginger
6 shiitake mushrooms, sliced, stems discarded
2 tsp unrefined sesame oil
4 cups water or vegetable broth
2 medium carrots, scrubbed and diced
1 potato, any kind or color, diced
1 cup of cooked white beans
1 bunch of dandelion greens, trimmed and chopped into 1-2-inch pieces
1 cup sugar snap peas, trimmed and chopped into ¾-inch pieces
1-2 cups cold water
2 TBS freshly minced dill or basil
1 lemon, cut into wedges, for serving

Place the onion, salt, garlic, ginger, mushrooms and sesame oil in a large pot and stir over medium heat for 5 minutes or until onions and mushrooms begin to soften. Add a tablespoon or two of water to keep from sticking, if necessary. Then add the water, carrots and potato and bring to a simmer. Cover and let simmer for 15 minutes. Then add the cooked white beans, dandelion greens and sugar snap peas. Simmer for 2 minutes, then remove from heat, adding 1-2 cups cold water to stop the cooking process and keep the greens green. Taste for salt, serve garnished with fresh dill or basil and a side of lemon wedges.

BRAZILIAN COCONUT SOUP

SERVES 6-8

This soup is a little rich because of the coconut milk and almond butter, but it is heavenly. Plus, it contains cancer-fighting ingredients (onion, garlic, shiitakes, spinach, carrots and tomatoes)!

1 TBS grated ginger
3 jalapenos, seeded and minced
1 medium onion, diced
3 garlic cloves, pressed
1 TBS tamari or shoyu (may substitute a ¼ tsp unrefined sea salt or Himalayan salt)
1 cup sliced shiitakes, stems discarded
1 ½ cups cooked white beans, drained
2 cups coconut milk (may substitute light coconut milk or part rice milk)
2 cups vegetable broth
2 cups chopped spinach
2 carrots, shredded
⅓ cup almond butter
2 limes, juiced
½ bunch of cilantro, cleaned, trimmed and minced
1-2 medium tomatoes, seeded and diced

Place the ginger, jalapenos, onions, garlic, tamari, shiitakes and beans in a large soup pot. Add a couple of tablespoons of the coconut milk and bring to a simmer over medium heat. Stir frequently, adding a little water if necessary to prevent sticking. Once the onions are softened and the mushrooms have given up their water, add the rest of the coconut milk, vegetable broth, spinach and carrots. Bring to a simmer for 5 minutes. Meanwhile, whisk together the almond butter and lime juice. Turn off heat and add this to the soup along with the cilantro and tomatoes. Taste for salt. Serve hot.

(GF) CREAMY MUSHROOM SOUP

SERVES 6-8

Use any mushrooms you like but be sure to always include the prized shiitake. Shiitake mushrooms help strengthen, detoxify and boost the immune system. They also help lower cholesterol and are a powerful cancer fighter.

1 medium kabocha squash, a.k.a. Japanese pumpkin (may substitute red kuri squash)
1 TBS olive oil (may substitute ¼ cup vegetable broth or water)
1 large onion, diced
2 celery stalks, diced
½ tsp unrefined sea salt or Himalayan salt
4 cups of mixed mushrooms, fresh (shiitake, chanterelle, porcini, maitake, etc.)
3 garlic cloves, pressed
2 bay leaves
2 tsp fresh thyme leaves (please don't use dried thyme here, it has a different taste)
6 cups of mushroom or vegetable broth
1 yukon gold potato, diced
½ cup raw cashews
½ cup hot water, plus more as needed
2 TBS freshly minced chives
2 TBS freshly minced parsley

Preheat oven to 375 F. Place the kabocha squash on a cutting board and carefully cut it in half. Discard seeds. Place cut side down on a baking dish and fill pan with enough water to cover the squash with approximately 1-inch of water. You may need two pans in order to fit both halves of the squash. Bake for 35-45 minutes or until you can easily pierce through the squash with a knife. Remove from pan, discard water and let the squash cool by turning it cut side facing up. Once cool enough to handle, remove from peel and dice squash into ½-inch cubes. Measure ¾ cup of cubed squash and set aside. Reserve the remaining squash for another use (add to miso soup, add to stir fries or other steamed vegetables for a side dish, mash and give to kids, mash and use to make spinach pancakes, purée with coconut milk and salt to make a creamy sauce for grains or vegetables).

Recipe continues on next page...

CREAMY MUSHROOM SOUP...

Meanwhile, place the oil, onion, celery and salt in a large soup pot and heat over medium heat for 5 minutes, stirring occasionally. Slice the mushrooms into attractive bite-size pieces and discard any tough stems (shiitakes). Add them to the pot and cook another 5 minutes, adding a little water to prevent sticking, if necessary. Add the garlic, bay leaves and thyme and cook another 2 minutes. Now add the 6 cups of broth and the potato and cover. Let simmer for 15 - 20 minutes over low heat. Once the potato is very soft, turn off heat and remove the bay leaves. Next use a potato masher to lightly mash the soup and break up the potato pieces. This will thicken the soup. Now add the cubed kabocha squash pieces (¾ cup). I like to leave them whole (unmashed) for color and texture.

Prepare the cashew cream by placing the raw cashews in a blender with just enough hot water to barely cover the cashews. Blend to break up the pieces, stopping to scrape down the sides of the blender if necessary. Then slowly add a little more water, up to 1 cup while the blender is blending to make it smooth and creamy until your desired thickness is achieved. I don't like it too thin so go slow with the water. You may need to let the blender run for 1-2 minutes to make it smooth. **Adding all of the water at once will make it hard to get a smooth cream unless you have a special high-powered blender.** Add cashew cream to the soup until your desired creaminess is met. You may not need all of the cream. Taste for salt and serve, garnished with chives and parsley.

Shiitake mushroom stems also contain incredible nutrition but are sometimes a little too tough to chew. I usually discard the stems and just cook with the caps. But, to increase the medicinal value of your meal, save the stems, mince them in a food processor and use them in any savory recipe for added healing power!

If your blender jar is plastic instead of glass use room temperature water.

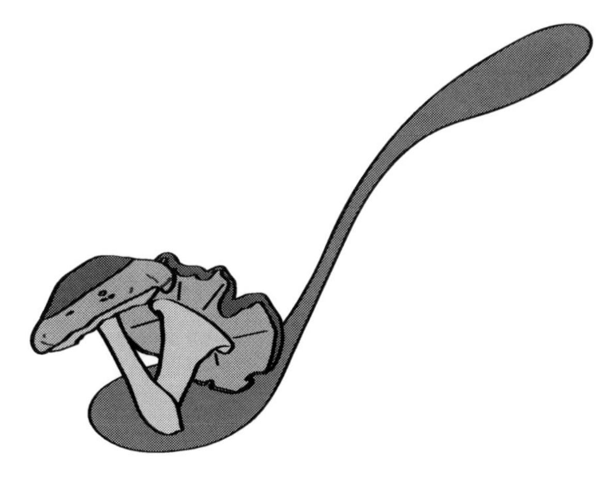

GF

CREAM OF BROCCOLI-KALE SOUP

SERVES 8

1 TBS olive oil (may substitute ¼ cup vegetable broth or water)
1 large onion, chopped
2 celery stalks, minced
4 garlic cloves, pressed
1 pinch red pepper flakes
1 quart vegetable broth (may substitute water)
1 lb of cauliflower, cut into small florets
3 lbs broccoli, stems peeled and cut into small chunks, tops chopped into florets
1 bunch kale, washed, chopped, stems discarded (may substitute chard, collard, spinach)
unrefined sea salt or Himalayan salt, to taste
1 lemon, zested and juiced

In a large, heavy bottomed soup pot, sauté the onions and celery in the olive oil over medium heat for 10 minutes. Then add the garlic and red pepper flakes and cook for 1-2 minutes. Slowly add the vegetable broth while stirring, then cover and bring to a boil. Add cauliflower, all of the chopped broccoli stems, ***all but 1 cup*** of the broccoli florets, and all of the chopped kale (the reserved broccoli florets are for garnish). Cook uncovered, until tender, about 10 minutes.

Meanwhile, cook the reserved broccoli florets for just a couple of minutes (steam, blanch or in a water 'sauté'). Rinse under cold water to keep the bright green color, then set aside. Using a hand held blender (stainless steel, no plastic), blend the soup until smooth and creamy. Taste and add sea salt, lemon zest and lemon juice to taste. Stir to combine then serve, garnished with broccoli florets and a bit more lemon zest.

For even creamier soups, there are several options: (1) You could use 1 medium potato (Japanese sweet potato or a new potato), diced small and added to the boiling broth. Just add it a few minutes before the cauliflower, broccoli and kale so it gets cooked all the way through. The smaller you dice the potato, the faster it cooks. (2) You could add ½ cup raw cashews to the soup when you add the cauliflower and then blend until smooth. (3) You could add about 1 cup of cashew milk or cashew cream to the soup when blending until desired creaminess is reached.

If you don't have a stainless steel hand held blender, then purée the soup in small batches in a glass blender. If your blending devise is made of plastic then wait until the soup is thoroughly cooled before puréeing.

SIMPLE THAI COCONUT CURRY SOUP (GF)

SERVES 6

This soup came about because I was in a super big hurry but wanted something delicious and nutritious. These ingredients are staples in my kitchen so I usually always have them on hand. I was still surprised by how wonderful this dish turned out. It's beautiful too!

2 tsp Thai red curry paste (can add more if you like it spicy)
1 can of light coconut milk
1 can or 1 ½ cups puréed sweet potato or yam, pumpkin or kabocha squash
1 cup mixed vegetables, fresh or frozen, any kind
1 can or 1 ½ cups adzuki beans (if using Eden foods brand can - no need to drain)
10 oz. frozen or fresh spinach, chopped (no need to thaw)
¼ cup goji berries, rinsed
1 lime, juiced
tamari, unrefined sea salt or Himalayan salt, to taste

In a large soup pan, whisk the curry paste with the coconut milk and pumpkin purée. Then place all of the ingredients except the lime and tamari in the pan and heat over medium heat until vegetables are heated through, but not overcooked. Add water if a thinner soup is desired. Then add lime juice and salt, to taste. If you have more time, also add diced onion and grated ginger or pressed garlic.

I like to serve this soup with a side of brown or black rice.

NAIROBI STEW

SERVES 6-8

Sweet potatoes or yams, are an excellent source of beta-carotene, a powerful antioxidant. This super food is sweet tasting but won't cause your blood sugar to spike. Anytime you see sweet potato or yam in a recipe you can use either one. Yams are actually a type of sweet potato.

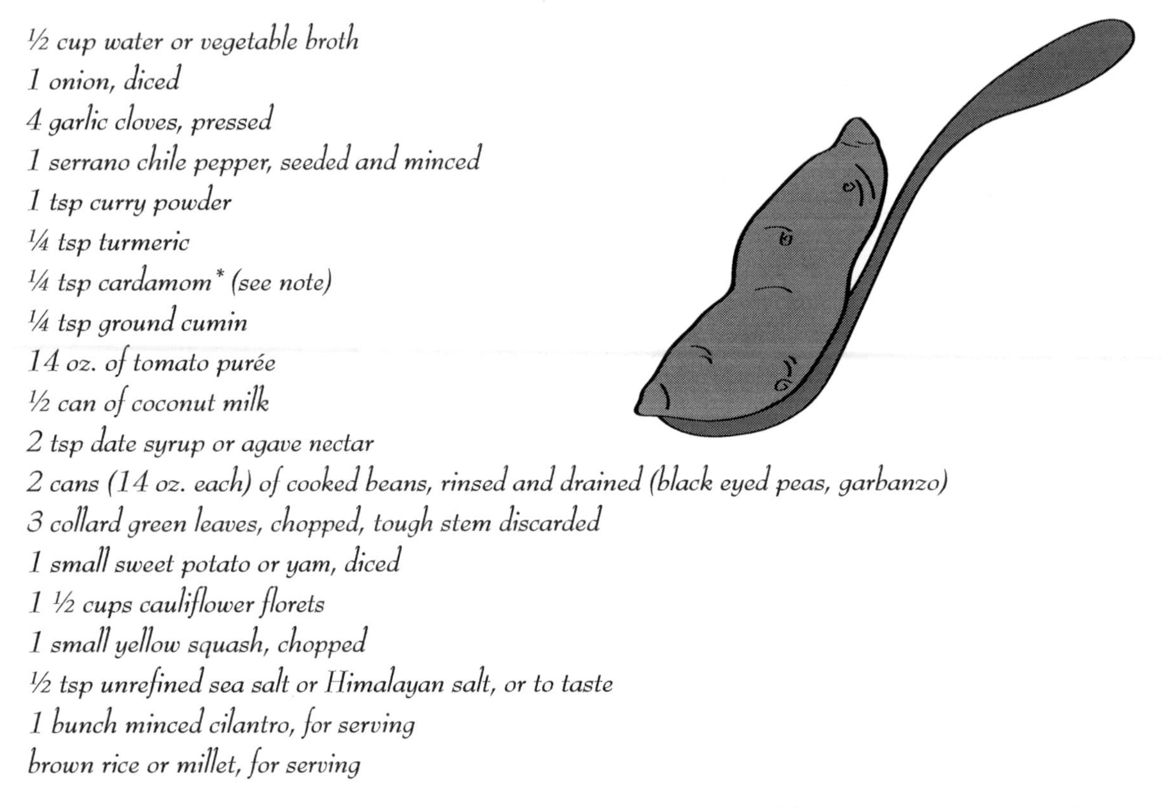

½ cup water or vegetable broth
1 onion, diced
4 garlic cloves, pressed
1 serrano chile pepper, seeded and minced
1 tsp curry powder
¼ tsp turmeric
¼ tsp cardamom (see note)*
¼ tsp ground cumin
14 oz. of tomato purée
½ can of coconut milk
2 tsp date syrup or agave nectar
2 cans (14 oz. each) of cooked beans, rinsed and drained (black eyed peas, garbanzo)
3 collard green leaves, chopped, tough stem discarded
1 small sweet potato or yam, diced
1 ½ cups cauliflower florets
1 small yellow squash, chopped
½ tsp unrefined sea salt or Himalayan salt, or to taste
1 bunch minced cilantro, for serving
brown rice or millet, for serving

Place the water, onion, garlic and chile pepper in a large pot and heat over medium heat for about 5 minutes or until the liquid is almost all absorbed. Add the dried spices and stir to coat. Cook for 1 minute, then add the tomato purée, coconut milk and sweetener and stir. Next add the remaining ingredients and bring to a simmer. Cover, reduce to low and let simmer for 15 minutes or until vegetables are tender. Add more water or broth if desired. Taste for salt and spice. Serve with brown rice or millet and cilantro.

If you can't find ground cardamom buy the whole cardamom pods and smash the pods open. Pick out the little brown seeds and grind these seeds in a spice grinder or a coffee grinder until you have ¼ tsp ground cardamom. The cardamom is the key flavor to this dish so don't skip it, but at the same time, don't add too much!

I came across some wonderful recipes while researching Kenya in 2008. This is my version of a powerful stew, dedicated to Barack Obama.

BLACK BEAN SOUP WITH SWEET POTATO AND GREENS

GF

SERVES 6

This hearty, warming soup reminds me of a vegetarian version of the Brazilian dish Feijoada but with a little twist. I like it over a bowl of brown rice.

2 tsp olive oil
2 large carrots, chopped
1 large yellow onion, chopped
3 stalks celery, chopped
3 bay leaves (fresh is nice but dried will work too)
2 cans black beans, organic preferred, or 3 cups cooked black beans
1 medium sweet potato or yam, peeled and cut into ½-inch cubes
2 garlic cloves, pressed
1 small jalapeno, seeded and minced
1 TBS minced fresh ginger
1 ½ TBS ground cumin
1 tsp dried oregano, or 1 TBS fresh
1 14-oz can diced tomatoes
½ tsp unrefined sea salt or Himalayan salt
½ tsp red pepper flakes
1 small head of broccoli, cut into florets
1 bunch collard greens, washed and chopped
1 lime, cut into wedges, for serving
1 bunch of cilantro or parsley, minced

Place the oil in a large soup pot over medium heat and add the carrots, onions, celery and bay leaves and sauté for 3 minutes. Add beans and their liquid plus 1-2 cups of water, depending on how thick you like it. Cover and simmer for 10 minutes. Add the sweet potato, garlic, jalapeno, ginger, cumin, oregano, tomatoes, salt and red pepper flakes. Cover and simmer about 8 minutes. Remove the bay leaves and add the chopped broccoli and collard greens and cook another 5 -7 minutes, uncovered. Adjust seasoning if necessary and serve hot with a squeeze of lime, garnished with cilantro.

(GF) CREAMY CHICKPEA SOUP WITH LEMON AND PARSLEY

SERVES 6

This recipe is simple and delicious, always a crowd pleaser. The tahini gives this a unique richness and flavor. If you like the flavor of hummus then you'll like this. I like to top the soup with a dollop of harissa then serve with crusty, whole grain bread, drizzled with olive oil and sprinkled with a little garlic and parsley.

1 large onion, chopped
2 carrots, diced
3 stalks celery, chopped
6 garlic cloves, pressed
2 tsp olive oil
2 tsp ground cumin
1 TBS white wine (may substitute water)
6 cups vegetable broth
2 cans garbanzo beans, drained, about 3 cups cooked beans (see note)*
½ cup tahini
3 TBS fresh lemon juice
2 cups of chopped arugula, sorrel or spinach
1 tsp unrefined sea salt or Himalayan salt
pinch cayenne
1 bunch parsley, minced
3 green onions, chopped
harissa, for serving

Cook the onion, carrot, celery and garlic in the olive oil in a large pot for five minutes over medium heat, stirring often. Add the cumin, stir to coat for 30 seconds then add the wine to deglaze the pan. Now add the vegetable broth and simmer for 10 minutes. Next add the garbanzo beans and simmer another 5 minutes. Whisk the tahini with the lemon juice together in a small bowl (or put in food processor, adding water if necessary to make smooth). Stir this back into stew until well combined. Now add the arugula, salt and cayenne, and stir to combine. Simmer for 1 minute then turn off heat. Taste for seasoning and garnish with parsley, green onions and a small swirl of harissa. Enjoy!

If using Eden brand canned beans–no need to drain or rinse because they are organic and have kombu seaweed in the water! Add seaweed to your food anytime you can to reap the benefits from the minerals and detoxifying properties of seaweed.

WHITE BEAN SOUP WITH ROSEMARY AND LEMON (GF)

SERVES 6

Can't have too many bean soup recipes! They are a great source of protein, fiber and are naturally low in fat. This recipe has the refreshing taste of rosemary, lemon and mint. Plus, it uses kombu seaweed which is full of minerals and helps increase the digestibility of the beans. See pg. 450 for more information on the healing properties of kombu.

1 ½ cups dried white beans (cannellini, navy, etc.)
2 bay leaves
3 sprigs of fresh rosemary
1-5-inch piece of kombu seaweed, rinsed
3 garlic cloves, pressed
1 tsp unrefined sea salt or Himalayan salt
dash of cayenne
2 cups arugula, cleaned well (may substitute spinach or nettles)
2 meyer lemons, zested and juiced
fresh mint leaves, optional garnish

Sort through the beans, removing any stones, then rinse and drain the beans.
Soak the beans for 8 hours in 6 cups of water. Then drain off and discard the water.
Add 4 cups of fresh water to the soaked beans and bring to a boil in a large pot. Add the bay leaves, rosemary and kombu. Reduce heat to low and cover. Simmer for 1-2 hours*, stirring occasionally. You want the beans to still hold their shape but be tender all the way through (not too hard and not too mushy). You may need to add water to the pot during the cooking process to keep them from sticking. Discard the bay leaves and rosemary sprigs (the kombu can remain in the soup, but chop into smaller pieces if it hasn't already disintegrated into little bits).

Place the garlic in a mortar and pestle with the salt and cayenne, and crush to make a paste. Add to the beans and simmer for three minutes. Chop the arugula and stir into the soup. Simmer for 1 minute or until the arugula is wilted but still bright green. Turn off heat, taste for salt, and serve in bowls topped with some zest, lemon juice and chopped fresh mint. Serve with crusty whole grain bread.

Recipe continues on next page...

WHITE BEAN SOUP WITH ROSEMARY AND LEMON...

Beans will vary in cooking time depending on how old they are. Just keep an eye on the pot to make sure they don't start to stick to the bottom. You may need to add more water.

You could use a vegetable broth instead of water to cook the beans, just be sure that it has **no salt** in it as using salt in the early stages of cooking may change the texture of the beans.

BORSCHT OF SORTS

SERVES 6-8

This will make you feel super charged and refreshed. Beets are excellent for helping to cleanse the liver. If you have cabbage leftover, use to make a sauerkraut or kimchi, or a cabbage slaw. You can add fresh horseradish to this dish for some added heat.

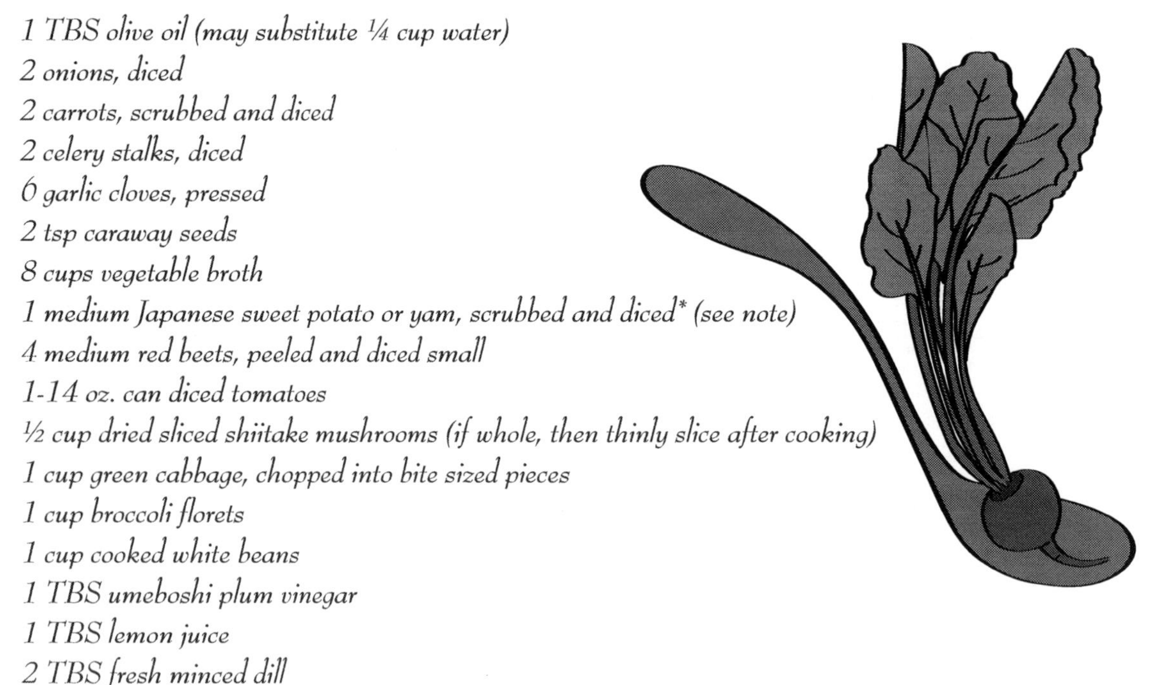

1 TBS olive oil (may substitute ¼ cup water)
2 onions, diced
2 carrots, scrubbed and diced
2 celery stalks, diced
6 garlic cloves, pressed
2 tsp caraway seeds
8 cups vegetable broth
1 medium Japanese sweet potato or yam, scrubbed and diced (see note)*
4 medium red beets, peeled and diced small
1-14 oz. can diced tomatoes
½ cup dried sliced shiitake mushrooms (if whole, then thinly slice after cooking)
1 cup green cabbage, chopped into bite sized pieces
1 cup broccoli florets
1 cup cooked white beans
1 TBS umeboshi plum vinegar
1 TBS lemon juice
2 TBS fresh minced dill

Recipe continues on next page...

BORSCHT OF SORTS...

unrefined sea salt, cayenne or white pepper, to taste
cashew sour cream, for serving *(see next page)*
toasted rye bread, for serving

Place the oil, onions, carrots, celery, garlic and caraway seeds in a large soup pot and sauté over medium heat for 3-5 minutes. Then add the broth, sweet potato, beets, tomatoes and dried shiitakes and bring to a boil. Cover, reduce heat to medium and let simmer for 20 minutes. Then add the cabbage, broccoli, white beans and simmer uncovered for 5 minutes. Turn off the heat, add the vinegar, lemon juice and dill. Taste for salt and pepper. Serve topped with a dollop of cashew sour cream and toasted rye bread.

Anytime you see sweet potato or yam in a recipe you can use either one because they are related and taste very similar to one another. Yams are actually a type of sweet potato.

Cashew Sour Cream

1 cup cashews, soaked 4-24 hours in plenty of water in the refrigerator, then drained
1 lemon
¼ tsp unrefined sea salt or Himalayan salt
dash of date syrup, agave nectar, brown rice syrup or yacon syrup
water
1 TBS nutritional yeast, optional

Place the drained cashews in a blender with the juice from ½ of the lemon, salt and sweetener. While machine is running, drizzle in a little bit of water, just enough to make the cashews whip up into a creamy mixture. Stop and taste for seasonings. Add more lemon or salt, if necessary, and blend again. Taste and then add the nutritional yeast if you desire a slightly nutty flavor.

Peel and grate the fresh horseradish into the dish at the end of cooking or grate it into the cashew cream with a dash of salt and some apple cider vinegar to taste.

(GF)

SQUASH APPLE SOUP

SERVES 6-8

Fall is definitely my favorite time of the year! Eating root vegetables gives you a sense of being grounded, which is a good thing, especially after a busy summer.

½ medium Kabocha squash (Japanese pumpkin) or Red Kuri squash, seeded
1 medium butternut squash, cut in half lengthwise, and seeded
1 TBS olive oil, plus more for oiling the pan
1 medium yellow onion, roughly chopped
½ tsp unrefined sea salt or Himalayan salt
1 TBS grated ginger
2 medium granny smith apples, cored, seeded and chopped
⅛ teaspoon allspice
¼ teaspoon cinnamon
¼ teaspoon red pepper flakes
dash or two of nutmeg, freshly ground is best
6 cups vegetable broth
1 lemon or orange, cut into wedges
toasted pumpkin seeds, for garnish (I like the green pepita seeds)

Preheat oven to 400 F. Roast squash pieces cut side down on a lightly oiled baking dish or sheet pan until very soft (about 30 minutes). While squash is roasting, place 1 TBS olive oil in a large pot over medium heat and add the onions and salt. Sauté until onions turn translucent, stirring frequently. Add ginger and apples, and sauté another five minutes or until the apples begin to soften. Add the allspice, cinnamon, red pepper flakes and nutmeg and stir to coat for 1 minute. Then deglaze the pan with 1 cup of the broth and simmer for 1 minute. Then add 5 more cups of the broth and bring to a simmer.

When squash is finished roasting, scoop it out, discarding skins and any seeds and add to the soup pot. Add more water if necessary to cover vegetables. Let simmer, covered, for 10 minutes. Add soup to glass blender in small batches and blend until smooth. Or you could purée using a hand held blender. Taste for seasoning. Serve with lemon or orange wedges and sprinkle with toasted pumpkin seeds.

Please be sure that blender container is not plastic. Never use plastic with hot foods, it can leach into the food and may be harmful to health.

MOROCCAN LENTIL VEGETABLE STEW OVER GRAINS

SERVES 8

This recipe looks like it has a lot of steps, but no need to chop anything in advance. Just start cooking the onions, and while they are cooking, prepare the next ingredients, add them and prepare the next group, and so on. Just be sure to have cooked grains already prepared (or start them just before you start the stew) so when the stew is finished, so are the grains. Try serving this stew over different grains such as millet, teff, amaranth or quinoa, or a combination of these.

1 medium onion, diced
2 TBS olive oil
½ tsp unrefined sea salt or Himalayan salt (see note)*

3 medium tomatoes, seeded and chopped (or use 1 can diced tomatoes)
2 garlic cloves, pressed
1 tsp ground cumin
1 tsp ground ginger
½ tsp red pepper flakes
½ tsp saffron (may substitute paprika)
½ tsp ground cardamom
½ tsp cinnamon
½ tsp turmeric

1 cup red lentils, sorted through to remove stones, then rinsed and drained
8 cups water
2 carrots, diced
1 celery, diced

1 ½ cups cauliflower florets
½ cup chopped dried apricots (may substitute golden raisins) (see note)*

1 ½ cups broccoli florets
1 cup of cooked chickpeas
1 cup green peas, fava beans, lima beans, or green beans, fresh or frozen

2 lemons, juiced
½ cup minced cilantro
¼ cup minced parsley, plus extra for garnish
1 TBS minced mint leaves, plus extra for garnish

4 cups cooked grains (millet, teff, amaranth, quinoa or whole wheat couscous)

Recipe continues on next page...

MOROCCAN LENTIL VEGETABLE STEW OVER GRAINS...

In a large soup pot sauté the onion in the olive oil and salt for 5 minutes over medium heat. Then add the tomatoes, garlic, cumin, ginger, red pepper flakes, saffron, cardamom, cinnamon, and turmeric. Stir and cook for 2 minutes. Next add the lentils, broth, carrots and celery. Cover and bring to a boil, then reduce heat and let simmer over medium low for 20 minutes, stirring frequently to prevent sticking. Then add the cauliflower and apricots and simmer another 10 minutes. Next add the broccoli, chickpeas and green peas and stir to combine. Turn off heat and let sit for 5 minutes. Then stir in the lemon juice, cilantro, parsley and mint. Taste for salt and spice. Serve in bowls over cooked grains, and garnish with more minced parsley and mint.

If using anything besides red lentils (such as dried split peas or mung beans, etc.), don't add any salt until the end of cooking.

As always, please use organic to avoid pesticides and sulfur dioxide on dried fruit.

SAFFRON BROTH WITH CHICKPEAS AND SWEET POTATOES

GF

SERVES 6

This soup will lift your spirits on a cold winter night. Please use real saffron for best flavor and allow it to "bloom" in liquid before adding to the dish. Adding cauliflower or cabbage to this recipe is recommended if you're looking for ways to increase your cruciferous vegetable intake.

¼ tsp saffron threads
½ cup white wine, or fresh apple cider
¼ cup olive oil
1 onion, in crescents
1 large fennel bulb, sliced thin (may substitute ½ tsp fennel seeds, crushed)
1 medium to large sweet potato, cut into half moons (see note)*
unrefined sea salt or Himalayan salt, to taste
1 can chickpeas, drained (unless using Eden brand, then use the liquid)
½ cup water
2 TBS cilantro, minced
¾ cup Italian plum tomatoes, seeded and chopped
3 artichoke bottoms (from a jar), rinsed and chopped
3 garlic cloves, pounded to a paste with ½ tsp salt in a mortar and pestle
cracked pepper, optional
2 TBS minced fresh parsley

Steep the saffron in the white wine for 30 minutes. Heat the oil over medium heat in a heavy bottomed pot. Add the onion, fennel, and sweet potatoes. Season with salt and stir well. Sauté, stirring often, until the potatoes are almost tender but not crispy, about 10 minutes. Reduce the heat, if necessary. Add the wine/saffron mixture, the chickpeas, water and cilantro. Add the tomatoes, the artichokes and the garlic paste. Cover and cook at a simmer until the potatoes are tender, about 5-10 minutes, adding more water, if necessary, to cover the vegetables. Season with pepper, if desired, and garnish with fresh parsley. Serve in a bowl with crusty bread.

Its not necessary to peel your sweet potatoes or most produce, especially if they are organic. A great deal of valuable nutrients and fiber are in the peel or just beneath it. So use whole sweet potatoes whenever you can. Just scrub and rinse well.

FRENCH ONION SOUP

SERVES 6

Think you need beef stock and cheese in order to make a great French onion soup? Think again! This soup might even kick your cold, too. Onions also help improve cholesterol, lower blood pressure and have anti-cancer, anti-viral, anti-biotic and anti-inflammatory properties.

6 yellow onions
2 TBS olive oil (may substitute ½ cup vegetable broth)
1 TBS fresh thyme leaves (no stems), or 1 tsp dried thyme (fresh is seriously preferred)
2 tsp fresh minced rosemary or ½ tsp dried rosemary
2 bay leaves
½ tsp toasted sesame oil
2 garlic cloves, pressed
2 TBS tamari or shoyu (may substitute ½ tsp unrefined sea salt or Himalayan salt)
5 cups water
2 TBS miso, whisked with 2 TBS water to make a slurry
2 TBS minced parsley
Nutritional yeast, for garnish
Toasted whole grain bread, to serve

Cut the onion in half then slice into long, thin strips. Cook the onions in a heavy bottomed soup pot with the olive oil, herbs and bay leaf, covered, over very low heat. Stir frequently and don't let them sizzle. They should cook slowly for about 30 minutes to bring out their sweet flavor. Once the onions are completely softened and sweet, add the toasted sesame seed oil, the garlic and the tamari and cook another 10 minutes over low heat. Slowly add the water and heat through. Remove the bay leaves. Then stir in the miso slurry and turn off the heat. Taste for salt. Serve hot garnished with parsley and nutritional yeast. Have toasted whole grain bread ready for soaking up the broth in your bowl. Be ready to want seconds!

YELLOW SPLIT PEA-YAM STEW

SERVES 6-8

This very simple split pea stew is so satisfying, delicious and easy on digestion. Roasting the shallot is an important step in creating the flavor of this soup.

1 cup yellow split peas, carefully picked through to remove stones
1 5-inch piece of kombu seaweed, rinsed
2 TBS grated ginger
½ tsp turmeric
8 cups water
2 cups of cauliflower florets
2-3 medium shallots (see note)*
1 TBS olive oil
1 medium yam or sweet potato (see note)*
2 tsp ground cumin
1 tsp ground coriander
1 tsp unrefined sea salt or Himalayan salt
1 bunch of arugula, washed well and trimmed
1 lemon, zested and juiced
2 TBS coconut milk or olive oil, optional
cilantro and green onions, chopped, optional
miso paste (sweet, mellow or white), optional (see note)*

Preheat oven to 375 F. After sorting through dried split peas to remove stones, rinse the peas and drain well. Place split peas, kombu, ginger and turmeric in a large heavy bottomed pan. Add water and bring to a boil. Reduce heat, cover and simmer until peas are cooked through, stirring frequently so they don't stick to the bottom (if you add salt or use salted broth the split peas will sink to the bottom of the pan and burn).

Meanwhile, place the cauliflower florets and the unpeeled shallots in a baking dish. Drizzle with olive oil, toss, and roast until soft, about 30-40 minutes. Remove from oven and let cool until able to remove skins from shallots and dice. Scrub the yam and dice into ½-inch pieces. Add yam to the split peas for the last 10 minutes of cooking, or when the peas are tender all the way through. Also, add the roasted cauliflower and the peeled and diced shallots.

In a dry pan, toast the ground cumin and coriander over medium heat just for a minute or two to bring out their flavor and then add to soup pot. Also add the salt to the soup and stir to incorporate. Remove the kombu seaweed and chop into tiny pieces and put back into the soup.

Recipe continues on next page...

YELLOW SPLIT PEA-YAM STEW...

Once everything is tender and cooked through, add the chopped arugula and simmer for another 2 minutes or until arugula is wilted but still bright green. Add the lemon zest and lemon juice and stir to combine. You could add 2 TBS coconut milk or olive oil for added richness. Serve soup garnished with cilantro and green onions, if desired.

You can substitute a yellow onion if you can't find shallots, just be sure to roast it first!

The typical yam you find in American grocery stores is actually a type of sweet potato. Use any variety you please.

1-2 TBS of miso paste may be added in place of some of the salt, if desired. Just remember not to add the miso until after the soup is finished and the heat is turned off so the beneficial bacteria or probiotics don't get destroyed. The easiest way to add miso is to whisk it with a little water in a small bowl before adding to the soup. This is called a slurry.

Cooking times may vary with dried peas and beans, depending on how old they are. I usually check at 30 minutes, then every 10 minutes after that. Peas are done when soft all the way through and have started to break apart. It could take up to 1 ½ hours to reach this stage. Remember to never add any salt to the peas or beans until they are thoroughly cooked!

ASIAN CURRY STEW WITH SOBA NOODLES

SERVES 8

8 oz. package of buckwheat soba noodles (look for 100% buckwheat)
1 onion, chopped
2 TBS grated ginger
4 garlic cloves, pressed
1 burdock root (the size of a medium carrot), scrubbed and diced
1 cup chopped shiitakes (stems discarded)
2 tsp unrefined sesame oil

Recipe continues on next page...

ASIAN CURRY STEW WITH SOBA NOODLES...

1 tsp unrefined sea salt or Himalayan salt
1 TBS Japanese curry powder
⅛ -¼ tsp cayenne pepper
2 TBS mirin (may substitute sake or water)
2 cups water
4 cups vegetable broth
½ medium kabocha squash (Japanese pumpkin), peeled, seeded and cut into crescents
1 cup broccoli florets
2 cups napa cabbage, chopped
¼ cup minced cilantro, plus extra for garnishing
3 green onions, sliced
1 cup chopped spinach (may substitute any dark leafy green vegetable)
1 TBS toasted sesame oil
1 tsp hot pepper sesame oil (optional)
½ cup peas, fresh or frozen
1 TBS date syrup, agave nectar, brown rice syrup or yacon syrup
1-2 TBS tamari or shoyu, if necessary
mung bean sprouts and extra cilantro for garnish

Cook the noodles according to package directions and set aside. In a large soup pot, sauté the onion, ginger, garlic, burdock and shiitakes in the oil and salt for 5 minutes over medium heat. Add the curry powder and cayenne and stir to coat. Cook another 2 minutes. Now add the mirin to deglaze the pot and let simmer gently until all liquid is absorbed. Put water and broth into the pot and bring to a boil.

Meanwhile, chop the kabocha crescents into smaller pieces (1-inch by ½-inch). Simmer for 3 minutes in the broth then add the broccoli and cabbage. Simmer for 5 minutes. Add the cilantro, green onions and chopped spinach and cook another 3 minutes. Remove from heat, add the oils, peas, syrup and add more tamari if necessary. Serve in bowls, adding as much of the cooked soba noodles to your bowl as you like. Garnish with mung bean sprouts and cilantro.

I usually store the cooked soba noodles separate from the soup until serving, otherwise they tend to break down and get too mushy.

Add cooked adzuki beans (for more protein) or add some wakame seaweed (for more cleansing properties) when you add the broccoli.

SAVORY GREEN SPLIT PEA SOUP

SERVES 6-8

This soup is hearty and creamy without any added oil. If you miss the smoky, salty taste of ham, look for tempeh bacon at your health food store and add a few tablespoons of it, diced, when you add the vegetables.

1 cup green split peas, dried
1 onion, diced
2 garlic cloves, pressed
2 tsp grated ginger
1 5-inch piece of burdock root, scrubbed and diced small
1 5-inch piece of kombu seaweed, rinsed
1 bay leaf
1 TBS fresh thyme leaves, no stems (fresh thyme is seriously preferred for taste)
1 TBS fresh marjoram or oregano leaves, minced (may substitute 1 tsp dried marjoram or oregano)
1 TBS fresh sage leaves, minced (may substitute 1 tsp dried sage)
5 cups water (may substitute no-salt vegetable broth)
2 carrots, scrubbed and diced
2 celery stalks, diced
2 cups broccoli florets
3 TBS miso, mellow, white, or sweet
¼ cup cilantro, minced

Sort through the peas to remove any stones. Rinse them and drain well. Place peas, onions, garlic, ginger, burdock, kombu, spices and water in a large pot. Bring to a boil then reduce heat and let simmer for a few minutes uncovered, skimming away any foam that appears on top. Then cover and let simmer for 40 minutes, stirring periodically to make sure nothing is sticking to the bottom. Add the carrots and celery and simmer another 10 minutes. Check to see if peas are cooked through. They should not be firm at all but almost a purée consistency. Cook longer if necessary, stirring often.

Once peas are cooked through, add the broccoli florets and simmer another 5 minutes. Then turn off heat and remove bay leaf and kombu. Chop the kombu into tiny pieces and add back to the soup. Discard the bay leaf. Prepare the miso slurry by whisking miso with a couple tablespoons of water in a small bowl until smooth. Add to soup, stir well to incorporate, and serve in bowls garnished with cilantro.

INDIAN DAHL WITH VEGETABLES

GF

SERVES 6

2 TBS coconut oil (may substitute unrefined sesame oil)
1 onion, minced
4 garlic cloves, pressed
1 TBS grated ginger
1 ½ cup yellow split peas, picked through to remove stones (may substitute red lentils)
2 tsp cumin seeds, toasted in a dry pan until fragrant, then coarsely ground (see note)*
1 tsp turmeric
¼ tsp ground cardamom
¼ tsp cayenne
6 cups water
2 cups diced butternut squash
1 cup cauliflower florets
2 medium tomatoes, seeded and diced
unrefined sea salt or Himalayan salt, to taste
1 bunch of cilantro, minced
1 lemon or lime, cut into wedges, for serving

Place the coconut oil, onions, garlic and ginger in a large soup pot and sauté over medium heat for 5 minutes. Meanwhile, sort through the split peas to remove stones then rinse well and let drain. Add them to the pot and stir to coat. Then add the toasted, ground cumin, the turmeric, cardamom and cayenne and stir to coat for 1 minute. Now add the water, cover and bring to a boil. Reduce heat and let simmer over medium-low heat for 40 minutes, skimming the foam off the top, and stirring often, until the split peas are tender and starting to lose their shape. This could take up to 1 hour depending on how old the split peas are. Once tender, add the butternut squash and cauliflower and let simmer another 10 minutes, adding more water if necessary. Add the tomatoes and salt to taste and let simmer until everything is tender and cooked through (once you add the salt, stir the dahl very frequently to prevent sticking). Serve garnished with cilantro and a side of lemon.

I've also added fresh or frozen spinach, green peas, green beans or broccoli when I add the cauliflower.

Recipe continues on next page...

INDIAN DAHL WITH VEGETABLES...

Please remember not to add any salt until the peas are thoroughly cooked to ensure best texture and consistency. You could use red lentils for this recipe, but reduce cooking time to 20 minutes before adding the vegetables.

Dry toast the cumin seeds first, then coarsely grind in a mortar and pestle or in a spice grinder/clean coffee grinder. Have this ready just before starting the recipe.

AFRICAN ALMOND STEW

SERVES 6-8

1 onion, chopped
1 TBS grated ginger
½ tsp unrefined sea salt or Himalayan salt
1 bay leaf
1 tsp ground coriander
1 medium sweet potato or yam, scrubbed and diced
4 cups water
1 green pepper, seeded and chopped (may substitute 2 stalks celery)
1 medium zucchini, diced
2 large tomatoes, peeled, seeded, and diced
1 tsp sweetener, optional (to balance out the tomatoes)
½ jalapeno, seeded, and minced (or more if you like spicy)
2 cups chopped green cabbage
1 bunch of collard greens, washed, chopped and stems discarded
½ cup raw almond butter
1 small bunch of cilantro, cleaned, trimmed and minced
1 lemon, cut into wedges

Place the onion, salt, bay leaf, coriander, sweet potato and water in a large covered pot and bring to a simmer over medium high heat for 5 minutes. Add the green peppers, zucchini, tomatoes, sweetener, jalapeno, cabbage, collard greens and let simmer for another 5 minutes, uncovered. Check to see if all the vegetables are tender and simmer another minute, if needed. Whisk together the almond butter with ¼ cup of water and add to the soup. Taste for salt and spice. Remove bay leaf. Sprinkle with cilantro and lemon juice and serve.

LENTIL VEGETABLE SOUP

SERVES 6

Adding the beet gives a beautiful color to this healthy soup. Just don't use canned beets, as they don't taste as delicious as fresh beets. Don't forget to use those beet greens too because they contain healthy antioxidants like beta-carotene and lutein.

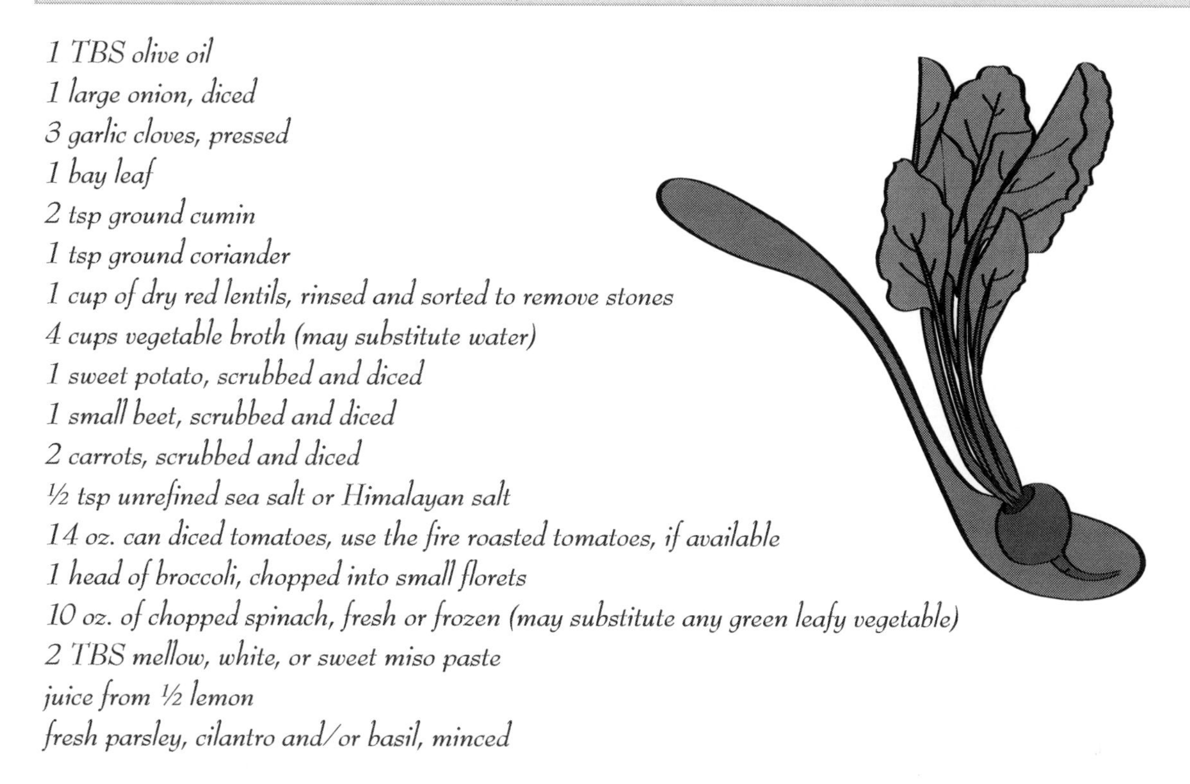

1 TBS olive oil
1 large onion, diced
3 garlic cloves, pressed
1 bay leaf
2 tsp ground cumin
1 tsp ground coriander
1 cup of dry red lentils, rinsed and sorted to remove stones
4 cups vegetable broth (may substitute water)
1 sweet potato, scrubbed and diced
1 small beet, scrubbed and diced
2 carrots, scrubbed and diced
½ tsp unrefined sea salt or Himalayan salt
14 oz. can diced tomatoes, use the fire roasted tomatoes, if available
1 head of broccoli, chopped into small florets
10 oz. of chopped spinach, fresh or frozen (may substitute any green leafy vegetable)
2 TBS mellow, white, or sweet miso paste
juice from ½ lemon
fresh parsley, cilantro and/or basil, minced

Sauté the onion in olive oil (or water) in a large soup pot over medium heat until soft, about 5-10 minutes. Then add the garlic, bay leaf, cumin and coriander and sauté another minute. Now add the drained lentils. Stir to coat with oil for 1 minute. Slowly add the vegetable broth, cover and simmer for 20 minutes, stirring from time to time to prevent sticking. Now add the chopped sweet potato, beet and carrots with the salt and canned tomatoes. Simmer another 10 minutes, stirring often. Remove the bay leaf. Add the broccoli and cook another minute. Then add the spinach and turn off the heat. Whisk together the miso paste and lemon juice. Pour back into soup and stir to combine. Taste for salt and spice. Top with fresh herbs and serve.

(GF) NORTH-EAST AFRICA SOUP

SERVES 6-8

I had a soup like this at a little café in Marin and then added a few of my favorite ingredients, like the harissa. It really adds a unique flavor, but start off slow since it can be spicy. Also, I don't add too much water while cooking this soup because I like it on the thick side. You can adjust to your liking. This soup is good anytime of the year!

1 onion, diced
2 TBS grated ginger
¼ tsp unrefined sea salt or Himalayan salt
2 TBS unrefined sesame oil (may substitute olive oil or coconut oil)
1 TBS garam masala
1 tsp harissa paste (may substitute cayenne, just a dash though)
2 medium sweet potatoes or yams, rough chopped
2 medium tomatoes, seeded, and chopped
water to cover
1 bag of frozen peas
½ pound of chopped spinach, cleaned thoroughly
3 green onions
1 lime, juiced
1 small bunch of cilantro, minced

Place the onions, ginger, salt and oil in a large soup pot and sauté over medium heat for 5 minutes. Add the garam masala and harissa and stir for 1 minute. Then add the sweet potatoes and tomatoes and stir to coat. Add water, just enough to cover the vegetables. Bring to a boil, cover, reduce heat to medium and let simmer for 20 minutes. Turn off heat and add ½ bag of frozen peas. Purée the soup in batches in a glass blender or with a hand held blender until smooth (or wait until thoroughly cooled if using plastic). Taste for salt and spice. Add the other ½ bag of peas, the chopped spinach and green onions. Heat until the spinach wilts and soup is heated through. Add the lime juice and chopped cilantro. Serve with more harissa on the side, if desired.

SWISS CHARD TOMATO SOUP (GF)

SERVES 8

A great spring time soup. If you can find green garlic (looks similar to a green onion), use 3 or 4 shoots and mince as you would a green onion, and add with the diced onion in this recipe for extra flavor and cancer fighting power.

1 onion, diced
1 TBS olive oil
½ tsp unrefined sea salt or Himalayan salt (see note)*
4 garlic cloves, pressed
8 cups vegetable broth (may substitute water)
¼ tsp red pepper flakes
3 TBS tomato paste, whisked together with ¼ cup water
2 cups peeled and cubed butternut squash (about ½-inch cubes)
1 celery stalk, thinly sliced
1 medium yellow squash, sliced into half moons, about ¼-inch thick
2 tomatoes, seeded and diced (canned is ok)
2 cups cooked chickpeas
8 cups chopped swiss chard, stalks included
1 lemon, juiced
2 TBS minced parsley

Place the onions, oil and salt in a large soup pot and sauté over medium heat for 5 minutes, then add the pressed garlic and sauté another 2 minutes, stirring often. Now add the broth, red pepper flakes, and tomato paste mixture and stir to combine. Bring to a boil and add the butternut squash, celery and yellow squash and let simmer, covered, for 5 minutes over medium heat. Next add the tomatoes, the cooked chickpeas and the swiss chard and cook uncovered for 5 minutes over medium heat. Turn off heat and add the lemon juice, to taste. Check for salt and serve garnished with parsley.

You can add a little miso (whisked together with a little bit of water until smooth) instead of using salt. Just make sure to add the miso at the end of cooking because boiling miso will destroy the beneficial bacteria or healthy flora.

MUSHROOM BARLEY BEET SOUP WITH ARAME

SERVES 6-8

You'll love this soup, I promise. It's hearty and super healthy, plus it tastes delicious. I use hulled barley instead of pearled, because hulled barley is a whole grain and has more fiber. Hulled barley is darker and a bit larger than pearled barley.

1 cup barley, hulled not pearled
1 onion, diced
3 garlic cloves, pressed
1 TBS grated ginger
1 TBS olive oil
½ tsp unrefined sea salt or Himalayan salt
1 bay leaf
8 cups vegetable broth (may substitute water)
½ cup sliced dried mushrooms, mix of shiitake, porcini, maitake, crimini, etc. (see note)*
2 celery stalks, diced
2 carrots, scrubbed and diced
1 medium beet, peeled and diced, plus beet greens if you have them
⅓ cup dried arame seaweed, ***soaked in 3 cups water for 15 minutes***
2 cups chopped spinach (may substitute arugula)
1-2 TBS mellow miso, whisked together with 1-2 TBS water
6 TBS minced parsley
3 TBS minced dill
1 lemon, juiced

Rinse and drain the barley, then set aside. In a large soup pot, sauté the onion, garlic and ginger in the olive oil and salt over medium heat for 5 minutes. Add the bay leaf, broth, dried mushrooms and barley and bring to a boil. Cover and reduce heat to medium and let cook for 30 minutes. Scoop out the soaked arame with a slotted spoon and place on a cutting board. Chop into small pieces and add to soup. Add the celery, carrots and beets and cook another 15 minutes or until vegetables and barley are tender. Remove the bay leaf and add the beet greens and/or spinach and cook just until wilted. Turn off the heat and add the miso slurry. Then add the parsley, dill and lemon juice. Serve hot.

If your dried mushrooms are not already sliced, cut them into small pieces with kitchen scissors before adding to the soup.

CARROT-GINGER SOUP WITH GOJI BERRIES (GF)

SERVES 6

Have you noticed that I like goji berries? And what's not to like… they're high in antioxidants and have been used for centuries in Tibet to promote a long, happy life free from illness. They have been used to help keep blood sugar levels stable, help protect vision, prevent cancer and heart disease, and help to slow the aging process. Look for the dried berries (they look like red raisins) and use in soups, grain dishes, salads, desserts, smoothies or just add a few to your tea.

1 TBS olive oil (may substitute coconut oil)
2 leeks, thinly sliced, cleaned well (see note)*
¾ tsp unrefined sea salt or Himalayan salt
6 medium carrots, scrubbed and chopped
½ lb sweet potato, chopped (may substitute butternut squash)
2 TBS grated ginger
7 cups vegetable broth (may substitute water)
½ cup goji berries
½ cup freshly squeezed orange juice
2 tsp orange zest
freshly ground white pepper, to taste
extra goji berries, to garnish
¼ cup fresh mint or parsley, chopped

In a large soup pot, sauté the leeks in the oil and salt over medium heat for about 5 minutes. Add the carrots, sweet potato, ginger and broth and bring to a boil. Cover and simmer until the vegetables are completely softened, about 20 minutes. Remove from the heat and add the goji berries and orange juice. In a blender or food processor, purée the soup in batches, until almost smooth, and return the soup to the pan. Alternatively, process with a hand held blender in the pan until the desired consistency is reached (wait until soup is cool if using plastic blender). Season with orange zest and white pepper. Serve warm, garnished with goji berries and fresh mint.

To properly clean leeks cut off the root end and the dark green end and discard. You are now left with the white and light green parts of the leek. Slice the leek in half lengthwise then place flat side down on a cutting board. Slice ¼-inch wide pieces and place in a large bowl of cold water. Use your hands to sort through the leeks looking for any dirt or sand trapped in between the layers. Let sand and dirt sink to the bottom of the bowl while clean leeks remain floating on the top. Scoop leeks out with a slotted spoon and move to a colander to drain until ready to use. Wash cutting board and knife because they may be sandy.

THAI COCONUT SOUP (RAW)

SERVES 6

Young coconut, a.k.a. Thai coconut or green coconut, can be found at natural grocery stores or at Asian super markets. They are off-white in color, as opposed to the mature coconuts that have a brown, stringy outside husk. Choose one that has no cracks, mold or soft spots. For instructions on how to open a young coconut find a website with pictures and proceed as directed. It can be tricky the first time so be sure to **use caution.** Once opened, if the flesh or meat of the coconut is anything but white in color, the coconut has gone bad. Discard and open a new one.

1 young coconut, water and meat (about 1 ½ c. water and 1 c. meat, but this may vary)
1 cup diced tomatoes
1 jalapeno pepper, seeded and chopped
4 kaffir lime leaves, chopped, center stems discarded
1 garlic clove, pressed
1 TBS grated ginger
2 TBS mellow, white or sweet miso paste
2 TBS shoyu soy sauce
1 lime, juiced
1 lemon, juiced
2 tsp raw, organic agave nectar, or yacon syrup, optional
more shoyu or Himalayan salt, if needed

½ cup grated carrot
½ cup thinly sliced raw shiitake mushrooms, stems discarded
1 small bunch of cilantro, minced
1 cup diced tomatoes, different colors would be nice
2 green onions, sliced
1-2 TBS dulse flakes
1 handful of sunflower seed sprouts, trimmed

Blend young coconut water, meat, tomatoes, jalapeno, kaffir lime leaves, garlic, ginger, miso, shoyu, lime and lemon juice, and sweetener in a blender until smooth. Taste and add more shoyu or salt, or perhaps more spice, if desired. If it is too thick add a little water and blend again. Pour into a bowl. Garnish with remaining ingredients and serve.

You can heat this soup gently over very low heat until it reaches just above room temperature.

By eating foods that are raw, or only heated to a temperature of 117 F or less, all of the enzymes are still present in the foods, making them easier to digest.

Dips & Spreads

VEGAN GARLIC "BUTTER" SPREAD

MAKES ABOUT 1 CUP

Great on everything from pasta to crackers, to roasted squash or steamed broccoli.

6 TBS raw pine nuts
½ cup cooked white beans
1-2 garlic cloves, pressed
salt, tamari, to taste (may substitute shoyu)
⅓ - ½ cup olive oil or flax seed oil (or a mixture of the two)
3 TBS minced chives
red pepper flakes, optional

Place the pine nuts, beans, garlic and salt in a blender and blend until combined. Slowly add the oil through the top of the blender while blending until it looks smooth and creamy. Taste for salt and garlic, adjusting if necessary. Remove to a bowl and fold in the minced chives and red pepper flakes, if using.

Add water to thin if desired (and to cut down on fat content).

Store in a sealed glass jar in the refrigerator.

TURKISH LENTIL "BUTTER" SPREAD

MAKES ABOUT 2 CUPS

½ cup red lentils, picked through to remove stones
1 ½ cups water
½ tsp unrefined sea salt or Himalayan salt
2 tsp olive oil
3 green onions, sliced thin
1 garlic clove, pressed
1 dash of cayenne
1 dash of turmeric
2 TBS minced parsley

Recipe continues on next page...

TURKISH LENTIL "BUTTER" SPREAD...

Combine lentils and water in a pot. Cover and simmer until lentils are soft and mushy, about 20 minutes. Drain if necessary and reserve water. Add the salt to the lentils and stir well to combine. Heat oil in a pan over low heat and cook the onions and garlic for a few minutes, just to soften. Be careful not to burn the garlic. Add the cayenne and turmeric and stir to coat. Add this mixture to the lentils along with the minced parsley, stirring well to combine. Taste for salt and refrigerate a few hours before serving. Spread on whole grain bread, crackers or use as a vegetable dip.

SIMPLE PINE NUT "CHEESE" SPREAD

MAKES ABOUT 1 CUP

1 cup pine nuts
2 TBS lemon juice
1 tsp mellow white miso
2 TBS nutritional yeast
unrefined sea salt or Himalayan salt, to taste

Soak 1 cup pine nuts for 4 hours in water to cover. Drain nuts, discard water and place lemon juice, miso and nutritional yeast in food processor with the drained pine nuts. Blend until almost smooth. Taste for salt and add if needed. Use this as a cheese substitute in lasagna, sandwiches, etc.

You could place this in a dehydrator to make a more solid cheese. Just spread about 1/8-inch thick on sheet liners and dehydrate at about 105 F for 5-6 hours, or until firm enough to handle. Then flip onto mesh screen and dehydrate for another 2-4 hours, or until desired firmness is reached.

See other cheese ideas under condiments.

CHEEZIE SPREAD

MAKES ABOUT 2 CUPS

Every good vegan has a cheese spread up their sleeve. This one is high in fiber, B vitamins, protein and a good source of probiotics and vitamin C.

1 can white beans, drained (navy beans, butter beans or cannellini beans)
5 TBS nutritional yeast flakes
4 TBS lemon juice
¼ tsp unrefined sea salt or Himalayan salt (or none if the beans are already salted)
1 TBS tahini
1 TBS miso paste (I like mellow, white or sweet miso)
1 tsp dijon mustard
dash or two of garlic powder, optional
4 TBS rehydrated, chopped sun-dried tomatoes, optional (see note)*

Place all ingredients, except sun-dried tomatoes, in a food processor and process until smooth. You may need to stop and scrape the sides of the bowl and process again. Add the rehydrated tomato pieces and pulse to combine, leaving small bits of tomato, or process until smooth.

If you don't want to use tomatoes, add a bit more lemon juice, miso, nutritional yeast and salt.

SIMPLE SAVORY CREAMY SPREAD

MAKES ABOUT 1 CUP

1 can of navy beans, or 1½ cups cooked, drained
1 garlic clove, pressed
1-2 TBS olive oil (may substitute water)
unrefined sea salt or Himalayan salt, to taste

Place beans in a food processor with pressed garlic. Process until smooth, gradually adding olive oil through the top of the food processor while machine is running until a creamy, smooth texture is achieved. Taste and add salt. Use this creamy spread on whole grain tortillas, breads, vegetables, grains, etc.

SUN-SEED AND SUN-DRIED TOMATO DIP

MAKES ABOUT 1 ¾ CUPS

½ cup sunflower seeds, soaked for 4 hours or up to 24 hours in refrigerator
¼ cup sesame seeds, soaked for 4 hours or up to 24 hours in refrigerator
½ cup sun-dried tomatoes, covered with hot water until softened (20 minutes)
1-2 garlic cloves, pressed
1 TBS nutritional yeast
1-2 TBS mellow miso
¼ cup lemon juice
unrefined sea salt or Himalayan salt, to taste
¼ cup freshly minced basil leaves

Drain the seeds and the sun-dried tomatoes and place in a food processor with the garlic, nutritional yeast, miso and lemon juice. Pulse to combine, add a bit of water to help make it smoother, if desired. Taste and add salt or more lemon, if necessary. Move to a serving bowl and fold in the minced basil.

Serve as a dip or use as a filling inside nori.

CHEEZY PINE NUT-TOMATO SPREAD

MAKES ABOUT 2 ½ CUPS

2 cups pine nuts, soaked for about 4 hours, then rinsed and drained (see note)*
1 garlic clove, pressed
¼ cup sun dried tomatoes, soaked in hot water for at least 30 minutes, drained
2 TBS lemon juice
2-3 TBS nutritional yeast, optional
1 TBS flax seed oil (may substitute water)
2 TBS mellow or white miso paste (see note)*
unrefined sea salt or Himalayan salt, if necessary

Place the drained pine nuts and garlic in a food processor and process until coarsely ground. Rough chop the sun-dried tomatoes and add them to the food processor with the lemon juice, nutritional yeast, oil and miso. Process until almost smooth and serve.

You could use sunflower seeds, pumpkin seeds or cashews instead of the pine nuts, however, the texture and color will be a bit different.

If you use a darker miso, start with less because it may be saltier than you like.

SPINACH BEAN DIP

SERVES 8

2 cans or 3 cups cooked white beans, unsalted
1 TBS lemon juice
½ cup salsa
¼ cup nutritional yeast
1 package of dry onion soup mix (buy organic brand to avoid hidden MSG)
1 package of frozen, chopped spinach, thawed and squeezed dry
¼ cup freshly minced parsley

Drain the beans and place in a food processor with the lemon juice, salsa, nutritional yeast and onion soup mix and process, adding water one tablespoon at a time until creamy and smooth (you could use the liquid from the canned beans if they are organic and no salt is added). Remove to a container and fold in the spinach and parsley. Refrigerate for 1 hour before serving.

If you can't find an organic dry soup mix, then make your own using dry minced onions (see below), or better yet, use freshly minced onions, pressed garlic and some salt.

Serve with raw vegetable pieces or your favorite whole grain, sprouted bread.

Homemade Dry Onion Soup Mix

This is equal to about 1 package

3 TBS dry minced onion flakes
2 tsp onion granules or powder
½ tsp garlic granules or powder
unrefined sea salt or Himalayan salt, to taste
1 dash of pepper
1 TBS nutritional yeast, optional
1 tsp sweetener of choice, optional

Mix all ingredients together.

(GF) WHITE BEAN AND ROASTED ARTICHOKE HEART SPREAD

SERVES 8

1 shallot, peeled and chopped
¼ cup olive oil
1 can white beans, rinsed and drained well (or 1 ½ cups cooked beans)
2 packages of frozen artichoke hearts, or 2 cans, rinsed and drained
1 TBS fresh thyme, chopped (fresh is seriously preferred over dried) (may substitute fresh oregano)
½ cup fresh basil leaves, roughly chopped
1 lemon, zest and juice
unrefined sea salt or Himalayan salt and cracked pepper, optional

Mix all ingredients together except for the fresh herbs and lemon. Place in a baking dish and bake at 325 F for 35 minutes, stirring halfway through. Remove from oven and let cool. Once **cooled**, add to food processor and blend until almost smooth. Some texture is good. Add the herbs, lemon zest and juice, and process a bit more to combine, but not too much. Add salt and pepper to taste. Serve as a dip with vegetables or spread on whole grain bread.

WASABI-BEAN SPREAD

SERVES 6

1 lb. shelled edamame, thawed (may substitute fava or lima beans)
1 lime, juiced
1 tsp umeboshi plum vinegar
1 TBS minced ginger
1 TBS mellow miso
2-3 tsp wasabi paste (or more if you like it hot) (see note)*
1 TBS tamari, to taste (may substitute unrefined sea salt)
1 ½ TBS brown rice vinegar
1 TBS toasted sesame oil
¼-½ cup water
toasted sesame seeds, black or tan, to garnish

Combine all ingredients, except the water and toasted sesame seeds, in a food processor. Process, adding the water slowly until smooth and creamy. You may not need all of the water. Garnish with toasted sesame seeds and serve chilled or at room temperature with vegetable crudités or rice crackers.

If using wasabi powder, follow directions on package to make wasabi paste. You may need to use hot or cold water when making the paste in order for wasabi to "bloom."

LIMA BEAN SPREAD

GF

MAKES ABOUT 3 CUPS

You might think you don't like lima beans, but wait,
here's a recipe that will make you love them!

3 cups cooked lima beans (fresh or frozen preferred, not canned) (see note)*
¼ cup lemon juice
2 TBS apple cider vinegar (organic, unfiltered and raw)
2 tsp umeboshi plum vinegar
2 TBS minced red onion
2 TBS minced parsley
2 TBS minced cilantro

Recipe continues on next page...

LIMA BEAN SPREAD...

½ tsp ground cumin
2 TBS flax seed oil
cayenne, to taste

Place all ingredients in a food processor and process until smooth. Taste and adjust spices if necessary.

You could also make this recipe using fava beans.

Serve as a dip with vegetables or as a sandwich spread.

HUMMUS WITH BASIL AND CARROTS

MAKES ABOUT 3 CUPS

There are a million different ways to make hummus. Here's one of my favorites.

2 large carrots, scrubbed and chopped (see note)*
2 cans garbanzo beans, drained or 3 cups cooked garbanzo beans, drained
3 cloves of garlic, pressed
¼ cup tahini
1 large lemon, juiced
1 TBS umeboshi plum vinegar
1 tsp ground cumin (more if desired)
1 small bunch basil
1 small bunch cilantro
3-4 green onions, sliced
unrefined sea salt or Himalayan salt, to taste

Lightly steam the carrots then move to a food processor. Add the drained beans, pressed garlic, tahini, lemon juice, umeboshi vinegar and cumin. Process until smooth, adding a bit of carrot steaming water if necessary to make it creamy. Clean the leaves of the basil and cilantro and add those to the food processor. Pulse to combine, but not completely smooth. Now add the green onions and pulse just to combine. Taste for salt and serve.

You could also just use the carrots raw instead of lightly steaming them. Just be sure to grate them first before adding to the food processor.

PUMPKIN HUMMUS

GF

MAKES ABOUT 2 ½ CUPS

1 garlic clove, pressed
1 ½ cups of cooked garbanzo beans or 1 can garbanzo beans, rinsed and drained
1 cup pumpkin purée
2 TBS tahini
1 lemon, juiced
1 tsp ground cumin
½ tsp ground coriander
½ tsp unrefined sea salt or Himalayan salt
dash of cayenne, optional
water, to thin
2 TBS or more, chopped fresh cilantro, parsley or sage
1 TBS toasted pumpkin seeds

Place the garlic and garbanzo beans in a food processor and pulse until chopped. Stop and scrape the sides of the bowl and process again. Next, add the pumpkin purée, tahini, lemon juice, cumin, coriander, salt and cayenne. Process until smooth, and gradually add water through the top of the machine while blending to make it smoother, if desired. Remove and place in a bowl. Garnish with chopped herbs and toasted pumpkin seeds.

TURKISH PEPPER DIP

MAKES ABOUT 2 CUPS

This is good with baked falafel patties or as a dip for vegetables or whole grain pita.

1 ½ cups raw walnuts, toasted lightly in oven, optional
1 slice whole grain bread
2 TBS water
1 jar (16oz) organic roasted red peppers, rinsed and drained well
2 TBS pomegranate syrup (may substitute tamarind paste)
1 TBS lemon juice, plus more if needed
½ tsp unrefined sea salt or Himalayan salt, or to taste
2 tsp date syrup, agave nectar or brown rice syrup
¾ tsp ground cumin
¼ tsp cayenne pepper (or less if you don't like spicy)

Recipe continues on next page...

TURKISH PEPPER DIP...

Toast the walnuts on a baking sheet in a 300 F oven for 10 minutes or until they are lightly toasted. Be careful not to let them burn. Once the walnuts are cool enough to handle, add to the food processor with the bread and pulse to combine. It should look like coarse breadcrumbs. Next, add the water and the roasted red peppers and process until smooth. Add the remaining ingredients and purée until smooth. Taste for lemon, salt and sweetener. Adjust seasonings, if necessary, and blend again to combine.

SWEET POTATO SPREAD

SERVES 6

Use as a dip for fruit or vegetables or use as a sandwich spread.

1 large sweet potato
2 TBS almond butter (may substitute hemp seed butter or pumpkin seed butter)
1 TBS mellow miso
water, as needed
optional ingredients: salt, freshly grated ginger, lemon juice and toasted sesame oil

You can roast or steam the sweet potato. On a cold day, I prefer to roast the potatoes. In the summer, I steam them. To roast, preheat oven to 375 F. Poke a few holes in the sweet potato and place directly on a rack in preheated oven. Roast until soft, about 35-45 minutes. Remove and let cool until able to peel off skin (or just leave the skin on), then chop.
If steaming the sweet potato, cut into small cubes (peeled or not) and steam over plenty of filtered water until very soft. Remove from heat, reserving the steaming water.

Place the roasted or steamed sweet potato, almond butter and miso in a bowl and mash together with a potato masher. Use a little of the reserved steaming water or regular water, if necessary, to make blending easier. Taste and add salt, ginger, lemon or sesame oil, if desired.

You can also place all items in a food processor and process until creamy, add water gradually until desired texture is reached. Just make sure the potato is cooled first.

VELVETY ROASTED RED PEPPER SPREAD

MAKES JUST UNDER 3 CUPS

Use to dip veggies or to spread on whole grain breads, crackers or as a sauce on vegetables, grains or noodles.

2 red bell peppers (may substitute 1 jar of roasted red peppers, organic)
½ cup raw cashews, soaked for up to 24 hours in fridge in plenty of water, then drained (see note)*
½ cup cooked beans (garbanzo, red lentils, pinto, adzuki or white beans)
¼ cup of sesame seeds (tan not white), lightly toasted is nice
⅓ cup nutritional yeast
1 large lemon, juiced
1 TBS miso paste (may substitute ½ tsp unrefined sea salt or Himalayan salt)
dash or two of cayenne, optional
1 garlic clove, pressed, optional
water, to thin, if necessary

Preheat oven to 425 F. Take red peppers and place them directly on your oven rack and roast at 425 F for 30 minutes, turning once or twice. Skin will blacken. You may want to place a pan on the shelf below the peppers to catch any juices that may drip from the peppers. (You can skip this step by just buying jarred roasted red peppers. Just make sure they are organic. Then rinse and drain the jarred peppers before proceeding with the recipe). Remove peppers from the oven once the skin is mostly black and the peppers are soft. Let cool until able to touch. Once peppers are cool enough to handle, remove and discard the skins and seeds.

Add pepper pieces to a blender then add the drained cashews, cooked beans, sesame seeds, nutritional yeast flakes, lemon juice, miso and the optional cayenne and garlic. Blend until smooth and creamy, add water slowly while machine is running to help blend, if necessary.

If you don't have time to soak your cashews then you can boil them for 3 minutes in enough water to cover, then drain and proceed. You just need the cashews to be very soft (by soaking or boiling) or they won't blend up as smooth.

Add more water if you want it to be a sauce or less water for a dip/spread.

THE CLEANSING OMEGA 3 SPREAD

MAKES ABOUT 1 CUP

Here is a great recipe for helping to cleanse the body while improving heart health through the consumption of a healthy fat known as Omega 3. Eating a handful of raw walnuts a day provides you with a healthy dose of this essential fatty acid. Using the optional flax seed oil will add even more of this heart healthy fat. Lemons and parsley are know for being cleansing and detoxifying. And the garlic has anti-cancer properties.

1 cup raw walnuts
2 garlic cloves, pressed
1½ lemons, medium (meyer lemons are nice!)
¼ cup minced parsley, or more, if desired
unrefined sea salt or Himalayan salt, to taste (may substitute 1 TBS mellow miso paste)
water or Flax seed oil, optional (see note)*

Place the walnuts and garlic in a food processor and process into small pieces. Stop and scrape down the sides of the bowl. Add the juice from 1 ½ lemons, the parsley and a dash of salt. Process again, adding a tablespoon of water (or flax seed oil) through the top of the machine while it is running. Stop and scrape the sides of the bowl again, if necessary, and process until smooth, add a bit more water if necessary to reach the consistency you like. Taste for salt and adjust, if necessary.

Serve as a sandwich spread or a dip for vegetables. This can also be used as a topping for soups, beans, burritos or whole grains. You'll love it!

Remember to always keep your flax seed oil refrigerated and never heat this oil or the beneficial properties will be destroyed.

WALNUT MISO SPREAD

MAKES ABOUT 1 CUP

Use this as a dip for fruit, vegetables or whole grain crackers or a spread on your favorite whole grain bread. I also use it as a sauce for roasted squash by adding a bit more water, then heating very gently in a saucepan until just warm.

1 cup raw walnuts, lightly toasted if desired
¼ cup sliced green onions
1 TBS grated ginger
1 tsp brown rice vinegar (may substitute orange juice)
1 TBS miso paste (mellow, white or sweet) (see note)*
3 TBS water, or more

Place the walnuts in a food processor and process until finely ground. You may have to stop and scrape the sides of the bowl a few times and process again. Add the remaining ingredients and process until almost smooth, add more water, if necessary to reach desired consistency.

Remember, never boil miso or the beneficial bacteria will be destroyed!

(GF) NUT-NOT-TUNA SPREAD

SERVES 8

Spread on whole grain toast and add lettuce, mustard and sprouts for the perfect sandwich!

2 cups raw almonds, soaked for up to 24 hours in plenty of water, in refrigerator
¼ cup raw sunflower seeds, soaked for up to 4 hours in plenty of water, in refrigerator
5 TBS lemon juice
water or nut milk (unsweetened), if necessary
½ cup minced red onion
3 green onions, sliced thin
3 TBS minced parsley
1 TBS minced dill
1-2 TBS capers
2 celery stalks, diced small
2 tsp dulse seaweed flakes
2 tsp kelp seaweed flakes
Umeboshi plum vinegar, to taste
Tahini, optional
Broccoli sprouts, optional (see note)*

Soak the almonds for 8-24 hours. Drain and rinse. Soak the sunflower seeds for at least 4 hours, then drain and rinse. Discard soak water. Place the almonds, sunflower seeds and lemon juice in a food processor and process a few times to pulverize. You may need to stop and scrape down the sides of the bowl and process again. Add a little water or nut milk, if necessary, and process until big pieces of nuts can no longer be seen. You want it to be creamy but not completely smooth. Move to a bowl and fold in the minced onions, parsley, dill, capers, celery, dulse and kelp. Taste for salt and tanginess. Stir in the umeboshi plum vinegar 1 tsp at a time and taste again until desired flavor is reached.

If you desire a creamier spread, add some tahini to the food processor with the almonds and sunflower seeds.

You can add more or less of any of the flavor ingredients depending on taste.

For additional nutrition, add 1 cup of broccoli sprouts to the food processor with the almonds and sunflower seeds and process until almost smooth.

NETTLE PESTO
MAKES ABOUT 1 CUP

All I can say here is "Wow!" Try making this during allergy season because nettles help to alleviate allergy symptoms.

¼ lb. fresh nettles (see pg. 252 for more info on handling nettles)
1 garlic clove, pressed
¼ cup raw walnuts (may substitute pumpkin seeds)
2 TBS lemon juice
2 TBS nutritional yeast
¼ tsp unrefined sea salt or Himalayan salt, or to taste
dash or two of cayenne
1 TBS flax seed oil, optional (may substitute water)

To wash the nettles place them in a large bowl of cold water and use tongs and scissors to discard any large, tough stems. Use a slotted spoon or tongs to scoop the nettles from bowl into a pot of boiling water. Boil for 1 minute, then remove and place in a separate bowl of ice water for 30 seconds. Remove from ice water and place in a colander to drain well (no need to squeeze dry, just let drain naturally). Place garlic and walnuts in a food processor and process until it is coarsely ground. Add the blanched nettles, lemon juice, nutritional yeast, salt and cayenne. Process to combine, then slowly add the oil (or just use water) while machine is running, until pesto comes together.

Have your ice water ready ahead of time.

GREEN PEA PESTO
SERVES 6-8

1 bunch of arugula, trimmed
1 bunch of basil, trimmed
1 cup of pea shoots
½ cup green peas, thawed
1 oz. hemp seeds
1 TBS umeboshi vinegar (may substitute lemon juice and salt, to taste)
1 TBS mellow white miso
2 TBS flax seed oil
2 TBS olive oil

Wash the arugula, basil and pea shoots well. Pat dry with a towel. Place in a food processor with peas, hemp seeds, umeboshi vinegar and miso and pulse to combine. With the machine is running, add the flax seed oil and olive oil gradually until it comes together. You may have to stop the machine and scrape down the sides of the processor bowl. Add water if necessary to help reach the consistency you desire. Store covered in refrigerator and use within 3 days.

Please do not heat this pesto. Heating flax seed oil and miso destroys the therapeutic value of these ingredients.

You can serve as a spread or on top of warmed grains or noodles.

DANDELION PESTO
MAKES ABOUT 5 CUPS

Every ingredient used in this pesto is a nutritional powerhouse; walnuts and flax seed oil for Omega 3, hemp seeds for protein and balanced Omega 6 and Omega 3, and garlic and broccoli sprouts for fighting cancer. However, the dandelion greens are quite impressive. They are used to help strengthen the liver, help purify the blood, gallbladder, kidneys, and cleanse the body. Dandelion is also great for treating anemia, reducing bad cholesterol and clearing skin. This is a tasty way to get dandelion into your diet.

Recipe continues on next page...

DANDELION PESTO...

2 garlic cloves, pressed
½ cup raw walnuts
1 bunch of dandelion leaves, cleaned, trimmed and chopped
1 bunch cilantro, cleaned, trimmed and chopped
1 bunch parsley, cleaned, trimmed and chopped
1 bunch basil, cleaned, trimmed and chopped
1 handful of arugula, cleaned, trimmed and chopped
¼ cup hemp seeds
1 large handful of broccoli sprouts
juice from ½ a lemon
1 tsp umeboshi plum paste or ½ of an umeboshi plum, pitted
¼ cup nutritional yeast
¼ cup (or less) flax seed oil or olive oil (may substitute water for a low-fat option)
unrefined sea salt or Himalayan salt, to taste

Process the pressed garlic and the walnuts in a food processor until they resemble small crumbs. Place all of the greens, hemp seeds, broccoli sprouts, lemon juice, plum paste and nutritional yeast in a large food processor and process to combine. You may have to stop and scrape down the sides of the work bowl. Add the oil while the machine is running, adding only enough oil just to bring it together. Taste the pesto and add a tiny bit of salt or more umeboshi plum paste if it needs salt or salty-tanginess. Refrigerate until ready to serve.

You will need a large food processor for this to work, otherwise, make the pesto in two batches.

This pesto should not be heated.

Try it as a dip, a sandwich spread or mixed with grains, tempeh, seitan or vegetables.

My favorite way to eat this is to mix it with boiled tempeh cubes. Serve pesto coated tempeh inside a whole grain pita pocket with tomato slices, shredded carrot and more broccoli sprouts, then say "Hello" to good health!

TOMATO-ARUGULA PESTO

SERVES 2-4

4 medium tomatoes, ripe * *(see note)*
1 bunch arugula, cleaned and chopped
3 green onions, sliced
¼ cup flax seed oil
1 TBS lemon juice
2 TBS nutritional yeast
2 garlic cloves, pressed * *(see note)*
3 TBS chopped fresh basil
¼ tsp unrefined sea salt or Himalayan salt, or to taste

Cut tomatoes in half and squeeze to remove seeds. Rough chop the tomatoes into smaller pieces. Place in food processor with arugula, green onions, oil, lemon juice, nutritional yeast, garlic, basil and salt. Process by pulsing until combined but still chunky. You may have to stop and scrape the sides of the bowl and pulse again. Add water one tablespoon at a time to make blending easier, if necessary. Taste for seasonings.

Tomatoes are best eaten in the summertime when they are in season, but if you crave this pesto outside of the summer months you may find that drained, organic, canned tomatoes work well.

You may use more or less garlic depending on your tastes.

Serve as a dip, a spread for sandwiches or a sauce for pasta or pizza.

CHERRY TOMATO BRUSCHETTA

MAKES ABOUT 2 CUPS

2 cups cherry tomatoes, any kind, a variety of colors is nice * *(see note)*
2 garlic cloves, pressed
¼ cup fresh basil, minced
2 TBS olive oil
1 lemon
1 lime
unrefined sea salt or Himalayan salt, to taste
whole grain bread, toasted

Cut tomatoes in half, add pressed garlic, basil, olive oil and a squeeze of lemon and lime juice. Add a sprinkle of salt. Toss to combine. Taste for salt and citrus and adjust to your liking. Place on top of toasted whole grain bread. Refrigerate any remaining tomato mixture and use within 3 days.

Toss in a few tablespoons of cooked white beans (any kind) for a heartier dish.

You can roast the cherry tomatoes ahead of time for a twist. Just cut them in half and place in an oven safe dish in a preheated 375 F oven. Toss with a dash of olive oil, balsamic vinegar and salt and roast for about 20 minutes. Then toss with the garlic, basil, 1 TBS olive oil and the citrus juices and spread on toasted bread.

BLACK-EYED PEA SALSA

MAKES ABOUT 3 CUPS

1 cup cooked black eyed peas, rinsed and drained
2 cups seeded and diced tomatoes
1 small bunch of cilantro, washed and minced
¼ cup minced red onion
1 TBS minced jalapeno, or more if you like it hot
1 garlic clove, pressed
2 TBS fresh lime juice
½ tsp ground cumin
½ tsp unrefined sea salt or Himalayan salt

Toss ingredients together in a medium bowl and refrigerate until serving. Use within 2 days.

GF

FRUITY AVOCADO SALSA

MAKES ABOUT 3 CUPS

This doesn't keep well so find a way to use it up once it's made (trust me, it won't be hard). I like it with baked tortilla chips, in a burrito or placed on top of brown rice and mixed greens.

1 cup chopped strawberries, organic of course!
¼ cup diced cucumber
¼ cup red onion, minced
½ small jalapeno, seeded and minced
¼ cup diced nectarine
2 TBS cilantro, minced
¼ cup lime juice, from about 2 limes
1 medium avocado, cut into small cubes
unrefined sea salt or Himalayan salt, to taste

Gently combine all ingredients and serve immediately.

CRISPY CRUNCHY APPLE SALSA

MAKES ABOUT 2 CUPS

1 medium granny smith apple, cut into ½-inch cubes (or smaller)
½ small lemon, juiced
1 celery stalk, diced small, like the apple
½ cup finely diced English cucumber, seeded (may substitute diced jicama)
2 TBS minced red bell pepper
1 green onion, minced
2 TBS cilantro, minced
¼ tsp ground ginger powder
unrefined sea salt or Himalayan salt, and cayenne, to taste

Place the diced apples in a bowl and toss with the lemon juice. Add the celery, cucumber, red bell pepper, green onion, cilantro, ginger, salt and cayenne and toss to combine. Chill until ready to serve.

Dressings, Sauces & Condiments

PICK A SAUCE, COOK A GRAIN, MAKE A MEAL...

Ok, let's break it down. Cooking healthy doesn't have to be complicated. There's a simple formula to it all.

WHOLE GRAINS = about one third to half of your plate at each meal. Choose the actual grains (quinoa, brown rice, hulled barley, millet, buckwheat, kamut berries, etc.) instead of bread or refined grains.

VEGETABLES = at least half of your plate or more! (a mixture of raw and lightly steamed, all colors).

PLANT PROTEIN = about a quarter of your plate at each meal (beans, lentils, split peas, tempeh, seitan, or a couple tablespoons of nuts and/or seeds).

SAUCE OR DRESSING = a good way to get herbs, ginger, garlic, miso, nutritional yeast and healthy fats into the meal (not too heavy, you don't want to be in the habit of always drowning your food in something. Properly cooked vegetables and whole grains have a wonderful flavor on their own).

FRUIT = eat as a snack or as a dessert.

To Thicken Sauces Using Kudzu or Arrowroot

There may come a time when you desire a thicker sauce, or when you have too much cooking liquid in your sauté pan and you want to use it to create a sauce. It's easy to do if you have kudzu or arrowroot powder in your pantry. Kudzu root and arrowroot are white powdery-like ingredients similar to cornstarch. You can use either one to thicken sauces. The key is to always whisk the kudzu or arrowroot with a little cool water in a separate bowl until smooth (this is called a slurry) before adding it to the hot soup or sauce.

Adjust the amount of kudzu or arrowroot depending on how much soup or sauce you are trying to thicken. For example, if you have 1 cup of soup broth that you wish to thicken, use 1 TBS kudzu or arrowroot whisked together with 2 TBS water. If you have ½ cup of soy ginger stir fry sauce use only ½ TBS of kudzu or arrowroot whisked together with 1 TBS water. Basically, 1 TBS of kudzu or arrowroot will thicken about 1 cup of soup or sauce.
Adjust accordingly.

Once the slurry is added to the soup or sauce let it simmer gently while stirring until it is thickened and no longer cloudy. Kudzu root powder may sometimes need to be finely ground before using in a recipe. Do this with a mortar and pestle or in a clean coffee grinder.

FAVORITE TEMPEH MARINADE
MAKES ABOUT 1½ CUPS OR ENOUGH FOR 16 OZ. TEMPEH

¼ cup olive oil (may substitute vegetable broth)
⅓ cup tamari (may substitute shoyu soy sauce)
4 green onions, chopped
3 garlic cloves, pressed
3 limes, juiced
½ tsp red pepper flakes
½ tsp ground cumin
3 TBS date syrup, agave nectar or brown rice syrup

Combine ingredients in blender then place in a shallow glass container. Add **16 oz. of cooked and cubed tempeh** to the container with the sauce. Marinate at least 1 hour or overnight in the refrigerator. Remove tempeh from marinade and bake on a parchment lined baking sheet or sauté in a skillet until warm.

Serve with vegetables and brown rice.

SAVORY MARINADE FOR BEANS OR TEMPEH
MAKES ABOUT ½ CUP MARINADE

2 TBS balsamic vinegar (see note)*
2 TBS lemon juice
2 tsp tamari (may substitute shoyu soy sauce)
2 tsp umeboshi plum vinegar (see note)*
2 tsp toasted sesame oil
2 garlic clove, pressed
½-1 tsp Thai chili paste

Whisk all ingredients together and pour over 2 cups cooked beans or 8 oz. steamed tempeh. Cover and let marinate in the refrigerator for at least 1 hour or all day.

Try fig balsamic vinegar if you can find it!

Serve chilled on salads, warm on top of grains or in stir fries.

SIMPLE SAUCE OR DRESSING FOR ANYTHING

MAKES ABOUT ½ CUP

Whisk together 1-2 TBS mellow miso (or sweet miso) and the juice from one orange until smooth.

For endless variations, add tamari, grated ginger, minced cilantro, and/or pressed garlic.

Pour over grains, vegetables, tempeh, beans, or noodles. My favorite way to use this sauce is to steam some greens (mixture of kale, collards, bok choy and chard) and then pour this sauce over the steamed greens and serve in a bowl with brown rice.

Just remember not to boil the sauce because the beneficial bacteria in the miso will be destroyed.

SWEET CHILE GARLIC SAUCE (GF)

MAKES ABOUT ½ CUP

Hot and garlicky!

6 red Thai chilies, stems discarded (fresh or dried chilies)
8 garlic cloves, pressed
3 TBS date syrup, agave nectar, brown rice syrup or yacon syrup
1 TBS umeboshi plum vinegar
3 TBS brown rice vinegar

Place chilies and garlic in food processor and process until combined. Stop and scrape the sides of the bowl. Add the other ingredients and process again until combined. Taste and adjust seasonings if necessary, adding more lemon, salt or sweetener if it's too hot.

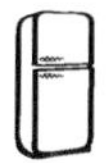

Keep covered and refrigerate any leftovers.

HOT GARLIC SAUCE

MAKES ABOUT ½ CUP

This is good on pretty much everything!

1 fresh minced chile pepper (Thai, Serrano or jalapeno pepper, seeded)
4 garlic cloves, pressed
2 TBS lemon juice
1 TBS sesame oil, optional
1 TBS minced fresh herbs (thyme, oregano, parsley)
1/8-¼ tsp unrefined sea salt or Himalayan salt

Combine all ingredients in a small bowl. Taste to adjust spice if necessary. Refrigerate until serving.

GF GINGER-GARLIC HOT SAUCE

MAKES ¼ CUP

This doesn't make a large quantity, so double it if serving for a large crowd. It tastes best when used within a day or two, so don't make more than you need.

1 TBS finely minced ginger (or use a microplane)
1 TBS garlic, pressed
1 TBS olive oil
1 TBS lemon juice
¼ tsp cayenne pepper (may substitute 1 tsp minced jalapeno) (see note)*
⅛ tsp unrefined sea salt or Himalayan salt

Combine all ingredients in a mortar and pestle.

Adjust the cayenne to suit your needs. I like medium spice.

Use to drizzle over soups, grains, beans or vegetables.

DIPPING SAUCE FOR SPRING ROLLS OR GYOZA

MAKES ABOUT ½ CUP

3 TBS brown rice vinegar
¼ cup tamari (may substitute shoyu soy sauce)
1 tsp date syrup, agave nectar, brown rice syrup or yacon syrup
1 green onion, chopped
1 tsp toasted sesame oil

Whisk all ingredients together and serve on the side for dipping.

WASABI PONZU SAUCE (GF)

MAKES ABOUT 1 CUP

⅓ cup orange juice
⅓ cup lemon (may substitute lime juice or grapefruit juice; freshly squeezed of course!)
3 TBS minced onion
1 garlic clove, pressed
1 TBS grated ginger
1-2 tsp wasabi powder (see note)*

Place all ingredients in a blender and blend until smooth. Refrigerate until ready to serve.

Go slow with the wasabi at first. Sometimes it takes 10 minutes or so for it to develop into full strength. Follow package directions for using wasabi. You may need to first whisk the powder with hot or cold water in order for it to "bloom." Look for 100% wasabi powder.

This spicy-citrus sauce could be used as a dipping sauce for spring rolls or drizzled over steamed vegetables and whole grains. It could also be used as a marinade for seitan, beans or tempeh (cook first, then marinate, then bake).

This sauce will keep for 1 week.

TERIYAKI SAUCE

MAKES ABOUT 1 ½ CUPS

⅓ cup tamari (may substitute shoyu soy sauce)
1 TBS ginger juice (from grating ginger and squeezing pulp)
2 garlic cloves, pressed
3 TBS lemon juice
2 TBS date syrup, agave nectar, brown rice syrup or yacon syrup
2 tsp orange zest
⅓ cup orange juice (freshly squeezed)
1 TBS toasted sesame seeds
2 tsp arrowroot (may substitute kudzu) (see note)*

Place all ingredients EXCEPT arrowroot in a saucepan and heat over medium heat. Whisk the arrowroot with 1 TBS water and pour into the saucepan while stirring. Let simmer for a couple of minutes until the mixture begins to thicken and is not cloudy anymore. Turn off heat and let cool.

Kudzu root powder may sometimes need to be finely ground before using in a recipe. Do this with a mortar and pestle or in a clean coffee grinder.

MISO-TAHINI SAUCE

MAKES ½ CUP

2 TBS miso (I like the mellow white or sweet miso)
4 TBS tahini (may substitute almond butter)
1 lemon, juiced
2 garlic cloves, pressed
water, as needed

In a small bowl whisk all ingredients together, except water, until smooth. Add water, one tablespoon at a time and continue whisking until desired texture is reached.

SWEET SESAME GINGER MISO SAUCE

MAKES ABOUT 1 CUP

2 TBS grated ginger
¼ cup miso paste (mellow white or sweet miso)
1-2 TBS date syrup, agave nectar, brown rice syrup or yacon syrup
¼ cup toasted sesame seeds, partially ground in a suribachi bowl, or spice grinder
water, to thin

Whisk all together until combined. Add more sweetener if desired.

CARROT GINGER SAUCE (GF)

MAKES ABOUT 1 CUP

1 cup chopped carrot
1 TBS grated ginger
1 garlic clove, pressed
¼ tsp red pepper flakes
1 cup vegetable broth (may substitute water)
unrefined sea salt or Himalayan salt, to taste

Combine all ingredients in a saucepan and heat over medium-high heat until carrot is softened and some of the liquid has been cooked off. Mash or purée with an immersion blender (**no plastic with hot foods**) until smooth. Season with salt, if desired.

Good for tossing with steamed vegetables and tempeh.

GF

HARISSA

MAKES ½ CUP

This is definitely my favorite condiment! It makes anything taste exciting.

6-8 hot red chilies, stemmed and seeded
1 TBS olive oil
3-4 garlic cloves, pressed
1 tsp ground coriander seeds (see note)*
1 tsp ground caraway (see note)*
½ tsp unrefined sea salt or Himalayan salt
3 TBS water
extra oil, for covering

Using gloves and scissors, cut the chilies in half lengthwise, removing stems and seeds (if using the dried peppers, cut, discard stems and seeds, and soak chilies in hot water for 20 minutes, then drain). Combine the chilies, oil, garlic, coriander, caraway, and salt in a food processor until a paste is formed. Now add the water and pulse until smooth.

Freshly grind the coriander and caraway in a spice grinder or coffee grinder just before using. Then toast the spices in a dry skillet over medium heat for a minute or two, being extra careful not to burn the spices. Immediately remove toasted spices to a plate to cool.

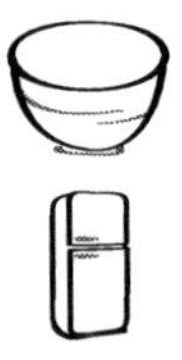

Add to any dish for extra spice.

Store covered in the refrigerator and use within a couple of weeks.

CHIMICHURRI SAUCE (GF)

MAKES ABOUT 1 CUP

Chimichurri is a popular sauce originally from Argentina used to season protein dishes and vegetables. It may also be used as a marinade. Legend has it the sauce was created by an Irishman named Jimmy McCurry, who lived in Argentina. This Irishwoman likes this sauce on top of grilled vegetables and toasted bread.

3 garlic cloves, pressed
¼ tsp unrefined sea salt or Himalayan salt
2 TBS of fresh oregano leaves, minced, or 2 tsp dried
1 bunch of parsley, minced
1 jalapeno, seeded and minced
1 lemon, juiced
splash of red wine vinegar
olive oil, start with a drizzle

Place the garlic and salt in a mortar and pestle and make a paste. Place in a small dish and add the minced oregano, parsley, jalapeno and lime juice. Toss with a splash of red wine vinegar and drizzle in olive oil until your desired consistency is reached.

Serve on vegetables, whole grains or legume dishes for a fresh and spicy delight. Use to marinate tempeh, beans, seitan or vegetables. Also use as a topping for your favorite soup.

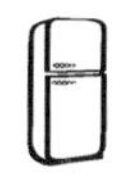

Refrigerate leftovers (if there are any) in an airtight dish and use within 3 days.

GF

CHERMOULA SAUCE

SERVES 8

This sauce, a.k.a. charmoula, is used in Moroccan, Algerian and Tunisian cooking to flavor many foods. You can experiment with different amounts of the ingredients below to create your own signature sauce.

2 garlic cloves, pressed
¼ cup almonds
1 small bunch of cilantro, cleaned and large stems discarded
1 small bunch of parsley, cleaned and large stems discarded
⅛ tsp cayenne
1 tsp ground cumin (toast in a dry skillet over medium heat for 1 minute)
1 pinch of saffron threads, softened in 2 TBS warm water for 5 minutes (see note)*
¼ cup lemon juice, from about 2 lemons
¼ cup olive oil, first cold press, as always
unrefined sea salt or Himalayan salt, to taste

Place garlic, almonds, cilantro, parsley, cayenne, cumin and saffron (plus the water) in a food processor and blend until combined, stopping if necessary to scrape down the sides of the bowl. With machine running, add the lemon juice and olive oil and process until almost smooth. Taste and add salt, if desired. Mixture should resemble chunky pesto.

Look for saffron threads that are deep orange-reddish in color, not yellow, and not the powdered stuff. You'll know it's real saffron because it will be real expensive. I do recommend seeking out real saffron because it will add a unique flavor to the dish.

Serve over roasted vegetables or on top of mixed grains.

ALMOND-GINGER-COCONUT SAUCE

MAKES ABOUT 1 ½ CUPS

½ cup coconut milk
¼ cup almond butter
1 TBS grated ginger
1 garlic clove, pressed
1 TBS lemon juice (may substitute lime juice)
1 TBS date syrup, agave nectar, brown rice syrup or yacon syrup
1 TBS umeboshi plum vinegar
2 tsp tamari (may substitute shoyu soy sauce)
1 TBS chopped mint leaves
¼ cup chopped green onions
¼ cup chopped cilantro
1 tsp Thai paste, optional

Whisk together all ingredients or combine in a blender and blend until smooth. Taste and add more spice or salt if desired.

This sauce is great over soba noodles and steamed vegetables.

To keep fat content low, you can skip the coconut milk and use unsweetened almond or rice milk instead.

CILANTRO-COCONUT SAUCE (GF)

MAKES ABOUT ¾ CUP

1 cup loosely packed cilantro leaves, cleaned and chopped
¼ cup coconut milk
2 TBS lemon juice
1 jalapeno, seeded and chopped
1 garlic clove, pressed
1 TBS grated ginger
¼ tsp unrefined sea salt or Himalayan salt

Recipe continues on next page...

CILANTRO-COCONUT SAUCE...

Place all items in a blender or food processor and blend until smooth. Add a tablespoon of water, if needed, to make blending easier.

So many variations... add any or all of the following options: toasted coconut flakes, almond butter, mango, kaffir lime leaves, lime juice or mint leaves and blend with the original ingredients to create your own twist on this sauce.

Use this sauce for rice, noodles, or any vegetable dish for a tropical twist.

GF

GREEK YOGURT SAUCE

MAKES ABOUT 1 ½ CUPS

1 cup rice yogurt, plain, ***unsweetened*** *(may substitute soy, coconut, or seed yogurt)*
⅛ tsp unrefined sea salt or Himalayan salt
1-2 garlic cloves, pressed
1-2 TBS fresh dill, minced
1 small cucumber, peeled, seeded and diced small

Stir to combine. Adjust seasonings if desired. Chill before serving.

YOGURT MINT SAUCE

MAKES ABOUT 1 ½ CUPS

1 cup rice yogurt, plain, ***unsweetened*** *(may substitute soy, coconut or seed yogurt)*
1-2 garlic cloves, pressed
3 TBS minced fresh mint
⅛ tsp unrefined sea salt or Himalayan salt
2-3 tsp lime juice from 1 lime
½ cup diced cucumber (peeled and seeded)
2 TBS fresh parsley/cilantro

Stir to combine. Adjust seasonings if desired. Chill before serving.

CRANBERRY-HORSERADISH SAUCE

GF

MAKES 3 CUPS

My friend Jolene gave me this recipe after she made it for Thanksgiving one year. It's fabulous!

2 cups fresh cranberries
¼ cup fresh horseradish, grated
1 small onion, diced
¾ cup rice or soy yogurt, plain
½ cup (more or less) date syrup, agave nectar, brown rice syrup or yacon syrup

Blend the cranberries with the horseradish in a food processor to make chunky. Then add the rest of the ingredients (adding sweetener to taste).

Make the day before you wish to serve it and let it rest in the refrigerator so the flavors can meld.

CRANBERRY AND BLOOD ORANGE RELISH

GF

SERVES 6-8

4 blood oranges, 1 zested, and all peeled
12 oz. fresh cranberries
2 tsp grated fresh ginger
⅓ cup date syrup, agave nectar, brown rice syrup or yacon syrup

Zest one of the oranges and set aside. Peel and separate the oranges into segments. Remove seeds, if necessary, and cut segments into bite-size pieces. Place cranberries, ginger and sweetener in a food processor and pulse to combine, with some chunks remaining, not smooth. Toss this with orange zest and oranges. Add more sweetener if desired. Chill before serving.

(GF)

CURRIED PISTACHIO-APRICOT RELISH

MAKES ABOUT 2 CUPS

4-6 fresh apricots, diced and pitted
¼ cup minced red onion
¼ cup roasted red pepper, diced (may substitute raisins)
2 TBS lemon juice
2 TBS olive oil
¼ tsp curry powder
1 tsp date syrup, agave nectar, brown rice syrup or yacon syrup
½ cup chopped pistachios (lightly toasted, if desired)
3 TBS fresh mint, chiffonade
unrefined sea salt or Himalayan salt, to taste

Combine all ingredients in a bowl and chill until ready to use.

Serve with Indian spiced rice, dahl and vegetables. Whole grain naan or chapatis would also be great with this relish if you can find them.

(GF)

TOMATO CHUTNEY

SERVES 8

1 medium onion, chopped
1 TBS unrefined sesame oil
1 garlic clove, pressed
½ tsp unrefined sea salt or Himalayan salt
2 large ripe tomatoes, seeded and diced
1 tsp curry powder
1 TBS tamarind paste
1 TBS lime juice

In a skillet, cook onion in oil over medium heat until soft. Stir in garlic and salt, and continue cooking for a few minutes. Stir in tomatoes, cover and cook until tomatoes are very soft. Stir in the curry powder, tamarind extract and lime. Cook for another minute or two. Taste for salt and tang. Adjust seasonings if desired. Let mixture cool then transfer to a food processor and pulse to combine, with some chunks remaining. Refrigerate for at least 2 hours before serving.

GINGER-COCONUT CHUTNEY

GF

MAKES ABOUT 2 CUPS

3 TBS fresh lime juice
3 TBS fresh orange juice
½ cup fresh ginger, peeled and coarsely chopped
½ cup grated, dried coconut, toasted in a dry skillet until lightly browned (see note)*
1 tsp unrefined sea salt or Himalayan salt
¼ cup goji berries
½ cup diced fresh mango (may substitute pineapple or apple)

Add lime juice, orange juice, ginger, coconut and salt to a food processor or blender and process until smooth. You may need to scrape down the sides of the container several times. Now add the goji berries and mango and pulse to combine. It's nice to leave some of it chunky. Refrigerate until ready to use.

Watch the coconut so that it does not burn. Use a heavy bottomed pan and stir frequently over medium-low heat. As soon as it begins to change from white to tan, move from the pan to a plate so it can cool. Then proceed with recipe.

Serve with Indian spiced rice or dahl.

BARBEQUE SAUCE

MAKES ABOUT 2 CUPS

I don't usually eat barbeque and I don't own a grill (my cousins in Kansas City are gasping at the thought of that). So I pretend by using this sauce to marinate cubes of boiled tempeh or seitan, which I then bake in the oven with the marinade until hot. I then place the cubes on skewers and serve on a plate with a side of sweet potato biscuits, cabbage slaw, corn on the cob, blueberry crisp and iced green tea sweetened with stevia.

2 TBS tamari (may substitute shoyu soy sauce)
2 TBS lemon juice
2 TBS apple cider vinegar
2 TBS molasses
1 TBS barley malt syrup
1 TBS Dijon mustard
dash of cayenne, or more if you like it spicy
1 small can of tomato paste (7oz.)
¾ cup vegetable broth (may substitute water)
fresh garlic and ginger, optional

Combine all ingredients together in a blender and blend until smooth and thick, adding additional water if necessary to reach desired thickness. Add some fresh garlic and/or ginger, if desired.

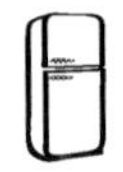

Keep sealed in the refrigerator until ready to use. Will keep for about a week.

ROMESCO SAUCE

GF

MAKES ABOUT 1 ½ CUPS

If you're not Italian, this recipe will make you think you are!
It's delicious as a dip or as a sauce.

¼ cup raw almonds (see note)*
¼ cup hazelnuts (see note)*
2 garlic cloves, pressed
½ tsp red pepper flakes (or more)
2 medium tomatoes, quartered and seeded
1 tsp paprika
¼ tsp unrefined sea salt or Himalayan salt
¼ cup olive oil (could use half flax oil)
½ TBS red wine (may substitute balsamic vinegar)
3 TBS chopped fresh parsley

Preheat oven to 300 F. Place almonds and hazelnuts on two separate baking sheets in the oven and toast for about 10-15 minutes, or until they smell nutty. Be careful not to burn the nuts! Move the hazelnuts to a damp kitchen towel and rub to remove their skins. Now place the nuts, the garlic, and red pepper flakes in a food processor. Process until finely ground. Add the tomatoes, paprika and salt then process to a smooth paste. Now slowly add the oil while the machine is running. Add the vinegar, to taste, by pulsing to combine. Transfer to a bowl and stir in the parsley. Cover and let rest at room temperature for 30 minutes.

Select almonds and hazelnuts that have not already been roasted.

Serve as a spread or a sauce on pasta, grains or vegetables.

Refrigerate leftovers in a tightly covered container and use within 3 days.

(GF) UN-TOMATO SAUCE

MAKES ABOUT 10 CUPS

You say "tomato" and I say "carrot and beet" sauce!

2 large onions, diced
4 garlic cloves, pressed
1 cup chopped shiitake mushrooms
2 celery stalks, chopped
2 TBS olive oil
¾ tsp unrefined sea salt or Himalayan salt
1 TBS Italian spice mixture (basil, oregano, rosemary, thyme)
4 medium carrots, scrubbed and chopped
2 cups of ***roasted*** *kabocha squash (Japanese pumpkin) from 1 medium squash* (see note)*
1 small beet, peeled and diced
1 lemon, juiced
1 small bunch of basil, leaves sliced
1 TBS minced fresh oregano, optional

Sauté the onions, garlic, mushrooms, and celery in the oil and salt in a large soup pot over medium heat for 5 minutes. Add the Italian spices and stir to coat for 1 minute. Add the carrots, 2 cups of the roasted kabocha squash and the beets. Now add enough water to just cover the vegetables. Bring to a boil, reduce heat, cover partially and let simmer for 30 minutes. Blend in a glass blender or with a stainless steel handheld blender until smooth. If you only have a plastic blender or food processor you must wait until the mixture is thoroughly cooled before blending. Once it is smooth, taste for salt and spices. Add a dash of cayenne, if desired. Season with fresh lemon juice, basil and oregano, then serve.

You need to roast the kabocha squash first. I usually poke a few holes in the squash and place the whole thing in a 375 F oven, right on the rack (you'll want to place something on the rack below the squash, like another dish or a piece of foil, to catch the drippings). Let roast for about 35-45 minutes, or until you can easily pierce it with a knife. Remove from oven. Cut in half and let squash cool until you can remove the seeds; scoop out the flesh from the skin into a glass measuring cup to equal 2 cups. Save any remaining squash to add to soups, grain dishes or vegetable dishes.

Freeze any leftover sauce for your next pasta or pizza night. Or use with any grain dish.

BUTTERNUT SQUASH SAUCE (GF)

Slice a medium butternut squash in half lengthwise. Roast squash, cut side down, on a lightly oiled baking dish for 45 minutes in a 375 F oven. Remove and let cool to room temperature. Scoop squash into a blender or food processor and add ½ cup coconut milk and a ½ tsp unrefined sea salt or Himalayan salt. Add water to thin to desired thickness. Taste and add more salt or coconut milk, if desired. Garnish with chopped chives.

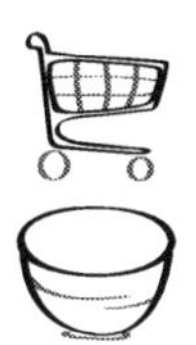

Add Thai curry paste, to taste, if you like some zippy heat!

Use this beautiful sauce on grains, vegetables or beans.

CREAMY CAULIFLOWER SAUCE (GF)

MAKES ABOUT 3 CUPS

This dreamy, creamy sauce is rich in taste, but super healthy!

1 medium head of cauliflower, chopped into florets (see note)*
1 medium onion, chopped
2 tsp olive oil
¼ tsp unrefined sea salt or Himalayan salt
water or vegetable broth, as needed

Roast or steam the cauliflower until soft. If roasting the cauliflower, mix the cauliflower, onion, oil and salt in a baking dish and cover with foil. Roast in a 375 F oven for about 30 minutes, or until vegetables are soft. Remove from oven and let stand, uncovered, until cool. If steaming the cauliflower, place florets in a steaming basket and steam until soft, being careful not to let the pan run out of water while steaming.

Meanwhile, sauté the onion and salt in the oil over medium heat until translucent. Let all ingredients cool. Now place all ingredients in a food processor and blend until smooth, adding a little water or vegetable broth while the machine is running to achieve a smooth and creamy sauce. Once it is creamy, taste for salt and add more if necessary. You can also add a drizzle of olive oil while it is blending for added richness. Add more water for a thinner sauce, if desired. Serve as a creamy sauce over grains, noodles or vegetables.

I also make the same sauce by substituting steamed carrots for the cauliflower.

By using less liquid you can fool your friends into thinking they're eating mashed potatoes!

TAHINI SAUCE FOR FALAFEL

MAKES ABOUT 1 CUP

½ cup tahini
1 TBS flax seed oil
2 medium lemons, juiced
1 TBS miso paste (I like mellow, white or sweet miso)
1-2 garlic cloves, pressed
1 TBS umeboshi plum vinegar
1 oz. hemp seeds
1 small bunch of parsley, minced

Combine all ingredients EXCEPT parsley in a food processor and process until smooth. Fold in the minced parsley.

Serve with falafel

CREAMY "CHEESE" SAUCE

MAKES 3 CUPS

½ cup oat flour (may substitute barley flour)
¼ cup olive oil (may substitute macadamia nut oil)
2 ½ cups water
2 TBS Dijon mustard
2 tsp granulated garlic
1 tsp white pepper
1 tsp unrefined sea salt or Himalayan salt
⅔ cup nutritional yeast flakes

Make a roux by placing the flour and oil in a pan and whisking them together over medium heat for a couple minutes until flour smells nutty. Slowly add the water, while whisking, until mixture is smooth. Add remaining ingredients EXCEPT nutritional yeast. Bring to a boil, reduce heat and simmer for a few minutes, stirring often, until smooth and creamy. Turn off heat and add nutritional yeast to the mixture and whisk well until smooth and thickened.

Pour over pasta or add to casseroles or any dish that desires a cheesy cream sauce.

BÉCHAMEL SAUCE

MAKES ABOUT 2 CUPS

Use this instead of milk based béchamel for creamy casseroles, noodles and soups.

½ onion, finely minced
1 garlic clove, pressed
1 tsp olive oil
½ tsp unrefined sea salt or Himalayan salt
2 TBS flour (kamut, barley or whole wheat)
1 TBS tahini
1 ½ cups water

Sauté the onions and garlic in the olive oil and salt for a few minutes to soften. Add the flour and tahini then stir to coat. Slowly whisk in the water until there are no lumps and bring to a boil. Reduce heat and simmer 15 minutes, stirring often, until thickened.

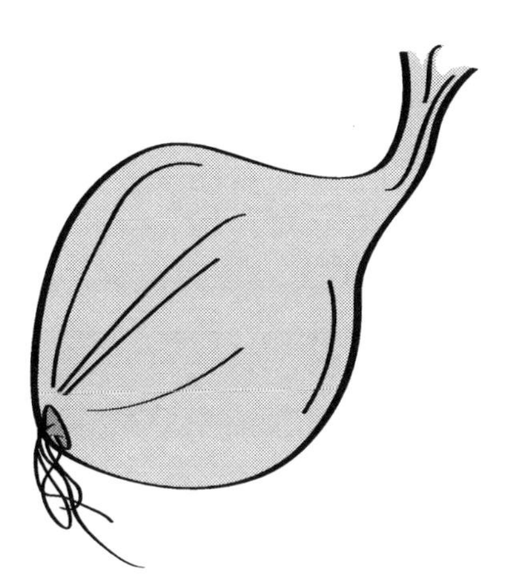

SHIITAKE-CASHEW GRAVY
MAKES ABOUT 3 CUPS

1 small yellow onion, diced
6 shiitake mushrooms, chopped, stems discarded
1-2 cups vegetable broth (may substitute water)
1 cup of cashews (soaked for 4 hours or boiled for 3 minutes, then drained)
1 TBS miso paste (I like sweet, mellow or white miso)
1 garlic clove, pressed

Place the onions, mushrooms and 1 cup of the broth into a saucepan and cook over medium heat, partially covered, for about 10 minutes, or until very soft. Add more broth or water, if needed, to prevent sticking. Remove from heat once softened and let cool, reserving any liquid remaining in the pan. Place 1 cup of cashews in a blender and cover with ½ cup broth (you can use any liquid remaining in the pan from the cooked onions and mushrooms). Blend until almost smooth. Add the onions, mushrooms, and miso paste. Blend again, adding broth one tablespoon at a time, until gravy is smooth and thickened to your liking. Taste for salt.

To reheat this gravy place in a small saucepan and heat over very low heat while stirring frequently until it is heated through. Don't boil this gravy!

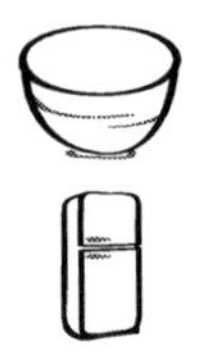

Serve over any grain or vegetable dish you wish.

Store in a sealed container in the refrigerator for up to a week.

ONION-MISO GRAVY

MAKES ABOUT 2 CUPS

1 TBS olive oil (may substitute ½ cup vegetable broth)
3 medium onions, ***finely minced*** *(can use a food processor)*
2 TBS tamari (may substitute shoyu)
2 TBS flour (try any kind you like; barley, brown rice or kamut)
1 cup vegetable broth (may use more if necessary)
1 TBS mellow, white miso
⅓ almond milk, ***unsweetened*** *(may substitute cashew cream or other non-dairy milk)*
salt and pepper to taste

Place the onions and oil in a heavy bottomed pan over very low heat and toss to coat. Cover and cook for about 30 minutes or until very, very soft. Whisk together the tamari and flour in a small dish then add to the onions, and cook for a couple of minutes. Next, add the broth in a slow, steady stream while whisking constantly. Simmer until sauce thickens. Meanwhile, in a small bowl whisk the miso with the almond milk. Turn off heat and stir to combine with gravy. Season if necessary with salt and pepper.

If it's too thick after adding the miso and almond milk slurry then whisk in a little more vegetable broth, one tablespoon at a time, until desired texture is reached.

Use a heavy bottomed pan for this recipe. Use a flame tamer under your pan if you can't achieve a steady, low heat on your stove top. You can check on the onions after 20 minutes to make sure they're not sticking to the pan.

Don't boil the gravy once the miso has been added or you will destroy the beneficial bacteria of the miso.

GLENN'S SALAD DRESSING

MAKES ABOUT 1 CUP OR MORE

When Glenn makes this dressing life is good!

1 garlic clove, pressed
1 tsp grated ginger
½ lemon, juiced
1 TBS mellow white miso (see note)*
2 TBS brown rice vinegar (may substitute apple cider vinegar)
a squirt of date syrup, agave nectar, brown rice syrup or yacon syrup
1 tsp dijon mustard
¼ cup flax seed oil (see note)*
1 handful of parsley, minced (may substitute cilantro)

Blend all of the ingredients **except** the flax seed oil and parsley in a blender or food processor until smooth. Slowly add the flax seed oil while blending, until desired thickness is achieved. Add the parsley and pulse to combine.

You may substitute water or more lemon juice for some of the flax seed oil for a lighter dressing.

Use on salads or grains.

Keep this dressing stored in an airtight container in the refrigerator.

Please do not heat this dressing or the beneficial properties of the miso and flax seed oil will be destroyed.

CAESAR SALAD DRESSING

MAKES ABOUT 1 CUP

The seaweed (dulse and nori) gives this vegan dressing an ocean taste, while adding cleansing properties to the dressing.

¼ cup raw cashews
2 TBS water
1 ½ tsp Dijon mustard
1 tsp dulse seaweed flakes
1 sheet of toasted nori seaweed, broken into pieces
2 TBS nutritional yeast
½ tsp date syrup, agave nectar or yacon syrup
2 TBS lemon juice
1-2 garlic cloves, pressed
1 TBS flax seed oil
½ umeboshi plum (may substitute 1 tsp umeboshi plum paste)
¼ tsp pepper

Blend the cashews and water together in a blender until smooth. Add remaining ingredients and blend until creamy.

Store refrigerated.

SIMPLE FAT FREE DRESSING IDEAS

Citrus
Squeeze fresh lemon, lime, orange or grapefruit juice over salad.

Sweet Mustard
Whisk rice vinegar with a little mustard and a dash of date syrup, agave or yacon syrup.

Orange Miso
Combine orange juice, miso, pressed garlic and grated ginger.

CREAMY RANCH DRESSING
MAKES 1 ½ CUPS

¾ cup cashew cream, see pg. 195 (may substitute ¾ cup puréed white beans)
3 TBS green onions, chopped
2 TBS parsley
2-3 TBS fresh dill or 1-1 ½ tsp dried
1 garlic clove, pressed
2 TBS lemon juice
1 TBS umeboshi plum paste
2 tsp tamari (may substitute shoyu soy sauce)
2 tsp olive oil (may substitute flax seed oil)
2 tsp brown rice vinegar
¼ tsp white pepper
⅛ cup to ½ cup water

Blend all ingredients, **except** water, in a blender or food processor until smooth. Add water gradually until desired thickness is obtained.

Serve as a dressing or a dip for vegetables.

APRICOT VINAIGRETTE
MAKES ABOUT ¾ CUP

½ cup organic apricot preserves
1 TBS shallot, minced
1 TBS lemon juice, plus more if desired
1 TBS olive (may substitute flax seed oil)
dash of unrefined sea salt or Himalayan salt

Place the apricot preserves in a small saucepan with the minced shallots and heat over medium-low heat for about 3 minutes. Turn off the heat. Whisk in the lemon juice, then add the oil and a dash of salt and whisk until well combined. Taste and add more lemon if desired. Let cool before serving.

Use on salads, grains, or over steamed vegetables. This is also a good dip for spring rolls!

CREAMY GINGER VINAIGRETTE

GF

MAKES ABOUT 1 ½ CUPS

2 TBS brown rice vinegar
3 TBS lime juice
1-2 garlic cloves, pressed
2 TBS grated ginger
1 Thai chili pepper, seeded and minced
1 TBS date syrup, agave nectar, brown rice syrup or yacon syrup
2 TBS tahini, optional
2 TBS toasted sesame oil
2 TBS sesame oil
2 TBS water
unrefined sea salt or Himalayan salt, to taste
1 small bunch of cilantro, minced
1 TBS chopped fresh mint

Place all items **except** salt, cilantro and mint into a food processor or blender and combine until smooth. You may also whisk ingredients together by hand. Add salt to taste, then stir in the minced cilantro and mint, then serve.

Delicious on any salad or vegetable dish. Try it on noodles or toss it with steamed tempeh too.

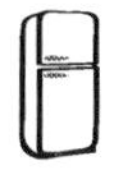

Refrigerate any leftover dressing in a tightly sealed container and use within 3 days.

BASIL SALAD DRESSING

MAKES ABOUT 1 CUP

¼ cup apple cider vinegar (may substitute lemon juice or red wine vinegar)
1 garlic clove, pressed
1 small shallot, minced
2 tsp whole grain mustard
2 tsp date syrup, agave nectar, brown rice syrup or yacon syrup
¼ tsp unrefined sea salt or Himalayan salt
¼ cup olive oil

¼ cup flax seed oil
2-3 TBS freshly minced basil
freshly ground pepper to taste

Blend all ingredients **except** basil and pepper in a blender until smooth. Fold in the basil and add some freshly ground pepper to taste.

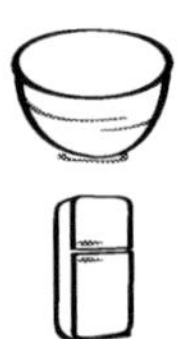

Serve over any salad greens, steamed vegetables, grain dishes or noodles.

Refrigerate any remaining dressing in a tightly sealed container and use within a few days.

You can lower the fat of this recipe by substituting water for some of the oil.

Do not heat this dressing- it contains flax seed oil, which cannot be heated or the precious Omega 3 will be destroyed!

ORANGE CURRY DRESSING (GF)

MAKES ABOUT ¾ CUP

½ cup orange juice
1 garlic clove, pressed
1 TBS apple cider vinegar
1 tsp curry powder
1 TBS flax seed oil
1 TBS minced cilantro
¼ tsp unrefined sea salt or Himalayan salt

Combine all ingredients in a blender until smooth, or just whisk together in a bowl until combined.

Serve over salads or grains. I also like this dressing mixed into cooked quinoa and tossed with toasted almonds, steamed broccoli, peas and carrots.

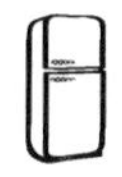

Store covered in refrigerator.

SESAME PLUM DRESSING

MAKES ABOUT ¾ CUP

You'll be surprised how delicious this dressing is. And, have I mentioned the amazing health benefits of the pickled umeboshi plum? You know the old saying "An umeboshi plum a day keeps the doctor away!" These sour, salty plums have a powerful alkalinizing effect on the body, and can be used to combat fatigue, headaches, indigestion and help eliminate toxins. Plus eating an umeboshi plum can help alleviate symptoms of a hangover or over indulgence. But please, buy from a health food store and make sure no artificial food colorings have been added.

¼ cup sesame seeds, tan not white
1 TBS brown rice vinegar
1 umeboshi plum, pitted
½ tsp dried dill (may substitute 1 TBS fresh dill)
½ cup water

Toast the sesame seeds in a pan over very low heat, stirring often, until they begin to smell nutty. Move them to a suribachi bowl or to your blender and pulse to grind them into small bits. Now add the remaining ingredients and grind or blend until smooth.

This dressing is great on vegetables or mixed into grain dishes.

STRAWBERRY BALSAMIC DRESSING

GF

MAKES ABOUT 1 ½ CUPS

This low fat, antioxidant rich dressing tastes amazing when strawberries are sweet and fresh.

1 cup chopped strawberries, organic of course! (see note)*
1 tsp date syrup, agave nectar, brown rice syrup or yacon syrup
1 small shallot, peeled and diced
3 TBS balsamic vinegar
¼ tsp unrefined sea salt or Himalayan salt
1 TBS flax seed oil (may substitute olive or walnut oil)
1 TBS chopped fresh basil (may substitute mint)

Combine all ingredients in a blender until smooth and creamy. Add a tablespoon of water if necessary to get the blender going.

You could also use raspberries in place of the strawberries, or half and half.

WASABI DRESSING

MAKES ABOUT ½ CUP

2 tsp tamari (may substitute shoyu soy sauce)
2 tsp wasabi paste (or make your own paste with wasabi powder and hot water)
⅓ cup brown rice vinegar (may substitute half apple cider vinegar)
1 TBS date syrup, agave nectar, brown rice syrup or yacon syrup
1 tsp sesame oil

Whisk all ingredients together in a small bowl. Refrigerate until ready to serve.

Goes great on a salad made of dandelion leaves, shredded carrot and sliced avocado.

TAHINI WASABI DRESSING
MAKES ABOUT 2 CUPS

2 TBS wasabi powder combined with enough water to make a paste (see note)*
½ cup tahini
2 TBS brown rice vinegar
2 TBS tamari (may substitute shoyu or soy sauce)
1 cup water, more or less

Place the wasabi in a small bowl and add with the appropriate temperature water to make a paste. Let sit for 5-10 minutes to let flavor develop. Meanwhile, place the tahini, brown rice vinegar and tamari in a food processor and process to incorporate. Gradually add the 1 cup of water while the machine is running until desired thickness is reached. You want it to be like gravy. Now add half of the wasabi paste and process again until smooth. Taste for spice, adding the rest of the wasabi paste if desired (I like to really taste the wasabi!). Refrigerate until needed. Serve on salads, vegetables and grain or noodle dishes.

Follow directions on package as certain wasabi powders need to be combined with hot or cold water in order for them to "bloom."

TAHINI MAYO
MAKES ABOUT ¾ CUP

¼ cup tahini
¼ cup water
1 TBS flax seed (may substitute olive oil)
2 TBS lemon juice
1 TBS mellow miso
1 garlic clove, pressed
1 ½ tsp date syrup, agave nectar, brown rice syrup or yacon syrup

Combine all ingredients in bowl and whisk until smooth. Or use a food processor or blender to combine until smooth.

GARLIC ALMOND MAYO

MAKES ABOUT 2 CUPS

(GF)

This mayo has a sharp garlic taste but will mellow out after chilling.

¾ cup raw almonds (see note)*
½ cup water
1-2 garlic cloves, pressed (see note)*
¾ tsp unrefined sea salt or Himalayan salt
½ cup flax seed oil
½ cup olive oil
3 TBS lemon juice
1 TBS apple cider vinegar

Drop the almonds into a pan of 2 cups boiling water for 30 seconds then remove with a slotted spoon and place in a bowl of ice water. Slip off the almond skins by squeezing each one between your thumb and fingers. Place the almonds, ½ cup water, garlic, and salt in a blender until very smooth. Slowly add the oils while the blender is running. Then add the lemon juice and vinegar and blend to combine. Add a bit more water while blending if you desire a thinner consistency.

Be sure to have your bowl of ice water ready in advance so it is easier to slip off the almond skins.

It can be made without the garlic, if desired.

Store in a tightly closed container in the refrigerator and use within 1 week.

CASHEW MAYO

MAKES ABOUT 1 CUP

½ cup cashews
3 TBS lemon juice (may substitute apple cider vinegar)
2 tsp date syrup, agave nectar, brown rice syrup or yacon syrup
½ tsp unrefined sea salt or Himalayan salt
½ tsp dry mustard powder
⅛ tsp white pepper, optional (do not substitute black pepper here)
water, as needed

Place the cashews in a pan and cover with water. Boil for 2 minutes, then drain and rinse with cold water. Drain again. Alternatively, you could soak the cashews in fresh water for up to 24 hours, then drain, rinse and drain. Place softened cashews in a blender with the remaining ingredients and blend until smooth, adding water slowly, blend until desired thickness is reached.

GARLIC MISO MAYO

MAKES ABOUT 1 CUP

4 TBS flax seed oil
4 TBS olive oil
3 TBS mellow white miso
2 TBS lemon juice
2 tsp apple cider vinegar
2 garlic cloves, pressed
1-2 tsp date syrup, agave nectar, brown rice syrup or yacon syrup
water, as needed

Blend all ingredients in a blender or food processor; drizzling in a tablespoon of water if needed to help make the blending easier. Blend until smooth and creamy.

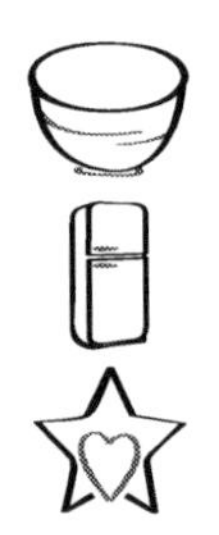

Serve as a spread for sandwiches or as a dip or dressing.

Store covered in the refrigerator.

Please do not heat this spread or the therapeutic properties of the flax seed oil and miso will be lost.

CURRIED CASHEW MAYO OR CURRIED CASHEW CREAM (GF)

MAKES ABOUT 1 CUP

Follow recipe for cashew mayo or cashew cream, but reduce sweetener in half and add about 1 TBS curry powder, then blend. Adjust seasonings and serve as a sauce for grains, beans, burgers, etc.

CASHEW CREAM (PLAIN, SWEET, LEMON OR SAVORY) (GF)

MAKES ABOUT 1 ½ CUPS

1 cup cashews, raw, organic preferred

Optional Ingredients

sweetener (dates, agave nectar, yacon syrup)
lemon juice
Himalayan salt

Place cashews in a dish and cover with water. Let soak for 4 hours or up to 24 hours in a cool dark place or in the refrigerator. Drain, rinse with fresh water and drain again. Place softened cashews in a blender. While machine is running, slowly drizzle in fresh water through the top of the blender until desired thickness is reached. * You will need a powerful blender to make it smooth. Otherwise try blending store bought cashew butter with water until creamy.

If you are short on time, take the cashews and place them in a pan and cover with water. Bring to a boil for 2 minutes, then drain, rinse with cold water and drain again. Blend as indicated above.

This cream can be used to replace cream in any recipe, sweet or savory, and can be adjusted depending on the type of dish you are serving. Serve it thick or thin by adjusting the liquid content, or add a sweetener, and/or lemon juice to serve as a creamy topping with dessert. Also experiment using salt, nutritional yeast, garlic and spices for a savory cream. The possibilities are endless. My favorite is to use this recipe as a base for a creamy sauce in casseroles.

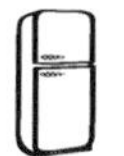

Refrigerate until ready to use. Use within 2-3 days.

(GF) GARLIC-LEMON-BASIL CREAM

MAKES ABOUT ¾ CUP

½ cup cashews (see note)*
1 garlic clove, pressed
1 lemon, zested and juiced
⅓ cup chopped fresh basil
2 tsp chopped fresh oregano
unrefined sea salt or Himalayan salt, to taste
cayenne, to taste

Place the cashews in a small saucepan and cover with water. Bring to a boil for 2 minutes. Then drain and rinse with cold water. Place in a blender with garlic, lemon zest and juice. Blend until smooth and creamy, add fresh water while blending until desired consistency is reached. Remove to a bowl and stir in the basil, oregano, salt and cayenne.

You can soak the cashews for 24 hours instead of boiling them if you desire a raw sauce.

You can adjust this recipe and use as a dip for vegetables by using less water. Or keep it thin to pour over pasta and steamed vegetables for a delicious cream sauce.

(GF) CASHEW SOUR CREAM

MAKES ABOUT 1 CUP

½ cup raw cashew pieces
¼ tsp unrefined sea salt or Himalayan salt
2-3 TBS lemon juice
water, as needed

Place the cashews in a saucepan with enough water to cover and boil for 2 minutes. Drain and rinse with cold water and drain again. Add cashews, salt and lemon juice to a blender and blend while gradually adding a little fresh water through the top of the blender (about 1 TBS at a time) until mixture is smooth. Taste for tang and salt, adding more lemon or salt if necessary, and refrigerate until ready to serve. Use within a few days.

CRÈME FRAICHE
MAKES ABOUT 1 ½ CUPS

1 cup raw cashews
1 TBS lemon juice
2-3 TBS date syrup, agave nectar, brown rice syrup or yacon syrup
3-5 TBS water
unrefined sea salt or Himalayan salt, to taste

Take the cashews and soak them in 2 cups water for up to 24 hours in a cool, dark place, or in the refrigerator. If pressed for time, boil the cashews in 2 cups of water for 3 minutes. Either way, once the cashews are softened drain them well and place in a blender with the lemon juice, 2 TBS sweetener, 3 TBS water, and a dash of salt. Blend until smooth, adding more water if necessary to achieve a thickened cream. Taste for lemon, sweetener and salt and adjust if necessary.

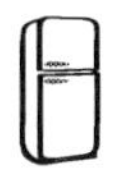

Keep sealed in the refrigerator until ready to serve.

TANDOORI SPICE MIX

MAKES ½ CUP

3 TBS paprika
1 TBS ground coriander
1 TBS ground cumin
1 TBS unrefined sea salt or Himalayan salt
1 tsp freshly ground black pepper
1 ½ tsp rapadura (unrefined sugar)
2 tsp ground ginger
½ tsp cinnamon
¼ tsp cayenne

Whisk all ingredients together in a bowl.

Use to flavor tempeh, beans or vegetables.

Transfer to jar and store in a cool, dry, dark place.

(GF) MARRAKESH SPICE BLEND

MAKES ABOUT ¼ CUP

Wow! Every ingredient in this Moroccan spice mixture has healing properties... good for digestion, increasing circulation and decreasing inflammation. Create ways to use this blend weekly on your favorite foods.

1 TBS ground ginger
1 TBS ground cumin
1 TBS cinnamon
1 TBS ground coriander
1 tsp turmeric
½ tsp ground cloves
¼ tsp ground cardamom
¼ tsp cayenne pepper

Whisk all ingredients together then place in a spice jar.

There is no salt in this spice blend so add salt when serving, if desired (it helps to bring out some of the other flavors). And, as always, use unrefined sea salt or Himalayan salt.

Adding lemon juice and/or a little sweetener to your dish also helps to bring out the flavors of this spice blend.

Use to flavor stews, grains, beans, salad dressings or cashew mayo.

AUTUMN SPICY MIX

MAKES ABOUT ¼ CUP

Adding a little spice to your life in the fall and winter helps to keep you warm!

2 TBS ground allspice
1 TBS cinnamon
2 tsp cayenne
2 tsp ground ginger
½ tsp ground cloves

Combine spices in a spice jar and stir to combine.

Use on any roasted vegetable, or in simmered fruit compote.

GOMASIO

MAKES ABOUT ½ CUP

This Macrobiotic condiment is used on top of vegetable, grain, and noodle dishes to give a salty taste without all the salt! Use unrefined sea salt or Himalayan mountain salt. Remember to love seaweed for its high mineral content (iodine, calcium, iron, etc.) and detoxification qualities.

½ cup sesame seeds (tan, not white)
¼ tsp unrefined sea salt or Himalayan salt
1 TBS dulse seaweed flakes (see note)*

Use a large, heavy bottomed pan and dry roast the sesame seeds, salt and dulse flakes; stirring almost constantly over very low heat so seeds do not burn. It will take 5-10 minutes until they are lightly roasted. If they are jumping out of the pan, the heat is too high. Once roasted, grind in suribachi bowl, or mortal and pestle, until about half the seeds are crushed. Remove and store in an airtight container in the **refrigerator**.

Use any type of seaweed flakes you desire: dulse, nori, kelp, etc.

You could also put the seeds into a coffee grinder or a food processor and pulse to partially grind the seeds. You don't want all the seeds to become ground because it's nice to have the crunchiness of some whole seeds.

How To Toast Sesame Seeds
Take desired amount of sesame seeds and rinse them in a fine mesh strainer. Drain well and move to a heavy bottomed pan. Turn heat to low and stir constantly until no moisture remains on the seeds. Now be sure the heat is at the lowest setting because the seeds can burn in an instant. Heat, stirring frequently, until they begin to smell nutty and start to pop. If they are popping out of control, the heat is too high. Remove from pan and use to sprinkle on foods or grind in a suribachi bowl (a mortar and pestel, but with grooves).

WALNUT "PARMESAN"

MAKES ABOUT ½ CUP

1 cup walnuts
2 TBS nutritional yeast
dash of unrefined sea salt or Himalayan salt

Lightly toast the walnuts on a sheet pan in a 300 F oven for 10 minutes, taking care not to burn the walnuts. Let cool completely and place in a food processor with the nutritional yeast and salt. Pulse to combine, until crumbly like bread crumbs.

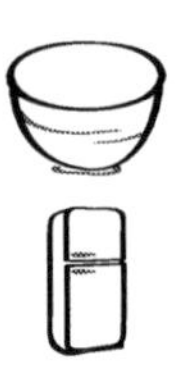

Use as a topping on pasta, salads, soups, etc.

Store in an airtight container in the **refrigerator**.

GARLIC-BRAZIL NUT "PARMESAN"

MAKES ABOUT ½ CUP

1 cup brazil nuts, roughly chopped
1 garlic clove, pressed
a pinch of unrefined sea salt or Himalayan salt
2 TBS nutritional yeast, optional

Place brazil nuts in a food processor with the garlic and salt and process by pulsing on and off until you have fine crumbs. You may have to stop and scrape the sides of the bowl and process again. Be careful not to over process into a paste. Add more salt if necessary and the nutritional yeast (if using) and pulse one more time to combine.

Best to make this in small quantities because it tastes best when eaten fresh. A little goes a long way.

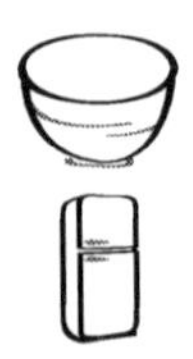

Serve on any dish where you desire parmesan.

Store leftovers in a tightly covered container in the **refrigerator** up to 3 days.

Salads

There is an entire section of Dressings, Sauces and Condiments that you can use to invent your own salad. Take your favorite lettuce or green leafy vegetable, raw or steamed vegetables, nuts or seeds, berries or sprouts, etc. and toss with whatever dressing you desire. I'll let you be the creator for this category! Here are a few composed salads to get you started.

"Health is not simply the absence of sickness."

~ Unknown

DANDELION GREENS WITH WASABI DRESSING

SERVES 6-8

Dandelion is not just any old weed. The greens are used to help strengthen the liver, help purify the blood, gallbladder, kidneys, and cleanse the body. Also great for treating anemia, reducing bad cholesterol and clearing skin. It can be bitter tasting so look for fresh greens at your farmer's market in springtime.

1 bunch of dandelion greens, chopped
1 avocado, sliced
1 lemon, cut into wedges
1 medium orange, peeled
½ cup wasabi dressing

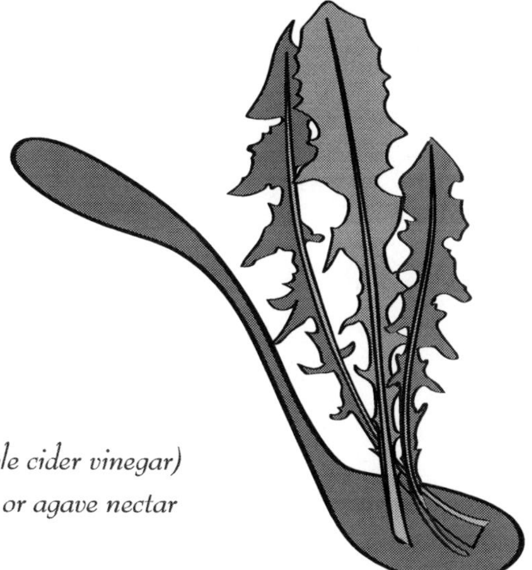

Dressing Ingredients *(makes about ½ cup)*
2 tsp tamari (may substitute shoyu soy sauce)
2 tsp wasabi paste (may make your own paste with wasabi powder and hot water)
⅓ cup brown rice vinegar (may substitute part apple cider vinegar)
1 TBS date syrup, brown rice syrup, yacon syrup, or agave nectar
1 tsp unrefined sesame oil

Wash and chop the dandelion greens, discarding the tough stems. Pat dry with a towel or spin dry with a salad spinner. Place greens in a serving bowl. Slice the avocado into long slices and place in a small bowl. Drizzle about 1 TBS of lemon juice onto avocado and toss gently to prevent browning; then add to the salad. Cut the orange into bite-size pieces (or supreme it) and add to the greens. Finally, whisk all dressing ingredients together in a small bowl. Gently toss the greens with half of the dressing. Taste and add more dressing if desired. Serve immediately; garnish with lemon wedges

DANDELION AND WATERCRESS SALAD WITH ZESTY GINGER DRESSING

SERVES 6

In your quest for zest remember that there's more to citrus fruits than the vitamin C-rich juice. The zest of lemons and limes contains powerful cancer-fighting compounds, and adds incredible flavor to your meal. Just remember to use organic produce to avoid exposure to pesticide residue.

3 cups torn dandelion leaves
1 bunch watercress, chopped, roots discarded (may substitute spinach)
1 medium carrot, scrubbed and grated
½ medium red onion, cut into slivers
½ cup chopped fresh cilantro
1 small cucumber, peeled

Dressing Ingredients
2 tsp date syrup, agave nectar, brown rice syrup or yacon syrup
2 tsp grated ginger
2 TBS fresh lime juice
Zest of 1 small organic lemon
2 tsp tamari (may substitute shoyu soy sauce)
1 tsp toasted sesame oil
2 tsp flax seed oil (may substitute hemp seed oil)
½ teaspoon chili-garlic sauce (may substitute ⅛ teaspoon crushed red pepper flakes)

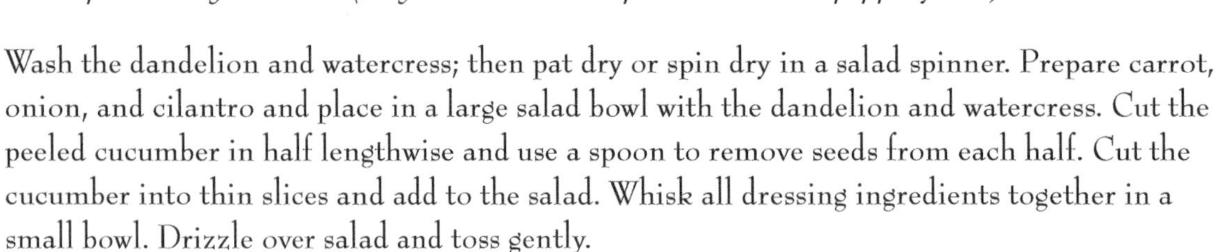

Wash the dandelion and watercress; then pat dry or spin dry in a salad spinner. Prepare carrot, onion, and cilantro and place in a large salad bowl with the dandelion and watercress. Cut the peeled cucumber in half lengthwise and use a spoon to remove seeds from each half. Cut the cucumber into thin slices and add to the salad. Whisk all dressing ingredients together in a small bowl. Drizzle over salad and toss gently.

PURSLANE AND TOMATO MEDLEY SALAD (GF)

SERVES 6

Although this leafy green vegetable is considered a weed in the U.S. (a.k.a. Pigweed or Little Hogweed), purslane is eaten elsewhere in the world and prized for its health benefits. It is high in Omega-3 EFA, vitamins A and C, magnesium, calcium, potassium and iron. It is helpful in lowering bad cholesterol, strengthening the liver, treating urinary tract infections, dysentery, and reducing inflammation in arthritis. You can use the tender stems, leaves and flower buds raw or cooked in any dish that calls for a leafy green vegetable (spinach, chard or kale). It has a slight lemony taste, which makes salads, spreads and sandwiches more interesting.

3 cups purslane leaves, tough stems discarded
3 heirloom tomatoes, chopped, seeded (a variety of colors is nice, especially green zebra) (see note)*
½ cup cherry tomatoes, halved (a variety of colors is nice, especially orange and yellow)
1 nectarine, sliced thin
1 white peach, sliced thin
3 green onions, finely chopped

Dressing Ingredients
1 TBS olive oil (may substitute flax seed oil)
1 TBS lemon (may substitute lime juice)
dash of unrefined sea salt or Himalayan salt
dash of cayenne, optional
6 medium basil leaves, sliced (may substitute parsley, cilantro or mint) (see note)*

Combine purslane, tomatoes, nectarine, peach and onions in a medium bowl. In a small bowl, whisk together oil, lemon, salt and cayenne. Drizzle over the purslane-tomato mixture, garnish with basil, and serve immediately.

It's best to make this when heirloom tomatoes and nectarines are in peak season so you can find all different varieties and colors.

The basil will start to turn brown soon after it is sliced so don't slice the basil until you are ready to serve. Also, anytime you add salt to fruit (or other watery foods), the salt will extract moisture from the fruit and you are left with wilted fruit and a bowl full of liquid. To avoid this, add the dressing just before serving, and only dress what you are going to eat.

In ancient Roman times Pliny the Elder could be seen wearing an amulet of purslane to expel all evil. That may have some benefit but I think I'll just stick to eating it.

(GF) BROCCOLI SEAWEED SLAW

SERVES 6-8

Learn to love seaweed! It's full of minerals and helps the body get rid of toxins. This is a good recipe for beginners because the seaweed is hardly noticeable.

1 small burdock root, scrubbed and diced (see note)*
½ cup vegetable broth (may substitute water)
3 broccoli stalks, peeled (see note)*
1 small beet, peeled
1 small daikon, scrubbed
2-3 medium carrots, scrubbed
2 cups rehydrated mixed seaweed, from about ¼ cup dry (follow package directions)
1 tsp ginger, grated on a microplane, catching juice as well as pulp
¼ cup minced cilantro
¼ cup sliced green onions
2 TBS vegan mayo (see pg. 194)
1 tsp umeboshi plum vinegar
1 tsp toasted sesame oil
1 TBS brown rice vinegar
dash of cayenne, optional (may substitute chili sauce)
2 TBS gomasio (sesame seed salt)

Place the diced burdock root in a pan with the water and let simmer for 5 minutes. Drain and let cool. Grate broccoli stalks, raw beets, daikon, and carrots (you could do this on a mandolin). Place in a large bowl with the burdock and the remaining ingredients except gomasio and toss to combine. Garnish with gomasio.

If you don't want the whole salad to turn the color of beets then soak the grated beets in a bowl of cold water for 10 minutes. Remove with a slotted spoon and drain well. Proceed as indicated.

To clean burdock root all you need to do is scrub it under cold water. You can trim away any blemishes or strings, but it is not necessary to peel it.

You'll want to peel the broccoli stalks because the outer layer can be tough to chew.

Serve chilled or at room temperature.

SPROUT SALAD WITH SESAME CHILI DRESSING

SERVES 4

Loaded with cruciferous vegetables this salad will help fight cancer. Broccoli sprouts in particular have 20 times the cancer-fighting compound, sulforaphane glucosinolate, compared to mature broccoli. Find ways to include cruciferous vegetables at each meal.

1 cup shredded purple cabbage
1 cup shredded green cabbage
½ cup shredded daikon radish
2 cups shredded carrots
1 cup sunflower seed sprouts, trimmed
1 cup broccoli sprouts
¼ cup chopped cilantro
2 TBS mint leaves, chopped
1 TBS toasted sesame seeds
(may substitute pumpkin seeds)

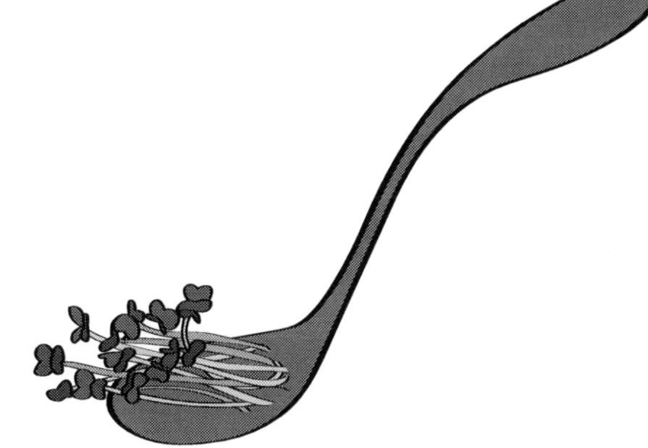

Dressing Ingredients
¼ cup lemon juice
2 tsp date syrup, agave nectar, brown rice syrup or yacon syrup
3 TBS flax seed oil
1 tsp toasted sesame oil
1 tsp mellow miso
½ tsp red pepper flakes (add more if you like it spicy)

Place all salad ingredients in a bowl and toss to combine. In a small bowl whisk together all of the dressing ingredients. You will have more dressing than you need for the sprout salad. Toss a couple tablespoons of the dressing with the salad and serve immediately.

Save remaining dressing in a tightly covered container in the refrigerator for up to 1 week.

(GF)

TRIPLE A SALAD WITH CHUTNEY DRESSING

SERVES 6

Apples, avocados and almonds, oh my!

2 tsp fresh lemon juice
1 granny smith apple; unpeeled, cored and thinly sliced
1 avocado, peeled and thinly sliced
½ almonds, chopped
¼ cup sliced green onions
8 oz. mixed salad greens, washed and spun dry

Dressing Ingredients
4 TBS lemon juice (may substitute lime juice)
2 TBS orange juice
1 TBS mango chutney (may substitute other favorite chutney)
½ tsp dry mustard
½ tsp unrefined sea salt or Himalayan salt
a dash of cayenne (add more if you like spicy)
4 TBS flax seed oil

Prepare salad by sprinkling lemon juice on the apple and avocado slices. Toss with the almonds, onions, and mixed greens in a large salad bowl. Prepare dressing by combining all ingredients, except oil, in blender. Add oil while blender is running in a slow, steady stream until smooth and creamy. Toss salad with dressing and serve immediately.

BURDOCK-BEET SALAD

SERVES 4

This recipe is good for nourishing the blood and the liver. Burdock is not the prettiest vegetable on the block but it just might be the healthiest.

6-inch piece of burdock, scrubbed well and cut into matchsticks (see note)*
1 small beet, scrubbed and shredded
1 medium carrot, scrubbed and shredded
1 tsp ginger juice (from squeezing freshly grated ginger over a strainer and bowl)
2 TBS brown rice vinegar (may substitute 1 TBS orange juice and 1 TBS lemon juice)
2 tsp umeboshi plum vinegar
1 TBS sesame seeds, toasted
2 green onions, minced
3 TBS cilantro, chopped

Mix all ingredients together and serve chilled or room temperature.

To clean burdock root scrub it under cold running water to remove most of the dark brown skin and strings. Cut into matchstick size pieces. If not eating the salad immediately, place cut burdock in a bowl of cold water for 10 minutes, then drain well, pat dry, and proceed with recipe. This will keep it from turning green.

(GF) FENNEL-ORANGE-BEET SALAD

SERVES 6-8

3 medium oranges
3 green onions, washed and thinly sliced
1 medium fennel bulb, trimmed and very thinly sliced may use a mandolin)
1 small bunch of parsley, chopped
1 TBS olive oil (an orange-infused oil is nice)
unrefined sea salt or Himalayan salt, to taste
10 oz. mixed greens
½ cup raw walnuts (may substitute ⅓ cup raw pumpkin seeds)
1 medium red beet, peeled and grated
¼ cup pomegranate seeds

Chop walnuts into small pieces. Peel the oranges and separate into segments, discarding any seeds. Cut segments in half and place in a large bowl. Add green onions, fennel, parsley, and oil; toss to combine. Season with salt, if desired. Let sit at room temperature for 30 minutes. To serve, toss the mixed greens with the orange mixture and sprinkle with walnuts, grated beets and pomegranate seeds.

(GF) PRESSED CABBAGE SALAD WITH LEMON

SERVES 6

When you salt and massage cabbage it wilts the cabbage, making it softer. This is a quick pickling method, but without the development of the prized healthy flora, the good bacteria that gets produced when making traditional raw sauerkraut or kimchee.

1 head of Chinese cabbage, about ½ lb., sliced
2 cups of sliced red cabbage
unrefined sea salt or Himalayan salt, as needed
juice from 1 lemon
3 green onions, sliced

Place the sliced cabbage in a large bowl. Sprinkle lightly with salt and knead gently for 3-5 minutes or until cabbage begins to wilt and lose its water. Move to a strainer and let water drain off, kneading and squeezing a bit more. Taste the cabbage, if it is too salty then rinse the cabbage and drain well. Move to a serving bowl and toss with the lemon juice and green onions and serve at room temperature or chilled.

BEAUTIFUL BEET "CARPACCIO"

GF

SERVES 4

Inspired by Italian Artist Vittore Carpaccio, this salad dish of thinly sliced raw beets is almost too pretty to eat!

1 cup arugula leaves, cleaned, and patted dry
1 medium golden beet, peeled and sliced into very thin circles * *(see note)*
1 medium red beet, peeled and sliced into very thin circles
1 small chiogga beet, peeled and sliced into very thin circles (may substitute watermelon radish)
12 basil leaves, torn into 1-inch pieces
2 tsp olive oil
1 tsp umeboshi plum vinegar (may substitute lemon juice and a dash of salt)
2 tsp hemp seeds

Arrange the arugula on a platter. Lay the beet slices on top of the bed of arugula alternating between yellow, red and pink. Sprinkle with basil, olive oil, umeboshi plum vinegar and hemp seeds.

Serve chilled or at room temperature.

Use a mandolin to slice the beets and radish into very thin circles. If you don't have a mandolin, see if your grater has a slicer blade or try using a vegetable peeler.

GF

JICAMA SALAD

SERVES 4

If you haven't tried jicama before, this is a great introduction to this tuberous root. Jicama has a refreshing, crunchy texture with a hint of sweetness. It is loaded with fiber so include it in any salad or use as a vehicle for hummus and other spreads to help increase your fiber intake.

1 lb. jicama, peeled and cut into matchsticks
1 carrot, scrubbed and grated
½ cup shredded red cabbage
2 tsp minced jalapeno pepper
1 tsp grated ginger
1 garlic clove, pressed
3 TBS orange juice
1 TBS lime juice
1 tsp rice vinegar
3 TBS minced cilantro
4 mint leaves, minced
unrefined sea salt or Himalayan salt, to taste
sweetener, optional

Place the jicama, carrot and cabbage in a serving bowl. In a separate bowl whisk together the jalapeno, ginger, garlic, juices, vinegar, cilantro, mint and a dash of salt. Taste and adjust if needed; adding a dash of sweetener, salt or spice. Pour over the jicama salad, toss gently, and season with more salt if desired. Serve immediately or cover and place in the refrigerator and serve within one day.

SPICY SLAW
SERVES 6-8

2 serrano peppers, seeded and minced
1 carrot, scrubbed and grated
1 red bell pepper, julienned
2 TBS mint, chiffonade
¼ cup cilantro, minced
3 green onions, chopped
1 medium head napa cabbage, shredded

Dressing Ingredients
1 TBS tamari (may substitute shoyu soy sauce)
juice of 1 medium lime
2 TBS flax seed oil
2 TBS brown rice vinegar
2 TBS apple cider vinegar
¼ cup raw almond butter
2 TBS ginger, grated

Whisk together the dressing ingredients until combined. Toss salad ingredients together with dressing and serve chilled or at room temperature.

(GF) CABBAGE-ALMOND SLAW

SERVES 6

A very good salad full of very healthy ingredients.

1 medium cabbage (napa, savoy, green), sliced into small, thin pieces, core discarded
6 green onions, cleaned and sliced
½ cup almond slivers, lightly toasted until fragrant, optional (see note)*
¼ cup sesame seeds, lightly toasted until fragrant, optional (see note)*

Dressing Ingredients
⅓ cup flax seed oil (see note)*
⅓ cup apple cider vinegar
½ tsp unrefined sea salt or Himalayan salt
3 TBS date syrup, agave nectar, brown rice syrup or yacon syrup

Toss salad ingredients together. Whisk dressing ingredients together or combine in a blender. Toss dressing with salad gradually as you may not need all of the dressing (depending on the size of your cabbage).

Toast the almonds and sesame seeds by placing in a dry skillet and heating over medium-low heat while stirring almost constantly until they begin to smell nutty. Immediately remove from the pan onto a plate to cool.

Save remaining dressing in a covered container in the refrigerator for up to 1 week. Slaw will keep for 3 days in the refrigerator.

Do not heat this dressing - flax seed oil should never be heated or the beneficial Omega-3 EFA (essential fatty acid) will be destroyed. Omega 3 is helpful for improving cholesterol levels.

KIMCHI OR KIMCHEE

GF

MAKES 1 QUART/LITER

You will need a large crock pot to make this recipe. You will also need a plate or glass lid to set directly on the vegetables inside the crock. Read entire recipe before starting to make sure you have all the necessary equipment. It takes cleanliness and patience to make kimchee. If done properly you will be rewarded with a naturally fermented raw salad full of the 'good bacteria', a.k.a. probiotics.

4 TBS unrefined sea salt or Himalayan salt
4 cups water
1 pound Chinese cabbage, rinsed and chopped (may substitute napa cabbage)
1 daikon radish, scrubbed
2 carrots, scrubbed
1 small lotus root, peeled and sliced
1 10-inch piece of burdock, scrubbed well
1 red onion
1 bunch of green onions
4 garlic cloves (or more)
3-4 hot red chilies, fresh or dried
3 TBS grated ginger

Make sure that you always use clean hands, utensils, cutting board and containers when making kimchi. Wash the large crock pot container in hot soapy water and dry well with a clean towel. Mix a brine of about 4 cups of water and 4 TBS sea salt in the crock pot. Stir to dissolve salt. Chop the cabbage, radish, carrots, lotus root and burdock into desired bite-size shapes. Place these in the brine in the crock pot and set a plate or glass lid directly on top of the vegetables so that they are submerged in the brine. You may need to weight down the plate in order to keep the vegetables completely submerged in the brine and not exposed to air. I usually use a plate weighted with a clean glass jar. Then place a clean towel over the crock to keep out dust and pests. Check the vegetables in a few hours (using clean hands or utensils) to see if they are softened. If not, keep submerged and covered with the towel overnight.

Once the cabbage and vegetables are softened, prepare the spices by chopping the onion, pressing the garlic, mincing the chilies (removing seeds to reduce spiciness), and grating the ginger. Take these spices and process them in a food processor to make a paste.

Recipe continues on next page...

KIMCHI OR KIMCHEE...

Now drain off the brine water from the crock and reserve in a separate, clean jar. Taste cabbage for saltiness. It should be salty, but if too salty, then rinse with water. If you don't taste salt, then sprinkle on some more and mix into the cabbage and vegetables with clean hands. Add in the onion paste and mix well to incorporate the spices. Place a plate and a weight on top of the cabbage mixture and press down on the vegetables until you see water rising. If necessary add a little of the reserved brine so that the cabbage and vegetables are submerged in liquid as before. Cover the plate and weight with a clean towel to keep out dust and pests.

Let rest for about one week in your kitchen or another warm place, but away from drafts or direct sunlight. Taste the kimchi every day. It will take more or less time depending on the temperature of your kitchen. When it is cold, it takes longer. You will know when it's ready because it will taste fermented and ripe. If it tastes bad, off, or is moldy, then it got contaminated and you should throw it out. Move the kimchi and brine to a clean, smaller glass container or jar with a lid, and place in the refrigerator.

Kimchi will last one month in refrigerator.

Serve a scoop of kimchi with every meal to improve digestion.

Just be sure to always use a clean slotted spoon or fork when reaching into the jar.

Vegetables

"I have no doubt that it is a part of the destiny of the human race, in its gradual improvement, to leave off eating animals."

~ Henry David Thoreau

RAW BURDOCK SALAD

SERVES 2

Please find ways to include this shy vegetable in your diet
to strengthen and clean your liver, blood and lungs.

4-inch piece of burdock, scrubbed and cut into matchsticks (see note)*
1 medium carrot, scrubbed and grated
2 TBS brown rice vinegar
1 tsp umeboshi plum vinegar
1 TBS sesame seeds, toasted
2 green onions, minced
2 TBS cilantro, chopped

Mix all ingredients in a bowl and refrigerate until serving.

To clean burdock root all you need to do is scrub it under cold water. You can trim away any blemishes or strings, but it is not necessary to peel it.

Best served when chilled.

(GF) DAIKON DIGESTION DISH

SERVES 6

This simple side dish helps you digest foods and just makes you feel fresh.

1 small daikon radish, scrubbed and grated
1 small carrot, scrubbed and grated
1 small bunch of cilantro, minced
1 tsp grated ginger
1-2 tsp lemon juice (may substitute apple cider vinegar)

Toss all ingredients together in a medium bowl.

Serve chilled or at room temperature as a side dish to any meal.

Refrigerate any leftovers and use within 2 days.

MACRO PICKLES

MAKES 1 ½ CUPS OF PICKLES

1 pound of radishes (red, daikon or watermelon radish)
2 TBS umeboshi plum vinegar

Slice radishes into thin slices equal in size. Toss with the vinegar and place in a small pickle press. Leave radishes to press and pickle overnight. They should be submerged in their own liquid. After 12-24 hours transfer radishes and their liquid to a clean glass jar and place in the refrigerator.

If you don't have a pickle press, place the radish slices and umeboshi vinegar in a crockpot and cover with a plate or something that fits inside the crockpot with a flat surface. Then place a can or a jar on top of the plate (to act as a weight) and finally cover the crockpot with a lid. The vegetables should soon be submerged in their own liquid. Let sit in a cool, dark place for 12-24 hours. Then proceed as indicated above.

Always remove pickles with **clean** tongs or a slotted spoon when serving.

These pickles will last one month if kept refrigerated.

MARINATED CARROTS

SERVES 6

6-8 carrots, quartered and sliced into 3-inch lengths
½ cup olive oil
¼ cup white wine vinegar
2 garlic cloves, pressed
1 tsp fresh basil, chopped (may substitute ½ tsp dried basil)
1 tsp unrefined sea salt or Himalayan salt
½ tsp freshly ground black pepper
juice of one lemon

Simmer the carrots in water to cover for 3 minutes. Drain and discard water (or use for a soup). Place carrots in a jar. Mix remaining ingredients in a small bowl and pour over carrots and refrigerate overnight. Drain thoroughly before serving.

BEETS WITH CRANBERRIES (GF)

MAKES 2 CUPS

A beautiful, refreshing side dish to any meal.

2-3 medium beets, peeled and diced
½ cup water
½ cup orange juice, freshly squeezed
1 TBS grated ginger
⅓ cup chopped fresh cranberries (can use frozen if necessary, no need to chop)
⅛ tsp unrefined sea salt or Himalayan salt
2 TBS chopped fresh mint or basil leaves

Combine the beets, water, juice and ginger in a saucepan. Bring to a boil then reduce heat to low and simmer 10-15 minutes or until beets are almost tender. Add the cranberries and salt and simmer for another 5 minutes. Remove beets and cranberries from the pan with a slotted spoon. Garnish with mint or basil.

Serve warm or chilled.

BEETS IN UMEBOSHI VINEGAR

SERVES 4

This dish is surprisingly simple and delicious! I know plenty of people who thought they didn't like beets but that was before they had this salad. You'll like them even more knowing that they help clean the liver and nourish the blood.

3 beets, scrubbed and cut into ½-inch thick wedges (no need to peel)
1 celery stalk, diced
½ red onion, sliced thin
2 TBS minced parsley
1-2 tsp umeboshi plum vinegar, to taste
1 TBS flax seed oil, or more to taste
(may substitute lemon infused olive oil)

Boil beets in water until soft. Drain and let cool. Once cool enough to handle, slip off the skins and discard. Toss beets with the celery, red onion and parsley. Sprinkle with a couple teaspoons of umeboshi plum vinegar and the oil and toss again.

Serve chilled.

NUTTY GARLIC SAUCE OVER BEET SALAD

SERVES 4-6

3 medium beets, sliced into 8 wedges
water, to cover beets in pan
½ cup diced daikon
1 baby bok choy, sliced and diced
1 celery stalk, diced
1 medium onion, chopped
1 garlic clove, pressed
¼ cup chopped walnuts, lightly toasted
¼ cup chopped parsley (may substitute cilantro leaves)
1 TBS miso paste, mellow, sweet or white miso
1 TBS apple cider vinegar
1 TBS lemon juice
½ tsp unrefined sea salt or Himalayan salt
½ tsp ground coriander
½ tsp ground cumin
dash of cayenne

Place the sliced beets in a pan of water and bring to a boil. Cover, reduce heat and let simmer for 10-15 minutes or until tender. Remove from water and rinse under cold water, removing and discarding the skins by slipping them off with your hands (they should slip off easily or use a peeler). Chop into bite-size pieces, if necessary.

Meanwhile, prepare the daikon, bok choy and celery and set aside in a medium bowl with the beets. Next, place the onion, garlic and toasted walnuts in a food processor and pulse until coarse crumbs. You may have to stop and scrape down the sides of the bowl. Then add the parsley, miso, vinegar, lemon juice, salt and spices in a food processor and process until smooth. Toss this nutty garlic sauce over the chopped beets and diced vegetables.

Serve this dish as a filling in wraps or on top of mixed grains, or as a side dish along with cabbage salad.

Keep chilled until ready to serve.

BRAISED GREENS WITH MARRAKESH SPICE

SERVES 6

This dish is exquisite!

½ cup vegetable broth, plus more as needed (may substitute water)
1 onion, sliced into strips
1 carrot, scrubbed and diced (or roll cut)
1 yellow squash, diced (may substitute yellow bell pepper)
1 TBS Marrakesh spice mixture (see pg. 198)
¼ tsp unrefined sea salt or Himalayan salt
2 TBS green raisins (may substitute dried apricots, diced or goji berries) (see note)*
1 bunch green kale, chopped, stems discarded
1 bunch collard greens, chopped, stems discarded
½ lemon
1 tsp date syrup, agave nectar, brown rice syrup or yacon syrup, optional
½ cup shredded red cabbage

Place the broth, onion, carrot, squash, Marrakesh spice mix and salt in a large pot and let simmer over medium heat for 5 minutes. Add the raisins, kale and collards and cover for 3 minutes (no more or the greens will lose their pretty green color). Add more broth or water if necessary to prevent sticking. After 3 minutes remove cover and stir. Greens should be wilted. Cook another 2-4 minutes or until greens are tender. Turn off heat and add the juice from half a lemon and the sweetener, if using, and stir well to combine. Taste for salt and spice, adding more salt, lemon or sweetener if desired. Toss with the shredded red cabbage and serve.

Always buy organic especially when it comes to dried fruit to avoid sulfur dioxide.

STEAMED VEGETABLES WITH SESAME-UME-DILL DRESSING (GF)

SERVES 4-6

5 cups of steamed vegetables (carrots, broccoli, squash, beets, mushrooms, green beans, burdock, daikon, kale etc.) (see note)*

Dressing Ingredients

1 tsp umeboshi plum paste
1 TBS toasted sesame seeds
1 TBS orange juice, freshly squeezed
2 TBS fresh dill, minced, or 1-2 tsp dried
2 TBS flax seed oil (see note)*
1 tsp date syrup, agave nectar, brown rice syrup or yacon syrup, optional
1-2 TBS water, optional, if too strong or thick

Clean and chop your vegetables then steam until tender. Set aside to cool slightly. Whisk together the umeboshi plum paste, toasted sesame seeds, orange juice, dill and oil. Taste and add the sweetener and water if needed. Toss vegetables with the dressing and serve warm.

Choose any vegetables you like. Steam each vegetable until tender. You may need to steam each vegetable separately because some vegetables require longer steaming times.

You could also pour this dressing on raw vegetables and let them marinate in the refrigerator until ready to serve.

Please don't heat this dressing because it contains flax seed oil which can't take the heat!

WILTED SPINACH WITH TAHINI SAUCE

SERVES 4-6

This is quick and tasty.

1 lb. of spinach, cleaned well and chopped (may substitute any green leafy vegetable)
2 TBS tahini
2 TBS tamari (may substitute shoyu soy sauce)
2 TBS lemon juice (may substitute orange juice)
1 TBS water
1 tsp date syrup, agave nectar, brown rice syrup or yacon syrup
2 tsp sesame seeds, lightly toasted

Place the spinach in a large pan with a few tablespoons of water and stir until it is wilted and bright green. Remove with tongs and place in a strainer. Meanwhile, whisk together the tahini, tamari, lemon juice, water and sweetener. Move spinach to a serving bowl and toss with the dressing. Garnish with toasted sesame seeds and serve.

Add pressed garlic to the pan with the spinach if you desire.

STEAMED BROCCOLINI WITH LEMON AND GARLIC (GF)

SERVES 6

2 pounds broccolini, cleaned and trimmed (see note)*
1 tsp toasted sesame oil
2 tsp olive oil
2 garlic cloves, pressed
1 tsp grated ginger (use a microplane)
¼ tsp red pepper flakes, optional
2 TBS lemon juice
2 TBS gomasio (toasted sesame seed condiment)

Steam broccolini for 3-5 minutes or until tender, taking care not to let it over cook. Uncover and remove from steamer to a serving bowl immediately so that it does not lose its pretty color. Meanwhile, heat the oil in a skillet over medium-low heat and add the garlic, ginger and red pepper flakes. Stir and cook for 2 minutes being careful not to let the garlic or ginger turn brown. Remove pan from heat and add the lemon juice to the skillet. Then use a rubber spatula to remove all of the garlic and ginger oil from the skillet and toss with steamed broccolini in a large bowl. Sprinkle with gomasio and serve warm.

Broccolini is a cross between broccoli and Chinese kale. You can also just use broccoli, kale or asparagus for this recipe.

WINTER KALE AND CHARD SAUTÉ

SERVES 6

This is my favorite way to eat greens.

2 TBS sesame seeds (tan, not white)
1 bunch kale, cleaned, center stem discarded, leaves torn into bite-size pieces (see note)*
1 bunch of rainbow chard, chopped (no need to discard stalks, just chop into small pieces) (see note)*
1 small firm fuju persimmon, cut into 1-inch long slivers (may substitute orange segments)

Dressing Ingredients
2 TBS toasted sesame oil
1 TBS tamari, to taste (may substitute shoyu soy sauce or unrefined sea salt)
1 TBS water
1 garlic clove, pressed
2 tsp grated ginger
1 tsp Dijon mustard

Place sesame seeds in a dry skillet and toast for 5 minutes over very low heat. Stir constantly to be sure they don't burn. When seeds are fragrant and nutty, remove to a plate to cool immediately to stop the cooking process. If the seeds are jumping out of the pan then the heat is too high.

Meanwhile, place the cleaned kale and chard leaves in a large sauté pan with a couple tablespoons of water and heat, covered, over medium-high heat for about 3-5 minutes. The greens will become bright green and begin to wilt. Add a little more water (a couple tablespoons) if necessary to keep greens from sticking to the pan. Remove greens while they are al dente with a slotted spoon and place onto a serving dish (no plastic with hot foods). Meanwhile, whisk together the dressing ingredients. Combine the steamed greens with the persimmon and dressing and toss gently. Sprinkle with toasted sesame seeds and serve warm or chilled.

You can use any dark green leafy vegetable.

Just be sure not to overcook the greens. Remove the lid and remove greens from the pan as soon as they are tender so they don't lose their pretty green color.

CREAMY THAI KALE

SERVES 4

1 cup carrot juice (may substitute vegetable juice)
1 onion, diced
2 carrots, diced
2 bunches of kale, collard greens or chard, cleaned well and chopped, stems discarded
2 TBS almond butter
1 lime, juiced
1 tsp date syrup, agave nectar, brown rice syrup or yacon syrup
1-2 tsp Thai chile paste (may substitute Vegetarian Tom Yum Paste, hard to find but yummy!)
unrefined sea salt, Himalayan salt, or tamari, to taste

Bring the juice to a simmer in a large pot and add the onions and carrots and cook for about 5 minutes, uncovered. Add the chopped greens and cook another 3-5 minutes. You want the vegetables to be tender but not mushy. **Carefully** pour off the liquid from the pot into a small bowl (no plastic), leaving the onions, carrots and greens in the pot. Measure out about ½ cup of this liquid, reserving the rest for another use.

In a small bowl place the almond butter, lime juice, sweetener, chile paste and salt and whisk together with the ½ cup of the cooking liquid. Taste and adjust the spices in the sauce accordingly (some chile pastes are more spicy than others, start slow and add more if desired). Pour this sauce back into the pot with the vegetables and stir to combine. Serve immediately!

If there is no liquid in the pot then just add a little water to the small bowl in order to whisk together the sauce. If there is too much liquid in the pot (more than ½ cup) use any extra to make a soup. You want the sauce you make to be thick, not watery.

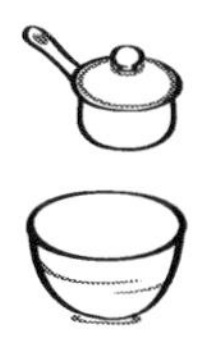

Be careful not to overcook the greens or they will lose their pretty green color.

I like to enjoy this with a side of short grain brown rice.

PRESSED KALE SALAD

SERVES 4-6

Kale, a Superfood, is a great source of calcium, fiber, vitamins K, C, E, beta-carotene and lutein. It helps keep our bones strong, protect our eyes against cataracts, and helps protect against lung cancer, arthritis and cancer. The anti-cancer compound, sulforaphane glucosinolate, in kale and other cruciferous vegetables, helps to boost the body's detoxification process, thus helping to clear carcinogenic compounds from the body. Studies consistently show that diets high in cruciferous vegetables are associated with lower risk of many types of cancer.

1 medium handful of arame seaweed, dried
2 bunches of kale (I prefer the dino kale for this)
1 small shallot, minced
1 garlic clove, pressed
1 medium lemon, juiced
⅛ tsp unrefined sea salt or Himalayan salt, or to taste
2-3 TBS hemp seeds
2 TBS olive oil (may substitute flax seed oil)
½ avocado, sliced, optional (may substitute ¼ cup raw pumpkin seeds)

Place the arame seaweed in a large bowl of cold water. Let soak for about 15 minutes. Remove seaweed with a slotted spoon and move to a clean towel to absorb some of the water. Then place on a cutting board and chop into bite-size pieces, if necessary. Clean the kale in a large bowl of cold water. Shake off any water remaining on kale or dab with a towel. Remove tough stems and discard. Chop kale into bite-size pieces. Place kale, arame, shallot, garlic, lemon juice and salt in a large serving bowl and knead the kale with your hands until the kale begins to wilt, about 1-2 minutes. Taste for salt or lemon. Now add the hemp seeds and olive oil and toss to combine.

Serve chilled or at room temperature.

Best to eat within 1-2 days of making this salad.

Please don't heat this salad if you're using hemp seeds or flax seed oil because the beneficial properties of these healthy fats are destroyed with heat.

SAUTÉED COLLARD GREENS (GF)

SERVES 6-8

The collard green, another prized vegetable from the powerful cruciferous family, is full of cancer-fighting power, calcium, beta-carotene and has a wonderful texture and taste.

3 bunches of collard greens
1 onion, sliced into long strips
1 TBS olive oil
3 garlic cloves, pressed
unrefined sea salt or Himalayan salt, to taste
a dash or two of red pepper flakes
1 lemon, cut into wedges

Thoroughly wash the greens and cut out the center stem and discard. Chop the greens into pieces about 2 x 1-inches and set aside. Sauté the onions and oil in a large skillet for 5 minutes over medium heat. Add garlic, some salt and red pepper flakes and stir for 1 minute. Add the chopped greens and stir. You may need to add a couple tablespoons of water to prevent sticking. Stir and cook until greens are slightly wilted, about 5 minutes. Remove from heat and serve with lemon wedges.

You may need to cook the greens in batches because they may not all fit in your pan at the same time.

Stir often to be sure the garlic doesn't burn.

(GF) GARLIC DANDELION GREENS WITH SHIITAKES AND SHISO

SERVES 6

1 cup thinly sliced shiitake mushrooms, stems discarded
4 garlic cloves, pressed
3 green onions, cleaned and sliced
1 medium burdock root, a.k.a. gobo root, scrubbed and cut into matchsticks (see note)*
1 TBS unrefined sesame oil (may substitute olive oil)
1 tsp grated ginger
¼ tsp unrefined sea salt or Himalayan salt
2 TBS mirin (may substitute sake or water)
½ tsp red pepper flakes, optional
1 bunch dandelion greens, cleaned and chopped, stems discarded
1 bunch kale, cleaned and chopped, stems discarded
water, as needed
2 TBS raw sunflower seeds
¼ cup sliced shiso leaves (a.k.a. Japanese basil or perilla) (see note)*
lemon wedges, to serve

Place the shiitakes, garlic, green onions, burdock, oil, ginger and salt in a large skillet or pot and cook over medium-low heat until mushrooms give off their liquid, about 5-8 minutes. Continue to cook until pan is almost dry, then add the mirin and red pepper flakes and stir to coat. Next add the dandelion and kale and stir to coat. Add a tablespoon or two of water if needed to help cook the greens and prevent sticking. Cover pan and simmer for 3 minutes. Remove lid, stir and continue to cook a few minutes or until kale is tender. Serve garnished with sunflower seeds, shiso leaves and a lemon wedge.

If you can't find shiso at your local Japanese grocery store or health food store, then substitute fresh basil or mint leaves. Slice the leaves just before serving so they don't brown.

Just scrub the burdock root before grating, no need to peel. Then julienne or cut into matchsticks and place in a bowl of cold water until ready to use/cook. This mellows out the flavor and prevents it from turning green or brown.

Recipe continues on next page...

GARLIC DANDELION GREENS WITH SHIITAKES AND SHISO...

Any liquid remaining in pan after cooking the greens can be reserved and used when making soups or grains.

This dish is nice with steamed asparagus and lotus root and a big bowl of soba noodle miso soup.

SPINACH "SUSHI" BITES

SERVES 2-4

1 lb. fresh or frozen spinach (or some nettles would be nice)
1-2 tsp tamari (may substitute shoyu soy sauce)
1 TBS lemon juice
½ tsp toasted sesame oil
1 TBS lightly toasted sesame seeds
1 sushi mat, for rolling the spinach

Clean and chop the fresh spinach, then place in a large pan with a couple of tablespoons of water. If using frozen spinach, remove from package and place in a large pan with a couple tablespoons of water. Cook over medium-high heat, stirring often until fresh spinach is completely wilted or frozen spinach is completely thawed. Drain well, let cool and squeeze out remaining liquid with your hands (reserving liquid for making soups or grains). Chop spinach well. In a large bowl add the spinach and sprinkle over it the tamari, lemon juice and the toasted sesame oil. Toss together and taste, adjusting seasonings if necessary. Roll the spinach up in a sushi mat to make a tight, long roll, then unroll and remove mat. Cut spinach into sushi-size pieces. Sprinkle with toasted sesame seeds and serve at room temperature.

This makes a nice accompaniment to an Asian inspired meal with miso soup, seaweed salad and a brown rice-vegetable bowl or vegetable sushi with a side of pickled ginger and wasabi.

LIVER CLEANSER DANDELION SAUTÉ

SERVES 4-6

Dandelion can have a very strong flavor, one that may seem too bitter to you if you've never had it before. Just remember that most bitter foods are very cleansing to the liver so learn to enjoy this flavor. If you want to take it more gradually, use half dandelion leaves and half chard or spinach and proceed.

1 small onion, minced
1 TBS grated ginger
2 garlic cloves, pressed
2 medium carrots, scrubbed and diced
¼ cup vegetable broth (may substitute water)
3 cups chopped dandelion leaves, tough stems discarded
1 tsp toasted sesame oil
2 tsp tamari (may substitute shoyu soy sauce)
½ lemon, juiced
½ cup diced green apple
½ cup grated raw red beet
2 TBS hemp seeds, for garnish

Place the onion, ginger, garlic, carrots and broth in a large skillet and let simmer, covered for 5 minutes over medium heat. Then add the dandelion and stir until wilted, about 3 minutes, uncovered. Turn off heat and add the sesame oil, tamari and lemon juice. Toss to combine, then serve topped with the green apples, beets and hemp seeds.

STIR FRY VEGETABLES WITH MARINATED TEMPEH

SERVES 4-6

6 cups cooked whole grains (barley, brown rice, spelt, etc.)
1-2 packages of tempeh, cubed and boiled for 15 minutes

Sauce
3 TBS tamari (may substitute shoyu soy sauce)
1 TBS brown rice vinegar
1 TBS date syrup, agave nectar, brown rice syrup or yacon syrup
1 tsp unrefined sesame oil
¼ tsp red pepper flakes
1 tsp arrowroot mixed in ¼ cup water to make a slurry (may substitute ground kudzu)

Stir Fry
1 TBS unrefined sesame oil (may substitute tea seed oil or coconut oil)
2 TBS grated ginger
2 garlic cloves, pressed
8 shiitake mushrooms, sliced, stems discarded
1 cup broccoli florets
1 medium carrot, cut into thin ovals
1 cup chopped red bell pepper
8 green onions, chopped
1 cup snow peas, trimmed
¼ cup sesame seeds

Prepare your whole grains and boil the tempeh before proceeding with the stir fry. Whisk the sauce ingredients together. Pour over the tempeh and let marinate for 30 minutes. Remove tempeh from marinade and set aside. Add the arrowroot slurry to the marinade and stir to combine. Set aside. Now heat your wok or skillet over medium-high heat and add the oil and ginger. Stir for 30 seconds, then add the garlic, shiitakes, broccoli and carrots and stir fry for 5 minutes, stirring frequently. Next, add the red bell pepper and cook for 2 minutes. Now add the green onions, snow peas, the tempeh and the marinade (with the arrowroot slurry) and stir to combine. Cook until sauce begins to thicken, about 3 minutes. Sprinkle with sesame seeds and serve over whole grains.

JAPANESE ODEN VEGETABLES

SERVES 4

This one pot hearty winter stew is traditionally cooked in a ceramic pot called a nabe. But it can also be made in a heavy bottomed stainless steel pot, just don't use aluminum.

4 strips of kombu seaweed, each about 5-inches long by 1-inch wide
¾ cup dried, sliced shiitake mushrooms
1 medium daikon radish, scrubbed and roll cut, or diced
1 medium sweet potato or yam, peeled and diced
1 medium turnip, peeled and chopped
8 lotus root discs, ¼-inch thick, peel first, rinse well
2 cups green cabbage, chopped (may substitute bok choy)
1 12-inch piece burdock root, scrubbed, cut on a diagonal, ¼-inch thick
3 carrots, scrubbed and cut on a diagonal, ½-inch thick
6 green onions, sliced
1 TBS grated ginger
1 TBS tamari (may substitute shoyu soy sauce)
1 tsp date syrup, agave nectar, brown rice syrup or yacon syrup
1 TBS sake, optional (may substitute mirin)
water
2 cups fresh spinach or other green leafy vegetable (watercress, nettles or chard)
1 TBS toasted sesame seeds
1 tsp dulse seaweed flakes (may substitute nori or kelp seaweed flakes)
Japanese hot mustard, for serving

Soak the kombu in a large bowl of water for 10 minutes. Remove pieces with a slotted spoon and discard soak water (or give to your house plants being that they don't mind if it contains a little sand). Tie each kombu strip into a simple knot. Place kombu and sliced shiitakes into the pot to fully cover the bottom of the pot. Then layer the daikon and sweet potato on top of that, followed by a layer of turnip and lotus root, then a layer of cabbage and burdock, and finally a layer of carrots. Sprinkle with the green onions, ginger, tamari, sweetener and sake. Add enough water to cover vegetables halfway. Cover pot and cook over low heat for 30-40 minutes without lifting lid. Then remove lid and top with spinach and cook until liquid has almost all evaporated.

Recipe continues on next page...

JAPANESE ODEN VEGETABLES...

This could also be made into a hearty soup by skipping the step where you remove the lid and let liquid evaporate. Instead, add enough water to make soup plus some cooked buckwheat soba noodles and cooked adzuki beans to the broth. Season with miso and serve.

Serve as a vegetable side dish topped with toasted sesame seeds, dulse flakes and a side of hot mustard.

BURDOCK KINPIRA

SERVES 2-4

This classic Japanese dish makes the burdock taste sweet from the slow simmering. Burdock is praised for its ability to purify the blood and aid in liver and gall bladder function.

2 pieces of burdock root (each the size of a medium carrot)
1 medium carrot
1 handful of arame (may substitute wakame seaweed)
1 tsp unrefined sesame oil
2 tsp tamari (may substitute shoyu soy sauce)
1 tsp date syrup, agave nectar, brown rice syrup or yacon syrup
1 tsp mirin (Japanese sweet cooking wine)
1 TBS sesame seeds, toasted

Scrub burdock root and rinse well. Trim away any strings but don't peel the burdock. Cut burdock root into matchstick-size pieces. Scrub the carrot and also cut it into matchsticks. Put the seaweed in a bowl of cool water and soak according to package directions. In a skillet heat the oil over medium heat. Add burdock and stir fry for a few minutes, then add the carrots and stir to coat. Add tamari, sweetener and mirin. Turn heat to low, cover and simmer until the vegetables are tender, about 20 minutes. Add a little water if necessary to prevent sticking. Remove cover and add the soaked and drained seaweed. Heat for another 3-5 minutes. Serve sprinkled with toasted sesame seeds.

(GF)

GARLIC-CURRY SWEET POTATO "FRIES"

SERVES 6-8

4 medium sweet potatoes, cut and scrubbed (see note)*
2 TBS tea seed oil (may substitute macadamia nut oil)
1 tsp unrefined sea salt or Himalayan salt
1 tsp garlic powder or granules
1 TBS curry powder
½ tsp cayenne pepper
¼ cup minced cilantro (may substitute parsley)

Preheat oven to 375 F. Prepare sweet potatoes by slicing into strips, about 3-4-inches long and ½-inch thick. In a large bowl combine the oil with the salt, garlic powder, curry powder and cayenne. Toss in the sweet potatoes and mix with hands until the potatoes are evenly coated. Place on a parchment lined baking sheet in a single layer (not touching) and bake for 15 minutes, flip each, fry and bake for another 10-15 minutes until tender and slightly crispy (you may need to flip again and bake longer, depending on thickness of pan and fries). Let cool slightly then garnish with chopped cilantro.

It helps to have a couple of heavy bottomed baking pans or sheet pans to ensure more even baking.

I usually rotate my pans halfway through baking in case my oven has a hot spot.

Try and cut the potatoes all the same thickness (not necessarily the same length) or the skinny fries will burn.

BUTTERNUT SQUASH AND TANGY APPLE SALAD

SERVES 6

A lovely side dish in the fall!

2 pounds of butternut squash, peeled and cut into ¾-inch cubes
2 medium granny smith apples, peeled and cubed, same size as squash
1 lemon
2 TBS date syrup, agave nectar, brown rice syrup or yacon syrup
1 TBS apple cider vinegar
1 TBS tamari (may substitute shoyu soy sauce)
2 TBS olive oil (may substitute flax seed oil)
1 sprig of fresh rosemary, leaves finely minced, stem discarded
1 small sweet onion, diced
2 TBS goji berries (re-hydrated in warm water, if necessary)
¼ cup chopped raw walnuts
¼ cup minced parsley

Steam the cubed squash for 5-10 minutes or until tender but not mushy. Cut the lemon in half and squeeze one half over the cubed apples and toss. In a small bowl whisk together the juice from the other lemon half, the sweetener, vinegar, tamari, oil and rosemary until combined. Toss dressing with steamed squash, apples, onions and goji berries. Top with walnuts and parsley and serve immediately.

Don't heat the dressing if you're using flax seed oil because heat will destroy the beneficial omega 3 properties of this fragile EFA (essential fatty acid).

GF

THAI SMASHED SWEET POTATOES

SERVES 6

Sweet potatoes are nutritionally superior to the standard white potato. Loaded with the antioxidant beta-carotene plus fiber and minerals. They have a low glycemic index, which means they provide steady energy and won't raise your blood sugar.

¼ tsp unrefined sea salt or Himalayan salt
3 garlic cloves, pressed
3 medium to large sweet potatoes, peeled (optional) and diced (see note)*
2-4 TBS coconut milk
¼ tsp unrefined sea salt or Himalayan salt
1-2 tsp Thai red curry paste, or more if you like spicy
3 green onions, sliced
¼ cup minced cilantro

Place salt, garlic and sweet potatoes in a pan of filtered, cold water and bring to a boil. Cover, reduce to a simmer and cook for 10 minutes or until potatoes are very soft. Scoop potatoes out of water and place them into another large pan (no plastic). Reserve the cooking water. In a small bowl whisk together the coconut milk, salt and curry paste and pour over the potatoes (start with just a teaspoon of the curry paste and then add more later on if more heat is desired). Smash with a potato masher, adding more of the reserved cooking water if necessary to reach desired creaminess. Taste for salt and spice. Serve warm. Garnish with green onions and cilantro.

If you desire a golden color instead of the bright orange color from regular sweet potatoes, use Japanese sweet potatoes, which are off-white on the inside.

You could use orange juice instead of the reserved cooking water if you desire a sweeter dish. Please use freshly squeezed juice from 1-2 oranges.

I serve these for the Holidays instead of regular mashed potatoes. They're a real crowd pleaser, even for the die-hard traditionalists!

SHREDDED BRUSSELS SPROUTS WITH CURRIED ONIONS

GF

SERVES 4

Brussels sprouts are hardly recognizable in this recipe.

1 onion, diced
1 TBS olive oil
¼ tsp unrefined sea salt or Himalayan salt
2 tsp mild curry powder
a dash of cayenne, optional
2 TBS lemon juice
1 TBS date syrup, agave nectar, brown rice syrup or yacon syrup
1 lb. Brussels sprouts (see note)*
1 bunch cilantro, minced

Sauté onions in oil and salt in a large skillet over medium heat for 5 minutes. Stir in the curry powder and optional cayenne and cook for 1 minute, then deglaze with lemon juice and the sweetener. Meanwhile, slice 1 pound of Brussels sprouts in half lengthwise then place flat side down and slice across each half into thin slices or shreds. Sauté the shreds in the onion mixture for 5 minutes then add 1 cup of water to the pan and cook over medium heat until sprouts are tender but not mushy and liquid is evaporated.

Try adding other vegetables too, like carrot or shiitakes, for added flavor and color.

I also make this exact recipe with sliced napa cabbage instead of the Brussels sprouts!

Serve hot, garnished with cilantro.

CURRIED CAULIFLOWER AND RUTABAGA

(GF)

SERVES 6

Rutabaga is a somewhat shy root vegetable that doesn't like to take center stage but certainly could! If you haven't tried it lately I encourage you to give it another try. It's surprisingly delightful! I often use it in place of white potatoes, which are in the nightshade family and may cause inflammation in the body. However, the rutabaga is in the cruciferous family which means you get cancer fighting power.

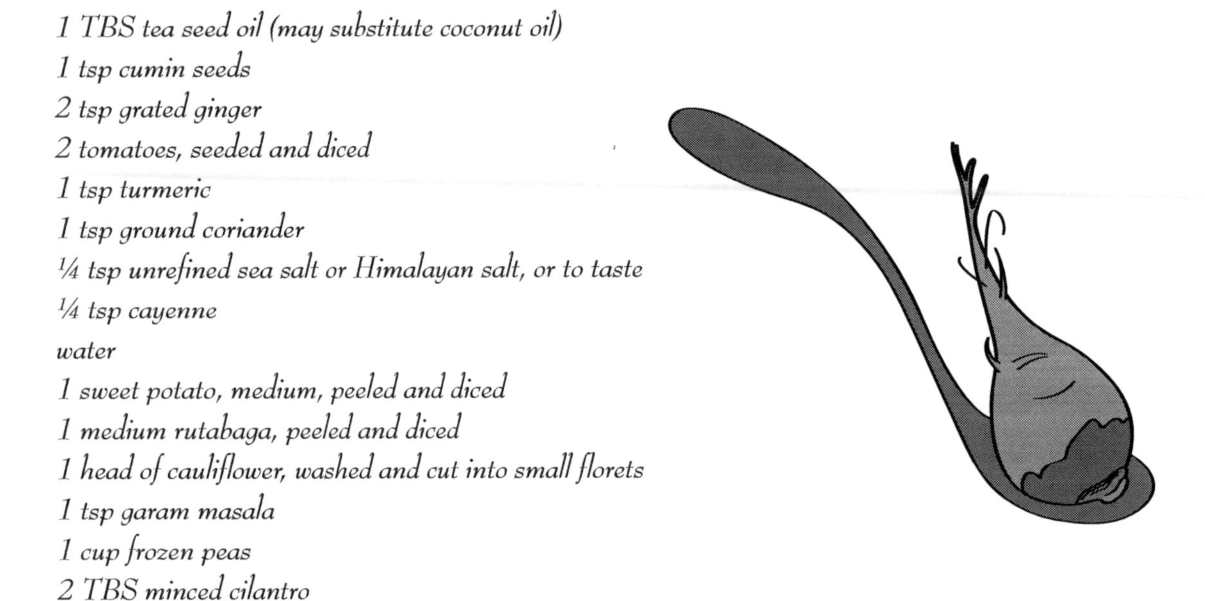

1 TBS tea seed oil (may substitute coconut oil)
1 tsp cumin seeds
2 tsp grated ginger
2 tomatoes, seeded and diced
1 tsp turmeric
1 tsp ground coriander
¼ tsp unrefined sea salt or Himalayan salt, or to taste
¼ tsp cayenne
water
1 sweet potato, medium, peeled and diced
1 medium rutabaga, peeled and diced
1 head of cauliflower, washed and cut into small florets
1 tsp garam masala
1 cup frozen peas
2 TBS minced cilantro

Heat oil in a pan over medium heat and add the cumin seeds, sauté for 1-2 minutes, then add the grated ginger and the tomatoes and cook for 2 minutes. Next add the turmeric, coriander, salt and cayenne. Stir well to coat and add about 2 TBS of water, the potatoes, rutabaga and the cauliflower. Mix well and cover for about 10 minutes and let cook over low heat. Check after 5 minutes to make sure vegetables are not sticking to the bottom, if so add two more TBS of water. After 10 minutes pierce the vegetables with a fork to see if they are tender. If not add a little bit more water, cover and cook a few more minutes. Once the vegetables are tender add the garam masala and peas and cook, covered for about 3 minutes. You want the liquid to be cooked off by now so if there is still liquid remaining in the pan then remove cover and let simmer a few minutes until there is no more liquid. Serve, garnished with cilantro.

COCONUT CURRY CAULIFLOWER AND SPINACH

GF

SERVES 4-6

2 TBS grated ginger
4 garlic cloves, pressed
2 tsp ground coriander
2 tsp cumin seeds
1 tsp paprika
¾ tsp unrefined sea salt or Himalayan salt
¾ tsp turmeric
¾ tsp red pepper flakes
½ cup coconut milk
2 cups cauliflower florets
4 10-oz. packages of frozen spinach

Place the ginger, garlic, spices, coconut milk and cauliflower in a large pan. Simmer, covered over medium heat until cauliflower is soft, adding a little water if necessary to keep from sticking. Next add the frozen spinach (no need to thaw or drain) and stir to combine. Continue to simmer until spinach is cooked through. Taste for salt and serve.

This goes well with a side of lentil dahl and brown basmati rice.

ROASTED CAULIFLOWER AND ONIONS

SERVES 4

This is absolutely my favorite way to eat cauliflower. It's simple and super delicious.

1 medium head of cauliflower, cut into florets
1 small onion, sliced
sprinkle of salt
cayenne, optional
1-2 TBS macadamia nut oil (may substitute tea seed oil)
nutritional yeast, optional (see note)*
1-2 TBS minced parsley, to garnish

Preheat oven to 375 F. Place vegetables in a roasting pan and sprinkle with salt and a dash of cayenne, if using. Then drizzle on the oil and toss to combine. Roast for 30 minutes, then stir and continue to roast another 15 minutes, or until tender. Garnish with nutritional yeast and parsley.

Nutritional yeast (different from brewers yeast) gives this simple dish a nutty, almost cheesy flavor. It also provides beneficial B vitamins, including the hard-to-get vitamin B12.

Use this method to roast any combination of vegetables you desire.

ROASTED FENNEL WITH FIGS AND OLIVES

GF

SERVES 6-8

4 small fennel bulbs, trimmed and chopped, core discarded
1 sweet onion, sliced into strips
¼ tsp unrefined sea salt or Himalayan salt
2 TBS olive oil
½ cup pitted green olives (I used cinnamon-cardamom spiced olives!)
12 fresh figs, trimmed and cut in half from stem to bottom
1 TBS each minced fresh oregano, parsley and rosemary

Preheat oven to 350 F. Prepare the fennel and onions and place in a large roasting pan. Toss with the salt and then the oil. Roast for about 45 minutes or until tender, stirring every 10 minutes to ensure even baking. Remove from heat and add the olives, figs and herbs. Toss gently to combine and serve warm or room temperature.

MUSTARD ROASTED ROOT VEGETABLES

SERVES 6

Read through the recipe and directions before beginning. You'll need to have enough baking pans for the root vegetables and then a separate pan for the green beans and garlic because they require less baking time.

¼ cup whole grain mustard
2 TBS olive oil
1 tsp lemon zest
1 TBS lemon juice
½ tsp unrefined sea salt or Himalayan salt
dash of cayenne, optional
1 sweet potato, peeled and cut into 1-inch dice (may substitute yam)
1 small turnip, cut into ½-inch wide wedges
1 6-inch piece of burdock, scrubbed and cut into thin diagonal slices
1 small beet, peeled and cut into ½-inch wide wedges
1 medium daikon, scrubbed and roll cut, or chopped
1 handful of green beans, trimmed and cut in half
2 garlic cloves, pressed
1 TBS freshly minced oregano
1 TBS freshly minced rosemary leaves

Preheat oven to 425 F. Line 2 baking sheets or large baking pans with unbleached parchment paper. Whisk the mustard, olive oil, lemon zest, juice, salt and cayenne together in a large bowl. Add all the vegetables (except the green beans, garlic and herbs) and toss to coat. Then place in a single layer on the prepared baking pans, reserving the remaining mustard sauce in the bowl. Roast the root vegetables for 20 minutes.

Meanwhile, place the green beans, garlic and herbs in the bowl with the remaining mustard sauce and toss to coat. After the root vegetables have roasted for 20 minutes, place the green bean mixture in a separate baking pan and roast for about 15-20 minutes. The root vegetables will need 40-45 minutes total baking time. The green beans will need about 15-20 minutes. Once all vegetables are tender, toss together gently and serve.

Winter squash and rutabaga make nice additions to this recipe.

AUTUMN SPICY KABOCHA SQUASH

GF

SERVES 6-8

I love kabocha squash, it may be my favorite squash, okay, it is my favorite squash (sorry butternut). Please buy in the fall and winter when they are in season, otherwise they won't have the same great sweetness or lovely texture.

1 medium kabocha squash, a.k.a. Japanese pumpkin (see note)*
2 tsp tea seed oil (may substitute macadamia nut oil)
1 tsp autumn spicy mix *(see pg. 198)*
¼ tsp unrefined sea salt or Himalayan salt
¼ tsp garlic powder or garlic granules (fresh garlic will burn if used)
cooked basmati brown rice, tamari, green onions and cilantro, for serving, optional

Preheat oven to 375 F. Line a baking sheet with unbleached parchment paper. Rinse the kabocha squash and cut in half. Scoop out the seeds and discard. You may peel the squash if it is not organic, otherwise you can leave the peel on because it is edible. Chop squash into 1-inch by 2-inch pieces and place in a large bowl. Toss with the oil and spices until evenly coated. Place on the baking sheets (not overlapping) and roast for 20-30 minutes. Test to see if squash is tender all the way through with a toothpick. Roast longer if necessary. Serve with basmati brown rice tossed with tamari, green onions and cilantro for a simple, delightful dinner!

You could substitute most winter squashes in this recipe.

Add adzuki beans to the rice for a more hearty dinner.

MISO GLAZED BUTTERNUT SQUASH AND EGGPLANT ROUNDS

SERVES 6-8

2 eggplants (for size see next line)
1 butternut squash, one with a long neck, about the same diameter as the eggplant
⅓ cup mirin (Japanese sweet rice wine) (may substitute apple juice)
5 TBS miso, mellow, white or sweet miso
1-2 TBS grated ginger
1 tsp red pepper flakes
4 garlic cloves, pressed
2 tsp toasted sesame seed oil
1 bunch green onions, minced

Preheat oven to 375 F. Prepare two baking sheets by lining them with oven safe racks (I use stainless steel cooling racks that fit perfectly into my cookie sheets but roasting racks would also work). Lightly oil the racks to prevent sticking. Slice the eggplant into ½ inch thick rounds. Do not peel. Place on a rack (over a baking sheet). Sprinkle both sides with salt and let sit for ½ hour. Rinse eggplant slices well to remove salt then pat dry. Place back onto the lightly oiled rack (oil the rack again, if necessary).

Meanwhile, bring a large pot of water to a boil on the stovetop. Slice the butternut squash into ½-inch thick rounds. Do not peel. Simmer the squash rounds for 3 minutes or until just about cooked but not mushy. Remove from water and place on one of the lightly oiled racks (over a baking sheet). Be careful not to break apart the squash rounds.

Now whisk together the mirin, miso, ginger, red pepper flakes, garlic and oil in a small bowl. It should be spread-able so add a dash of water if it is too thick. Spread a teaspoon or two of the miso glaze on each piece of eggplant and squash. Place the pans (and racks of course) in the oven and bake for 30 minutes or until the eggplant and squash are tender and lightly browned. Sprinkle with green onions and arrange on a large plate, alternating eggplant and squash.

Serve as a side dish to any meal.

FAVORITE SHIITAKE MUSHROOMS

Shiitakes are famous for their ability to boost the immune system and to help fight cancer. Be sure to include this superfood into your diet weekly.

In a medium saucepan place 1-2 cups fresh mushrooms (cleaned, sliced, stems discarded) in 2 cups orange juice, 2 TBS tamari or shoyu soy sauce, 1 TBS minced ginger and 3 cloves of pressed garlic. Have a lid partially covering the pan and let simmer over low heat for about 30 minutes or until liquid is reduced to about ½ cup or less. Simmer slowly and keep your eye on it so it doesn't burn. Use a slotted spoon to scoop out the mushrooms and serve.

Use any remaining liquid in pan to make salad dressings or sauces.

Use mushrooms in lots of different recipes like stir fries, salads, burritos or toss with noodles or brown rice for a very tasty treat.

FAVORITE PORTOBELLO MUSHROOMS

You'll need 1 portobello mushroom per person. Then something to flavor and marinate the mushrooms like balsamic vinegar, red wine vinegar, brown rice vinegar, lemon juice, and tamari or shoyu soy sauce. Break off the stems and reserve for another use (soup, stir fries, etc.). Clean the mushrooms by running them under water. Shake off excess water. Place whole mushrooms in a baking dish, stem side facing up, preferably in a single layer. Add the vinegars or lemon juice, plus a dash of something salty like tamari or shoyu. You'll want to add enough marinade to reach about half way up the mushrooms. Let marinate at room temperature for about 2 hours using a baster or a spoon every 20 minutes to distribute the marinade over the mushrooms. Then place the baking dish with the mushrooms and the marinade into the oven and let bake for about 30 minutes at 350 F. The mushrooms will begin to shrink a bit but should never look dry. If they do, baste again with the marinade.

Serve these mushrooms whole on a bun with all the usual burger fixings or slice and add to any savory dish. You'll never know what hit you!

GF ROASTING SQUASH

Cut squash in half and remove seeds. Rub cut side lightly with oil (macadamia nut oil or tea seed oil). Place cut side down on a baking pan or sheet pan and roast in a preheated 375 F oven for 30 minutes. Check to see if squash is tender all the way through with a fork. If not, roast until tender. Use in any recipe that calls for roasted squash.

For hard-to-cut squash (too large or tough to safely cut through with a knife) you can also roast it whole by poking a few holes in the squash and then placing the whole squash on a sheet pan in a preheated 375 F oven for about 30 minutes or until squash can easily be pierced with a fork. Remove from oven, cut in half and let cool. Remove seeds and serve as desired.

To serve squash filled with stuffing: place **roasted** squash halves on a baking sheet and fill with **prepared** stuffing or grain salad. Bake in a 350 F oven until warm, about 10-20 minutes.

GF OVEN ROASTED TOMATOES

An inexpensive way to have that sun-dried tomato flavor but even better!
This is a great way to use up tomatoes when your garden is overflowing with them.

This recipe is for 2 lbs. of tomatoes. Adjust to meet your needs.

Preheat oven to 200 F. Take your tomatoes and cut them into wedges, approximately the same size. Toss them in a bowl with 1 TBS of your best balsamic vinegar and 1 TBS of your best olive oil. Sprinkle with a dash of salt and toss again. Place a cooling rack over a sheet pan. Place seasoned tomatoes cut side up on the rack and bake for 4-6 hours or until they begin to shrink and get chewy. Watch carefully so they don't burn or get too crispy. Once they are roasted and dried to your liking remove from oven and add to any recipe for depth and explosive flavor!

Invest in a cooling rack that has a small grid pattern so that the tomatoes won't fall through the cracks once they start to shrink.

After the tomatoes are dried to your liking, you can toss with freshly minced herbs such as rosemary, oregano and basil. Serve over whole grain noodles or on top of baked polenta discs.

Store any leftovers in a sealed container in the refrigerator and use within 5 days.

CARROT CURL GARNISH (GF)

Using your favorite vegetable peeler shave 4-inch long pieces of carrot and place in bowl of ice water for 30 minutes or until curled. Drain well and use as a garnish on top of soups, grains or salads at your next party to impress your friends.

SPROUTING BROCCOLI SEEDS TO MAKE BROCCOLI SPROUTS (GF)

Broccoli sprouts may just be your best defense against cancer, at least when it comes to using "food as medicine." It's because broccoli sprouts are super high in a cancer fighting compound called sulphoraphane glucosinolate. Sulphoraphane mobilizes the body's natural cancer fighting resources and may reduce the risk of developing cancer. Sulphoraphane is also found in other cruciferous vegetables such as broccoli, cauliflower, cabbage, collard greens, kale, turnips and Brussels spouts but is most concentrated in broccoli sprouts.

Broccoli sprouts look just like alfalfa sprouts and can be used in sandwiches, pita pockets, burritos or on salads. If you can't find the sprouts in the refrigerated section of your grocery store then sprout your own broccoli seeds.

There are many websites and sprouting books available for more in-depth instructions on how to sprout seeds (I highly recommend researching this before proceeding). Here's a quick summary just to give you an idea of what you'll need to do to make broccoli sprouts. Obtain organic broccoli seeds on-line or at your health food store. Sterilize your sprouting jar. Soak the seeds for 8 hours. Drain. Allow to sprout 3-4 days, rinsing every 8 hours. Once fully sprouted move to the refrigerator and use within 5 days.

GF

NETTLES

The stinging nettle is a highly nutritious plant that gets overlooked because of its sting! The bristles on the leaves and stems will irritate the skin if you touch them so see tips below for how to handle this incredible green and start using it A.S.A.P.!

Here are a few health benefits to help you get over your fear of this stinging plant:

- High in chlorophyll; calcium; magnesium; silicon; sulphur; copper; chromium; zinc; cobalt; potassium; phosphorus; vitamins A, C, D, E, K; B1 and B2.
- Nettles are high in iron and can be used to help treat anemia.
- Used to help treat rheumatoid arthritis.
- It strengthens hair and protects against hair loss.
- Helps to purify and remove toxins from the blood.
- Helpful in dissolving kidney stones.
- Can be used as a diuretic.
- Helps to reduce blood sugar.
- Useful in treating asthma and expelling phlegm from the lungs.
- Reduces allergies.
- Helps kill intestinal worms and treats dysentery and diarrhea.

Tips for Handling Nettles

- If picking wild nettles for eating, harvest only the top four inches of the plant.
- Don't touch fresh nettles with your bare hands. Always use tongs or wear gloves.
- You may want to remove and discard the thick stems before cooking (I use scissors to trim leaves from stem).
- Wash the leaves in a large bowl of cold water, allowing sand and dirt to settle on bottom of the bowl. Lift clean nettles out of water with tongs and place in a strainer. Rinse and let drain.
- Always cook nettles until they are completely wilted before eating. This can be achieved by blanching them for 1 minute in boiling water or by cooking in a sauté pan with a bit of water. Once completely wilted the stingers are de-activated.
- Cooked nettles can be substituted in any dish that calls for other greens such as chard, spinach, kale, collards or purslane. They are **great** in pesto, soups, grain dishes, tomato sauce or just on their own sautéed with lemon and garlic.

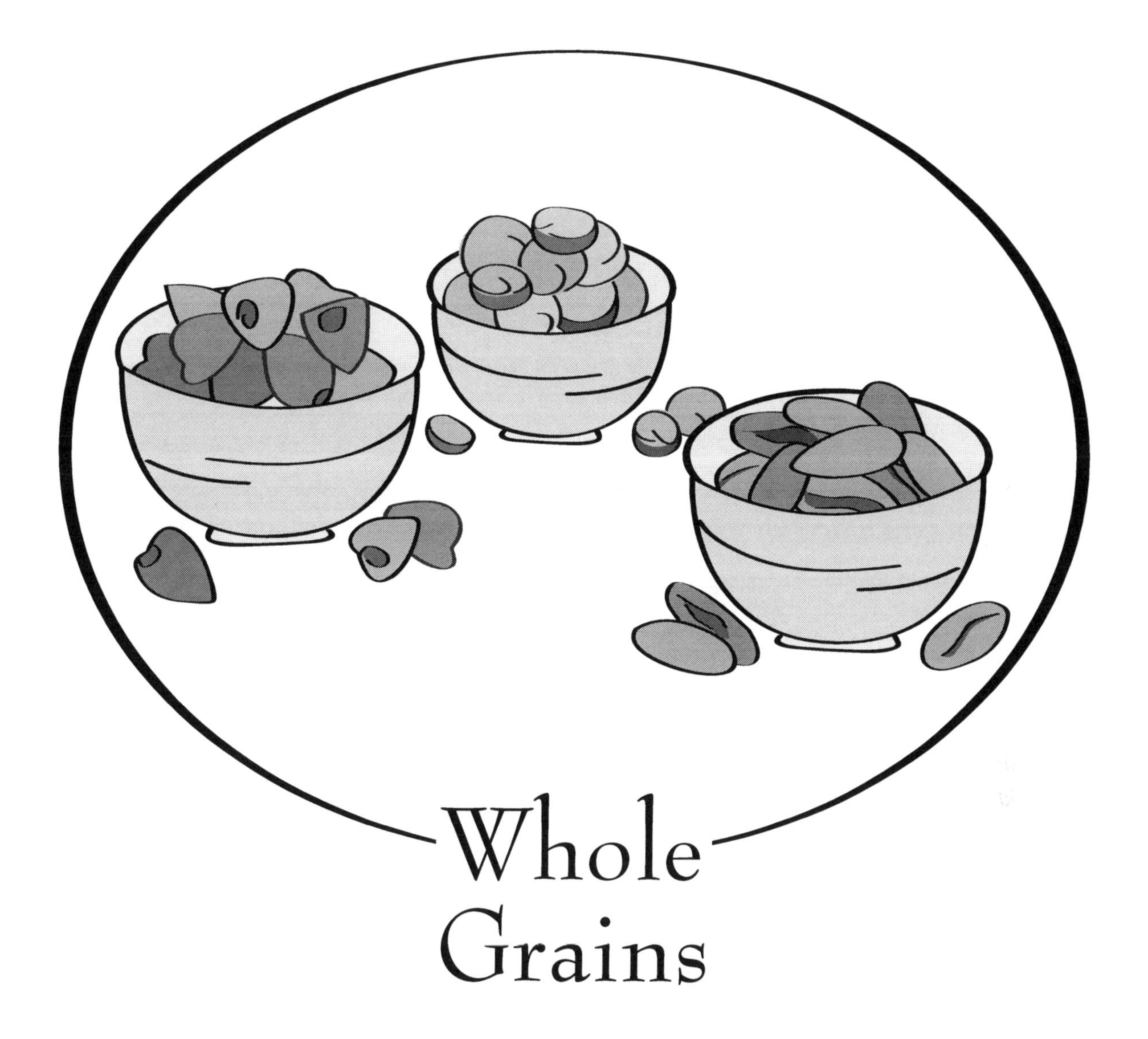

Whole Grains

The biggest mistake that I see people make is that they don't include a whole grain at each meal (and they eat too much protein!). Without the whole grain you will be missing valuable fiber and nutrients that will help keep blood sugar levels stable and cravings for unhealthy foods at bay.

Filling up on bread as your 'whole grain' is not what I had in mind either. You will need to go out and buy the actual grains. Buy a rice cooker and use it several times a week to make a variety of whole grains. Once the whole grain is made half of your meal is ready!

Also, wheat is not the only grain out there! Really! Many people suffer from mild to severe wheat allergies. If you feel tired, bloated or have indigestion after consuming wheat or gluten then it would be a good idea to avoid anything containing these foods. Even if you aren't gluten sensitive or allergic to wheat opt for the gluten-free grains used in this chapter more often than not.

Gluten-free grains featured in this book: amaranth, brown rice, black rice and red rice, buckwheat (or kasha), hato mugi (Job's tears), millet, quinoa, teff and wild rice.

Soaking Whole Grains: To make your whole grains more alkaline, easier to digest and the minerals easier to absorb you may soak grains in room temperature water for up to 24 hours. Phytic acid and enzyme inhibitors are neutralized when grains are soaked. To soak brown rice, place 1 cup of rinsed rice in a pot with 2 cups of water. Add 1 TBS of lemon juice. Cover and let sit on counter for up to 24 hours. Cook rice with the soak water (cooking time may be shortened due to soaking). Most of the recipes in this book do not list the soaking directions. Plan ahead so that your grain is already soaked and ready. Then use in recipes (but cook for less time).

Combining Grains In Your Pot: I have a stainless steel rice cooker that I use to cook most grains. I mix and match certain grains. Here's a rough guide of which grains can be cooked together in the same pot or rice cooker. As always, rinse and soak your grains before cooking.

Quicker Cooking Grains: Quinoa, millet, amaranth, teff and buckwheat (kasha)

Longer Cooking Grains: Hulled barley, brown rice, red rice, black rice, wild rice, rye, spelt, kamut and oat berries, and hato mugi (Job's tears).

BASIC QUINOA

SERVES 2-4

GF

While not truly a grain, this seed is known as the "mother grain" in Peru because of its high protein and nutrient content. It is a complete protein, high in fiber, phosphorus, magnesium and iron. I love it because it only takes 15 minutes to make.

1 cup of quinoa
2 cups of vegetable broth (may substitute water)
a pinch of unrefined sea salt or Himalayan salt

Rinse the quinoa well with cold water and let drain. Place in a pan with the broth and salt. Cover, bring to a boil, reduce heat to low and let simmer for 10-15 minutes, or until water is absorbed into the grain.

Quinoa has a bitter coating, called saponin, which needs to be thoroughly rinsed away to make it palatable.

BASIC MILLET

SERVES 2-4

GF

1 cup of millet
2 ¼ cups vegetable broth (may substitute water)
pinch of unrefined sea salt or Himalayan salt

Rinse your millet and drain well. Place millet in a heavy bottomed pan and heat over medium heat for about 5 minutes, stirring often. This is to toast the millet. You'll know when it's toasted because it will begin to smell nutty. Don't let the millet burn or turn brown. Turn heat down and stir often. Once the millet is toasted, add the water, **slowly**, because it will most likely splatter all over the place and may burn you. Add the salt, bring to a boil, cover and reduce to low. Let the millet simmer for 22 minutes. Turn off heat and let stand, covered, for another 5 minutes. Fluff gently with a fork and serve!

BASIC BROWN RICE

To Serve 2-4

1 cup short grain brown rice or long grain brown rice

2 cups water

1 5-inch piece of kombu seaweed (or any mild tasting seaweed you like), rinsed (see note)*

a pinch of unrefined sea salt or Himalayan salt, optional

To Serve 6-8

2 cups of short grain brown rice or long grain brown rice

3 ½ cups filtered water

1 5-inch piece of kombu seaweed (or any mild tasting seaweed you like), rinsed

a pinch of unrefined sea salt or Himalayan salt, optional

2 TBS sesame seeds, toasted lightly in a dry skillet over very low heat, optional

To make the rice, place the rice in a bowl, cover with lots of cold water and swoosh around with a wooden spoon. Let rice settle to the bottom of the bowl, then pour off the water and anything that was floating on top of the water. Repeat until water runs clear. Let drain well through a fine mesh strainer. Place rice and water in a pan with the seaweed and optional salt. Bring to a boil, cover and reduce to a simmer for 40 minutes. Turn off the heat but do not lift the lid. Let sit for another 10 minutes before lifting lid. Add the toasted sesame seeds just before serving.

Although kombu is famous for helping to digest beans when cooked together, you can also cook your whole grains with this sea vegetable to add minerals to your dish.

BLACK RICE WITH THAI RED CURRY SAUCE

GF

SERVES 6-8

1 ¾ cups black rice (a.k.a. forbidden rice, or Thai black rice), rinsed
3 ¼ cups water
1 medium sweet potato, scrubbed and diced
1 cup of broccoli florets
½ cup coconut milk (may substitute almond milk)
¾ tsp Thai red curry paste, plus more if desired
¼ tsp unrefined sea salt or Himalayan salt
1 red bell pepper, diced
½ cup green peas, fresh or frozen
3 green onions, minced
a handful of fresh Thai basil leaves, thinly sliced, or other basil

Place the rice and water in a medium saucepan and bring to a boil. Cover, reduce heat to low and let simmer for 30 minutes. Remove from heat and let rest another 10 minutes. Meanwhile, dice the sweet potato and place in a medium pan with enough water to cover the sweet potatoes halfway. Bring to a boil, cover and reduce to medium heat. Let cook for 5 minutes, remove lid and add the broccoli. Cover and let cook another few minutes or until vegetables are tender.

Remove vegetables from the pan with a slotted spoon, leaving any remaining water in the pan for another use (add to a soup), and place vegetables into a serving bowl. Add the cooked rice to the serving bowl. Then in a small bowl whisk together the coconut milk, red curry paste and salt until smooth. Pour this over the rice and toss. Next add the red bell peppers, green peas, green onions and Thai basil leaves. Taste for salt and spice, adding more if desired.

BHUTANESE RED RICE WITH KALE AND COCONUT

SERVES 6

If you can't find red rice use short grain brown rice. It won't be as pretty, but it will taste the same and be just as nutritious.

3 ½ cups water
2 cups Bhutanese red rice, rinsed
2 kaffir lime leaves, minced (center vein discarded) (see note)*
½ tsp unrefined sea salt or Himalayan salt
1 TBS unrefined sesame oil (may substitute coconut milk)
1 small onion, diced
4 garlic cloves, pressed
2 carrots, diced or shredded
1 tsp tamari (may substitute shoyu soy sauce or a dash of salt)
2 cups chopped kale, any kind
water
1 TBS lime juice
2 tsp apple cider vinegar
1-2 tsp Thai curry paste, red or green (more if you like it hot!)
1 bunch of cilantro, minced
2 TBS dried, shredded coconut, toasted (see note)*

In a medium pan, bring the water, rice, minced kaffir lime leaves and salt to a boil. Cover, reduce heat and let simmer for 45 minutes. Turn off heat and let sit another 10 minutes before lifting lid. Meanwhile, in a skillet, heat the oil, onion, garlic, carrots and the tamari for 10 minutes over medium heat. Add the chopped kale and a few tablespoons of water to prevent sticking. Cover and cook for 5 minutes. Remove cover and cook a couple more minutes until most of the liquid is absorbed (if liquid is absorbed but the kale is not yet tender, add a little bit more water and continue to cook until tender).

Meanwhile, in a small bowl, whisk together the lime juice, vinegar and curry paste. Remove the rice from the heat and toss with the vegetables and sauce mixture. Taste to adjust seasonings and serve warm or at room temperature. Garnish with cilantro and toasted coconut.

If you can't find kaffir lime leaves (oh, what a pity), then use lime juice instead of water when cooking the kale.

Recipe continues on next page...

BHUTANESE RED RICE WITH KALE AND COCONUT...

Try not to have the lid on the vegetables for too long once the kale has been added. Anytime you are cooking green vegetables, only have them covered for a short time because cooking anything green for a lengthy amount of time while covered will cause the greens to lose their color and look less appetizing.

To toast dried coconut, place in a dry skillet over medium heat and stir with a wooden spoon until the coconut begins to turn light brown and smell toasted. Remove coconut immediately and place on a plate to stop the cooking process and prevent burning. Let cool and then sprinkle on the finished dish. I normally don't like dried coconut, but toasted coconut is a different story completely - I love it!

LEMON RICE WITH INDIAN SPICE

SERVES 6

This dish is wonderful and fresh tasting. Lemon, although acidic in taste, actually has an alkalizing effect on the body. When the body is alkaline cancer cells cannot grow.

2 cups brown basmati rice
3 ½ cup water
½ tsp unrefined sea salt or Himalayan salt
1 TBS oil (unrefined sesame, olive, coconut or tea seed oil)
½ tsp ground coriander
½ tsp turmeric
1 tsp cumin seeds
1 lemon, zested and juiced
½ cup green peas, fresh or frozen, optional

Recipe continues on next page...

LEMON RICE WITH INDIAN SPICE...

Wash the rice well and drain. Place in a pan with the water and salt and bring to a boil. Cover, reduce heat and simmer over low heat for 40 minutes. Turn off heat but do not lift lid. Let rice steam for another 10 minutes. Meanwhile, place the oil, coriander, turmeric and cumin in a large pan and stir to coat over medium-low heat for 3 minutes. Do not let spices burn. Add the cooked rice to the pot and stir gently to coat. Then fold in the lemon zest and juice and the green peas, if using. Serve warm or chilled.

You can soak the rice in plenty of water for up to 24 hours in the refrigerator or other cool, dark place. Soaking grains makes them easier to digest, more alkaline-forming and faster to cook.

GINGER-GARLIC BROWN RICE

SERVES 6

This is by far my favorite way to have rice. Keep these ingredients on hand because it may be your favorite way too! This makes a wonderful accompaniment to Asian or Indian meals.

2 TBS unrefined sesame oil (may substitute olive oil)
2 TBS grated ginger
½ cup chopped green onions
½ cup chopped green garlic (may substitute 6 garlic cloves, pressed)
a few TBS vegetable broth (may substitute mirin Japanese rice wine)
tamari or shoyu soy sauce, to taste
*3 cups **cooked** brown rice (I like a combo of short grain brown rice and red rice)*
1 bunch cilantro, chopped

Heat the oil over **very** low heat and cook the ginger, green onions and garlic just until the onions are tender and bright green, about 8 minutes. Stir often so that garlic doesn't burn. Deglaze with vegetable broth or mirin and cook another few minutes. Add tamari to taste and mix into cooked brown rice. Add cilantro to garnish. YUM!

This is **amazing** with shiitakes and green peas. Add 1 cup of sliced shiitake mushrooms to the pan with the ginger, green onions and garlic and cook as directed above. Add ½ cup of peas (frozen works) at the end of cooking and then toss with the rice and cilantro.

THAI LEMONGRASS RICE (GF)

SERVES 6

2 ½ cups brown basmati rice
1 TBS unrefined sesame oil (may substitute coconut oil, melted)
3 TBS grated ginger
2 lemongrass stalks (see note)*
3 garlic cloves, pressed
2 TBS grated coconut, dried
4 cups vegetable broth
2 kaffir lime leaves, minced, center vein discarded
½ tsp unrefined sea salt or Himalayan salt
¼ tsp red pepper flakes
1 bunch of cilantro, minced

Place rice in a large bowl of cold water and stir. Pour off the water and anything that's floating on top while leaving the rice in the bottom of the bowl. Repeat until water is clear. Heat oil over medium heat and add ginger, lemongrass and garlic. Stir for 1 minute, then add the rice and coconut and stir for a couple minutes to coat and toast. Now add the broth, kaffir lime leaves, salt and red pepper flakes. Bring to a boil, reduce to low, cover and cook for 45 minutes. Turn heat off but don't lift the lid. Let stand for another 10 minutes, then fluff with a fork. Sprinkle with cilantro and serve.

When using fresh lemongrass you only use a small portion of the stalk. You want to cut off the hard root end and remove the outer leaves until you see the inner, tender part of the bottom ⅓ of the stalk. Take that and mince it finely, discarding the rest of the lemongrass.

(GF) NORI WRAPPED RICE BALLS WITH UMEBOSHI SURPRISE

MAKES ABOUT 8 RICE BALLS

The surprise is the tangy, salty, sour treat in the center of each ball, known as umeboshi plum. Umeboshi plums are actually made from salted, aged and fermented green apricots that date back over 2000 years in China's culinary and medicinal history. They have a strong salty and tart flavor that is surprising and unique. It took me a little while to love these pink little gems but once I learned about their medicinal qualities they instantly became more delicious. Here are a few of the prized health benefits: they help to alkalize the body, they aid in digestion, they help relieve migraines and headaches, they reduce muscle soreness from lactic acid buildup, they help relieve body aches present with the flu, they help stimulate appetite, and they help stimulate the liver and kidneys to cleanse the blood. Plus I heard they are helpful for relieving a hangover! You know the old saying "An umeboshi plum a day helps keep the doctor away!"

2 sheets toasted nori (the kind used to make sushi)
2 cups cooked short grain brown rice
2 umeboshi plums, pitted and sliced
or 2 TBS umeboshi plum paste (see note)*
2 TBS toasted sesame seeds
small bowl of water with ¼ tsp salt dissolved in it

Wave the sheets of nori over your stove top burner for a few seconds until the nori turns from black to green. Fold each sheet and cut into two. Then fold each in half lengthwise and cut again. You should have 8 long strips. Wet your hands in the bowl of salted water and make a rice ball by forming a handful of rice into a firm ball, about 2-inches in diameter. Press a hole into the center with your thumb and place a small piece of umeboshi plum or ½ tsp umeboshi plum paste in the center. Sprinkle a ½ tsp of toasted sesame seeds on top then close up the hole and compact the ball again until it is firm and round. Wrap a nori strip around the diameter of the rice ball and seal it by moistening the ends with water. You may need to trim the nori strips. Serve immediately or tightly wrap each one individually in wax paper and store in refrigerator.

I've seen jars of umeboshi plums containing food coloring and preservatives at some Asian grocery stores so be sure to always get your umeboshi plums and umeboshi plum paste at a health food store.

Umeboshi plum *concentrate* is a supplement that can be taken for health reasons and contains no salt. However, the concentrate *cannot* be used in place of the umeboshi plums or the umeboshi plum paste in recipes.

PUMPKIN BARLEY AUTUMN "RISOTTO"

SERVES 6-8

Risotto is usually made with a starchy rice, such as arborio, a type of refined white rice. This recipe uses hulled barley, which is less starchy and less creamy but equally as tasty, plus it's healthier for you! This whole grain is loaded with fiber and is beneficial in lowering blood sugar and insulin and improving cholesterol levels. Please be sure to include barley in many dishes and remember to chew this hearty grain well.

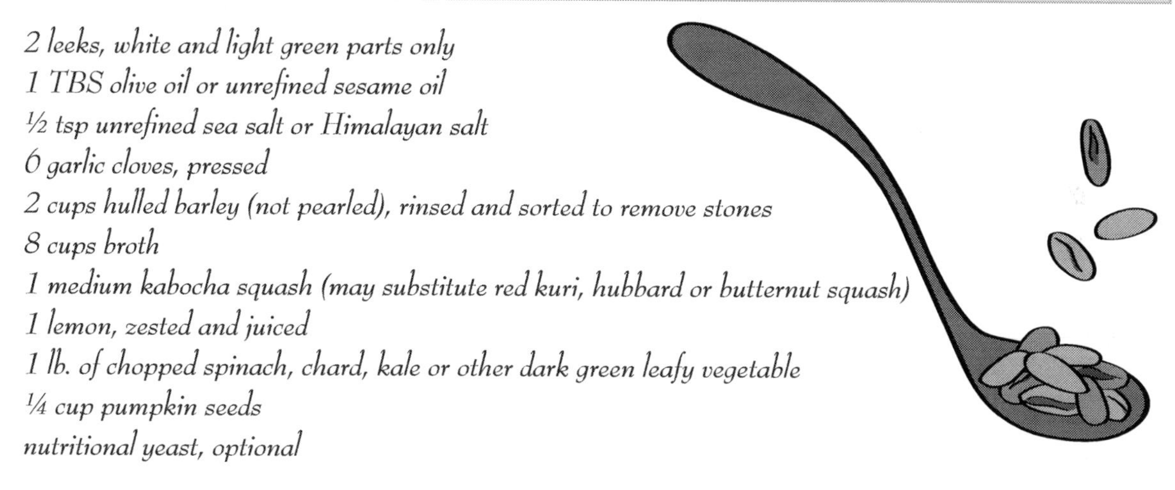

2 leeks, white and light green parts only
1 TBS olive oil or unrefined sesame oil
½ tsp unrefined sea salt or Himalayan salt
6 garlic cloves, pressed
2 cups hulled barley (not pearled), rinsed and sorted to remove stones
8 cups broth
1 medium kabocha squash (may substitute red kuri, hubbard or butternut squash)
1 lemon, zested and juiced
1 lb. of chopped spinach, chard, kale or other dark green leafy vegetable
¼ cup pumpkin seeds
nutritional yeast, optional

Slice the leek in half lengthwise, then across in ¼-inch pieces. Place chopped leeks in a large bowl of cold water. Swoosh around with your hand to loosen the sand from the leeks and let the sand sink to the bottom of the bowl. Scoop out the leeks with a slotted spoon and move to a colander to drain. Then place leeks in a large, heavy bottomed soup pot with the oil and salt. Sauté over medium heat for 5 minutes, then add the garlic and stir to combine. Cook another minute or so, then add the rinsed barley and stir to coat. Add the vegetable broth and bring to a boil. Cover, reduce to low and let simmer for 40 minutes, skimming any foam from the top several times and stirring occasionally.

Recipe continues on next page...

PUMPKIN BARLEY AUTUMN "RISOTTO"...

Meanwhile, prepare the squash by cutting it in half, scooping out the seeds, peeling it and dicing into ½-inch pieces. Add the squash to the barley after the barley has been cooking for about 40 minutes and stir to combine. Add more water if necessary so that the barley and squash are just covered in liquid. Cover and cook for another 15-20 minutes, checking often to see if it needs more water. If there is too much water, remove the lid and continue to simmer uncovered to let some liquid cook off. If there is still too much liquid when the barley and squash are finished cooking, carefully pour off the liquid into another pan and reserve for use in a soup. Once the barley is tender and the squash is soft, add the zest and juice of 1 lemon and the chopped greens. Stir to combine and let simmer a few minutes or until wilted but still bright green. Serve in bowls topped with toasted pumpkin seeds and sprinkled with nutritional yeast.

"Food is the key to health and health is the key to peace."

~ George Ohsawa

BROWN RICE SPRING "RISOTTO"

SERVES 6

(GF)

Asparagus is used to help expel toxins and excess water from the body. Also, in some studies, asparagus has been very beneficial in fighting cancer and protecting against heart disease.

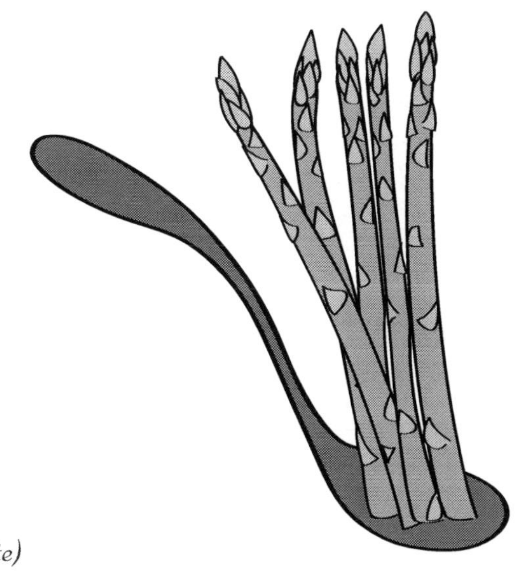

1 onion, diced
1 TBS olive oil
2 cups short grain brown rice, rinsed and drained well
4 cups vegetables broth
1 cup white wine (see note)*
1 tsp olive oil
dash of unrefined sea salt or Himalayan salt
2 cups sliced shiitake mushrooms, stems discarded
1 medium fennel bulb, small dice, core discarded
1 bunch of asparagus (see note)*
½ cup green peas, thawed
zest and juice from 1 large lemon
pinch of nutmeg
fresh basil, parsley or mint, minced, for garnish (see note)*

Sauté the onion in 1 TBS olive oil in a medium skillet for 3-5 minutes over medium-low heat. Add the brown rice and stir to coat for 1-2 minutes. Mix the wine with the broth in a separate bowl. Add this mixture to the rice gradually in ¼ cup to ½ cup additions, stirring after each addition then covering the pan partially with a lid. Add more broth once the previous addition of broth is absorbed into the rice. Keep doing this, and stirring often, until all of the broth/wine mixture is added to the rice and the rice is cooked through. You may need to add more water and cover the pot completely if the rice is not cooking all the way through. Either way, just be sure to stir the rice often to prevent sticking.

Meanwhile, in a sauté pan, add the olive oil, salt, mushrooms, fennel and asparagus and cook for 3-5 minutes. Add sautéed vegetables to the risotto once the rice is thoroughly cooked. Sprinkle with green peas, lemon zest, juice and a dash of nutmeg. Top with fresh herbs and serve.

White wine is not necessarily a therapeutic ingredients so you may substitute apple juice, water or vegetable broth.

Recipe continues on next page...

BROWN RICE SPRING "RISOTTO"...

Please be sure to use fresh herbs, not dried, for better flavor and presentation.

Hold asparagus spears in one hand and break off the root ends where they naturally want to break. Discard the root ends. Place remaining part of asparagus in a large bowl of cold water and shake gently to remove any sand that may be lurking in the asparagus tops. Rinse well and drain. If stalks feel tough and thick, peel them with a vegetable peeler. Young asparagus is more tender and thin and will not need to be peeled. Chop asparagus into 1-inches pieces and proceed with recipe.

ANCIENT GRAINS OVER MIXED GREENS

SERVES 6-8

Quinoa and kamut berries, the ancient grains in this recipe, are delicious together. Cook them in separate pots for the best results. Also, if you don't want the salad to look pink, add the grated beets at the end.

1 cup kamut berries (this is the name of whole grain kamut)
1 cup quinoa
1 small handful of dried wakame, crumbled or cut into very small pieces (use scissors)
2 cups broccoli florets, steamed lightly
2 carrots, scrubbed and diced, steamed lightly
1 cup cherry tomatoes, halved
1 4-inch piece of daikon, scrubbed and grated (see note)*
1 small beet, peeled and grated
1 bunch of parsley, minced
3 green onions, sliced
½ cup almonds, chopped into small bits
10 cups of mixed greens

Recipe continues on next page...

ANCIENT GRAINS OVER MIXED GREENS...

Dressing Ingredients
2 garlic cloves, pressed
1 TBS grated ginger
1 tsp Dijon mustard
a dash of sweetener
¼ cup lemon juice
1 TBS mellow miso
2 TBS apple cider vinegar
1 TBS brown rice vinegar
½ cup flax seed oil (may substitute olive oil)

Rinse the kamut and place in a pot with 3 cups of water and the wakame. Bring to a boil, cover and reduce heat to medium low. Let simmer, stirring frequently, for 40 minutes. Check to see if the kamut is tender all the way through. You may need to add more water and cook longer. If the kamut is finished, but there is still cooking liquid, strain off the liquid into another pan and reserve to make soup.

To make the quinoa, rinse it well and place in a pan with 2 cups of water. Bring to a boil, cover, reduce heat to low and let simmer for 15 minutes. Remove lid, stir and check to see if quinoa is cooked through. You may need to add a little water to prevent sticking, or cook longer.

Once both grains are cooked, place them in a large glass or stainless steel bowl (no plastic), stir to combine and let cool a bit. Meanwhile, make the dressing by placing all ingredients except the oil into a blender or food processor and blend until combined. While machine is running, slowly add the oil through the top until well incorporated. Add the steamed broccoli, carrots, cherry tomatoes, daikon, beet, parsley, green onions and almonds to the bowl with the kamut and quinoa. Toss to combine.

To serve, toss the mixed greens with half of the salad dressing and place on a plate topped with the grain and vegetable mixture. Drizzle with a bit more dressing and serve at room temperature or chilled.

Please do not heat this dressing if you are using flax seed oil because heat destroys the beneficial properties of this delicate oil.

To prevent daikon from turning green or brown after grating, place in a bowl filled with cold water until ready to use.

WILD RICE AND BARLEY WITH LEMON-PARSLEY DRESSING

SERVES 6-8

This wonderful recipe can stand alone as your main meal or be served as a side dish. It makes a perfect stuffing for roasted squash halves.

1 cup wild rice, rinsed
1 cup barley (hulled, not pearled), rinsed
5 cups vegetable broth (may substitute water)
1 bay leaf
½ tsp unrefined sea salt or Himalayan salt
½ cup sweet onion, small dice
3 stalks celery, small dice
1 cup of shredded red cabbage (may substitute ½ cup kimchi)
2 carrots, grated
¾ cup raw walnuts, chopped
1 cup dried cherries, cranberries, and/or goji berries (see note)*
1 large bunch of parsley, cleaned, trimmed, and chopped
2 TBS tamari (may substitute shoyu soy sauce)
¼ cup lemon juice
3 TBS olive oil
1 tsp Dijon mustard

Combine the wild rice and barley with the broth in a large pan, then add the salt and the bay leaf. Bring to a boil, reduce heat to low and cover. Simmer for 45 minutes to 1 hour. Stir periodically to make sure nothing is sticking to the bottom of the pan, adding more water if necessary. Once the grains are cooked through, drain well (if necessary) and remove the bay leaf. Move grains to a large glass, ceramic or stainless steel bowl (no plastic with hot foods). Add the onions, celery, cabbage, carrots, walnuts and dried fruit. In a food processor, combine the parsley, tamari, lemon juice, olive oil and mustard. Pulse to chop the parsley and bring the dressing together. Toss this with the rice mixture and serve chilled or at room temperature.

The goji berries are sometimes a little drier than one would like for this salad. If so, place them in a bowl of room temperature water and let soak for 5 minutes, just to soften and rehydrate them slightly. Then drain and pat dry before adding to the salad.

HATO MUGI GRAIN SALAD (A.K.A. JOB'S TEARS)

SERVES 6-8

This grain, hato mugi or Job's tears, looks like a tear drop shaped barley. It may even be referred to as Chinese barley however it is actually the grains from a tropical Asian grass. Either way, this grain has been used to help treat painful joints, reduce swelling and as a general body tonic.

1 cup hato mugi, rinsed and drained
½ cup hulled barley, rinsed and drained
3 cups vegetable broth (may substitute water)
1 TBS grated ginger
1 TBS tamari (may substitute shoyu soy sauce or ½ tsp unrefined sea salt)
1 cup cubed butternut squash or kabocha squash
1 medium onion, diced
1 cup daikon, diced small
2 cups broccoli florets
2 stalks celery, diced
½ cup frozen peas
2 TBS goji berries, soaked for 10 minutes, if necessary to soften
2 TBS hemp seeds
½ cup minced cilantro (may substitute parsley)
1 lemon, zested and juiced
3 green onions, minced

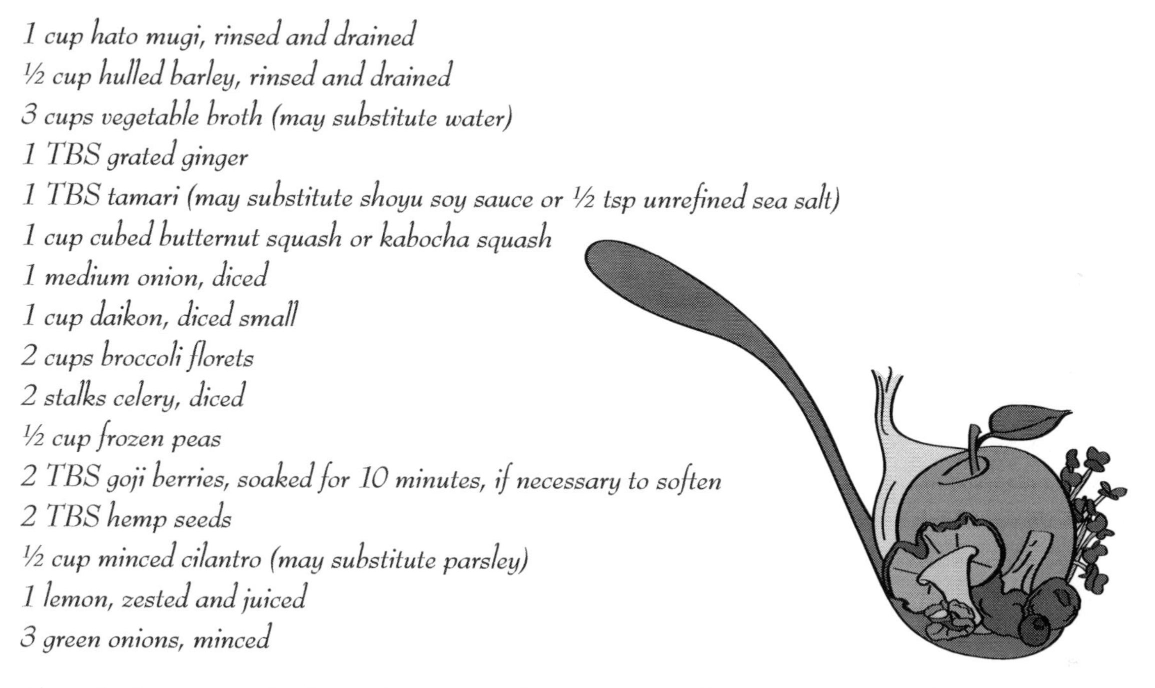

Place the hato mugi, barley and water in a heavy bottomed pot. Bring to a boil, cover, reduce heat and let simmer for 45 minutes over low heat. Check after 30 minutes and add a little water if necessary to prevent sticking. If there is still water left in the pan after the grains are cooked through, drain off the water and reserve for another use. Toss the cooked grains with the grated ginger and tamari. While the grains are cooking, prepare the vegetables and lightly steam the squash, onion, daikon and broccoli until tender (you can also do a water sauté, adding the broccoli during the last 3 minutes of cooking because it cooks quicker than the other vegetables). Use a slotted spoon and move the steamed vegetables to the cooked grains. Also add the celery, peas, goji berries, hemp seeds, cilantro, lemon zest, juice and green onions. Toss to combine and serve warm or at room temperature.

SPELT AND WATERCRESS SALAD

SERVES 4-6

Spelt, as well as kamut, are ancient relatives to wheat, and can sometimes be tolerated and digested more easily than wheat. They still contain gluten though so celiac sufferers should avoid all forms of wheat, including spelt and kamut.

1 cup spelt berries (may substitute kamut berries)
4 cups water
½ tsp unrefined sea salt or Himalayan salt
2 TBS apple cider vinegar
2 TBS lemon juice
2 tsp grated ginger
2 tsp mellow miso
2 tsp toasted sesame oil
1 small shallot, minced
4 baby bok choy, sliced thin
1 bunch watercress, coarse stems removed, chopped, (may substitute arugula)
1 small cucumber, peeled, seeded and diced
¼ cup goji berries, rinsed and dried with a towel

Rinse the spelt berries and drain well. Bring the water, spelt and salt to a boil in a saucepan. Cover, reduce heat to medium-low and simmer about 1 hour, checking a few times to see if it needs more water. They are done when tender, not hard or mushy. Let cool by rinsing the grains with cold water. Drain well then place in a large bowl.

Meanwhile, whisk the cider vinegar, lemon juice, ginger, miso, oil and shallot together in a small bowl until combined. Wash and chop the bok choy and place in a medium pan of boiling water. Boil the bok choy for 1 minute then remove to a strainer and rinse with cold water. Next, rinse and chop the watercress. Pat dry with a towel or spin dry in a salad spinner. Toss the watercress, bok choy, cucumber, goji berries and the dressing with the spelt berries. Serve at room temperature or chilled.

FAVA BEAN AND DANDELION GREENS OVER BARLEY

SERVES 4

Using fresh fava beans still in their pods is a little time consuming, but well worth it for their fresh and delicate flavor. So grab a friend to help get the fava beans prepped for this recipe (be sure to read through the directions thoroughly before proceeding).

1 lb. of fresh fava beans, in their pods
1 TBS olive oil
1 large leek, sliced, cleaned well and drained
a dash of unrefined sea salt or Himalayan salt
3 medium tomatoes, seeded and chopped
3 garlic cloves, pressed
½ tsp red pepper flakes
2 tsp fresh oregano (may substitute ½ tsp dried oregano)
1 bunch of dandelion greens, washed and chopped
3 TBS minced parsley
additional salt, to taste
1 lemon, cut into wedges, for garnish
3-4 cups cooked hulled barley (may substitute hato mugi) (see note)*

Prepare the fava beans by removing the fava beans from their pods, discarding the long pod. Place the fava beans in a pot of boiling water and boil for 1 minute. Move the beans from the boiling water with a slotted spoon and place into a bowl of ice water to stop the cooking process. Then move to a strainer. Next, peel off and discard the outer cream-colored shell of the fava bean to reveal a bright green, soft fava bean. The beans are now ready to be used in the recipe.

In a large skillet place the olive oil, sliced leek and a dash of salt and heat over medium heat for 5-8 minutes, stirring occasionally. Add the chopped tomatoes, pressed garlic, red pepper flakes and oregano. Stir and cook for 1 minute. Next, add the chopped dandelion greens and stir to combine. Add a small amount of water (about 2 TBS) and cook, stirring often, until the dandelion leaves are wilted but still bright green, about 3-5 minutes. Add more water, if necessary, to prevent sticking. Add the parsley and the peeled fava beans and toss to combine. Taste and add more salt, if necessary. Serve over a bed of cooked barley (or half barley, half hato mugi) and garnish with fresh lemon wedges.

Recipe continues on next page...

FAVA BEAN AND DANDELION GREENS OVER BARLEY...

To cook hulled barley (or hato mugi), rinse and drain 1 cup of grain. Place in a heavy bottomed pan with 3 cups of water and bring to a boil. Cover, reduce heat to low and let simmer for 40 minutes. Check to see if grains are tender. Add more water if necessary and continue to cook until grains are cooked through. If the grains are cooked through but there is still liquid in the pan carefully strain off the liquid.

QUINOA SALAD WITH ORANGE JUICE DRESSING

SERVES 2-4

This recipe is just plain good for you! Cleansing, nourishing and complete.

1 cup quinoa, rinsed well and drained
2 cups vegetable broth (may substitute water)
2 tsp grated ginger
1 beet, grated
¼ cup avocado, chopped
½ cup cucumber, chopped
½ cup mung bean sprouts
1 orange, juiced
2 tsp mellow miso
1 TBS flax seed oil
¼ cup minced parsley

Cook quinoa with the broth and ginger for 15 minutes or until the water is absorbed. Prepare the vegetables. Whisk the orange juice with the miso and flax seed oil. Season with spices if desired. Add the vegetables to the cooked quinoa. Toss with the dressing. Top with minced parsley. Serve chilled or at room temperature.

SWEETHEART QUINOA BEET SALAD (GF)

SERVES 6

Beets add a touch of sweetness to this dish and promote a healthy liver and heart!

1 ½ cups quinoa
¼ tsp unrefined sea salt or Himalayan salt
3 cups water
1-2 medium beets, peeled and grated
1 large red onion, finely chopped
1/2 -1 bunch flat-leaf parsley, cleaned and minced
2 celery stalks, diced
1 TBS red wine vinegar
1 lemon, juiced
1 TBS flax seed oil
2 tsp umeboshi plum vinegar
3 green onions, minced
2 TBS hemp seeds

Rinse the quinoa well and let drain. Then place in a pan with 3 cups of fresh water and ¼ tsp salt. Bring to a boil, cover, reduce and simmer for 15 minutes or until cooked through and all water is absorbed into the grain. Transfer cooked quinoa to a large glass or stainless steel mixing bowl to cool.

Meanwhile, prepare the onions, beets and parsley (can place in a food processor for quick chopping) then place in a large bowl with the cooked quinoa. Add the diced celery. Whisk together the vinegar, lemon juice, oil and umeboshi vinegar and pour over the quinoa. Toss gently. Sprinkle with green onions and hemp seeds. Add more of the vinegars or some lemon juice if needed. Serve chilled or room temperature.

Don't let the quinoa overcook. As soon as it is cooked through remove from heat and place in a large glass or stainless steel bowl (no plastic with hot foods), draining off any water, if necessary, and *gently* fluff the quinoa to allow it to cool.

(GF)

QUINOA WITH SPICY BERRY DRESSING

SERVES 6

This dish is great on a hot summer day. Serve with mixed greens for a beautiful meal.

1 cup quinoa, rinsed and drained
2 cups water
¼ tsp unrefined sea salt or Himalayan salt
1 bunch of asparagus, cleaned, chopped into bite sized pieces (bottoms discarded)
½ cup green peas (thaw if necessary by simmering with the asparagus)
1 lemon, juiced
4 ripe nectarines, diced (may substitute peaches, diced)
1 carrot, scrubbed and grated
1 celery, diced small
½ cup minced parsley
¼ cup minced chives
¼ cup chopped almonds
extra blueberries or chopped strawberries, for garnish
¼ cup fresh mint leaves, finely minced

Dressing Ingredients
½ cup fresh blueberries or strawberries, cleaned and chopped
2 TBS chopped shallot
3 TBS balsamic vinegar
1 TBS date syrup, agave nectar, brown rice syrup or yacon syrup
2 TBS walnut oil (may substitute flax seed oil)
a dash or two of cayenne pepper
½ orange, peeled and seeded

Combine the quinoa, water and salt in a medium saucepan over high heat and bring to a boil. Cover and reduce heat to medium-low and let simmer for 15 minutes or until all the water is absorbed and the quinoa is light and fluffy, not mushy. Meanwhile make the dressing by blending all dressing ingredients together in a blender until smooth. Set aside. Remove quinoa and spread out on a clean sheet pan or large baking dish to let cool to room temperature. *Gently* fluff every few minutes to speed the cooling process. In a separate pot (large enough for the asparagus), bring about 4 cups of water to a boil.

Recipe continues on next page...

QUINOA WITH SPICY BERRY DRESSING...

Add the asparagus (and green peas, if frozen) and cook for 2 minutes, then remove with a slotted spoon to a strainer and rinse under cold water. Drain and place in a large serving bowl with 1 TBS lemon juice. Add the nectarines, carrots, celery, parsley, chives and almonds to the bowl (plus green peas, if using fresh). Add the cooled quinoa to the bowl and add about **half** of the dressing. Toss gently to combine all ingredients. Garnish with extra berries and the mint and serve at room temperature or chilled.

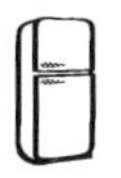

You will have more dressing than you need. Store the extra dressing in a sealed jar in the refrigerator and use within 5 days.

QUINOA WITH SAFFRON, LEMON AND ASPARAGUS (GF)

SERVES 4-6

2 cups quinoa
4 cups vegetable broth (may substitute water)
½ tsp saffron threads, crumbled
unrefined sea salt or Himalayan salt, to taste
1 lb. fresh asparagus, washed well to remove sand from tops
1 lemon, zested and juiced
¼ cup minced parsley
harissa, optional

Rinse the quinoa well and let drain. Place drained quinoa, broth and saffron in a medium large pot. Add ¼ tsp salt -or omit it if you used broth that contained salt. Bring to a boil, cover, reduce to low and let simmer for 10 minutes. Meanwhile, trim away the bottom ends of the asparagus and discard. Then chop the asparagus into bite-size pieces. Add the asparagus and the lemon zest to the quinoa after it has cooked for 10 minutes. Cover and cook for about 5 more minutes, adding a little more water if necessary to prevent sticking. Once asparagus is tender, turn off heat and add lemon juice (about 2 TBS) and parsley. Toss and serve with a drizzle of harissa.

Adding a cup of cooked chickpeas and a cup of steamed, diced carrots or sweet potato to this dish is a wonderful way to make a complete meal.

QUINOA TABOULEH

SERVES 6

Tabouleh is a middle-eastern dish typically made with bulgur wheat. This recipe uses quinoa, the 'mother grain' from South America for just a little extra boost in minerals and protein. Plus it contains lots of parsley, which is high in vitamins A and C, and iron, and is helpful in cleansing the blood, aiding in digestion and freshening the breath.

1 ½ cups quinoa
3 cups vegetable broth (may substitute water)
2 garlic cloves, pressed
3 medium lemons, zest from 1, and juice from all 3
¼ tsp unrefined sea salt or Himalayan salt
2 bunches fresh parsley, cleaned, trimmed, and rough chopped
¼ cup fresh mint leaves
2 TBS olive oil
2 TBS flax seed oil
*4 green onions, **finely** chopped*
2 cups of diced tomatoes, seeded (multi-colored cherry tomatoes, halved, are nice)
*1 medium fennel bulb, **finely** chopped, core discarded*
1 carrot, scrubbed and shredded
1 cucumber, seeded and diced

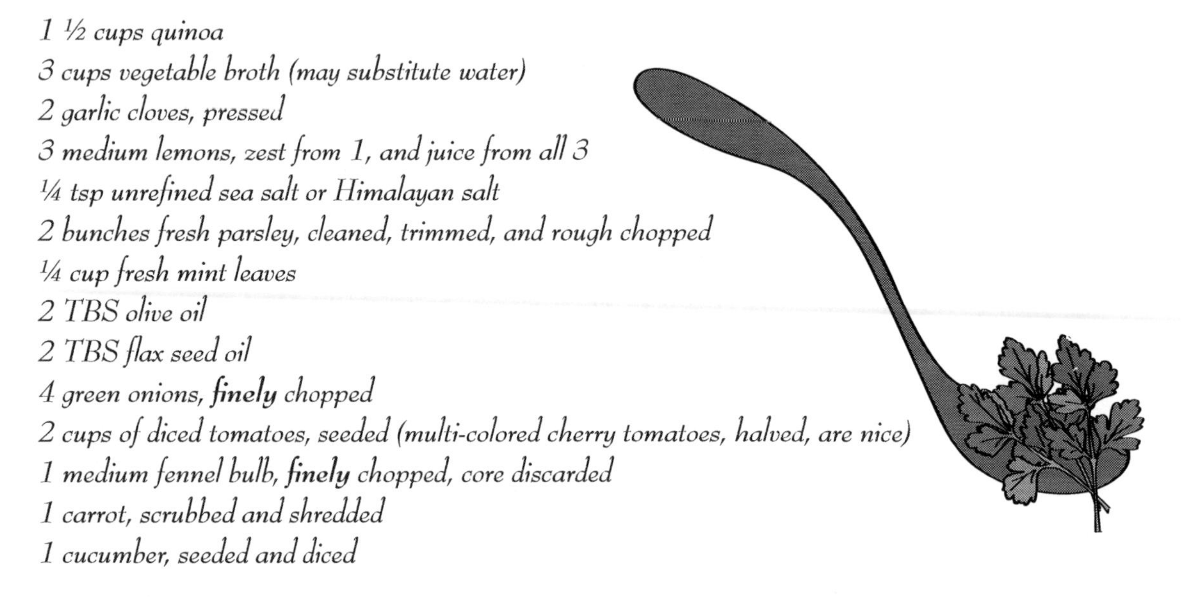

Rinse quinoa **thoroughly** in a bowl of cold water. Pour off excess water. Drain well in a fine mesh strainer. Bring broth to a boil with the drained quinoa. Cover the pot and simmer for 15 minutes over low heat. Do not overcook the quinoa. Once it is tender remove from heat and transfer to a large glass or stainless steel bowl, draining if necessary to keep from getting mushy. *Gently* fluff with a fork and let cool.

Meanwhile, place garlic, lemon zest, juice, salt, parsley, mint and oils in a food processor and pulse to combine (you may need to do this in batches if you have a small food processor). Toss this mixture with the cooled quinoa and add the green onions, tomatoes, fennel, carrot and cucumber. Serve chilled or at room temperature.

To make this dish a little more hearty you could add 1 cup of cooked chickpeas when you add the green onions.

AMARANTH "GRITS"

SERVES 4

Amaranth, also know as kiwicha in the Andes, is often referred to as a grain because it looks, tastes and cooks like a grain. But amaranth is actually a seed. Amaranth is a good source of protein, fiber, iron, magnesium, phosphorus, copper and manganese.

1 cup amaranth
1 garlic clove, pressed
1 medium onion, finely chopped
3 cups vegetable broth (may substitute water)
¼ tsp unrefined sea salt or Himalayan salt
1 TBS minced jalapeno, optional
nutritional yeast, optional (see note)*
2 TBS minced parsley, to garnish

Combine the amaranth, garlic, onion, broth, salt and optional jalapeno in a medium saucepan. Bring to a boil then reduce heat to low and simmer, covered, until most of the liquid has been absorbed and amaranth is cooked through and thickened, about 20 minutes. Mix in a couple tablespoons of nutritional yeast and garnish with parsley. Serve hot with a side of steamed vegetables and beans.

Some brands of nutritional yeast are gluten-free, some aren't. Read your labels and if you aren't sure just leave it out.

MILLET-CAULI MASH

SERVES 8

These sure remind me of mashed potatoes but without all the weight! Forget the turkey, just serve these topped with a miso gravy along with some baked tempeh and something green, then call the family over for Sunday supper!

1 medium onion, minced fine
1 TBS olive oil
2 cups millet (may substitute quinoa, amaranth or teff, in any combination)
4 cups cauliflower florets
½ tsp unrefined sea salt or Himalayan salt
4 garlic cloves, pressed
5 cups water, plus more as needed
nutritional yeast, to garnish
3 TBS minced parsley, to garnish
miso gravy, for serving *(see pg. 183)*

Sauté the onion in the olive oil over medium heat in a large pot for 5 minutes. Add the grains (be sure to thoroughly rinse the millet or quinoa first, then drain well before adding to pan) and stir to coat with olive oil and onion. Cook for 5 minutes, stirring frequently, until grains are lightly toasted and smell nutty. Then add the cauliflower, salt, garlic and 5 cups water (**add slowly, it will splatter**). Stir well, cover pot and cook over medium heat for about 20 minutes or until grains have absorbed all the water. Check often to make sure nothing is sticking to the bottom of the pan. You want the grains to be very soft and moist so add more water and cook longer if necessary. Once cooked through, use a potato masher to mash together until you get a smoother consistency. Serve in place of mashed potatoes, topped with nutritional yeast and minced parsley. Serve with a side of miso gravy.

WARM WINTER SQUASH AND COCONUT CURRY MILLET (GF)

SERVES 6

Roast your squash ahead of time to make this recipe go quicker.

1 cup of millet, rinsed
1 cup of quinoa, rinsed
¼ tsp unrefined sea salt or Himalayan salt
2 tsp curry powder
4 ½ cups vegetable broth (may substitute water)
1 small head of broccoli, cut into florets
½ of a small head of cauliflower, cut into florets
1 small beet, peeled and grated
½ of a winter squash, chopped and ***roasted*** *(kabocha, red kuri or butternut)*
½ can of coconut milk, shake well before measuring
a dash of salt
½ cup of cooked adzuki beans, green peas or shelled edamame, drained
1 bunch of cilantro, minced
3 green onions, minced
fresh lemon or lime wedges, for serving

Place the rinsed quinoa and millet in a pan with the salt, curry powder and water. Cover and bring to a boil. Reduce heat to low and let simmer for 20 minutes. Let stand for another 5 minutes. Meanwhile, steam the broccoli and cauliflower until tender, then set aside. Place the grated beet in a bowl of cold water for 5 minutes, then drain well and set aside (this will help minimize the magenta stain beets give off).

Place about 1 ½ cups of roasted squash and ½ can of coconut milk in a food processor and process until smooth, thick and creamy. You may need to add more squash or coconut milk until desired texture is reached. I like a thick gravy-like consistency. Taste and add a dash of salt, if desired, and blend again. Pour this sauce over the cooked quinoa-millet and stir to combine. Toss in the steamed broccoli and cauliflower, the grated beets and the beans. Gently toss and serve garnished with cilantro and green onions. Serve with fresh lemon or lime wedges.

GF

RUSSIAN KASHA AND BEET SALAD

SERVES 4

Kasha is another name for toasted buckwheat groats, an edible fruit seed of a plant related to rhubarb. Buckwheat gives strong, warming energy and is a good blood-building food. This gluten-free 'grain' is beneficial for stabilizing the blood sugar and helps to reduce the risk of heart disease by improving cholesterol levels. Buckwheat is rich in B vitamins as well as phosphorus, magnesium, iron, zinc, copper and manganese.

1 cup kasha (toasted buckwheat groats), rinsed
2 cups vegetable broth (may substitute water)
¼ cup minced red onion
2 celery stalks, diced
1 carrot, shredded
1 small beet, shredded
3 kale leaves, steamed and chopped
1 TBS minced dill
1 tsp umeboshi plum vinegar, plus more, if desired
1 TBS flax seed oil, optional
1 lemon, cut into wedges
2 TBS minced parsley

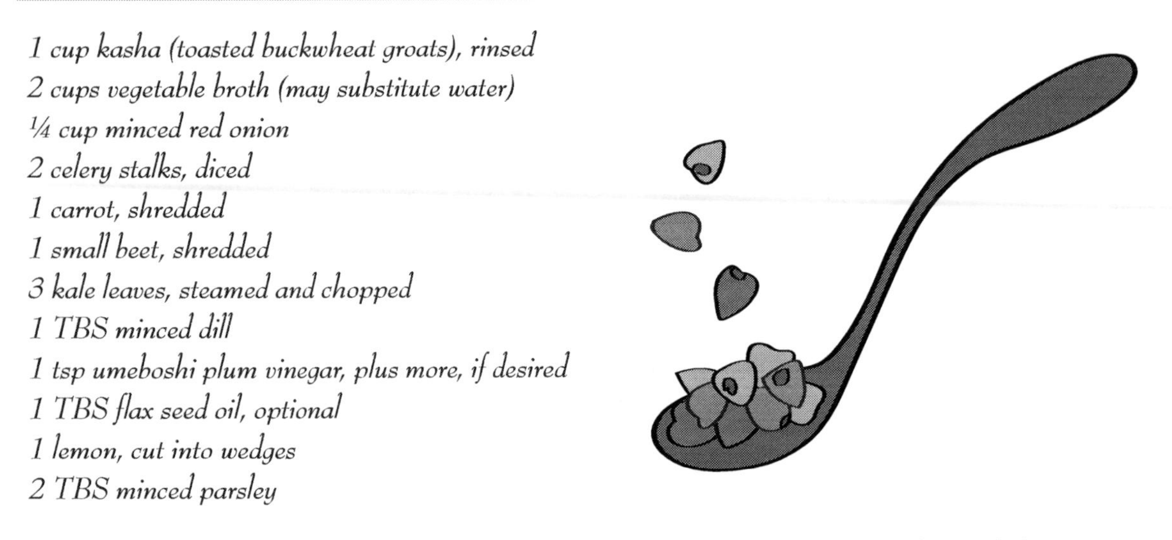

Place kasha and broth in a pan and bring to a boil. Cover and reduce to low, let cook for 12-15 minutes. Uncover and test to see if grain is tender, adding more broth and cooking longer if necessary. Be careful not to add too much broth or over cook the grain because it can get mushy. Drain off excess liquid if necessary. Once grains are cooked through move them to a serving dish and *gently* fluff and spread them out in the dish to cool a bit. Then prepare and add the remaining ingredients to the dish, tossing gently and adding lemon juice to taste. Garnish with parsley and serve warm or chilled.

Beans & Other Legumes

SIMPLE LENTIL CURRY

SERVES 6

So many ways to use lentils, so little time.
Memorize this recipe because you'll want to make it all the time.

1 large onion, chopped
1 TBS grated ginger
2 TBS water
1 tsp ground cumin
¼ tsp turmeric
6 cups water
1 ½ cup red lentils, picked through to remove stones, then rinsed and drained
½ cup coconut milk
3 TBS tomato paste
1 TBS lemon juice
¾ tsp unrefined sea salt or Himalayan salt
cayenne, to taste
½ cup minced cilantro, for garnish

Place the onions, ginger, and 2 TBS water in a large, heavy bottomed soup pot. Cover and cook over medium heat. Let cook, stirring occasionally for 5 minutes, adding a little more water if necessary to prevent sticking. Next add the cumin and turmeric and stir to coat for 1 minute. Add the lentils and the 6 cups of water. Bring to a boil and then reduce heat. Let simmer, covered, for 20-25 minutes, or until lentils have started to break down (higher altitudes may require longer cooking times). You may need to skim the top of the soup to remove any foam that forms.

Meanwhile, in a small bowl whisk together the coconut milk, tomato paste, lemon juice, salt and cayenne until smooth; then add to the soup and stir to combine. Heat another 5 minutes, then serve garnished with cilantro.

Serve with a side of brown rice, braised collards, and roasted squash. This is real comfort food!

SIMPLE LENTIL AND HERB SALAD

(GF)

SERVES 2-4

I use this recipe as a base and then add whatever vegetables, nuts, dried fruit and dressings I have on hand. Or just keep it simple. The possibilities are endless!

*2 cups **cooked** lentils (**not** the red/orange lentils)* (see note)*
½ cup freshly minced parsley
2 TBS freshly minced basil
1 TBS freshly minced dill
1 tsp freshly minced mint
½ cup freshly minced red or green onions
1 lemon, juiced
unrefined sea salt or Himalayan salt, to taste
micro greens, to garnish

Add lentils, drained and cooled, to a bowl and toss with the remaining ingredients. Toss in any additional items you desire. Then top with micro greens or sprouts and serve chilled or at room temperature.

Drain any liquid from the cooked lentils with a strainer and let the lentils cool thoroughly before mixing with other ingredients.

GF SAVORY BROWN LENTILS

SERVES 6-8

If you have rosemary or lavender salt, use this to season the lentils. You will be glad you did!

2 cups brown lentils (these are the larger, flat lentils, light brownish-greenish in color)
1 large onion, diced
1 medium leek, cleaned well and chopped
1 TBS olive oil
4 garlic cloves, pressed
2 tsp fresh thyme leaves (please don't substitute dried thyme leaves)
2 fresh rosemary sprigs, leaves minced
4 cups vegetable broth (may substitute water)
4 celery stalks, diced
3 carrots, scrubbed and diced
1 medium yellow squash, diced
½ tsp unrefined sea salt or Himalayan salt
2-3 TBS tomato paste
2 TBS red wine vinegar
¼ cup minced parsley
2 TBS minced basil

Sort through the lentils to remove any stones or foreign matter. Rinse well and let drain. Heat a large soup pot over medium heat with the onions, leeks, and olive oil for 5 minutes. Add the garlic, thyme, and rosemary and stir for one minute. Next add the drained lentils and the vegetable broth. Cover and let simmer for 15 minutes. Add the chopped celery, carrots, squash, salt, and tomato paste. Stir and let cook another 5-8 minutes or until vegetables and lentils are tender. If lentils are not cooked through, but there is no liquid left in the pan, add a few tablespoons of water, cover the pan, and let simmer a few minutes until softened, but not mushy (higher altitudes may require longer cooking times). Strain off any remaining liquid if necessary. Once everything is perfectly cooked add the vinegar and herbs and gently toss to combine. Taste and adjust seasonings if desired.

Over-stirring of this dish will cause the lentils to break apart and get mushy so be gentle.

LEBANESE LENTILS

SERVES 6

Lentils are an excellent source of low-fat protein and complex carbohydrates. They are loaded with fiber and minerals too. They are easier to digest than other legumes (beans) and require no soaking. Enjoy the flavor and health benefits of the lentils, olive oil, onion, mint, parsley and lemon in this simple recipe!

1½ cups brown lentils (see note)*
4 cups water
½ tsp unrefined sea salt or Himalayan salt
2 TBS olive oil
1 yellow onion, diced small (may substitute sweet onion)
1 green bell pepper, diced (may substitute 2 celery stalks, diced)
2 TBS minced mint leaves
1 medium bunch of parsley, cleaned, trimmed, and minced
1 large lemon, zested and juiced

Sort through the lentils to remove any stones or foreign matter. Rinse well and let drain. Place lentils in a pan with the water. Bring to a boil, reduce to medium low heat and simmer for 25 minutes or until lentils are cooked through but not mushy (higher altitudes may require longer cooking times). It may be necessary to add more water while they are cooking. Once the lentils are cooked, rinse them in cold water to stop the cooking process so they will hold their shape. Drain well. Sprinkle on the salt and olive oil. Toss with diced onion, green bell pepper, mint, and a few tablespoons of the minced parsley (or more). Add the lemon zest and juice and toss to combine. Taste for salt and serve at room temperature or chilled.

Although all lentils are good for you the red (orange colored) lentils will not work here. Look for the larger brown lentils for this recipe.

(GF)

LENTIL RADISH CUCUMBER SALAD

SERVES 6-8

This is refreshing and light, yet filling.

2 cups lentils, black beluga or French green preferred, sorted to remove stones
2 tsp olive oil
4 cups vegetable broth (may substitute water)
1 bay leaf
½ tsp unrefined sea salt or Himalayan salt
¼ cup or more brown rice vinegar
2 tsp umeboshi plum vinegar
1 cucumber, peeled, seeds removed, and diced
1 bunch of radishes, diced small (may pulse in a food processor)
1 cup shredded red cabbage
2 carrots, minced or grated
2 TBS hemp seeds
1 bunch chives, minced fine
mixed greens, for serving
1 lemon, cut into wedges

Rinse the lentils well in a large bowl of water. Pour the water off and drain well. Toast the lentils in a dry saucepan to remove any remaining water. Add the olive oil carefully and toss to coat, for 1-2 minutes. Slowly add the broth and the bay leaf. Bring to a boil and then reduce to a simmer cooking for 20 minutes. It's important that the lentils hold their shape and are firm, not mushy. Test after 15 minutes. If they are finished cooking and there is still broth remaining in the pan, pour off the broth into another pan or glass container and reserve for another use. If there is no broth left in the pan and the lentils are still too hard then add more water, 2 TBS at a time (higher altitudes may require longer cooking times). Add the salt at the last few minutes of cooking, but not before. Remove the bay leaf, drain if necessary, and let the lentils cool by spreading them out on a large sheet pan.

Meanwhile, add the cucumber, radishes and cabbage to a separate bowl and marinate in the vinegars for 20-30 minutes, stirring occasionally to evenly coat. Gently toss the lentils with the cucumber mixture, adding as much of the vinegar marinade as you desire. Toss in the carrots, hemp seeds and chives. Serve this salad over a bed of mixed greens with a lemon wedge.

COLORFUL 4-BEAN SALAD

SERVES 10-12

This dish is great to bring to a potluck party because it can be made ahead of time, eaten at room temperature and makes enough to feed a small crowd. Guests will certainly be impressed with your cooking skills by the taste and presentation of this simple dish!

1 can or 1 ½ cups of cooked garbanzo beans, rinsed and drained
1 can or 1 ½ cups of cooked adzuki beans, rinsed and drained
1 can or 1 ½ cups of cooked black beans, rinsed and drained
1 cup of shelled fava beans, fresh or frozen, not canned (may substitute lima beans)
1 ½ cups of grated carrots, from about 2 carrots
1 ½ cups of cherry tomatoes, cut in half (multi-colored if possible)
6 green onions, sliced thin
¼ cup diced red onion
½ cup sliced red cabbage
½ cup grated red beet (yes, raw)
1 bunch of cilantro, minced (may substitute parsley)
2 cups spinach, roughly chopped (may substitute arugula or watercress)
1 cup of broccoli florets, lightly steamed
1 lemon, juiced
2 tsp umeboshi plum vinegar
2 TBS apple cider vinegar
3 TBS flax seed oil
1 tsp mustard, any kind
dash of date syrup, agave nectar or yacon syrup
Salt, cayenne, miso, ginger, and garlic, optional

Prepare all of the vegetables being sure to wash the cilantro and spinach well in a large bowl of cold water, allowing the sand and dirt to fall to the bottom of the bowl. Scoop out the greens and chop as directed. Place all the prepared beans and vegetables in a large bowl. Place the lemon juice, vinegars, oil, mustard and sweetener in a small bowl and whisk until combined. Add optional dressing ingredients to your taste. Pour dressing over salad and toss to combine. Let rest at least ½ hour before serving or overnight in the refrigerator. Serve this dish chilled or at room temperature.

You must rinse and thoroughly drain the cooked beans, especially if using canned beans, or it will turn out too gooey.

CHICKPEA SALAD
SERVES 6

Ok, so I love chickpeas, but any bean would work in this recipe.

4 cups cooked chickpeas, drained
½ small red onion, minced (see note)*
1 red bell pepper, roasted, seeded and chopped (see note)*
1 jalapeno, seeded and minced (use only half if you don't like spicy)
3 green onions, sliced thin
3 cups of arugula, washed and chopped
1 small bunch of parsley, minced

Dressing Ingredients:
⅓ cup lemon juice
⅓ cup olive or flax seed oil (see note)*
3 garlic cloves, pressed
1 tsp ground cumin
½ tsp unrefined sea salt or Himalayan salt (use less if the beans contain salt)
1 TBS mellow miso

Place the chickpeas, red onions, roasted red pepper, jalapeno, green onions, arugula and parsley in a large bowl and toss to combine. In a small bowl (or in a small blender), combine the lemon juice, oil, garlic, cumin, salt, and miso. Whisk or blend until combined. Gradually toss about half of this dressing with the salad and taste. You may not need all of the dressing. Serve salad chilled or at room temperature.

You may substitute ½ cup rehydrated sun-dried tomatoes or 1 grated carrot for the red pepper.

If you don't love the taste of raw red onion, soak the diced onion in water for 15 minutes, then drain to help take the edge off the onions.

Please don't heat this salad if using flax seed oil because it can't take the heat!

UN-TUNA SALAD

SERVES 4

Better than the real thing, this sandwich spread contains fiber, protein and minerals. The two types of seaweed in the recipe give the chickpeas an 'ocean' flavor, while helping the body to detoxify.

1 ½ cups cooked chickpeas, rinsed and drained
¼ cup arame seaweed, rehydrated for 15 minutes in 3 cups of water (see note)*
2 tsp umeboshi plum vinegar
½ tsp kelp seaweed powder/flakes
½ cup minced parsley
4 green onions, minced
½ cup almond mayo or cashew mayo *(see pg. 193-4)*
¼ cup nutritional yeast, optional
1 cup celery, diced fine
2 TBS capers

Place the chickpeas in a medium bowl and mash with a potato masher. Scoop out the arame seaweed from its soaking water with a slotted spoon. Place on a cutting board and finely mince. Add the minced arame and remaining ingredients to the mashed chickpeas and mix well. Serve in place of tuna salad in sandwiches or on salads.

You could also use hijiki seaweed in place of the arame if you desire a stronger ocean flavor but you will need to boil the hijiki in water for 15-20 minutes to soften it, then scoop out and mince as directed above.

SIMPLE CURRIED BEANS AND BROCCOLI

SERVES 4-6

We all know by now that beans are good for protein and fiber but the broccoli is not to be overlooked here. Broccoli is high in vitamins C, A, K, calcium, fiber and phytonutrients which help protect against cancer, heart disease, cataracts, and help to keep bones strong.

2 tsp olive oil
1 onion, chopped
1 TBS fresh ginger, grated
1 tsp cumin seeds
2 tsp curry powder
1 can of diced tomatoes (15 oz) undrained
¼ tsp unrefined sea salt or Himalayan salt
1 cup diced sweet potato
½ cup water
2 cups of broccoli florets
1 can black beans (15 oz), rinsed and drained
1 can garbanzo beans (15 oz), rinsed and drained
⅓ cup chopped fresh cilantro
1 TBS lemon juice

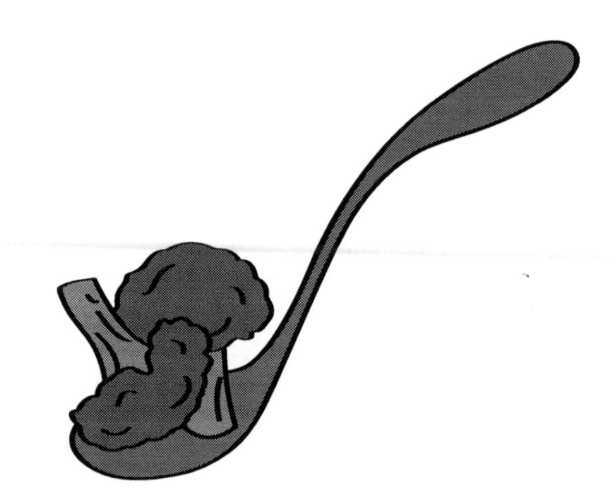

Place the oil and onion in a large skillet over medium heat and cook for 5 minutes. Add the ginger and cook another 2 minutes. Stir in the cumin seeds and curry powder and cook for 1 minute. Add tomatoes and their juice, salt, sweet potatoes, and water. Cover, reduce heat and simmer for 5 minutes. Add the broccoli and beans and simmer, uncovered, for 5 more minutes, stirring occasionally. Remove from heat, add the cilantro and lemon juice and serve.

TUSCAN BEANS AND GREENS (GF)

SERVES 6-8

This recipe is loaded with healthy ingredients. The onion and garlic contain allicin, which helps fight cancer; the carrots contain the antioxidant beta carotene; the beans and greens provide healthy amounts of calcium; while the lemon and parsley add vitamin C and iron, among other valuable nutrients. Serve this over quinoa or barley and you have a super healthy, high fiber, low fat meal guaranteed to keep you healthy!

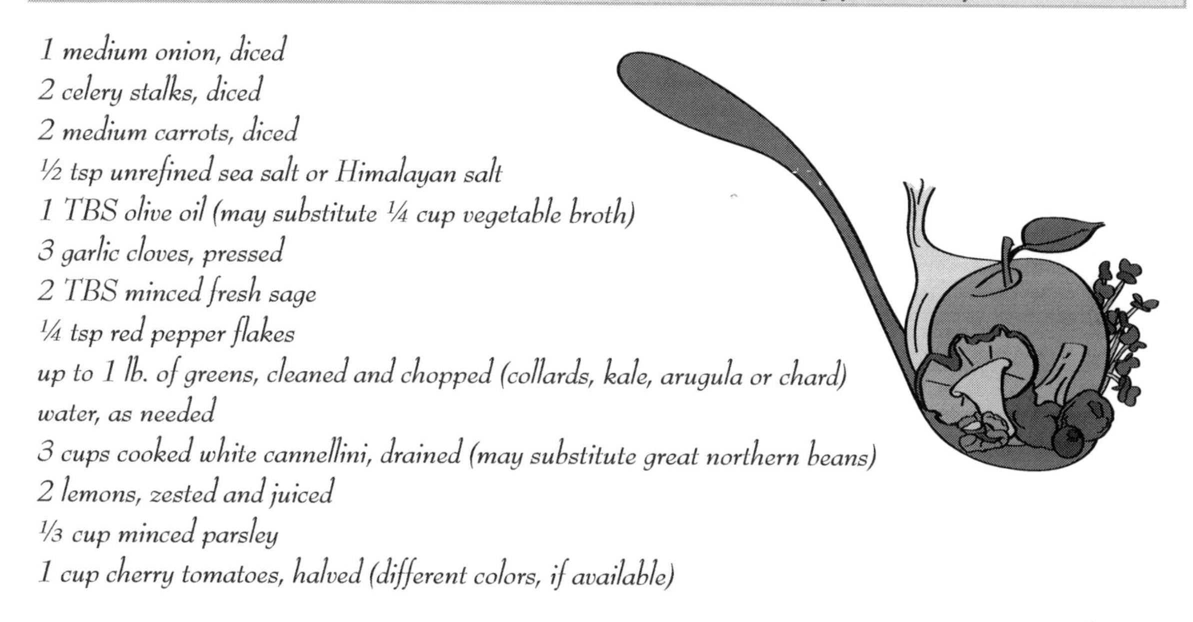

1 medium onion, diced
2 celery stalks, diced
2 medium carrots, diced
½ tsp unrefined sea salt or Himalayan salt
1 TBS olive oil (may substitute ¼ cup vegetable broth)
3 garlic cloves, pressed
2 TBS minced fresh sage
¼ tsp red pepper flakes
up to 1 lb. of greens, cleaned and chopped (collards, kale, arugula or chard)
water, as needed
3 cups cooked white cannellini, drained (may substitute great northern beans)
2 lemons, zested and juiced
⅓ cup minced parsley
1 cup cherry tomatoes, halved (different colors, if available)

Place the onions, celery, carrots, salt, and oil in a large skillet. Heat over medium heat, while stirring, until tender, about 5 minutes. Add the garlic, sage, and red pepper flakes and stir to coat for 1 minute. Add the chopped greens and a few tablespoons of water. Continue to cook over medium heat until greens are wilted and water is cooked off. Be careful not to overcook the greens; you want them to be tender but still bright green. Also, only add a small amount of water at a time to cook the greens; you don't want there to be extra water in the pan after cooking. Now add the drained, cooked beans; lemon zest and juice; and parsley. Toss to combine and serve warm or at room temperature, garnished with cherry tomatoes.

(GF) LOUISIANA BLACK-EYED PEAS

SERVES 6-8

Simple and delicious, and good for the soul!

1 lb. dried black-eyed peas, sorted through to remove stones
5 cups NO SALT vegetable broth (may substitute water)
1 5-inch strip of kombu seaweed
1 TBS creole seasoning (NO SALT)
1 tsp garlic powder
1 tsp chili powder
1 tsp black pepper
1 bay leaf
2 TBS green onion, minced
unrefined sea salt or Himalayan salt, to taste
1 bunch parsley, chopped

Cover the dried peas with lots of water and let sit for 6 hours or overnight. Drain and discard the water (or use to water your plants). Now add broth, kombu, spices and bay leaf. Bring to a boil, cover and simmer for 45 minutes to 1 hour, or until cooked through, but not mushy. Stir occasionally to prevent sticking. Add or drain off water if necessary. Toss with green onions, salt, and parsley then serve.

Serve with braised collard greens and brown rice.

ADZUKI BEANS: TO SPREAD...OR NOT

MAKES ABOUT 2 ½ CUPS

Sometimes I'm in the mood for these flavors in a spread. Sometimes I like the beans whole so I can serve them over brown rice with a side of roasted kabocha squash and onions. Try it both ways and decide for yourself!

1 cup dried adzuki beans, soaked for 4-8 hours in 6 cups of water * *(see note)*
3 cups water
1-5-inch piece of kombu seaweed, rinsed
¼ tsp unrefined sea salt (may substitute Himalayan salt)
1 TBS olive oil (may substitute unrefined sesame oil)
1 medium onion, diced
2-3 garlic cloves, minced
1 TBS grated ginger
1 tsp ground cumin
1 tsp tamari (may substitute shoyu soy sauce)
1 TBS miso paste (I like mellow white or sweet miso)
1 TBS lemon juice
2 TBS minced parsley
2 TBS minced cilantro

Drain the beans and discard soak water (use to water your house plants). Place beans in a large soup pot with 3 cups of water and the kombu seaweed. Bring to a boil over high heat. Reduce the heat to medium-low, cover and simmer for 1 ½ hours, or until beans are tender (it may take more or less time depending on how old the beans are). Add more water if needed. Stir in the salt and simmer uncovered for 5 minutes more. Turn off heat. Remove the kombu seaweed and chop it into small pieces then return it to the beans. Drain the beans, reserving any cooking liquid, and set aside.

Meanwhile, in a medium skillet, heat the oil over medium heat. Add the onion, garlic, ginger and cumin and sauté for 3 to 5 minutes, or until softened. Stir in the tamari and a couple tablespoons of the reserved broth. Turn off the heat. Whisk together the miso and lemon juice, then add it to the onion mixture. Add this to the beans and toss with the minced parsley and cilantro. Now you can either mash or purée everything to make a spread OR serve as is (without mashing) over whole grains with a side of roasted squash.

You can use canned adzuki beans to make this recipe go faster. Just look for organic beans. I like the Eden brand.

"I don't understand why asking people to eat a well-balanced vegetarian diet is considered drastic, while it's medically conservative to cut people open or put them on powerful cholesterol-lowering drugs for the rest of their lives."

~ Dr. Dean Ornish in "Healthy at 100"

Tempeh

Originating in Indonesia, tempeh is made by naturally culturing and fermenting whole soybeans. It differs from tofu in that it uses the whole soybean and undergoes a fermentation process, which make it nutritionally superior to unfermented and refined soy foods. Tofu is made from coagulated soy milk so it is not a whole food. Diets high in refined foods are linked to health problems so aim to have nearly all of your foods be whole, and when it comes to soy always choose whole and fermented soy foods (tempeh, miso and natto) to avoid the health risks associated with processed soy (see more on pg. 7). Tempeh is high in protein, fiber, healthy fat, vitamins and the beneficial antioxidant isoflavone. Tempeh can be used to replace meat in most recipes. It can be marinated, baked, grilled, stir-fried, cubed and crumbled to provide wonderful texture and heartiness to any meal. However, in order to be able to digest tempeh you must cook it first before using in a recipe.

How to Prepare Tempeh

Always boil tempeh for 15 minutes in enough water to cover the tempeh by an inch. You can also add a 5-inch strip of kombu seaweed and 1 TBS grated ginger to help aid in digestion. Also 1-2 cloves of pressed garlic add a nice flavor to this otherwise plain tasting protein. Flavorings are up to you, the most important thing to remember is to boil it for 15 minutes then discard the cooking water before proceeding with any recipe. This will reduce the strong flavor of tempeh and also make it easier to digest.

GF

Some tempeh contains added whole grains and seasonings. If you have a sensitivity to gluten read your labels to make sure the tempeh you purchase is gluten-free.

CURRIED BROCCOLI-TEMPEH SALAD

SERVES 4-6

Broccoli, like other cruciferous vegetables, is high in sulforaphane glucosinolate, an anti-cancer nutrient. Low in calories but high in fiber, vitamin C, vitamin A, vitamin K, folate and calcium, this vegetable is best eaten raw or lightly steamed to retain its healing powers.

4 oz. tempeh, cut into small dice
4 cups broccoli florets (about 1 inch or smaller in size)
1 tsp tamari or shoyu soy sauce (may substitute 1/8 tsp unrefined sea salt)
½ cup diced onion, any kind
½ cup dried pitted cherries, coarsely chopped (may substitute dried cranberries)
¼ cup raw sunflower seeds
¼ cup raw cashews, coarsely chopped
½ cup almond or cashew mayo (see pg. 193-4)
2 tsp curry powder
2 TBS apple cider vinegar (may substitute lemon juice)

Boil the tempeh in water to cover for 15 minutes. Discard cooking water. Let tempeh cool. Steam the broccoli for 3 minutes then remove and rinse under cold water to stop the cooking process. Set aside to drain. Toss tempeh with the tamari. Add the drained broccoli, onion, dried cherries, sunflower seeds and cashews. In a small bowl whisk together the mayo, curry powder and vinegar. Pour this dressing over salad, toss to coat and taste for salt. Chill before serving.

This tastes best if made at least 4 hours in advance and allowed to chill.

Nice as a sandwich filling or on top of your favorite whole grain.

TEMPEH SAUSAGE

SERVES 4

There is also a similar recipe under "Breakfast and Baking."

1 TBS flax seeds, ***freshly*** *ground (may substitute chia seeds, freshly ground)* (see note)*
¼ cup water
8 oz. package of tempeh
1 tsp each ground cumin, onion and garlic powder
½ tsp each dried sage, marjoram and thyme
⅛ tsp cayenne
1 TBS nutritional yeast
1 TBS flour, any whole grain kind
1 TBS juice (may substitute date syrup, agave nectar or water)
1 TBS olive oil
1 TBS tamari (may substitute shoyu soy sauce)

Preheat oven to 350 F. In a small bowl whisk together the ground flax seeds and ¼ cup water and let sit for 15 minutes, or until thickened. Meanwhile, chop the tempeh into cubes and boil it in enough water to cover for 15 minutes. Remove the tempeh from the water, discard water, and place tempeh in a medium glass or ceramic baking dish. Use a potato masher to combine the boiled tempeh pieces with remaining ingredients, including the flax seed mixture. Use wet hands to form it into patties or meatball shapes. Place on a parchment lined baking sheet and bake for 25 minutes. Flip and bake another 5-10 minutes.

Always buy whole flax seeds and chia seeds and grind them yourself in a spice grinder or in a clean coffee grinder. This means buying the seeds whole, not already ground, and grinding only what you need as you need it. Once these seeds are ground they are exposed to air which causes the omega 3 oil in the seed to go rancid. Rancid food is not good for you!

If the mixture is too wet add more whole grain flour. If too dry, add a little water.

To clean a coffee grinder, place a tablespoon of uncooked rice (one way to use up any white rice you still have in your house) and grind it until pulverized. Throw away the ground rice and wipe clean. This will remove most of the coffee flavor and grounds.

MUSTARD TEMPEH, KALE, SWEET POTATO AND GOJI BERRIES

SERVES 3-4

8 oz. package of tempeh
1 5-inch strip of kombu seaweed
water
1 small head of cauliflower, chopped into small florets (see note)*
½ cup whole grain dijon mustard, divided
1 small red onion, sliced
2 garlic cloves, pressed
2 TBS grated ginger
1 cup vegetable broth
2 tsp tamari (may substitute shoyu soy sauce)
1 medium sweet potato, peeled and diced
1 bunch of kale, cleaned and chopped, stems discarded
¼ cup goji berries (may substitute Chinese dates)
1 lime, juiced
2 cups cooked brown rice
2 TBS hemp seeds, to garnish

Preheat oven to 375 F. Cut tempeh into 3 or 4 pieces. Place in a pan with enough water to cover. Add kombu and bring to a boil. Let simmer for 15 minutes. Remove tempeh from water and set aside to cool. Discard cooking water. Chop the cauliflower and toss with **half** of the mustard in a medium bowl, then move to a baking dish. Once tempeh is cool, coat both sides with the remaining mustard then place in the baking dish. Bake in the oven for 30 minutes. Flip tempeh once during baking. In a skillet over medium heat cook the onions, garlic and ginger in the vegetable broth and tamari for 2 minutes. Add the sweet potato. Reduce heat to a simmer, cover and cook for 10 minutes. Add the chopped greens and cook, covered, until tender, about 5 minutes, adding more broth or water if needed to prevent sticking (should not be soupy). Finally, add in the goji berries and lime juice and toss.

Make sure to cut the cauliflower into small pieces or it won't bake all the way through.

If there is any liquid left in the skillet strain off into another pan and whisk in a kudzu slurry (1 tsp of kudzu powder whisked together with 1 TBS water) and heat over medium-high heat until the liquid is thick. Use this as a sauce for the rice.

Serve on a bed of brown rice with the mustard baked cauliflower and tempeh filets. Garnish with hemp seeds.

IDONESIAN TEMPEH STIR FRY

SERVES 6-8

Listen to me now and believe me later: This recipe is GOOD!

½ cup lime juice
¼ cup date syrup, agave nectar or brown rice syrup
3 TBS tamari (may substitute shoyu soy sauce)
8 small red chilies (may substitute red pepper flakes, about 1 tsp)
4 garlic cloves, pressed
2 TBS grated ginger (see note)*
16 oz. tempeh, cut into thin strips, ***boiled*** *for 15 minutes*
1 onion, diced
1 medium head of broccoli, chopped (may substitute 1 bunch of broccoli rabe, chopped)
1 red bell pepper, cut into long strips
2 medium carrots, cut into ovals
½ can coconut milk, shake well before using
1 TBS kudzu root powder (may substitute arrowroot)
¼ cup cilantro, minced
2 TBS almonds, chopped
3 cups cooked whole grains (quinoa, brown rice, millet, wild rice, buckwheat soba, etc.)

Make the sauce by combining lime juice, sweetener, tamari, chilies, garlic and ginger in a blender until smooth. In a large skillet, cook the tempeh, onions, broccoli, bell pepper and carrots in the sauce mixture for 3-5 minutes or until the vegetables are tender. Remove all vegetables and tempeh from the pan with a slotted spoon to a large bowl, keeping the sauce in the pan. In a separate small bowl, whisk together the kudzu powder with the coconut milk and add to the pan with the sauce liquid. Cook over medium-high heat for a couple of minutes. The sauce will thicken. Turn off the heat and pour sauce over the tempeh and vegetables. Gently toss to combine. Top with cilantro and chopped almonds.

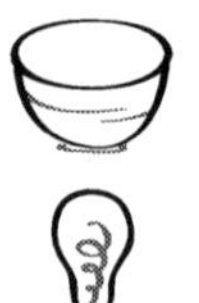

Serve over cooked whole grains.

Many times you will have little pieces of ginger leftover after you grate what is needed for a recipe. An easy way to use these up is to simply mince and place in a pan with water and let simmer for a few minutes and voila, you have ginger tea!

TEMPEH CHILI

SERVES 6

(GF)

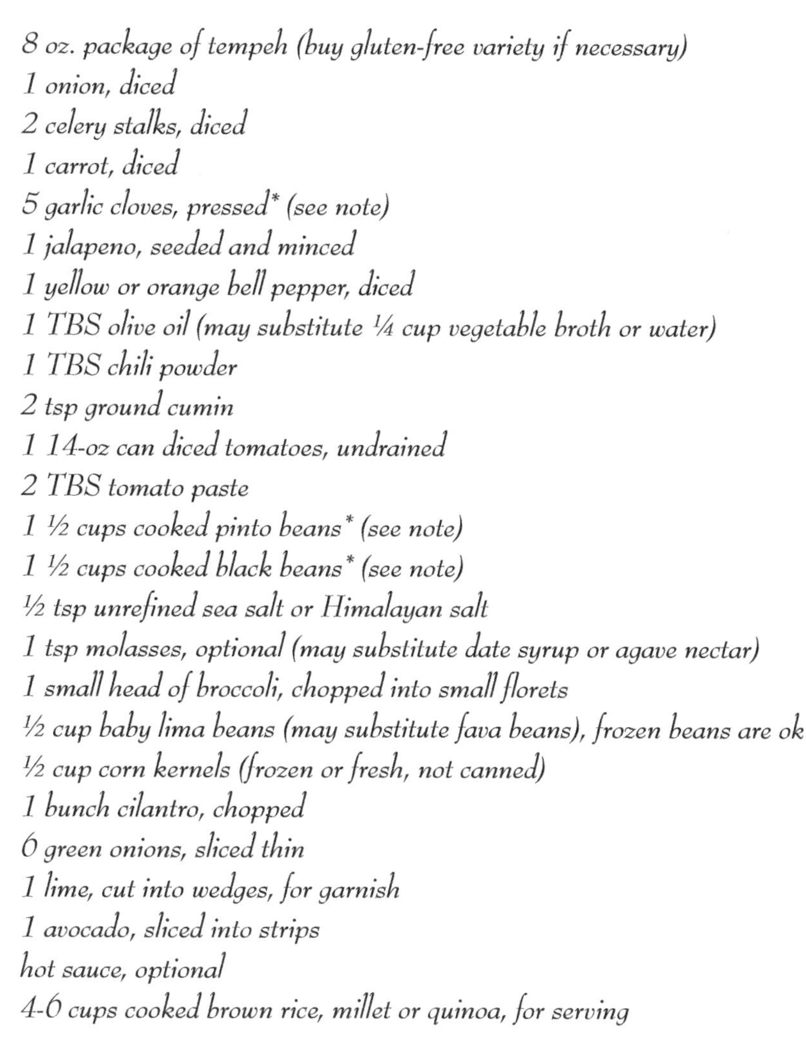

8 oz. package of tempeh (buy gluten-free variety if necessary)
1 onion, diced
2 celery stalks, diced
1 carrot, diced
5 garlic cloves, pressed (see note)*
1 jalapeno, seeded and minced
1 yellow or orange bell pepper, diced
1 TBS olive oil (may substitute ¼ cup vegetable broth or water)
1 TBS chili powder
2 tsp ground cumin
1 14-oz can diced tomatoes, undrained
2 TBS tomato paste
1 ½ cups cooked pinto beans (see note)*
1 ½ cups cooked black beans (see note)*
½ tsp unrefined sea salt or Himalayan salt
1 tsp molasses, optional (may substitute date syrup or agave nectar)
1 small head of broccoli, chopped into small florets
½ cup baby lima beans (may substitute fava beans), frozen beans are ok
½ cup corn kernels (frozen or fresh, not canned)
1 bunch cilantro, chopped
6 green onions, sliced thin
1 lime, cut into wedges, for garnish
1 avocado, sliced into strips
hot sauce, optional
4-6 cups cooked brown rice, millet or quinoa, for serving

Boil the tempeh for 15 minutes then drain off and discard the cooking water. Let the tempeh cool. Once cool enough to handle, crumble into little pieces with your hands or mash with a fork. In a large, heavy bottomed pot sauté the onion, celery, carrot, garlic, jalapeno and bell pepper in the oil (or broth) for 5 minutes over medium heat. Add the chili powder and cumin and stir to coat for 1 minute. Add the tomatoes and paste, beans, salt and the crumbled tempeh. Cover, reduce to low and simmer for 20-30 minutes, stirring every ten minutes to prevent sticking. Add the molasses, broccoli, lima beans and corn then simmer, uncovered another 5 minutes. Taste for salt.

Recipe continues on next page...

TEMPEH CHILI...

You could use canned beans but always look for organic. If you find the Eden brand canned beans you can use the liquid too. If the canned beans are not organic I would rinse and drain the beans before adding them to the pot.

Serve on a bed of whole grains, garnished with cilantro, green onions, lime wedges, avocado slices and hot sauce.

Always remember to press your garlic and let rest for at least 10 minutes on your cutting board to allow the cancer-fighting compound to activate.

MOCK CHICKEN SALAD WITH TEMPEH

SERVES 8

Broccoli sprouts are a powerful cancer fighting food. They contain 20 times the amount of the beneficial sulforaphane glucosinolate as mature broccoli. They look like alfalfa sprouts but are made from sprouted broccoli seeds. Try sprouting your own seeds if you can't find a store that carries the sprouts.

2 packages tempeh, boiled for 15 minutes
1 cup cashew or almond mayo (see pg. 193-4)
1 large carrot, grated and chopped
4 green onions, sliced, thin
2 stalks celery, diced, fine
1 TBS lemon juice
1 garlic clove, pressed
2 TBS minced parsley
1 package sprouted whole grain pita bread
1 TBS dijon mustard
*1 cup **broccoli sprouts***
tomato slices, optional

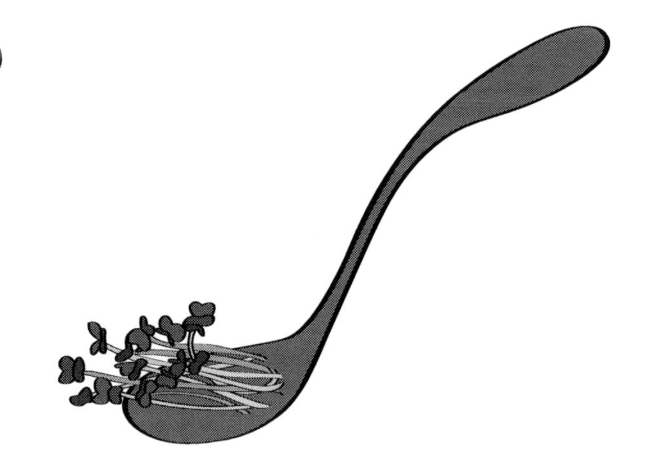

Boil the tempeh for 15 minutes then drain off and discard the cooking water. Let tempeh cool. Lightly toss the cooled tempeh with the mayo, carrot, onions, celery, lemon juice, garlic and parsley. Serve in pita pockets with mustard, broccoli sprouts and tomatoes. Enjoy.

TOKYO BAKED TEMPEH

SERVES 4-6

16 oz. tempeh, cubed and boiled for 15 minutes
2 TBS tamari (may substitute shoyu soy sauce)
1 TBS unrefined sesame oil
¼ cup freshly squeezed orange juice
¼ cup brown rice vinegar
2 TBS brown rice syrup
2 TBS grated ginger
2 garlic cloves, pressed
¼ tsp red pepper flakes (may substitute wasabi paste, to taste)
4 cups chopped vegetables (shiitakes, onion, broccoli, burdock, cauliflower, carrot, daikon) (see note)*
3 green onions, sliced
1 bunch of cilantro, cleaned, trimmed and minced
miso, optional, for serving (see note)*

Preheat oven to 350 F. After the tempeh has cooked for 15 minutes, remove from heat, discard the cooking water and place tempeh in a baking dish. Combine the tamari, oil, juice, vinegar, brown rice syrup, ginger, garlic and red pepper flakes in a bowl and whisk to combine. Pour over the tempeh and then top with the 4 cups of chopped vegetables. Cover with a lid (or unbleached parchment paper and foil) and bake for 15 minutes. Uncover and continue baking another 10 minutes, or until the vegetables are tender. Remove from oven, move to a serving plate and garnish with green onions and cilantro.

Cut the vegetables into bite-size pieces, approximately equal in thickness to ensure even cooking.

Anything remaining in the baking pan can be made into a sauce by adding a little bit of miso and whisking until combined. Add more orange juice if it's too thick. Serve this sauce on the side.

This dish is very satisfying when served over whole grains or buckwheat noodles.

BUCKWHEAT SOBA NOODLES WITH TEMPEH CROUTONS

SERVES 6

Once you have the tempeh crouton recipe up your sleeve you'll find yourself using it in lots of different recipes, adding different spices and flavors each time.

1 package of tempeh (8 oz.), cut into 1-inch cubes, boiled for 15 minutes
2 tsp tea seed oil (may substitute unrefined sesame oil)
1 TBS tamari (may substitute shoyu soy sauce)
dash of cayenne pepper or ginger powder, or both

8 oz. buckwheat soba noodles (look for 100% buckwheat)
2 cups broccoli florets, lightly steamed
1 cup of shredded carrot
1 red bell pepper, julienned
½ cup shredded daikon radish (may substitute cabbage, red or green)
½ cup mung bean sprouts, ends trimmed
3 green onions, sliced thin
1 bunch of cilantro, washed, trimmed, and chopped
2 TBS almonds, chopped

Dressing Ingredients
⅓ cup almond butter (see note)*
2 TBS lime juice, freshly squeezed (may substitute orange juice, freshly squeezed)
1 TBS date syrup, agave nectar, brown rice syrup or yacon syrup
¼ tsp red pepper flakes
2 TBS tamari (may substitute shoyu soy sauce)
¼ cup water
2 TBS toasted sesame seeds

Preheat oven to 375 F. Toss the cooked tempeh cubes in the oil and tamari. Add a dash of cayenne or ginger powder if desired. Bake on a parchment lined sheet for 25-30 minutes or until slightly crispy on the outside (it helps if they are not touching one another while baking). Remove from oven and set aside to cool. Cook the noodles according to package directions. Be careful not to overcook. Rinse with cold water and drain well, then transfer to a large bowl. Add the steamed broccoli, carrot, red bell pepper, daikon and cabbage. Toss to combine.

Recipe continues on next page...

BUCKWHEAT SOBA NOODLES WITH TEMPEH CROUTONS...

Whisk the dressing ingredients together and toss with the noodles and tempeh croutons. Top with bean sprouts, green onions, cilantro and almonds. Serve at room temperature or chilled.

You can omit the nut butter if desired. Just combine the lime juice, sweetener, red pepper flakes and tamari in a bowl and whisk to combine. You won't need the water but you may want to add more juice for flavor. Taste, and then add the toasted sesame seeds.

KALE AND TEMPEH WITH ORANGE MISO GLAZE

SERVES 6

16 oz. tempeh, cubed and boiled for 15 minutes
1-2 TBS grated ginger
4 garlic cloves, pressed
2 TBS balsamic vinegar
1 TBS tamari or shoyu soy sauce
2 tsp olive oil
2 bunches of kale (could sub. mustard greens, dandelion, chard, nettles, collards)
1 onion, diced
¼ cup vegetable broth or water
1 red bell pepper or carrot, thinly sliced
½ cup orange juice
2 TBS mellow white miso
1 TBS toasted sesame seeds or raw hemp seeds, for garnish

Place the drained, cooked tempeh cubes in a shallow baking dish with the ginger, garlic, balsamic, tamari and oil and let marinate, covered, in the refrigerator for 1-4 hours. Remove the stems from the kale and clean leaves in a bowl of cold water. Tear into bite sized pieces. Place the kale, onion and broth in a large pan and simmer, partially covered for 4-5 minutes. Remove cover and add the tempeh and its marinade. Cook uncovered for 2-3 minutes, adding a bit more water if necessary to keep from sticking. Once kale is tender and still bright green, add the red bell pepper and toss to combine. Turn off heat. Whisk together the orange juice and miso paste to make a slurry. Add to the kale and serve garnished with seeds.

TEMPEH BOURGUIGNON

SERVES 4

I don't always love the taste of tempeh. But this recipe is the best tempeh recipe in the book. How could it not be? It's bathed in red wine! Is red wine therapeutic? If it's organic (pesticide and sulfite free) and it makes you happy, then yes!

8-oz package of tempeh, cut into 1-inch cubes
2 cups dry red wine (Burgandy)
1 onion, chopped
2 carrot cut into ½ inch dice
3 garlic cloves, pressed
1 TBS tamari (may substitute shoyu soy sauce)
3 TBS olive oil, ***divided***
½ tsp herbes de Provence
1 bay leaf
3 TBS tomato paste
7 oz. sliced fresh shiitake mushrooms (stems discarded)
salt and pepper, to taste
3 TBS chopped parsley, for garnish
2-3 cups cooked brown rice, for serving

Boil cubed tempeh in enough water to cover for 15 minutes. Drain off and discard the cooking water. Combine the wine, tempeh, onion, carrot, garlic, tamari, 1 TBS olive oil, herbes de Provence and bay leaf in a large bowl. Cover, and refrigerate for 1-4 hours. Strain the wine marinade from the vegetables and tempeh, reserving the marinade in a medium bowl.

Heat the remaining 2 TBS oil in a large, heavy bottomed pan over medium heat. Add the tempeh and vegetable mixture (onions, carrots and garlic) and cook 5-7 minutes, until pan is dry. Then add ¼ cup of the reserved wine marinade and stir to deglaze the pan. Whisk together the tomato paste and the rest of the reserved wine marinade and add to the tempeh. Also add the sliced mushrooms. Reduce heat to medium-low, cover and simmer 20 minutes or until vegetables are tender, stirring occasionally. Add water, one tablespoon at a time, if mixture seems too dry. Season with salt and pepper. Sprinkle with parsley and serve over brown rice, while dreaming of France.

The Main Dish

"If beef is your idea of 'real food for real people' you'd better live real close to a real good hospital."

~ Dr. Neal Barnard

A FEW SAVORY CRUSTS...
Turn your dinner into something extra special by serving up a savory pie as the main dish. Use these different crust recipes and fill with your favorite vegetable and bean mixture. Experiment with different fillings found in the book or make up your own (I like using leftover roasted squash, beans and onions as a simple savory pie filling).

BARLEY AND CORNMEAL CRUST

MAKES 1 9-INCH CRUST IN A PIE PAN OR TART PAN

1 1/3 cups barley flour, plus more for kneading
1/3 cup yellow cornmeal
1/2 tsp unrefined sea salt or Himalayan salt
a dash of cayenne, optional
1/4 cup olive oil
1/4 cup cold water, more or less

Preheat oven to 375 F. Lightly oil a 9-inch round pie pan or tart pan (with removable bottom). In large bowl mix the flour, cornmeal, salt and optional cayenne with a fork. Gradually stir in the oil. With your fingertips, blend mixture until crumbly. Sprinkle in the cold water, one tablespoon at a time, tossing with a fork until mixture holds together when squeezed between your fingers and thumb. Knead dough for a minute or two on a lightly floured board. Roll out dough into a circle, slightly larger than the pan.

Carefully move dough to the pan and press dough evenly into the bottom and sides of the pan. Run rolling pin over rim to trim edges; use trimmings to patch crust if necessary. Pierce bottom of crust in several places with fork. Place pan in the oven (if using a tart pan first place on a baking sheet for easier transport) and bake for 12-15 minutes or until lightly browned. Let cool in pan on wire rack before filling, then bake again as indicated in your desired recipe.

You can place the dough between two sheets of waxed paper or unbleached parchment paper to make rolling easier. Just remove top sheet of paper before flipping the dough into tart pan, then remove the other sheet of paper-which is now on top!

HERBED CRUST OR DOUGH FOR POCKET PIES

ENOUGH TO MAKE 1 9-INCH PIE OR 4 POCKET PIES

1 cup whole wheat pastry flour
1 cup barley flour, spelt flour or any kind you have
2 tsp minced fresh basil
1 tsp minced fresh parsley
1 tsp minced fresh rosemary
⅛ tsp unrefined sea salt or Himalayan salt
dash of cayenne, optional
¼ cup olive oil
½ cup water, or more, if necessary

Crust

Mix the flours together with the herbs, salt and cayenne. Slowly drizzle in the oil while stirring until you have coarse crumbs (it helps to place a damp towel underneath the bowl to prevent slipping while stirring). Then slowly add the water while mixing until the dough forms a ball. Don't add too much water; you don't want it to be sticky. Add more flour if necessary and lightly knead the dough on a floured board. Roll out the dough to slightly larger than your pie dish and place in your lightly oiled pie dish. Cut away the excess dough folded over the edges of the pie dish and use your fingers or a fork to decoratively crimp the edges. Fill with desired savory filling and bake in the oven according to recipe instructions or until lightly browned.

Dough for Pocket Pies

Make the dough as indicated above. Divide dough into 4 sections and roll out each section into a circle, about ¼ thick or less. Place a couple tablespoons of desired filling in the bottom half of the circle, leaving room for crimping. Use water to moisten the edge of the dough then fold top half of the circle over the filling to make a semi-circle pocket. Use a fork to crimp and seal the edges. Make a slash in the top of the dough and place on a baking sheet to bake for 25-30 minutes or until lightly browned.

I always make more dough than I need, form the remaining dough into crackers or mini cups (in ramekins or muffin tins) and bake off to use for appetizers.

(GF)

MILLET CRUST

MAKES 1 9-INCH PIE CRUST

This is simple and gluten-free!

1 medium onion, chopped
2 garlic cloves, pressed
1 cup millet, rinsed and drained
3 cups water
unrefined sea salt or Himalayan salt, to taste (start with 1/8-¼ tsp)

Place the onion and garlic in a food processor and pulse until finely minced. You may have to stop and scrape down the sides of the bowl a couple of times. Place minced onion, garlic, millet, water and a little salt in a medium saucepan and bring to a boil. Cover and reduce heat to low. Let simmer for 30 minutes. Millet should be kind of like firm oatmeal. Let cool slightly then press the millet into a lightly oiled pie pan using wet hands to form a pie crust. Fill with desired filling and bake as directed.

SPINACH CRUST

MAKES 1 9-INCH PIE CRUST

1 TBS coconut oil, melted in a small pan if necessary
10 oz. frozen spinach, thawed and squeezed dry
½ medium onion, chopped
¾ tsp unrefined sea salt or Himalayan salt
¼ cup oat bran (may substitute rice bran)
¾ cup quinoa flakes
½ cup raw pumpkin seeds
½ tsp baking powder
a pinch of nutmeg, freshly ground on a microplane is best

Preheat oven to 350 F degrees. Oil a 9-inch pie dish. Process all ingredients in a food processor until combined. Then press into oiled pie pan. Bake for 15 minutes, then fill with desired filling. Bake again, protecting the crust with foil or a silicon pie crust protector, if necessary, to prevent overbrowning of the crust.

SAVORY SPELT CRUST

MAKES 1 9-INCH PIE CRUST

1 ½ cups spelt flour, plus more for rolling
½ tsp baking powder
¼ tsp unrefined sea salt or Himalayan salt
dash of cayenne, optional
¼ cup olive oil
⅓ cup water, more or less

Preheat oven to 350 F. Whisk together the flour, baking powder, salt and the optional cayenne. Drizzle in the oil while stirring with a wooden spoon (it helps to place a damp towel underneath the bowl to prevent slipping while stirring), until mixture resembles coarse crumbs. Then add the water, one tablespoon at a time while stirring, just until the dough is moist enough to hold together when pinched between your thumb and fingers. Move the dough to a lightly floured board and roll out dough about ⅛ inch thick and slightly larger in diameter than your pie pan.

Carefully move crust from the board to the 9-inch pan and press into place. Prick the surface with a fork in several places and place in the preheated oven for about 5 minutes. Remove and set aside until ready to fill.

CORNBREAD CRUSTED CHILI CASSEROLE

SERVES 8

*8 cups of **prepared** vegetable chili, with beans or tempeh (see pg. 301)*

Cornbread

1 ½ tsp egg replacer powder mixed with 2 TBS warm water
1 cup unsweetened almond milk (may substitute any non-dairy milk)
1 TBS lemon juice
3 TBS olive oil (may substitute macadamia nut oil or unrefined sesame oil)
2 tsp date syrup or agave nectar
1 cup whole wheat flour (may substitute barley flour)
1 cup finely ground cornmeal
1 TBS baking powder
¾ tsp unrefined sea salt or Himalayan salt
a dash of cayenne (or more)
½ cup corn kernels, fresh or frozen
3 TBS sun-dried tomato bits (cut with scissors until ½ inch or less) (see note)*
1 bunch of cilantro, minced

Heat oven to 350 degrees. Have the chili already made and place in the bottom of a medium casserole dish (about 8x8).

Cornbread Directions

Whisk together the egg replacer powder and water and set aside. Then in a small bowl whisk together the milk and lemon juice and let sit for 10-15 minutes. Then add the oil, sweetener and egg replacer mixture and whisk to combine. In another bowl whisk together the flour, cornmeal, baking powder, salt and cayenne. Add the wet ingredients to the dry and stir just until combined. Fold in the corn kernels, sun-dried tomatoes and half of the minced cilantro. Place batter on top of chili in the baking dish and bake for 35-40 minutes or until lightly browned. Remove from oven and let rest 5-10 minutes before serving. Garnish with remaining cilantro.

May substitute chopped olives in place of the sun-dried tomatoes, if desired.

CHICKPEA CASSEROLE

SERVES 6

2 ½ -3 cups cooked chickpeas, drained
3 cups broccoli, cut into florets
2 carrots, diced
4 medium shiitake mushrooms, sliced, stems discarded
1 small onion, diced
3 garlic cloves, pressed
1 ½ cups cashew cream (see pg. 195)*
½ cup amaranth, uncooked (may substitute quinoa but rinse and drain the quinoa well)
½ tsp unrefined sea salt or Himalayan salt
a dash or two of cayenne pepper
1 TBS minced fresh rosemary
1 TBS minced fresh oregano
1 TBS minced fresh basil
2 TBS minced fresh parsley, plus extra for garnish

Topping
¾ cup whole grain bread crumbs (see directions below)
¼ cup sunflower seeds (may substitute pumpkin seeds)
¼ cup sesame seeds
1 TBS oil (olive, macadamia or tea seed oil)

Preheat oven to 350 F. Prepare all ingredients, except the topping ingredients, and toss in a bowl until well combined. Add 1/4 cup water and stir. Transfer to a medium casserole dish. Cover with a lid or foil and bake about 50-60 minutes. Meanwhile, prepare the topping and place in a small bowl, stirring well to combine. Remove casserole from oven after 50 minutes, remove the cover and spread the topping evenly over the top of the casserole. Bake uncovered another 10 minutes. Let cool slightly before serving. Garnish with more freshly minced herbs.

Bread Crumbs

To make your own bread crumbs take about 4 pieces or more of whole grain bread (I save my bread ends and freeze them until ready to make bread crumbs) and tear into smaller pieces, about 1 inch by 1 inch. Place bread in a single layer on baking sheets and place into a preheated 300 F oven. Bake for 15-25 minutes (depending on how thick the bread is) or until the bread is toasted all the way through. Remove from oven, let cool thoroughly, then place in a food processor (in batches, if necessary) and process until you have bread crumbs. Store your bread crumbs in a sealed container in the freezer. Use within 2 month.

CARROT-BEAN-ASPARAGUS "QUICHE"

MAKES FILLING FOR A 9-INCH PIE CRUST

Okay, so not exactly like quiche, but this one is free of all the saturated fat and cholesterol that usually comes with traditional quiche. And it has asparagus, which is beneficial for removing toxins and excess water from the body. Also, in some studies, asparagus has been shown to help fight cancer and protect against heart disease.

6 carrots, scrubbed and chopped (see note)*
1 medium onion, chopped
2 garlic cloves, pressed
2 tsp curry powder
½ tsp unrefined sea salt or Himalayan salt
2 cups cooked white beans, drained
1 TBS egg replacer powder
2 TBS nutritional yeast
2 TBS tahini, optional
1 cup cooked garbanzo beans, drained
½ cup asparagus tops (2 inch pieces), cleaned well to remove sand
minced cilantro or parsley, to garnish
1 spinach pie crust recipe (see pg. 310)

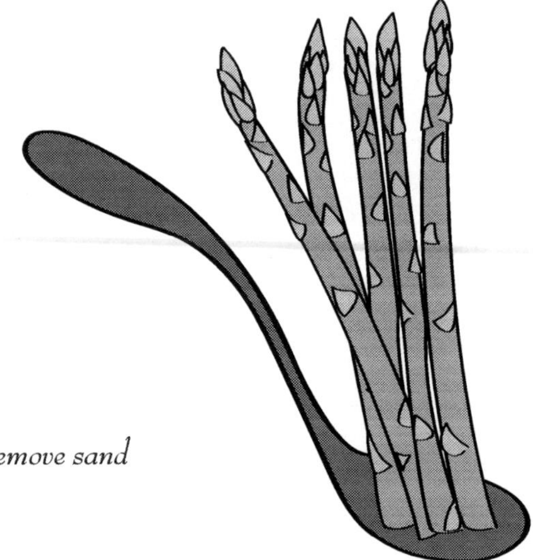

Preheat oven to 350 F. Steam the carrots until very soft. Reserve the steaming water. Cook the onions, garlic, curry powder and salt in a pan with ¼ cup of the steaming water over medium heat until onions soften and there is no liquid in the pan. Place the drained white beans, egg replacer powder, nutritional yeast, optional tahini and steamed carrots in a blender or food processor and blend until smooth. Add a tablespoon or two of the reserved steaming liquid if necessary to make it smooth. Now add the onion mixture and the garbanzo beans, pulse to combine but leave some chunks. Fold in the asparagus tops. Pour this mixture into the pre-baked spinach crust and bake for 30 minutes or until set.

You may need to protect the edges of the pie crust from browning too much by placing a foil ring or silicone ring around the exposed crust.

Recipe continues on next page...

CARROT-BEAN-ASPARAGUS "QUICHE"...

You could also use cauliflower in this recipe. Replace the carrots with 1 medium to large head of cauliflower and steam as indicated above. Then use peas in place of the asparagus.

You can decorate the top of this quiche with roasted cherry tomatoes, sautéed shiitakes, minced green onions, parsley, cilantro, etc. The possibilities are endless!

BRAISED GREENS WRAPPED IN PHYLLO CRUST

MAKES 1 PIE, ABOUT 8 ½ INCHES IN DIAMETER

To make this recipe go smoothly, you will need an 8 ½ inch spring-form pan, a pastry brush, a large flat surface and, if possible, a friend to help with the phyllo, preferably a friend like Deb - the co-creater of this recipe.

1 large onion, sliced into long strips
2 tsp olive oil
¼ tsp unrefined sea salt or Himalayan salt
2 lbs. of collard greens, chopped, stems discarded (may substitute chard, kale, nettles)
2 baby bok choy, sliced
2 cups chopped arugula
1 lb. of chopped frozen spinach
¼ cup sun dried tomatoes, cut into small pieces with scissors (see note)*
¼ tsp red pepper flakes, optional
1 medium to large lemon, zested and juiced
1 ½ cups cooked white beans, drained (may use 1 can of white beans, drained)
8-12 sheets of whole wheat or spelt phyllo dough, thawed properly
olive oil, for brushing, about ½ cup
2 TBS sesame seeds, tan or black
tahini-parsley sauce, for serving (see pg. 180)

Recipe continues on next page...

BRAISED GREENS WRAPPED IN PHYLLO CRUST...

Preheat oven to 375 F. Lightly oil an 8 ½ inch spring-form pan and set aside. Place the onions and oil in a large, heavy bottomed pan and stir to coat. Heat, covered, over very low heat for 30-40 minutes. Stir a couple of times just to make sure they are not sticking. Add a bit of water if necessary and continue to cook until the onions look and taste caramelized (brown and soft, but not burned, blackened or crunchy).* (see note)

Meanwhile, prepare the greens by washing and chopping them. Add the salt to the pan once the onions are caramelized and turn up the heat to medium-high. Add the collard greens and bok choy. Stir and cook for a few minutes. Once the collards are wilted but still bright green, add the arugula and stir to coat. Let them cook until wilted and add the chopped spinach, sun dried tomatoes and red pepper flakes. Stir and cook for two more minutes then turn off heat. Now take the white beans and place in a medium bowl or in a glass blender (no plastic). Add in the lemon zest and juice, plus any liquid remaining in the pan of braised greens (press the greens with a large wooden spoon while tilting the pan to pour off as much liquid as you can). If there is no liquid to be had, that is okay! Mash or blend the beans, lemon and braising liquid until smooth. Stir this bean sauce back into the pot of greens and stir to combine.

Get ready to oil the phyllo dough by taking two clean dish towels and dampening them with water. Also pour the olive oil into a small bowl and place next to your pastry brush. Take the thawed phyllo and remove from package. Place the sheets on a damp towel. Remove one sheet and place in front of you, then cover remaining sheets with the other damp towel. Lightly brush the sheet with oil, then carefully retrieve another sheet of phyllo. Again, cover remaining phyllo with the damp towel and place the second sheet on top of the first sheet.

Lightly brush with oil. Repeat process until 8 sheets have been lightly oiled. Carefully move all 8 sheets to the prepared pan so that it is centered over the pan. Gently press down on the phyllo around the bottom edge of the pan so there are no gaps between the phyllo and the sides of the pan. Now fill with the braised greens, gently pressing down on the greens as you fill the pan. Fold the phyllo ends into the center of the pan to enclose the greens. Sprinkle with sesame seeds and bake for 30-40 minutes or until lightly browned. Remove from oven and place on a cooling rack. Carefully remove the spring-form ring of the pan and let pie cool for 10-15 minutes before slicing.

Recipe continues on next page...

BRAISED GREENS WRAPPED IN PHYLLO CRUST...

For this recipe I recommend the dry sun-dried tomatoes over the ones packed in oil. It is not necessary to re-hydrate the tomatoes because they will absorb the moisture of the greens. Hopefully you have kitchen shears or scissors to make cutting the dried tomatoes easier!

If you don't have a spring-form pan you can use a regular pie pan. However, I would place unbleached parchment paper on the bottom on the pie pan so you can remove the phyllo pie from the pan after baking. Cut the parchment paper the same size as the phyllo sheet. You'll proceed as indicated above only you will bake the phyllo sheets on top of the parchment paper in the pan. Then fold in the phyllo sheets, but leave the parchment paper hanging out of the pan. Bake it until lightly browned and then remove the pie from the pan by picking it up by the parchment paper and moving it to a cooling rack. Then carefully pull out the parchment paper from underneath the phyllo (as if you were pulling a tablecloth from a table full of dishes, only gentler). Let pie cool 10-15 minutes before cutting.

If your pan is larger than 8 ½ inches, then you will need the extra four sheets of phyllo (each lightly brushed with oil) to place on top of the pie, like a lid, 4 sheets thick. I usually place this lid on top of the pie once I have it in the pan. Trim to fit the top, then wrap the sides up and over the lid so it is more secure. Top with sesame seeds and bake and cool as usual.

Slice the onion and get that cooking while you prepare the other vegetables. You want the onions to caramelize or cook so slowly that they eventually become naturally sweet.

TOMATO PIE WITH SPELT CRUST

MAKES 1 9-INCH PIE

1 Savory Spelt Crust (see pg. 311)
2 medium tomatoes, or 3-4 smaller tomatoes (see note)*
unrefined sea salt or Himalayan salt, for prepping the tomatoes (to release their juices)
¼ cup vegetable broth (may substitute water)
1 medium onion, cut into strips
2 garlic cloves, pressed
¼ tsp unrefined sea salt or Himalayan salt
1 tsp herbes de provence
¼ tsp red pepper flakes
1 bunch of collard greens, chopped, stems discarded (may substitute kale)
2 TBS balsamic vinegar
¼ cup uncooked bulgur wheat (may substitute whole wheat couscous)
1 cup cooked beans, drained if necessary
2 TBS Dijon mustard
2 TBS minced parsley
2 TBS minced basil
a sprinkling of lavender salt, optional

Prepare the crust as directed and set aside.

Slice the tomatoes about ⅓ of an inch thick. Gently remove most of the seeds then place tomato slices on a cooling rack and sprinkle both sides of the tomatoes with salt. You'll want to place a sheet pan underneath the rack because the tomatoes will begin to release their juices. I let them sit for about 20-30 minutes. Then rinse off the salt and gently pat the tomatoes dry with a clean towel.

Meanwhile, place the broth in a medium pan with the sliced onion, garlic, salt and spices. Let simmer for about 8 minutes over medium heat, uncovered. Add the chopped collard greens and stir. Cook another few minutes, until the greens are softened, adding more vegetable broth if necessary to prevent sticking. Once the greens are cooked, drain off any liquid left in the pan and reserve for another use. Add the balsamic vinegar, bulgur and beans to the pan and stir to combine. Spread the mustard on the bottom of the pie crust then fill with the onion-collard-bean mixture.

Recipe continues on next page...

TOMATO PIE WITH SPELT CRUST...

Lastly, top pie with the prepped tomato slices to make a pretty pattern (alternating colors is nice) and place in the preheated oven for about 25 minutes. If crust starts to brown too much, place a pie crust protector around the edge of the pie (or make one out of foil). Remove pie from oven and let rest for 10 minutes on a cooling rack. Sprinkle with the minced herbs and a dash of lavender salt, if using, and serve.

Seek out ripe heirloom tomatoes in different colors if possible.

I move my dough from the board to the pan by carefully folding the dough in half, then in half again (very loosely), then lifting the dough into the pan and unfolding it into place.

The herbed crust at the beginning of the chapter could also be used to make this pie.

POCKET PIES
SERVES ABOUT 6

These are great to take to work or on a picnic.

Dough

3 ½ cups barley flour, plus more for rolling (may substitute spelt or whole wheat flour)
4 TBS oil (olive, sesame, macadamia nut or tea seed oil)
1 TBS date syrup or agave nectar
1 tsp unrefined sea salt or Himalayan salt
1 cup water
cornmeal, for sprinkling on baking sheets

To make the dough, place flour in a mixing bowl and drizzle with the oil. Stir gently with a wooden spoon until flour resembles coarse crumbs. In a small bowl whisk together the sweetener, salt and water. Stir this into the flour bowl until the dough begins to form. Move to a floured board and knead until dough is soft and elastic, adding more flour if needed to prevent sticking. Divide into six small balls of dough and roll each one out to about 6-8 inches in diameter and ¼ inch thick.

Place a scoop (about 2 TBS) of your favorite filling (see mine below or make up your own from leftovers) in the center of a dough circle. Spread filling out evenly leaving about an inch border free for sealing the edges. Brush the perimeter of the dough lightly with water then fold the top half of the dough over the filling to make a half circle. Crimp the edge with a fork to seal. Cut a slash in the top of the pocket and place on a parchment lined baking sheet, sprinkled with cornmeal. Repeat with remaining dough and filling. Bake at 350 F for about 30 minutes or until lightly browned.

Be creative with your filling. Any bean and vegetable combination works or try fruit compote for a dessert pocket.

Make a bunch and freeze the leftovers for a rainy day. Let cool completely if freezing, then wrap each one in tightly and freeze for up to 2 months. To reheat wrap pocket in unbleached parchment paper and place frozen pocket in a 350 F oven until warm, about 30-40 minutes.

See another dough recipe on pg. 309.

Recipe continues on next page...

POCKET PIES...

Savory Bean And Creamy Vegetable Pocket Filling

About 2 cups vegetable broth, heated (may substitute water)
¼ cup dried shiitake mushrooms, preferably sliced
½ tsp unrefined sea salt or Himalayan salt
1 medium onion, diced
3 garlic cloves, pressed
1 celery stalk, diced
1 medium carrot, scrubbed and diced
1 small rutabaga, peeled and diced
1 medium zucchini, diced
1 medium yellow squash, diced
1 bay leaf
¼ tsp red pepper flakes, or a dash or cayenne
1 TBS freshly minced rosemary
1 TBS freshly minced oregano
1 TBS freshly minced basil
1 cup of cooked white beans
1 cup non-dairy milk, cashew is nice
½ cup white wine (may substitute vegetable broth)
2 TBS olive oil
2 TBS barley flour
½ cup peas
extra basil or parsley for garnish

In a small bowl cover the dried mushrooms with **hot** vegetable broth and let steep for 15 minutes. When softened, slice and if necessary, discard stems. Reserve soak water. In a medium saucepan or heavy bottomed pot combine the mushrooms, onion, garlic, celery, carrot, rutabaga, zucchini and yellow squash in a small amount of the reserved mushroom water. Add salt and cook over medium-high heat for 5 minutes, adding more liquid a tablespoon at a time when the pan starts to get dry. This is called a "water sauté." Add the bay leaf, red pepper flakes, herbs and white beans and stir to coat for 1 minute.

Meanwhile, in a medium bowl whisk together the milk, wine, olive oil and flour. Pour into the pot and reduce heat to medium low. Let cook until vegetables are tender and sauce is thickened, about 15 minutes. Turn off heat, remove the bay leaf and add the peas. Stir to combine.

Use as a filling for pocket pies or pour into a casserole dish topped with your favorite biscuit batter and bake until golden brown.

LENTIL LOAF

SERVES 4

You'll need already cooked lentils and millet for this recipe.

2 cups cooked lentils, any kind, drained well if necessary
½ cup rolled oats
½ cup cooked millet
½ cup onion, minced
1 medium carrot, scrubbed and grated
1 celery stalk, diced small
2 garlic cloves, pressed
1 cup tomato sauce (or the 'Un-Tomato' carrot-beet sauce purée from pg. 178)
2 TBS minced parsley, plus extra for garnishing
½ tsp unrefined sea salt or Himalayan salt
2 tsp dried spice (curry, Cajun, Italian, etc.)
2 TBS nutritional yeast, optional

Preheat oven to 350 F. Lightly oil a medium loaf pan. Combine all ingredients in a bowl. Add more rolled oats if mixture looks too goopy. It should look like cookie dough, not cake batter. Mix thoroughly and press mixture into prepared pan. Bake 50 minutes. Garnish with minced parsley. Let cool 10 minutes before slicing.

You can also make this in a muffin pan lined with unbleached parchment paper cups. Just reduce baking time to 30-40 minutes and let cool 10 minutes before serving.

CELTIC SHEPHERDS PIE WITH MISO GRAVY

SERVES 4-6

This recipe has a-whole-lotta healthiness going on.

Roasted Vegetables

1 medium onion, diced
1 small head of broccoli, cut into bite sized florets
½ head of cauliflower, cut into bite sized florets
1 cup of chopped green cabbage
1 medium turnip, scrubbed and diced
2 carrots, diced
2 cups of shiitake mushrooms, sliced, stems discarded
½ cup frozen peas
2 TBS olive oil
¼ tsp unrefined sea salt or Himalayan salt

Wash and chop the vegetables as indicated. Place in a medium casserole dish and toss well with olive oil and salt. Roast for ½ hour at 375 F, stirring occasionally.

Miso Gravy

4 TBS flour
2 TBS olive oil
1 cup vegetable broth
1 tsp Dijon mustard
3 garlic cloves, pressed
3 TBS miso (I like mellow white miso), whisked together with 2 TBS water
½ -¾ cup nutritional yeast

Put the flour and oil in a heavy bottomed pan and whisk over medium heat until the flour begins to smell nutty. Slowly pour in the broth while whisking and bring to a boil. Stir in the mustard and the pressed garlic and let simmer for about 2 minutes. Turn off the heat and whisk in the miso slurry and the nutritional yeast.

Whipped Potatoes

2 medium yukon gold potatoes, scrubbed and chopped (don't peel)
2 medium rutabaga, peeled and chopped

Recipe continues on next page...

CELTIC SHEPHERDS PIE WITH MISO GRAVY...

4 garlic cloves, pressed
½ tsp unrefined sea salt or Himalayan salt
2 TBS olive oil

Place potatoes, rutabaga, garlic and salt in a large pot with enough cool water to cover. Bring to a boil and then reduce to a simmer. Cook for about 10 minutes or until tender. Move potatoes/ rutabaga and garlic to a glass bowl or another pan with a slotted spoon, reserving the cooking water. Mash the potatoes/rutabaga with a potato masher. Add about ¼ cup of the reserved cooking water and the olive oil and mash again, until almost smooth. It may be necessary to add a bit more cooking water to make smooth. Add salt to taste.

To Assemble
Once the vegetables have been roasted, spread the mashed potatoes on top of the roasted vegetable in the baking dish and bake for another 10 minutes, uncovered. Remove and let cool ten minutes before serving. Serve topped with the miso gravy.

D.I.Y. BURRITO BAR

This is fun for feeding a big crowd because everyone gets to put together their idea of a perfect burrito.

Sprouted whole grain tortillas (can warm them in a dry skillet for a few minutes)
Your favorite salsa (see note)*
Avocado slices or guacamole
Mixed greens or shredded cabbage tossed in lime juice
Brown rice or Quinoa
Minced green or red onions
Black beans or pinto beans
Organic corn
Minced cilantro
Steamed yam and broccoli pieces
Hot sauce, optional

I like mango-green apple salsa (chop and mix tomato, red onion, green apple, cilantro, mango, jalapeno, salt, and lime).

BLACK BEAN AND GARLIC BURRITO

SERVES 2-3

1 cup fresh shiitake mushrooms, cleaned, chopped, stems discarded
1 tsp olive oil
1 garlic clove, pressed
dash of unrefined sea salt or Himalayan salt
1 can of black beans, drained, reserving the liquid if organic
1 cup broccoli florets
2 garlic cloves, pressed
1 tomato, or 2 tomatillos, diced
1 bell pepper, any color, diced, (may substitute 1 carrot, grated)
hot sauce, optional
1 lemon
sprouted whole grain tortillas, 1 per person (see note)*
1 avocado, sliced
mixed greens (may substitute broccoli sprouts)
salsa, optional, on the side
cashew sour cream, optional, on the side (see pg. 196)

Sauté the shiitakes in a skillet with the olive oil, 1 garlic clove and a dash of salt for 3-5 minutes over medium heat. Then set aside. Heat the black beans and broccoli florets in a separate pan over medium heat with 2 cloves of pressed garlic and some of the reserved bean liquid or water (about 1 TBS). Cook for 5 minutes, stirring now and then to prevent sticking. Remove beans from the heat and add tomatoes, bell pepper, hot sauce (to taste) and a squeeze of lemon juice and stir to combine.

Heat tortillas in a dry skillet over medium heat just to soften and heat through, about 2 minutes on each side. Make your own burrito by filling with some bean mixture, mushrooms, avocado slices and mixed greens. Roll up and serve with salsa or cashew sour cream on the side.

Please seek out a sprouted tortilla or a whole grain tortilla at your local health food store. There are many varieties out there besides the unhealthy white flour tortilla. And, as always, avoid any tortilla containing partially hydrogenated oil!

LENTIL DAHL WRAPS

SERVES 4

1 medium onion, chopped
1 TBS freshly grated ginger
1 cup red lentils, sorted through to remove stones, then rinsed and drained
3 cups water
¼ tsp red pepper flakes
1 tsp ground cumin
½ tsp turmeric
1 cinnamon stick
1 lemon or lime, juiced
½ tsp unrefined sea salt or Himalayan salt
4 sprouted whole-grain tortillas
1 cup grated carrots
1 small cucumber, sliced
2 cups mixed greens, spinach or arugula (may substitute broccoli sprouts)
1 bunch of cilantro, washed and minced
yogurt mint sauce, for serving *(see pg. 172)*

Place the onion, ginger, lentils, water, red pepper flakes, cumin, turmeric and cinnamon in a medium pot. Bring to a boil, then reduce to medium low and let simmer for about 30 minutes, removing any foam that forms on top of the water. Once the lentils are cooked through (may take longer at higher altitudes) and all the water has been absorbed (be careful not to let them burn!), add the lemon or lime juice, to taste, plus the salt. Cook for another few minutes to combine. Remove the cinnamon stick, turn off the heat and let the lentils cool.

Once cooled, warm the tortillas by placing them in a dry skillet over medium high heat for about 2 minutes on each side (don't let them get crispy or you won't be able to roll them up). Spread about ½ cup of lentil dahl in each tortilla and follow with ¼ cup grated carrots, some cucumber slices, mixed greens and cilantro. Fold sides in and roll the tortilla up and secure with a toothpick until ready to serve. Serve with a side of vegan yogurt mint sauce.

Add some cooked brown rice to these wraps and any other vegetables you desire.

Make the dahl ahead of time and let cool before assembling wraps.

PEACEFUL PIZZA

SERVES 4

Make your own pizza on whole grain pita bread, sprouted tortillas or cornmeal crusts and top with tomato sauce, pesto or hummus, then choose from a variety of toppings below. Assemble, bake until crust is heated to your liking and serve.

sliced roasted potatoes
sun-dried tomatoes
olives
roasted cauliflower, squash, or onions
steamed broccoli or arugula
marinated mushrooms
seitan or tempeh sausage (no TVP, or TSP, or soy protein isolate please)
chopped basil, parsley, oregano
pressed garlic
nutritional yeast, Walnut Parmesan (see pg. 200) or Pine-Nut Cheese (see pg. 139)

SQUASHED SPINACH PATTIES (GF)

MAKES ABOUT 8 4-INCH PATTIES

10 oz. of spinach (fresh or frozen), chopped
½ of a small kabocha squash, a.k.a. Japanese pumpkin, ***roasted***
1 tsp favorite spice mix (Cajun, curry, etc.)
¼ tsp unrefined sea salt or Himalayan salt

Preheat the oven to 350 F. Line a sheet pan with unbleached parchment paper. Place the chopped spinach in a pan with a couple tablespoons of water. Let spinach cook a few minutes, while stirring, until wilted. Remove the seeds and skin from the roasted kabocha squash (if you haven't already done so) and chop into bite-size pieces. Scoop the wilted spinach out of the pan, leaving any remaining water in the pan for another use (in a soup), and place the spinach in a mixing bowl with the chopped squash. Using a potato masher mash the squash, spinach, spices and salt together until well combined. Now form mixture into small pancakes or patties and place on the lined baking sheet. Moisten hands with water to keep mixture from sticking to hands. Bake in a 350 F oven for 20 minutes or until lightly browned. Remove and let cool before serving.

MO-CHEEZE PIZZA POCKETS

MAKES 6 POCKETS

4 oz. of mochi, grated (see note)*
½ onion, chopped
4 basil leaves, minced
1 TBS chopped fresh oregano, or 1 tsp dried
1½ cups chopped arugula
6 sprouted grain tortillas
14 oz. of pizza sauce or tomato sauce
6 garlic cloves, pressed
2 TBS nutritional yeast

Preheat oven to 450 F. Prepare 6 sheets of unbleached parchment paper roughly about the size of the tortilla, but square, not round. Grate the mochi just as you would grate cheese. Prepare the onion, basil, oregano and arugula. Now that everything is ready take a tortilla and place about ⅓ cup of chopped arugula in the center of the tortilla. Then add a tablespoon of chopped onion, a sprinkle of basil and oregano, followed by 2 tablespoons of tomato sauce, then press 1 clove of garlic over the sauce. Next add about ¼ cup or less of grated mochi. Sprinkle on a little bit of nutritional yeast, about 1 teaspoon. Then finish with another tablespoon or so of the sauce.

Fold in the sides, then the top and bottom so that you have an enclosed pocket. Wrap this in the parchment paper and place on a baking sheet. Repeat with the remaining tortillas until all are filled. Bake in a 450 F oven for 15 minutes. Remove and let cool before eating. The mochi will have melted and will be VERY HOT!!!!!!!

Mochi is made from pounded brown rice. It can be found in the refrigerated section of your health food store, usually in packages of about 12 oz. Use plain mochi or garlic-sesame mochi.

It's much easier to grate the mochi if it's at room temperature so take the mochi out of the refrigerator about 4 hours before you want to use it.

SPINACH ONION "QUESADILLAS"

MAKES 3 QUESADILLAS, SERVES 6

Onions contain allicin, which has been shown to help eliminate cancer cells from the body. To activate the cancer-fighting power in onions please chop and let rest for at least 10 minutes on your cutting board before cooking. All types of onions and garlic are beneficial so don't be shy. And if you are shy follow each onion and garlic meal with a handful of parsley to help freshen your breath.

6 sprouted grain tortillas
¼ cup water
1 onion, chopped fine
5 oz. of baby spinach leaves, chopped
¾ cup prepared hummus
¼ cup nutritional yeast
Harissa or hot sauce, for serving

Place the water and onions in a medium saucepan or skillet and cook over medium-high heat until onions are soft and water is almost all evaporated. Add the chopped spinach and heat until wilted, stirring often. Remove from heat, draining off any remaining water, if necessary. Add the nutritional yeast to the hummus and stir well to combine. Spread about ¼ cup of the hummus mixture onto a tortilla. Top with ⅓ of the spinach-onion mixture. Top with another tortilla and heat in a dry skillet over medium heat for 3 minutes. Carefully flip and cook for another 2-3 minutes. Remove to a plate then repeat with remaining tortillas. Cut into wedges and serve garnished with a drizzle of harissa or your favorite hot sauce.

The hummus mixed with nutritional yeast gives these a cheesy flavor while adding B vitamins, including hard-to-get vitamin B12.

CARROT GINGER PANCAKES

SERVES 6

2 TBS flax seeds or chia seeds, freshly ground then mixed with ⅓ cup water
3 cups shredded carrots (from about 4-6 medium carrots)
½ cup shredded zucchini (from about 1 small zucchini)
½ cup minced green onions
2 garlic cloves, pressed
2 tsp grated ginger
¼ tsp unrefined sea salt or Himalayan salt
¼ cup amaranth or oat flour (make by placing uncooked amaranth or rolled oats in a blender or coffee grinder and blend until flour consistency)
coconut oil, for oiling pan, if necessary

Preheat oven to 350. Line a baking sheet with unbleached parchment paper. Combine the ground seeds with water and set aside. In a large bowl combine the carrots, zucchini, green onions, garlic, ginger and salt. Toss well to combine. Then add the flour and the seed/water mixture and stir to combine well. Let sit for 5-10 minutes to let the flour absorb some of the moisture.

Then heat a skillet over medium heat. Lightly oil the pan, if necessary, with coconut oil then spoon about ¼ cup of batter on to the skillet. Press down very, very gently and spread to make a 4-inch pancake. If you press down too hard it may cause the pancake to stick to the pan. Cook for about 3 minutes on each side, or until lightly browned. Repeat until all pancakes are cooked. Now place the pancakes on the sheet pan and bake in the oven for about 15-20 minutes or until lightly crispy on the outside.

These go well served with cilantro coconut sauce (see pg. 171).

MUNG BEAN FLAT CAKES WITH GARLIC AND GINGER

SERVES 6-8

1 cup dried mung beans, soaked for 8-12 hours in 4 cups cold water
3 garlic cloves, pressed
1 TBS grated ginger
1 handful of mung bean sprouts
2 tsp umeboshi plum paste
1 TBS red Thai curry paste
1 tsp tamari (may substitute shoyu soy sauce)
water
5 green onions, minced
¼ cup minced cilantro

Drain the mung beans and discard the water. In a blender combine drained beans with garlic, ginger, bean sprouts, umeboshi paste, Thai paste, tamari and 1 TBS of water. Blend until smooth, adding a bit more water if necessary. Then move to a bowl and fold in the green onions and cilantro. Pour batter into pancake sized ovals onto a lightly oiled pan or griddle over medium heat and cook for 2-3 minutes on each side or until lightly browned.

Serve these with a spicy dipping sauce and a crisp vegetable salad.

LENTIL PATTIES

MAKES 16-20 PATTIES

1 cup millet, teff or quinoa, rinsed
½ cup red lentils, sorted through to remove stones, rinsed and drained
¾ tsp unrefined sea salt or Himalayan salt
¼ tsp red pepper flakes
½ tsp turmeric
3 ½ cups water
1 TBS unrefined sesame oil (may substitute coconut oil)
1 tsp cumin seeds
2 cups minced onion (can use food processor)
2 garlic cloves, pressed
cilantro coconut sauce, optional for serving (see pg. 171)

Place millet, lentils, salt, red pepper flakes and turmeric to a heavy bottomed pot with the water. Bring to a boil. Cover, reduce to a simmer and cook 20 minutes. Remove lid, stir to prevent sticking and continue to cook a few more minutes, if necessary, until there is no more liquid left in the pan (watch carefully so it doesn't burn at the bottom of the pan). Turn off heat.
In a skillet sauté cumin seeds in the oil over medium heat for 1 minute. Add the onion and garlic, stir to coat, and sauté for 10 minutes. Add onion mixture to the lentil mixture and stir. Spread this out on a large plate to cool until able to handle. Preheat oven to 350 F.
Line a baking sheet with unbleached parchment paper. Form lentil-onion mixture into patties (about 1/4 cup each) with wet hands. Place on baking sheet and bake for 25 minutes. Flip and bake another 10 minutes, or until done. Serve with cilantro coconut sauce.

These have a mild Indian flavor and are nice with a side salad or steamed vegetables.

Another Simple Patty Idea

Combine 3 cups cooked millet, ½ cup tahini, 1 TBS favorite dry spice mix (Cajun, Moroccan, Italian, etc.), ¼ cup minced parsley or cilantro, salt, to taste. Add a tablespoon of lemon juice if mixture seems too dry. Should remind you of cookie batter. Use wet hands to form into patties and bake on a parchment lined baking sheet in a preheated 350 F oven for 20 minutes. Flip and bake another 5-10 minutes or until lightly browned on the outside.

MOM'S FAVORITE VEGGIE BURGERS

MAKES 4 BURGERS

2 garlic cloves, pressed
1 TBS grated ginger
⅓ cup of ***hydrated*** *sun-dried tomatoes, chopped small*
¼ cup minced green onions
¼ cup freshly minced parsley
1 can of garbanzo beans, rinsed and drained (about 1 ½ cups)
1 can adzuki, pinto or black beans, rinsed and drained (about 1 ½ cups)
3 TBS flaxseeds or chia seeds, freshly ground
2 TBS tahini (may substitute almond butter or tomato paste)
½ tsp unrefined sea salt or Himalayan salt
dash of cayenne pepper
½ cup (or more) ***cooked*** *whole grains (quinoa, brown rice, millet or amaranth)*
4 whole grain buns
lettuce, broccoli sprouts, tomato slices, mustard, ketchup, pickles, kimchi, etc.

Preheat oven to 350 F. Place the garlic, ginger, sun-dried tomatoes, green onions, parsley, beans, ground flaxseeds, tahini, salt and pepper in a food processor and pulse to combine. Scrape down sides and pulse a few more times. You want the mixture to still have some texture to it, not completely smooth. Transfer to a bowl and add the cooked grains. Shape into patties using wet hands. Place on a parchment lined baking sheet and bake for 20 minutes, flip and bake another 10 minutes. Serve on buns with all the fixings.

If burgers seem too loose and won't form into patties, add more cooked grains to them. If too dry, sprinkle in a little water.

These are good with baked sweet potato "fries!"

I like to bake a few batches of these, let them cool completely on a rack, and then tightly wrap each one in waxed or unbleached parchment paper and freeze them in a freezer bag. This way I always have some on hand in case there's an unexpected barbeque party to attend.

BEAN BEET BURGERS

MAKES 12 BURGERS

2 cups cooked beans, drained and mashed with a potato masher (adzuki, black, pinto)
⅔ cup ground oats, sunflower or pumpkin seeds (see note)*
½ cup grated raw beets
2 TBS onion, finely minced
3 garlic cloves, pressed
1 tsp seasoning of choice (curry powder, Italian, chili powder, etc.)
1 tsp unrefined sea salt or Himalayan salt
3 TBS tomato paste (may substitute almond butter or tahini)
¼ cup nutritional yeast
½ cup or more of wheat germ (may substitute oat bran or quinoa flakes)
¾ cup sesame seeds (tan not white)

Preheat oven to 350 F. Combine all the ingredients, adding enough wheat germ to hold the shape. Form into 12 patties using wet hands. Coat with sesame seeds on all sides. Place on a baking sheet lined with unbleached parchment paper and bake for 25 minutes, flip and bake another 5-10 minutes, or until done.

Grind in blender or food processor until you have fine crumbs.

SOUTHWEST BEAN AND SEED BURGER

MAKES ABOUT 12 BURGERS

¾ cup raw sunflower seeds
½ cup cooked brown rice
1 ½ cups cooked black beans (or 1 can), rinsed and drained
2 TBS minced cilantro
½ red onion, minced or diced very small
4 garlic cloves, pressed
1 medium carrot, grated
1 small bell pepper, any color, diced very small (may substitute celery)
1 jalapeno, seeded and minced (use less if you don't like spicy)
1 TBS olive oil
½ tsp unrefined sea salt or Himalayan salt
2 tsp ground cumin
2 tsp chili powder
rolled oats, if needed

Preheat oven to 350 F. Line a baking sheet with unbleached parchment paper. Place the sunflower seeds in a food processor and process until seeds are ground, resembling bread crumbs. Remove and place in a large bowl with the cooked brown rice, black beans and cilantro. In a sauté pan, cook the onion, garlic, carrots, bell peppers, jalapeno, oil and salt over medium heat for 8-10 minutes or until vegetables are soft. Then add the spices and stir to coat for one minute.

Remove from heat and toss in the bowl with the beans and rice mixture. Use a potato masher to mash beans and blend ingredients together. Taste for salt and spice. Mixture should be thick and moldable. If mixture is wet or goopy, take about ½ cup rolled oats and place them in a food processor and process to make oat flour, then add oat flour gradually to the burger mixture until the mixture is no longer wet. If the mixture is too dry, sprinkle water into it while mashing with the potato masher. Once ready, form into 3-4 inch patties using wet hands. Place on baking sheet lined with parchment paper. Bake 25 minutes, flip and bake another 5-10 minutes.

Serve with all your favorite burger fixings!

TURKISH LENTIL BALLS

SERVES 6-8

1 cup coarse bulgur, rinsed (may substitute millet, quinoa or teff for gluten-free)
1 cup red lentils, rinsed and sorted to remove stones
1 onion, minced
1 tsp unrefined sea salt or Himalayan salt
1 TBS olive oil
2 TBS ground cumin
2 TBS tomato paste
½ tsp garlic granules or 2 garlic cloves, pressed
dash of cayenne
1 lemon, juiced
1 cup finely minced parsley
1 bunch of green onions, finely minced
lettuce or endive leaves, for serving
tahini sauce, for serving *(see pg. 180)*

Cook lentils and bulgur in 4 ½ cups water for 25 minutes over medium-low heat (or until cooked through - which may take longer at higher altitudes). Turn off heat and set aside. Drain if necessary, you don't want there to be any liquid left in pan. Meanwhile, sauté the onion in the oil and salt for 5 minutes over medium heat. Add the cumin and sauté for 1 minute, then add the tomato paste, garlic, cayenne and the lemon juice. Mix the lentil/bulgur mixture with the onion mixture in a large glass bowl. Taste for salt, adjusting if necessary. Let rest for 1 hour in the refrigerator or until cool enough to handle. Add parsley and green onions and shape into 1½ inch balls using wet hands. Serve on lettuce or endive leaves as an appetizer, drizzled with tahini sauce.

I have also baked these balls on a parchment lined sheet at 350 F for 20 minutes, or until lightly browned. I do this when I'm in the mood for something a little crispy and then serve it with toothpicks next to a tahini sauce. Either way is delicious!

BUCKWHEAT "MEATBALLS"

SERVES 6-8

I like this recipe. It is meat-free and wheat-free, and full of vegetables and lots of healthy ingredients that will make you feel like a hundred bucks. Plus it tastes really good!

2 cups cooked buckwheat * *(see note)*
½ cup cooked millet * *(see note)*
1 TBS olive oil
¼ cup finely minced onion
¼ cup finely minced carrot (may substitute red bell pepper or celery)
¼ cup finely minced shiitake mushrooms
2 garlic cloves, pressed
2 tsp Italian seasoning, dry
dash of cayenne
1 tsp unrefined sea salt or Himalayan salt
¼ cup finely minced parsley (or up to ½ cup)
2 TBS tahini or almond butter
2 TBS nutritional yeast, optional
2 TBS tomato paste
1 cup rolled oats or quinoa flakes, if necessary * *(see note)*

Preheat oven to 350 F. Place the olive oil, vegetables, Italian seasonings, cayenne and salt in a pan and sauté over medium heat for 5 minutes, or until softened. Take this mixture and place in a large bowl with the parsley, tahini, nutritional yeast, tomato paste and the cooled buckwheat and millet. Mix well (using your hands works best) and taste for salt. Add more salt if necessary. Form into 1 inch balls (using wet hands)* and place on a parchment lined baking sheet. Bake for about 30 minutes or until lightly browned and crispy on the outside.

Cook the grains by rinsing them and placing in a medium pan with 4 cups of water. Bring to a boil then reduce heat to low and let simmer for 15 minutes. Drain if necessary and let cool.

If mixture is really wet and won't form into round balls, then place the dry rolled oats in a food processor and process until it resembles coarse crumbs (not necessary if using quinoa flakes). Add 1 TBS at a time to the meatball mixture until you are able to shape into balls (using wet hands).

Serve with your favorite marinara sauce and whole grain pasta.

GF

LENTIL "MEATBALLS"

SERVES 6

1 ¾ cups water
½ cup lentils, any kind, sorted and rinsed
½ tsp each chili powder, basil, oregano, cumin and red pepper flake
2 garlic cloves, pressed
¼ cup sun-dried tomatoes, soaked in hot water for 15 minutes
¼ tsp unrefined sea salt or Himalayan salt
¼ cup finely chopped carrot
¼ cup minced onion (process in a food processor with the carrot)
½ cup minced parsley, cilantro or a mixture of them and arugula
1 ¼ cup rolled oats (or quinoa flakes for gluten-free), ground (see note)*

In a saucepan, combine water, lentils, spices and garlic. Bring to a boil, cover, reduce heat and let simmer over medium-low heat for 20 minutes. Meanwhile, drain the sun-dried tomatoes and chop into tiny pieces. After the lentils have cooked for 20 minutes, uncover them and add tomatoes, salt, carrot and onion and continue to cook until lentils are cooked through and all liquid is gone (higher altitudes may require longer cooking and more water). Mash the lentil mixture with a potato masher then add the minced parsley. Stir to combine then add most of the ground rolled oats and mix well. Let rest for about 15 minutes so the oats can soak up some moisture and the mixture is cool enough to handle. Preheat oven to 350 F.

Use wet hands to form into balls, about 1 to 1 ½ inches in diameter, adding more of the ground oats if necessary (or a sprinkle of water if too dry). Place on a parchment lined baking sheet and bake for about 20-25 minutes or until lightly browned and crispy on the outside.

Before adding oats to the meatball mixture you'll need to place the dry rolled oats into a clean and dry food processor and whirl until they resemble coarse crumbs. If using quinoa flakes you can skip this step. In your food processor first ground your rolled oats, then set aside. Second, add the carrots and onions and process those by pulsing and scraping the sides of the bowl once or twice until finely chopped (but not mush), then set aside. Third, add the parsley or other greens to the food processor and pulse those until they are minced.

Serve with toothpicks as an appetizer or serve on top of whole grain pasta with a vegetable marinara sauce for a super healthy rendition of an old favorite!

PASTA DELLA CASA

SERVES 6

I used to work at an Italian restaurant in Jackson Hole and everyday that I worked I would order the same dish, Pasta Della Casa. Here's a dairy free version of this simple, yet delightful dish. Yup, that's salad in the pasta sauce. Try it, you'll like it.

1 lb. of whole grain pasta
4 cups of your favorite tomato sauce
½ cup cashew cream, more or less (see pg. 195)
freshly ground black pepper, to taste
6 large handfuls of mixed salad greens, or arugula (1 large handful per serving)

Cook the pasta according to package directions and let drain well. Heat the tomato sauce in a pan and stir in a little cashew cream until your desired creaminess is reached. Continue to simmer gently, add the pepper and stir until incorporated. Turn off, add the salad greens and stir into the sauce to let them wilt down. Serve immediately.

If you're not going to serve all the pasta and sauce at one time, leave the salad greens out and add them to the heated sauce just before serving. You just want them to wilt into the sauce, so don't let them simmer in it or they'll get too soggy.

SIMPLY SUMPTUOUS GARLIC NOODLES

SERVES 3-4

Impress your friends with a super quick dinner that tastes amazing. They'll think you went to cooking school in Italy. It's a very simple recipe using ingredients that you probably already have on hand. Not your typical saucy pasta but different and delightful.

1 package whole grain pasta (I like brown rice spaghetti noodles)
4-6 garlic cloves, pressed
2 TBS olive oil (lemon infused olive oil is nice!)
unrefined sea salt or Himalayan salt, to taste (use less if the beans are already salted)
1 ½ cups of cooked white beans, drained well (rinse and drain if canned)
¼ tsp red pepper flakes (more or less depending on taste)
½ cup minced parsley
1 lemon, zested and juiced

Cook your favorite pasta noodles according to directions on package and let drain well. In a large skillet, heat the garlic, oil and salt over low heat for about 5 minutes. Don't let the garlic turn brown or it will taste terrible, so stir often and keep heat low. Then add the beans, red pepper flakes and parsley and stir to combine for 1 minute. Turn off the heat, add 1 tsp of lemon zest and a squeeze of lemon juice and stir to incorporate. Now toss with **some** of the noodles and taste, adjusting seasonings or adding more noodles if needed. Serve at once.

Don't forget to press your garlic and let it sit on the cutting board for at least 10 minutes before heating it so the cancer-fighting allicin can stay activated.

PASTA WITH LENTIL-TOMATO SAUCE

SERVES 4

Lentils are loaded with protein, healthy complex carbohydrates, fiber and minerals. They are naturally low in fat and full of flavor. Plus they are easier to digest than other legumes (beans) and require no soaking. They make a healthy substitute for ground meat in this recipe.

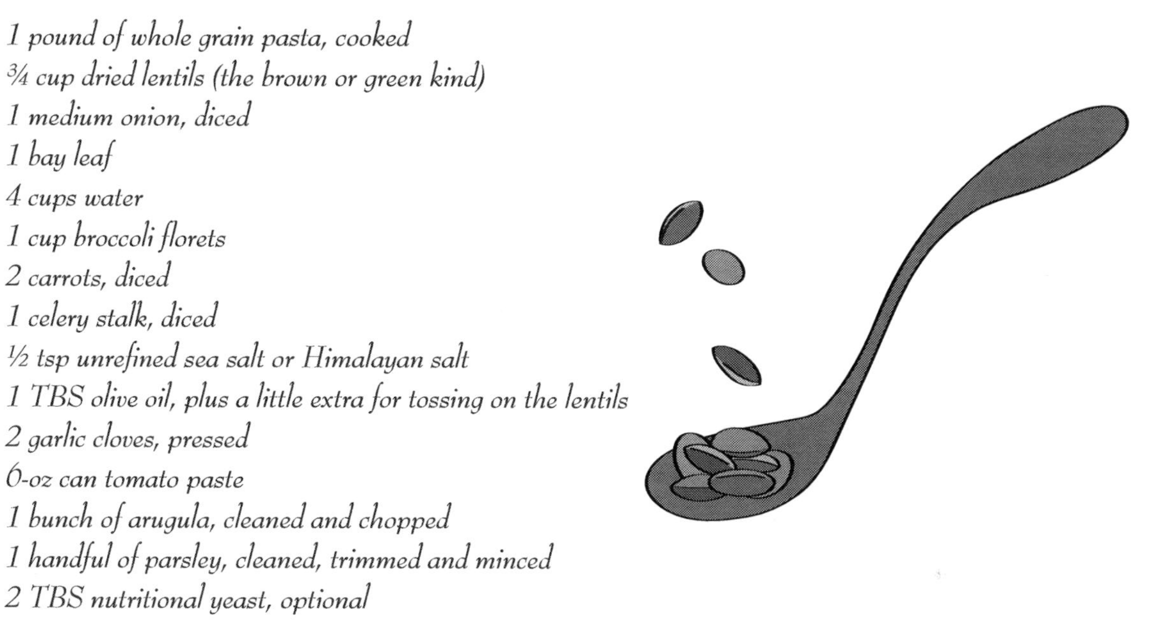

1 pound of whole grain pasta, cooked
¾ cup dried lentils (the brown or green kind)
1 medium onion, diced
1 bay leaf
4 cups water
1 cup broccoli florets
2 carrots, diced
1 celery stalk, diced
½ tsp unrefined sea salt or Himalayan salt
1 TBS olive oil, plus a little extra for tossing on the lentils
2 garlic cloves, pressed
6-oz can tomato paste
1 bunch of arugula, cleaned and chopped
1 handful of parsley, cleaned, trimmed and minced
2 TBS nutritional yeast, optional

Cook your whole grain pasta according to package directions, then drain and set aside. Carefully sort through the lentils, discarding any small stones, then rinse well and drain. Place the lentils, onions and bay leaf in a medium sauce pan with 4 cups of water and simmer, covered, for 25 minutes. Add the broccoli, carrots, celery and salt and simmer another 5-10 minutes, or until the lentils are soft but still hold their shape (higher alititudes may require longer cooking times). Carefully pour any remaining cooking water from the lentils into a glass dish to reserve. Remove the bay leaf. Toss the lentils with a dash of olive oil and set aside. In a small bowl whisk together the tomato paste with 1 cup of the reserved lentil cooking water until smooth.

In a large skillet heat 1 TBS of olive oil over medium heat. Sauté the garlic for about 30 seconds then add the tomato paste mixture. Let simmer for a couple of minutes. Then add the lentil mixture and reduce heat to low. Add the chopped arugula, cover, and let simmer for 3 minutes, adding a little more of the reserved cooking water if necessary to keep a sauce consistency. Taste for salt. Add red pepper flakes if you like it spicy. Toss the pasta with lentil-tomato sauce. Serve garnished with parsley and nutritional yeast.

EASY POLENTA LASAGNA

MAKES 9 SMALL PIECES

16 oz. sun-dried tomato polenta, (already prepared in a tube) sliced evenly into 18 rounds
1 jar of your favorite organic tomato sauce
2-3 cups of lightly sautéed vegetables (onions, garlic, peppers, zucchini, mushrooms, carrots, yellow squash, kale, beets, broccoli, etc.)
*1 recipe of **pine nut cheese*** (see directions below)*
3 TBS vegan pesto, optional

Make the pine nut cheese ahead of time and keep stored in a glass container in the refrigerator until ready to assemble.

Preheat oven to 350 F. Place a small amount of tomato sauce on the bottom of an 8 x 8 or 9 x 9 baking dish. Alternate layers of polenta, sauce, vegetables and cheese, then repeat. Top with pesto and bake, covered, for 30 minutes. Let cool for 10 minutes before cutting.

Pine Nut Cheese

Soak 1 cup pine nuts in water to cover for 4 hours. Drain, rinse and drain again, then place in food processor with 2 TBS lemon juice, 1 tsp mellow miso, 2 TBS nutritional yeast and salt to taste. Blend until almost smooth. This is Pine Nut Cheese! Feel free to add a small amount of fresh or dried herbs to your liking such as parsley, oregano, rosemary, etc.

TOKYO TORTILLA LASAGNA

G

SERVES 6-8

An interesting mix of my favorite Asian ingredients in a Mexican dish.

Adzuki beans are common in macrobiotic cooking for their flavor and nutritional benefits. They are low in fat, and contain healthy amounts of protein and fiber. They help reduce cholesterol, regulate blood pressure, and inhibit tumor development. They strengthen and nourish the kidneys, bladder and reproductive functions. Adzuki beans also help detoxify the body and reduce swelling and edema.

Enchilada Sauce

14 oz. can of tomato purée
1 TBS date syrup, brown rice syrup or agave
6 garlic cloves, pressed
1 tsp dried oregano
2 tsp chili powder
1 tsp ground cumin
a dash or two of cayenne
1 TBS apple cider vinegar
unrefined sea salt or Himalayan salt, to taste

The Filling

½ cup vegetable broth (may substitute water)
1 onion, diced
1 jalapeno, seeded and diced
4 shiitake mushrooms, sliced, stems discarded
1 4-inch piece of burdock root, scrubbed and diced
1 TBS grated ginger
4 garlic cloves, pressed
2 tsp ground cumin
1 tsp ground coriander
1 ½ cups cooked black beans, drained (or 1 can, drained)
1 ½ cups cooked adzuki beans, drained (or 1 can, drained)
1 carrot, diced
1 small head of broccoli, cut into florets
½ cup of corn kernels, fresh or frozen
unrefined sea salt or Himalayan salt, to taste

Recipe continues on next page...

TOKYO TORTILLA LASAGNA...

1-2 packages of organic corn tortillas (sprouted corn tortillas are preferred)
1 lb. of arugula, washed and chopped
16 oz. of hummus (sun-dried tomato, roasted red pepper, olive, something tangy)
1 small bunch cilantro, minced, for garnish

To prepare the enchilada sauce place the tomato purée, syrup, garlic, oregano, chili powder, cumin and cayenne in a medium saucepan and heat gently over medium heat for about 10 minutes, stirring often to prevent sticking. Stir in the vinegar and salt, to taste. Let simmer for another couple of minutes. Taste for salt, spice and depth. If it's too sour add a little more sweetener. You want it to be tangy and flavorful.

To make the filling place the water, onions, jalapeno, mushrooms, burdock, ginger, garlic, cumin and coriander in a large pan and heat over medium heat for 10 minutes, adding more broth if necessary to prevent sticking. Then add the beans, carrot, broccoli, corn and salt and let cook for about 5 minutes or until vegetables are tender. Taste for salt and spice and adjust if necessary.

Preheat oven to 350 F. Spread about ½ cup enchilada sauce to cover the bottom of an 8 x13 baking dish. Place a layer of corn tortillas to make the bottom layer of the lasagna. You may have to tear some tortillas in half to fit. It doesn't have to fit perfectly. Next spread about ½ of the hummus on top of the corn tortillas. Place about ½ of the bean and vegetable mixture on top of the hummus. Next sprinkle about ½ of the chopped arugula on top of the beans and vegetables, and finish by spreading about ½ of the enchilada sauce. Repeat by starting with a layer of corn tortillas, hummus, beans and vegetables, the arugula, and the enchilada sauce. Finish by garnishing with any remaining tortillas (torn into little decorative pieces) and sprinkling with cilantro. Cover the lasagna with a lid, place into the preheated oven and bake for about 30 minutes. Remove from oven and let cool for about 5-10 minutes before cutting.

LENTIL LASAGNA
SERVES 6-8

*2 cups **cooked** brown or green lentils, drained well*
12 lasagna noodles (spelt, brown rice or whole wheat noodles)
4 cups of vegetables (onion, garlic, shiitakes, carrot, zucchini, broccoli)
1 package of mochi, about 12 oz., plain or savory (see note)*
unrefined sea salt or Himalayan salt, to taste
1 TBS Italian spice mix
6-8 cups of your favorite tomato sauce
1 small can of tomato paste
¼ tsp or more of red pepper flakes
1 cup raw walnuts
2-3 TBS nutritional yeast
fresh basil and oregano, minced, for garnish

Preheat oven to 350 F. Have your lentils cooked and drained. Cook the lasagna noodles until they are al dente, then strain. After cooking the noodles I keep them in a strainer and occasionally sprinkle them with water to prevent them from drying out or sticking together in case I'm not ready to assemble the lasagna immediately. Meanwhile, sauté your vegetables in a large skillet over medium heat until tender (you can "sauté" in ⅓ cup water and a dash of salt instead of using oil). Take the mochi and cut into small cubes and place in a small saucepan with enough water just to cover the mochi cubes. Heat over medium-high heat while stirring with a wooden spoon. The mochi will begin to melt and get thick and gooey, like melted cheese. Add salt and Italian spices, stir and turn off heat. In another pan or bowl whisk together the tomato sauce with the tomato paste and red pepper flakes until incorporated.

To assemble, place a small amount of tomato sauce on the bottom of a 9 x 13 inch lasagna pan. Then place a single layer of lasagna noodles to cover the bottom of the pan. Top with ⅓ of the lentils, ⅓ of the vegetables, ⅓ of the mochi cheese and ¼ of the tomato sauce. Then repeat for 2 more layers. The last layer will just be the noodles and then some sauce. Cover the pan with unbleached parchment paper, then foil and bake for 30 minutes or until heated through. Remove from oven and uncover. Let rest for 10 minutes before cutting.

Meanwhile, make the walnut parmesan by taking the walnuts on a baking pan and toasting them in the oven for a few minutes. Watch closely so they don't burn. If they do, discard and start again. Once they are lightly toasted, place in a food processor with the nutritional yeast and pulse until it resembles coarse crumbs. Add a little salt, to taste, and pulse again. It should taste like parmesan cheese. Don't over-process or it will turn to butter. Top the cooked lasagna with the walnut parmesan and sprinkle with minced herbs.

Recipe continues on next page...

LENTIL LASAGNA...

When assembling you may substitute 2 cups of Pine Nut Cheese for the cooked mochi (see pg. 139).

If I have leftover ingredients I make lasagna roll-ups by taking a cooked lasagna noodle and placing a little of the sauce, vegetables and lentils on one end of the noodle, then rolling it up and securing with a toothpick. These can be messy but they make fun snacks. I don't usually put the mochi cheese in these roll-ups but instead I'll use a little walnut parmesan, or pine nut cheese, if I have some available.

(GF) MINI POLENTA PIZZAS

Make mini pizzas by taking tubes of already prepared polenta and slicing into ½ inch thick disks. Lightly brush both sides of each polenta discs with olive oil and place on a parchment lined baking sheet. Bake in a preheated 350 F oven for 20 minutes, then carefully flip each one and bake for another 10 minutes or until lightly crispy on the outside but still soft on the inside. Remove and top with your choice of sautéed vegetables, beans, tomato sauce, dandelion pesto and/or pine nut cheese.

TROPICAL LEAF WRAPS

MAKES 6 WRAPS

This is a perfect dish for a hot day.

6 large lettuce or shiso leaves (may substitute collards, kale or cabbage leaves) (see note)*
½ tsp toasted sesame oil
1 TBS date syrup, agave nectar, brown rice syrup or yacon syrup
3 TBS tamari (may substitute shoyu soy sauce)
1 garlic clove, pressed
1 TBS grated ginger
2 limes-1 juiced, and the other cut into wedges
¼ cup almonds, chopped small
2 TBS pumpkin seeds, rough chopped

Recipe continues on next page...

TROPICAL LEAF WRAPS...

2 TBS hemp seeds
2 Thai chilies, seeded and minced (may substitute Serrano chilies)
3 green onions, sliced
1 bunch of cilantro, cleaned and minced
½ cup shredded red cabbage
½ cup diced mango
½ small cucumber, peeled, seeded and diced small
2 TBS minced mint leaves
1 avocado, diced, then sprinkled with lime juice from 1 lime wedge
broccoli sprouts, to garnish at first, but then for eating

Prepare the leaves by cleaning them and removing hard stems or center stalks. If you're using collard greens, kale or cabbage you will need to lightly steam the leaves to make them more pliable.

To make the dipping sauce combine the oil, sweetener, tamari, garlic, ginger and the juice from 1 lime in a small bowl and set aside. Place the chopped almonds, pumpkin seeds, hemp seeds, Thai chilies, green onions, cilantro, red cabbage, mango, cucumber, mint and avocado in a large bowl and toss to combine. Place a small amount of this mixture in the center of each leaf. Fold in the sides and roll to close. Secure with a toothpick and place on a platter on top of a bed of broccoli sprouts. Serve with the dipping sauce and a side of the remaining lime wedges.

You could use pickled shiso leaves but be sure to thoroughly rinse off any salt and pat dry before using.

It takes a little practice to form these into perfect little wraps; so have toothpicks on hand to hold them together.

Save a little of the dipping sauce so you can sprinkle on the broccoli sprouts and eat as a salad.

JAPANESE MACROBIOTIC MEAL

- miso soup with adzuki beans, wakame, shiitakes and green onions and cilantro
- vegetable sushi with brown rice, tempeh and assorted vegetables
- pressed cabbage and seaweed salad with gomasio
- pickled daikon and ginger

MAKI SUSHI ROLLS

SERVES 6

1 cup short grain brown rice
1 cup red rice (may substitute more brown rice)
3 ½ cups water
½ tsp unrefined sea salt or Himalayan salt
2 TBS brown rice vinegar, optional
2 TBS brown rice syrup, optional
10-12 toasted nori sheets
assorted filling ingredients (see list below)*
wasabi paste and pickled ginger, about 1 TBS of each, per person

Place brown rice and red rice in a medium saucepan on the stovetop (or in a rice cooker). Add water and salt, bring to a boil, cover and reduce heat to low. Let simmer for 40 minutes, then turn off heat and let sit undisturbed for another 10 minutes.

"Sticky Rice" option: To make rice more sticky for rolling sushi take about a quarter of the cooked rice out of the pot and place in a bowl with 2 TBS rice wine vinegar and 2 TBS brown rice syrup. Mash to combine then mix this back with the rest of the rice. Spread out on a sheet pan to let cool. I've made these sushi rolls with this sticky rice option and with just regular cooked brown rice. Either way will work, this sticky rice version just adds a slightly different texture and flavor to the rice.

Prepare an Assortment of Fillings

- *Steam some greens (kale, chard, spinach, etc.) then squeeze dry and chop*
- *Slice a bunch of green onions*
- *Roast a yam or sweet potato then mash*
- *Marinate sliced shiitakes with lime juice, shoyu, mirin, garlic and ginger*
- *Shred a carrot, beet, daikon or burdock*
- *Cut a cucumber into 3 inch long sticks, about ¼ inch wide*
- *Boil and cube some tempeh, then season with teriyaki sauce*
- *Mince some cilantro*
- *Chop almonds or walnuts*
- *Slice an avocado and sprinkle with lemon juice*
- *Other filling ideas: umeboshi plum paste, broccoli sprouts, asian hot sauce*

Recipe continues on next page...

MAKI SUSHI ROLLS...

Have a bowl of cool water next to you (for sealing nori and to keep rice from sticking to your hands). Also, have all of your filling ingredients ready to go (mise en place). Place a nori sheet, shiny side down, on a bamboo mat. Spread about ½ cup of the sticky rice in a thin layer onto the nori, leaving about ½ inch of nori uncovered at the bottom of the nori sheet (closest to you) and at the top of the nori sheet. Place your filling ingredients along the bottom of the nori (closest to you), about ½ inch thick. Roll up the sushi by starting with the bottom (closest to you) and rolling away from you, making sure to roll it tight and even (go to your nearest sushi restaurant and sit at the bar to study how to do this!). When you reach the top, dab the nori with wet fingers to seal it shut. Then use a sharp knife to cut the sushi into six or eight discs. Place on a platter with pickled ginger, wasabi paste and shoyu soy sauce.

Pickled Ginger for Sushi

Ginger is a whole body tonic-it improves overall health. It has been used for immune system enhancement, to boost circulation, to reduce inflammation, to prevent platelet aggregation, to help treat nausea and to aid in digestion.

2 large young ginger roots, peeled (use a small spoon to peel away the ginger skin)
1 tsp unrefined sea salt or Himalayan salt
1 cup rice vinegar
4 TBS rapadura (unrefined sugar)

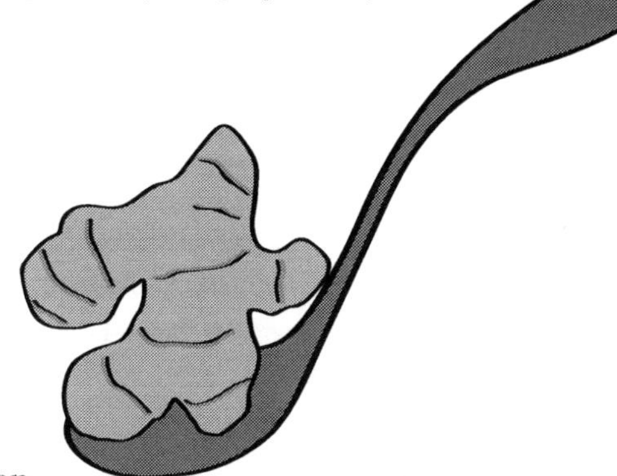

Slice into paper thin slices across the grain. Place ginger slices in a bowl and toss with salt. Let sit for 1 hour. Then rinse and pat dry. Sterilize a mason jar (big enough to hold the ginger slices plus 1 cup liquid) by submerging in boiling water for a few minutes. Let the jar drain on a clean towel. Then place ginger slices into the jar. In a medium saucepan mix rice vinegar with rapadura. Bring to a boil for 1 minute then pour the vinegar mixture over the ginger slices, making sure the ginger is submerged in the vinegar liquid. Cover and let cool. Then move to the refrigerator. Pickled ginger will be ready in 1 week and will turn pink.

Young ginger has thinner, smoother and lighter skin than regular ginger.

Pickled ginger will keep for 2 months in the refrigerator.

When serving, always remove ginger slices with a clean utensil.

ROASTED SQUASH FILLED WITH WILD RICE STUFFING

SERVES 6

3 small winter squash (see ntoe)*
oil, for brushing on squash (macadamia nut oil or tea seed oil)
½ cup wild rice, rinsed
1 cup brown rice, rinsed (see note)*
3 cups vegetable broth (may substitute water)
1 TBS grated ginger
½ cup finely diced celery
¼ cup finely diced carrot
2 firm pears, cut into ½ inch cubes
½ cup hazelnuts, chopped
1 TBS olive oil
¼ cup green onions, thinly sliced
¼ cup minced parsley
2 TBS fresh lemon juice
2 TBS dried cranberries, cherries, goji berries, or chopped figs (see note)*
unrefined sea salt or Himalayan salt, to taste

Preheat oven to 375 F. Rinse the squash and pat dry. Carefully cut each squash in half so that you have two "bowls." You may have to slice off a small bit from the tops and/or bottoms so that they will sit flat on a plate. Scoop out the seeds (and save for roasting, if desired) and rub cut sides of the squash with a small amount of oil. Place hollow side down on a baking dish and place in oven. Let roast for about 20-30 minutes or until a fork can easily pierce through the squash. Remove and turn over so they will cool.

Place the wild rice and brown rice in a medium saucepan with the broth. Bring to a boil, then cover, reduce heat to a simmer and cook 40 minutes. After 40 minutes, turn off heat but do not lift the lid for another 10 minutes. Meanwhile, sauté the ginger, celery, carrots, pears and hazelnuts in 1 TBS of olive oil for 5-8 minutes over medium heat or until tender. Turn off heat and add green onions, parsley, lemon juice and dried fruit. Toss and taste for salt. Stuff into the roasted squash halves and serve.

Recipe continues on next page...

ROASTED SQUASH FILLED WITH WILD RICE STUFFING...

There are many different squashes that can be used in this recipe: acorn, ambercup, autumncup, buttercup, carnival, delicata, gold nugget, green hubbard, kabocha (a.k.a. Japanese pumpkin) or sweet dumpling squash. Try them all!

You can also use heartier grains such as barley, kamut or spelt berries in place of the brown rice. Cook these with the wild rice but these grains require an additional ½ cup of water and 10-20 minutes longer cooking time. Unlike cooking rice, you can check on these grains after ½ an hour of cooking and then every 10 minutes to see if they need more water or longer cooking time.

If the dried fruit is tough, soak in water for about 5 minutes until softened, but not mushy. Then drain and pat dry before adding to recipe.

COCONUT CURRY WITH CHICKPEAS

SERVES 4

1 medium onion, diced
1 TBS grated ginger
½ tsp unrefined sea salt or Himalayan salt
¼ cup vegetable broth, plus more, if needed (may substitute water)
2 tsp cumin seeds, freshly ground in a spice grinder (or a clean coffee grinder)
1 TBS curry powder
1 tsp tamarind paste whisked together in 1 TBS water
2 kaffir lime leaves, minced, center vein discarded
1 cup seeded and diced tomatoes
2 cups cooked chickpeas (or use 1-2 cans, drained)
1 small sweet potato or yam, diced
1 cup of cauliflower florets
water
2 cups chopped kale
1 TBS lemon (may substitute lime juice)
1 tsp date syrup, brown rice syrup or agave nectar
½ cup coconut milk
1 tsp garam masala
4 cups cooked brown rice, for serving
1 small bunch of cilantro, minced

Place the onion, ginger, salt and water in a large pan and heat over medium heat for 5 minutes. Stir in the cumin seeds and curry powder and cook for 3 minutes. Next add the tamarind paste, kaffir lime leaves, tomatoes, chickpeas, sweet potato, cauliflower and water to partially cover the vegetables. Cover and let simmer for 10 minutes, stirring occasionally. Add more water, if necessary, to prevent sticking. Uncover and add the kale, lemon juice, sweetener, coconut milk and garam masala. Stir to combine and let simmer until kale is tender, about 5 minutes. Taste for seasonings, adding more salt, spice or lemon if desired and serve over a bed of brown rice, garnished with cilantro.

THAI PUMPKIN CURRY

SERVES 6-8

Kabocha squash (a.k.a. Japanese pumpkin) is preferred in this recipe for its texture, flavor and color, but most winter squashes or pumpkins will work. The kabocha squash, popular in macrobiotic cooking, is high in beta-carotene, vitamin C and fiber. You can eat the whole squash; skin, flesh, seeds and pulp.

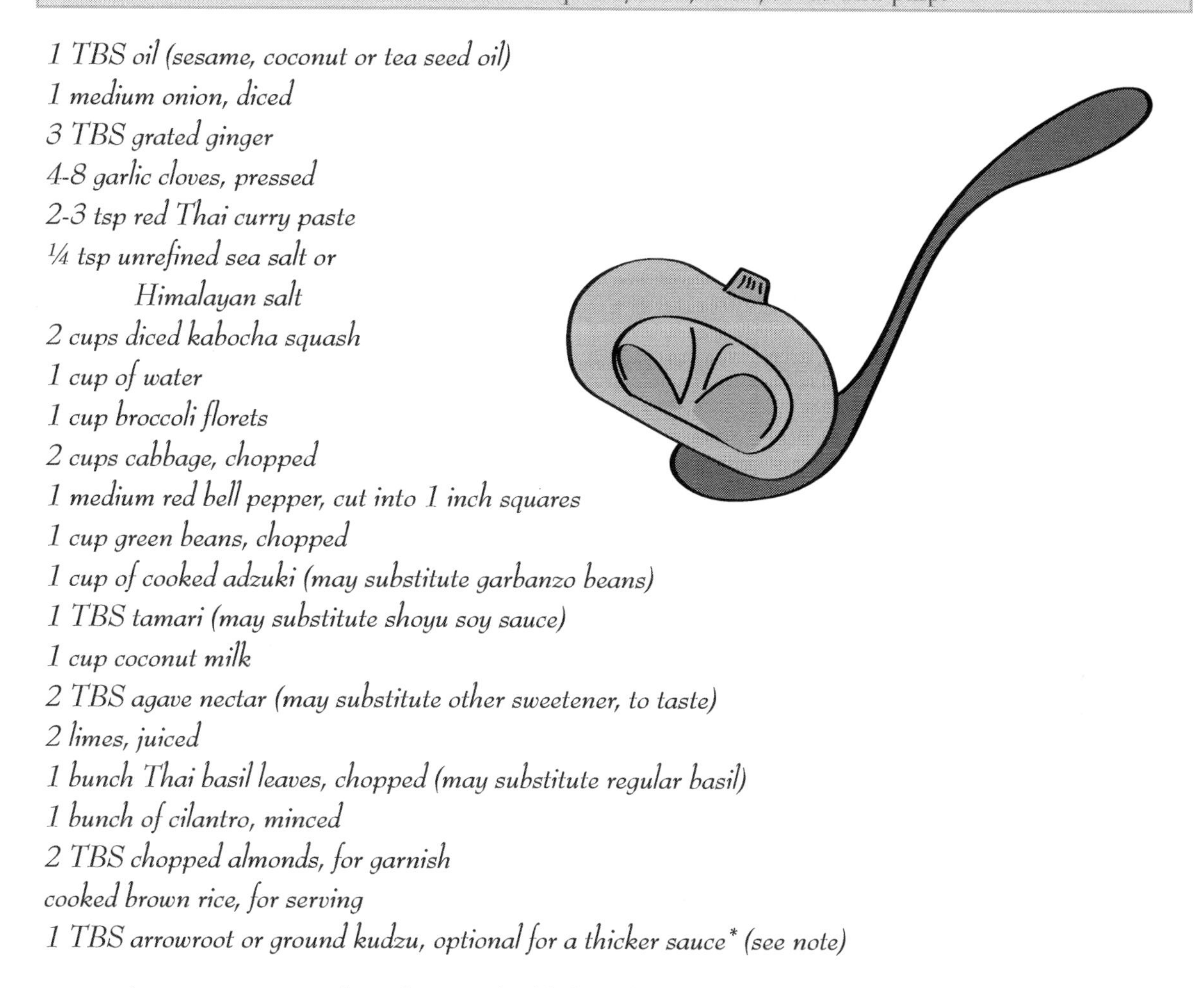

1 TBS oil (sesame, coconut or tea seed oil)
1 medium onion, diced
3 TBS grated ginger
4-8 garlic cloves, pressed
2-3 tsp red Thai curry paste
¼ tsp unrefined sea salt or Himalayan salt
2 cups diced kabocha squash
1 cup of water
1 cup broccoli florets
2 cups cabbage, chopped
1 medium red bell pepper, cut into 1 inch squares
1 cup green beans, chopped
1 cup of cooked adzuki (may substitute garbanzo beans)
1 TBS tamari (may substitute shoyu soy sauce)
1 cup coconut milk
2 TBS agave nectar (may substitute other sweetener, to taste)
2 limes, juiced
1 bunch Thai basil leaves, chopped (may substitute regular basil)
1 bunch of cilantro, minced
2 TBS chopped almonds, for garnish
cooked brown rice, for serving
1 TBS arrowroot or ground kudzu, optional for a thicker sauce (see note)*

Heat a large pot over medium heat and add the oil, onion, ginger, garlic, curry paste and salt. Sauté for 5 minutes, stirring occasionally, being careful not to burn the garlic. Add a little water if it starts to stick. Then add the kabocha and 1 cup of water. Cover pot and let simmer for 8 minutes. Next add the broccoli and cabbage and let simmer, uncovered, for 3 minutes. Now add the green beans, red bell pepper, beans, tamari, coconut milk and agave and simmer, uncovered, another 3 minutes. Turn off heat and add the lime juice, basil and cilantro, and stir to combine. Taste for spice. Serve over brown rice or your favorite grain or noodle, sprinkle with chopped almonds.

Recipe continues on next page...

THAI PUMPKIN CURRY...

If you prefer a thicker sauce, before adding the lime juice, basil and cilantro, pour off most of the liquid in the pot and place in a small saucepan over medium-high heat. Then in a small bowl, take 1 TBS arrowroot or ground kudzu and whisk it together with 2 TBS cold water to make a slurry. Pour the slurry into the small saucepan and bring to a simmer. Let simmer until thickened and no longer cloudy. Pour this sauce back over the pumpkin curry mixture and then add the lime juice, basil and cilantro and serve as directed.

GF

RICE WITH YELLOW SPLIT PEAS AND GARLIC

SERVES 6-8

½ cup yellow split peas, sorted through to remove stones
3 cups brown basmati rice
1 TBS olive oil (may substitute coconut oil)
1 onion, sliced into strips
4 garlic cloves, pressed
1 inch cinnamon stick
1 bay leaf
3 pieces of cloves
5 cups water
½ tsp unrefined sea salt or Himalayan salt
chopped cilantro, optional, for serving

Rinse the split peas and rice and set aside to drain. Heat the oil in a heavy bottomed soup pot over medium heat. Add the onion, garlic, cinnamon stick, bay leaf and cloves and cook for 5 minutes, stirring often. Be careful not to let the garlic burn. Add drained rice and split peas. Stir for a few minutes then add 5 cups of water. Bring to a boil, then cover and reduce heat to a simmer and cook for 40 minutes. Lift lid to check softness of split peas and rice. Add more water if necessary and cook longer or turn off heat and let sit for 5 minutes before serving. Remove bay leaf, cinnamon stick and cloves, then add the salt and stir to incorporate. Top with chopped cilantro if desired.

THAI RICE SALAD

SERVES 6

4 cups cooked brown rice (I like short grain brown rice)
1 cup cucumber, diced, and tossed in a small bowl with ¼ tsp of salt
½ cup shredded coconut, lightly toasted in a dry pan
1 carrot, scrubbed and shredded
1 cup cooked edamame beans, out of pods
1 cup diced granny smith apple, sprinkled with lemon juice or lime juice
1 cup shredded red cabbage
3 green onions, sliced
1 large handful of mung bean sprouts, trimmed
½ cup almonds, chopped

Dressing Ingredients
2 stalks lemongrass, trimmed so that only the tender, inner pulp remains
4 kaffir lime leaves, center vein discarded
3 TBS tamari (may substitute shoyu soy sauce)
3 TBS fresh lime juice (from about 2 limes)
¼ cup pineapple juice (fresh or canned)
¼ cup pineapple chunks
3 TBS chopped cilantro
3 garlic cloves, pressed
1 tsp grated ginger
½ jalapeno, seeded and chopped
1 tsp toasted sesame oil

Place the cubed cucumber in a small bowl with the salt for about 20 minutes to season it. Meanwhile, prepare the remaining salad ingredients and toss in a large bowl to combine. Place all dressing ingredients in a blender and make smooth. Taste and add more jalapeno or pineapple, if desired. Add **half** of the dressing to the salad and toss. Rinse the cucumber and add to the salad. Taste salad for spice, salt and lime and adjust if necessary.

Serve at room temperature with extra dressing on the side.

SPINACH AND BEANS OVER WHOLE GRAINS

SERVES 2-4

1-15 oz. can garbanzo beans, rinsed and drained
2-3 TBS lemon juice, freshly squeezed of course
1 TBS capers (may substitute chopped olives)
1 TBS balsamic vinegar
1 garlic clove, pressed
2 TBS water
6 oz. baby spinach, chopped
dash of red pepper flakes, optional
unrefined sea salt or Himalayan salt, to taste
cooked whole grain pasta or whole grains, for serving

Combine beans, lemon juice, capers and balsamic in a bowl and set aside. Then place the garlic and water in a skillet and heat for 2 minutes over medium heat. Add the chopped spinach and optional red pepper flakes and stir for 1 minute or until wilted, adding a sprinkle of water if needed to prevent sticking. Toss with the bean mixture and let rest for 1 hour.

Serve at room temperature tossed with whole grain pasta, quinoa or brown rice.

You could also purée beans, lemon juice, capers and vinegar until smooth then toss with the wilted spinach and serve as a spread.

CAROLINA BEANS, GREENS AND RICE

GF

SERVES 6

The collard green is an impressive leafy green in the cruciferous family. Famous for helping to prevent cancer, this green also contains a healthy amount of calcium and the antioxidant, beta-carotene. Eat your beans and greens and you'll get all the calcium you need for strong bones!

1 bunch of collard greens, cleaned and chopped
½ cup vegetable broth (may substitute water)
2 garlic cloves, pressed
1 carrot, scrubbed and grated
1 ½ cups cooked black eyed peas (or approximately 1 can, rinsed and drained)
2 cups cooked brown rice
4 green onions, chopped
2 celery stalk, sliced thin
1 large tomato, seeded and diced, or 1-2 cups of halved cherry tomatoes, no need to seed
¼ cup parsley, minced
6 TBS lemon juice
1-2 TBS olive oil
¼ tsp unrefined sea salt or Himalayan salt
dash of cayenne, optional

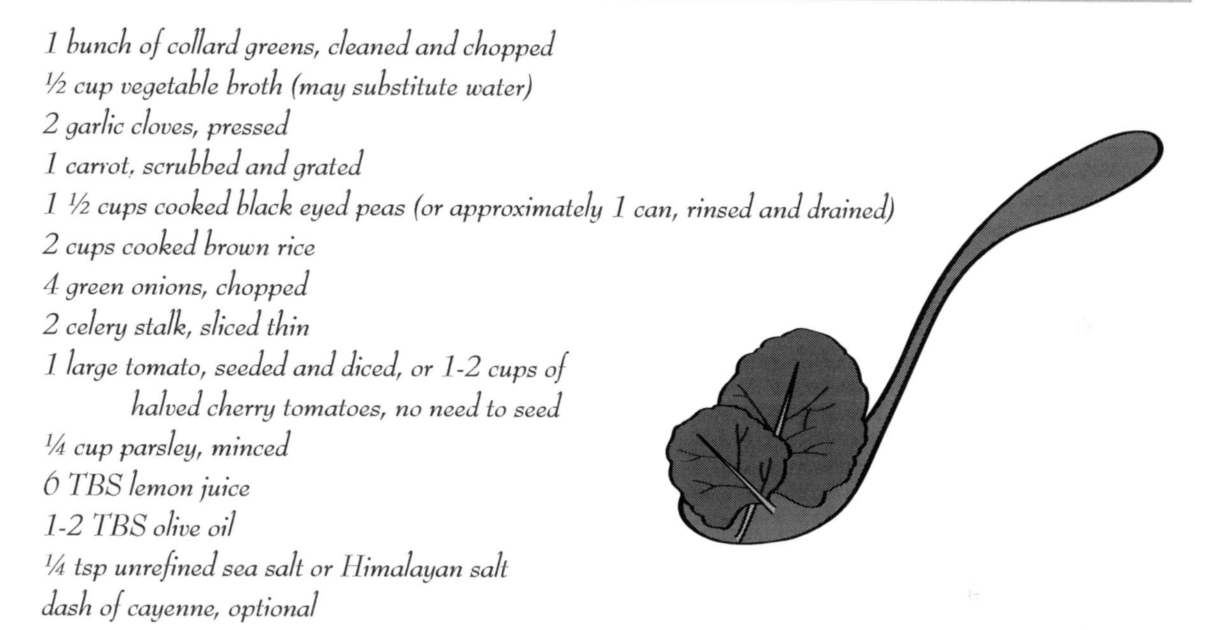

Place the chopped collard greens in a skillet with the water and bring to a simmer over medium-high heat. Cover and let simmer for 3 minutes. Uncover and add the pressed garlic and grated carrot. Stir and cook another few minutes until greens are soft, adding a little bit more water if necessary to prevent sticking. In a large bowl or serving dish (no plastic), combine cooked collard greens, garlic, carrot (use a slotted spoon to remove vegetables from pan, saving any remaining liquid in the pan to make soup), cooked black eyed peas, rice, onions, celery, tomato and parsley in a salad bowl. In a small bowl whisk together the lemon juice, olive oil, salt and cayenne. Pour over salad and toss to mix.

MUSTARD SEITAN WITH ONIONS, ARAME AND KABOCHA

SERVES 4-6

Look for seitan at your health food store. If you wish to use homemade seitan, cook your seitan first before starting this recipe.

1 tsp sesame oil, unrefined, organic
1 large yellow onion, sliced into strips
2 cups sliced kabocha squash, a.k.a. Japanese pumpkin, (about 1x2 inches), peeled or just scrubbed
2 cups sliced seitan
1 small handful of arame seaweed, rinsed
2 TBS Dijon mustard
½ cup vegetable broth
2 TBS shoyu or tamari soy sauce (see note)*
2 baby bok choy, sliced in half lengthwise, keeping bottoms intact (see note)*

Place the sesame oil and then the onions in the bottom of a large pot. Top with the kabocha squash and then the seitan and arame. Whisk together the mustard, broth and shoyu and pour into the pot. Place a lid on the pot and bring to a boil. Reduce to low and let simmer for 15 minutes. Then remove lid and add the baby bok choy and let simmer uncovered a few more minutes or until softened. Add a bit more broth, if necessary, to keep from sticking.

You may substitute ½ teaspoon of unrefined sea salt or Himalayan salt instead of soy sauce, if desired.

Wash the bok choy in a large bowl of cold water making sure to shake away any sand that may be trapped in the root ends.

Serve with a side of whole grains (or better yet, with a side of Millet-Cauli Mash from pg. 278).

BAKED SEITAN CHIMICHURRI
SERVES 4

8 oz. package of prepared seitan, chopped
1 recipe of chimichurri sauce *(see pg. 169)*
4 cups steamed vegetables, for serving
3 cups cooked whole grains, for serving

Place the chopped seitan in a baking dish and toss with ¾ of the chimichurri sauce. Stir to coat. Cover and let marinate in the refrigerator for 2-4 hours. Then place baking dish in the oven and turn heat to 350 F. (Don't preheat oven or your baking dish may crack from going from cold to hot so quickly). Let bake for 30-40 minutes, stirring occasionally. Remove and toss with the remaining ¼ cup of chimichurri sauce. Serve with the steamed vegetables and whole grains.

ROASTED CHILE SEITAN OVER QUINOA
SERVES 6

My friend Becky gave me this recipe. She is known for impressing her friends with her cooking skills, especially when she uses roasted peppers.

1 fresh jalapeno pepper (may substitute other spicy pepper of choice)
1 fresh poblano pepper
1 15-oz. can roasted tomatoes (whole or crushed)
1 red onion, chopped
3 cloves garlic, pressed
1 tsp freshly grated ginger
a pinch of unrefined sea salt or Himalayan salt
2 carrots, sliced
3 cups small broccoli florets
1-2 TBS olive oil (may substitute coconut oil)
1 TBS apple cider vinegar
1 TBS chili powder
1 TBS ground cumin
2 tsp ground coriander

Recipe continues on next page...

ROASTED CHILE SEITAN OVER QUINOA...

1 tsp dried oregano
pinch of red pepper flakes, optional
8 oz. package of prepared seitan, chopped
1-2 tsp date syrup, yacon syrup or agave nectar, if desired
*6 cups **cooked** quinoa, for serving*
1 small bunch cilantro, minced, for serving

Broil the jalapeno pepper and the poblano pepper in oven (or toaster oven if you have one), rotating which side of the peppers are exposed to the heat source so that the skin of the peppers becomes blackened. Once the peppers are blackened, remove from oven and let them rest until cool enough to handle. Then peel off the charred skins and chop the peppers, discarding the seeds. Empty the can of roasted tomatoes into a blender or food processor along with the chopped roasted peppers and blend until almost smooth.

Meanwhile, in a large pan, cook the onions, garlic, ginger, salt, carrots and broccoli in the oil over medium heat for 5 minutes, then add the apple cider vinegar and the spices, stir well and cook for another minute. Then add the chopped seitan and the blended tomato-pepper mixture, and cover. Let simmer over medium heat for 5-10 minutes. Taste and add sweetener, if needed to balance out the tomatoes and the spice. Serve over a bed of quinoa and top with chopped cilantro.

Snacks & Treats

BAKED KALE CRISPS

SERVES 4-8

Kale, a Superfood, is a great source of calcium, fiber, vitamins K, C, E, beta-carotene and lutein. It helps keep our bones strong, protect our eyes against cataracts, and helps protect against lung cancer, arthritis and cancer. The anti-cancer compound, sulforaphane glucosinolate, in kale and other cruciferous vegetables, helps to boost the body's detoxification process, thus helping to clear carcinogenic compounds from the body. Studies consistently show that diets high in cruciferous vegetables are associated with lower risk of many types of cancer.

3 TBS unrefined sesame oil
½ tsp toasted sesame oil
2 TBS brown rice vinegar
2 TBS apple cider vinegar
2 TBS agave nectar
2 tsp garlic powder
½ tsp unrefined sea salt or Himalayan salt
½ tsp nori or dulse flakes
a dash or more of cayenne
2 medium bunches of curly kale, washed, chopped into 1-inch pieces, stems discarded

Preheat oven to 300°F. Line two or three baking sheets with unbleached parchment paper. Whisk all the dressing ingredients together in a small bowl. Place kale in a salad spinner to remove all moisture. Place chopped kale into a large bowl (you may need two large bowls) and drizzle with the dressing. Use clean hands to massage the kale, evenly coating the dressing. This will also soften the kale a bit. Spread kale onto baking sheets trying not to overlap too much. Bake for 10 minutes. Flip kale crisps over and return to oven for another 10 minutes. Then check and stir every few minutes or until evenly crisp but not brown. Some pieces may crisp up before others so remove these and continue to bake the rest. The kale will crisp up a little more while cooling. Let cool on a rack before serving.

Pay close attention to these while they're baking as kale can turn from pretty green to burned in no time. Burned kale is neither healthy nor delicious.

Recipe continues on next page...

BAKED KALE CRISPS...

If your bowl is not large enough to hold all of the kale then place half of the kale into a bowl and drizzle with half of the dressing, then move to baking sheets and repeat until all kale is dressed. Also, if you only have one baking sheet, wipe it with a paper towel in between batches so there is no buildup of dressing on the parchment paper.

You could also make these in your food dehydrator. Follow the recipe but place them on the mesh dehydrator trays and dry for about 4-6 hours at 110 F.

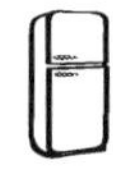

Keep stored in a covered container and eat within 1 day.

CHEESY RAW KALE CHIPS

SERVES 2-4

I have a dehydrator just for this recipe and it's worth it!
An incredibly healthy snack that will please even those green-vegetable-phobia types.

1 bunch or ½ lb. curly leaf kale, cleaned and chopped, stems discarded
1 large red bell pepper, chopped
1 lemon, juiced
¾ cup raw cashews, soaked for up to 24 hours, then drained
¼-½ cup nutritional yeast
a dash or three of cayenne
¼-½ tsp Himalayan salt (or miso paste, to taste)

Place the red bell pepper, lemon juice, cashews, nutritional yeast, cayenne and salt in a blender and blend until smooth. You may have to stop and scrape the sides of the blender and blend again. Taste for salt and spice. It should be tangy and cheesy. Put the kale in a large bowl then pour the cashew mixture over it. Massage the kale with clean hands until the leaves are slightly softened and totally coated with the cashew sauce. Place the kale in a single layer on dehydrator trays lined with sheets and dehydrate at 110 F. After about 2 hours move the kale chips to the mesh sheets, dehydrate for another 6 hours, or until crispy!

Store in a covered container at room temperature for up to 5 days, but trust me-they'll never last more than 5 minutes!

BAKED TORTILLA CHIPS

SERVES 8

1 package of sprouted grain tortillas
olive oil spray or mister
unrefined sea salt or Himalayan salt

Cut the tortillas into chip-sized pieces. Mist lightly with olive oil and sprinkle with a pinch of salt. Spread out in a single layer on a parchment lined baking pan(s). Bake at 375 F for 10 minutes, or just until lightly browned. Watch carefully during the last few minutes of baking as chips can **burn easily**. Remove from oven and let cool. They will crisp up as they cool.

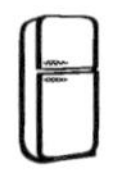

Store in a covered container and eat within 2 days. You may store for up to five days in the refrigerator, but you will need to re-crisp by placing chips on a baking sheet in a 300 F oven for just a couple of minutes.

MAGIC POPCORN

SERVES 4

¼ cup organic popping corn
1 TBS flax seed oil
hot sauce, to taste
2 tsp kelp, nori or dulse seaweed flakes
2 TBS nutritional yeast
unrefined sea salt or Himalayan salt, to taste (may substitute tamari or shoyu soy sauce)
garlic power, optional
agave nectar, optional

Place popcorn in an air popper. Once popped, toss in a large bowl with flax seed oil (drizzled on whilst tossing), a few dashes of your favorite hot sauce, seaweed flakes, nutritional yeast and salt, to taste. I also like to add a little garlic powder. Adjust seasonings to suit your desires.

If you prefer a sweet and spicy popcorn, toss popcorn with hot sauce and agave nectar and perhaps a dash of salt.

This popcorn does not store well so make only what you need.

ONION RINGS
SERVES 6

¼ cup flour (any kind)
1 tsp unrefined sea salt or Himalayan salt
2 TBS panko bread crumbs (Japanese bread crumbs)
2 medium to large onions

Set oven to 475 F. Slice onions into thin rounds, preferably on a mandolin. Place the flour, salt and bread crumbs in a large bowl. Whisk to combine. Add the onion rings, separating them into individual rings. Toss with the flour mixture and place on a parchment lined baking sheet. Bake for 30 minutes, stirring every 10 minutes, or until golden brown and crispy.

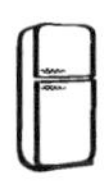

These don't store well so consume soon after making.

SPICED SEEDS
SERVES 2

GF

The spices used in this recipe are good for aiding digestion.

½ cup raw pumpkin seeds
1 tsp date syrup, agave nectar or yacon syrup
1 tsp fennel seeds
1 tsp caraway seeds
1 tsp cumin seeds
dash of unrefined sea salt or Himalayan salt

Place the pumpkin seeds in a dry skillet and dry toast for a few minutes over medium heat until they begin to toast and smell nutty. You must stir constantly or they could burn. Once toasted, immediately remove seeds from the skillet to a bowl and toss with the sweetener. Let cool a bit. Meanwhile, place the fennel seeds, caraway seeds and cumin seeds in a coffee grinder or spice grinder and make into a powder. Add a dash of salt to the spices and toss with the sweetened seeds.

Eat as a mid-day snack.

Store in a covered container in the refrigerator for up to 3 days.

CHICKPEA "FRIES"

SERVES 4-6

The dough will need to chill completely before baking these fries so make the dough the night before you wish to serve them.

2 cups chickpea flour (about ½ pound)
3 TBS minced parsley
1 garlic clove, pressed
1 small shallot, minced fine
¾ tsp unrefined sea salt or Himalayan salt, to taste
½ tsp spice of choice (I use Marrakesh Spice Blend, see pg. 198, but chili powder could work)
2 cups water
¼ cup olive oil
2 TBS lemon juice
oil spray
Harissa cashew mayo or garlic almond mayo for dipping (see note)*

In a heavy medium saucepan, combine the chickpea flour with the parsley, garlic, shallot, salt and spice. Whisk in the water, oil and lemon juice in a thin stream until a smooth paste forms. Heat the mixture over medium high heat, whisking constantly, until very thick, about 8-10 minutes. Be careful not to let it burn. Then switch to a wooden spoon and stir until smooth.

Move the dough onto a lightly oiled cookie sheet with a spatula, then use clean, wet hands to spread dough about 1/2 inch thick and make smooth and even on top. Pat the top of the dough with a towel to soak up any moisture. Let cool to room temperature, then press a piece of unbleached parchment paper or waxed paper (if cooled completely) directly onto the surface of the chickpea mixture. Refrigerate, tightly covered with additional foil or plastic wrap, until cold and firm, about 6 hours or overnight.

Preheat oven to 400 F. Remove chickpea dough in sections and place onto a cutting board. Slice into ½ -inch-wide by 3 inch long sticks (or slice right in the pan, if easier). Place fries on a parchment lined baking sheet and spray lightly with oil. Bake until lightly browned and crispy, about 30 minutes. Carefully flip each one and bake another 10 minutes. Serve with side of harissa spiced cashew mayo.

Keep an eye on the fries when they're in the oven because some ovens have hot spots and may cause uneven cooking. Rotate pan half way through baking.

I highly recommend making a harissa spiced mayo by whisking 1 tsp of harissa into ¼ cup of cashew or garlic almond mayo.

CHICKPEA SNACKS

GF

MAKES ABOUT 1 CUP

This low-fat alternative to a bowl of nuts makes a great, little appetizer for your next dinner party. Or add to trail mix for an interesting twist.

1 can of chickpeas (organic preferred), rinsed and drained
½ TBS macadamia nut oil (may substitute tea seed oil)
1-2 tsp spices (curry, Cajun, wasabi paste, mustard, 5-spice powder, Old Bay, etc.)
tamari soy sauce or unrefined sea salt, optional

Drain the chickpeas well and then toss with enough oil to coat and sprinkle with your favorite spices. Add a dash of tamari or a sprinkle of salt if desired. Spread the chickpeas on a baking sheet and bake at 400 F for 45 minutes. Stir frequently to ensure even cooking. They should be crunchy, similar to roasted nuts when finished, but be careful not to burn. Remove from oven and let cool.

Experiment with your favorite spice to season these any way you like.

Store in a covered container for up to 3 days.

NUTTY NORI BRITTLE

SERVES 8-12

5 TBS sesame oil (may substitute macadamia nut oil or tea seed oil)
¼ cup agave nectar
¼ cup brown rice syrup
¼ tsp unrefined sea salt or Himalayan salt
a dash or two of cayenne (highly recommended)
2 cups of chopped nuts and seeds (any combination of sesame seeds, sunflower seeds, pumpkin seeds, sliced almonds, chopped cashews or chopped pistachios)
5 sheets of nori seaweed, cut into 1 inch pieces (I use scissors)

Preheat oven to 350 F. Line two baking sheets with unbleached parchment paper. Place the oil, sweeteners, salt and cayenne in a medium saucepan and bring to a boil. Stir constantly while mixture is boiling. Once it is frothy (happens very quickly) turn off heat and stir in the nuts, seeds and the nori. Pour onto the prepared sheets in a thin and even layer. Place in the oven and bake for 10 minutes, watching carefully so that the edges don't burn. Remove and let cool completely before breaking apart into smaller pieces and serving.

Store in a covered container in a cool place for up to 3 days.

TRAIL MIX
MAKES ABOUT 6 CUPS

Learn to love seaweed! Seaweed is full of minerals and helps the body clear toxins.

1 cup bullwhip kelp pieces, cut into small pieces (see note)*
1 cup of whole grain pretzel pieces, such as spelt
1 cup almonds
½ cup baked chickpea snacks (see pg. 367)
½ cup raw walnuts
½ cup raw sunflower seeds
½ cup raw pumpkin seeds
½ cup dried cherries (may substitute cranberries)
½ cup goji berries
½ cup raw cacao nibs (may substitute dark chocolate chips or carob chips)

Mix together and serve as an appetizer or snack.

It's important to buy seaweed that has been harvested from clean water. Visit your health food store or order on-line from macrobiotic suppliers and start experimenting with all the different types of seaweed out there. You may substitute sea lettuce, dulse or 4 sheets of nori seaweed, cut into small pieces.

Store in a covered container in a cool place for up to 3 days.

NORI CIGARS

These are basically sushi rolls but because you don't slice them they end up looking like cigars! Take a toasted nori sheet and place on a sushi mat. Top with cooked brown rice, avocado slices, grated carrots, teriyaki baked tempeh, sautéed shiitakes, broccoli sprouts and raw kimchi. Tightly roll and seal to close. Serve with a side of wasabi-tamari dipping sauce and pickled ginger (see pg. 349 recipe for Maki Sushi Rolls)

CHOCOLATE CEREAL NUGGETS

MAKES 12 LARGE NUGGETS

1 ¼ cups of dark chocolate chips (may substitute carob chips)
1 tsp vanilla extract
a dash of unrefined sea salt or Himalayan salt, optional
¼ cup chopped walnuts, raw
¼ cup pumpkin seeds, raw (may substitute sunflower seeds)
1 cup wheat germ, raw (not technically a 'whole food' but I like it in this recipe)
1 cup rolled oats
2 cups of cereal (something high fiber and low sugar), crushed lightly (see note)*

Place unbleached parchment paper cups into a muffin pan and set aside. Fill the bottom pan of the double boiler halfway with water. Place the chocolate chips in the top of the double boiler (or in the stainless steel bowl) and place over the pan of water. Heat until the chocolate melts, stirring until smooth. Once melted remove from heat and add the vanilla and dash of salt, if using. Stir to combine, then toss in the walnuts and seeds and stir again. Next, add the wheat germ, oats and crushed cereal. Stir well.

Place cereal mixture into the parchment-lined muffin pan and press firmly with a damp spoon to pack down the mixture into the pan. Place pan into the refrigerator and let chill for at least 30 minutes before serving.

To crush your cereal, place it in a bag and crush gently with a rolling pin. You want the cereal to be roughly the same size as the rolled oats.

If you don't have a double boiler just use a stainless steel bowl that rests on top of a saucepan. Be careful not to get any water into the chocolate.

Store in a covered container in the refrigerator for up to 1 week.

CHOCOLATE GOJI BERRY DROPS

MAKES 12 DROPS

Mesquite powder is made from the ground seed pods of the mesquite plant, a legume traditionally used by Native Americans. Mesquite powder is highly effective at balancing blood sugar levels and is safe for people with diabetes. It tastes sweet and nutty, and is a good source of fiber, protein, iron and calcium. Use it in smoothies (1 TBS per person) and in baked goods (substitute ¼ cup of mesquite powder for ¼ cup of flour in sweet recipes).

You'll need 1 mini muffin pan lined with 12 mini-muffin unbleached parchment paper cups ready to go before starting this recipe.

1 cup chocolate chips
¼ cup goji berries
2 TBS mesquite powder (see note)*
2 tsp green powder (combo of wheat grass, barley grass, spirulina, chlorella, etc.)
a pinch or two of unrefined sea salt or Himalayan salt
a dash of cayenne, optional

Heat water in the bottom of a double boiler. If you don't have a double boiler use a stainless steel bowl that sits comfortably on top of a saucepan. Place chocolate chips in the top of the double boiler or in the bowl. Don't let water get into the chocolate. Heat until the chocolate is beginning to melt. Stir with a spatula until the chocolate is smooth. Remove from heat and add the remaining ingredients. Stir to combine. Taste for salt.

The Himalayan salt should be noticeable but not overbearing. If it's too salty add a teaspoon more of the mesquite powder. Once it tastes to your liking use two spoons to neatly place about 1 ½ TBS of the mixture into each of the parchment paper cups. Place the muffin pan into the refrigerator until completely cooled and set before serving. These are amazing.

Mesquite powder may be hard to find. Ask at your health food store or order on-line.

Store in a covered container in the refrigerator for up to 1 week.

CHOCOLATE BANANA POPSICLES

MAKES 8 POPSICLES

3 cups bananas, chopped
⅔ cup unsweetened almond milk (may substitute hemp seed or rice milk)
3 TBS cocoa powder (may substitute raw cacao powder)
1 tsp vanilla extract
1 dash of unrefined sea salt or Himalayan salt
3 TBS date syrup, agave nectar, brown rice syrup or yacon syrup, optional

Place ingredients in a blender or food processor and blend until smooth. Pour mixture into popsicle molds and insert handles. Freeze until solid (8 hours or more).

GF FRUITY YOGURT POPSICLES

MAKES ABOUT 6 POPSICLES
(DEPENDING ON THE SIZE OF YOUR MOLDS)

16 oz. plain soy yogurt (may substitute rice, coconut or seed yogurt)
½ cup chopped fresh fruit of choice
¼ cup date syrup, agave nectar, brown rice syrup or yacon syrup, optional

Place ingredients in a blender or food processor and blend until smooth. Pour mixture into popsicle molds and insert handles. Freeze until solid (8 hours or more).

Breakfast & Baking

NOTES ON BAKING AND DESSERTS

There are a few ways in which we can sweeten foods without the harmful side effects associated with sugar and high fructose corn syrup. First, I must point out that ultimately we should aim to be in the habit of not having to use sweeteners on everything we ingest and instead enjoying foods in their natural state. If you have been eating the standard American diet (S.A.D.), which is laced with sugars and artificial sweeteners, natural foods may taste bland at first. Routinely eating processed foods changes your taste buds and suddenly nothing is satisfying unless it's loaded with sugar, salt and fat. You will need to take a few weeks to adjust your taste buds. Aim to avoid all processed foods and foods with added sugars for three weeks. Replace with whole plant foods; fresh fruits, vegetables, whole grains, beans, lentils, nuts and seeds. After three weeks of eating real foods your taste buds will have changed and you will appreciate food without all the additives and chemicals. You will also feel much better too. This is a promise.

There will always be times when a baked good or a dessert is necessary. Luckily you have this book full of healthier recipes so you can avoid the processed sugars, refined flours and artery-clogging fats found in most baked goods. The sweeteners used in these recipes are safe even for people with diabetes, however, that doesn't give any of us the green light to eat as much dessert as we want. Date syrup, agave nectar (please buy raw and organic to avoid cheap imitations), brown rice syrup, yacon syrup and stevia will not raise blood sugar levels, but we should still only consume them in small amounts. They cannot always be used interchangeably with each other so follow directions closely. These sweeteners replace sugar, corn syrup, honey and maple syrup but

NOTES ON BAKING AND DESSERTS...

require a different ratio when substituting. So if you're trying to convert an old baking recipe from sugar to agave you will need to use less agave than sugar, and then decrease the other wet ingredients by 1/3. It will take some experimenting but it's not impossible. If you don't like to bake or have time to bake then always choose fresh fruit as the best choice for a healthy dessert.

Here are some other tips to help you get started:

Get a plunger type measuring cup for measuring things like date syrup, molasses, agave nectar, nut butters and oils.

Always sift your dry ingredients together (use a fine mesh strainer if you don't have a sifter). This is key to evenly distribute ingredients such as baking powder and salt, and aerate the flour resulting in a light, fluffy product.

Don't over-stir your baked goods batter. This will cause any gluten in the batter to develop resulting in a tough product.

When grinding flax seeds and chia seeds: 1 TBS of whole flax seeds or chia seeds will yield about 2 TBS ground chia seeds. Follow recipe and measure accordingly (some recipes you measure before grinding, some recipes you measure after grinding). Please only buy whole flax seeds or chia seeds instead of already ground seeds because they spoil quickly once ground. This is important.

When grinding oats or other grains to make your own "flour" measure according to the recipe directions. For example, some recipes call for 1 cup of oats, ground. So measure the oats to 1 cup then grind and proceed. Some recipes call for 1 cup amaranth flour. In this case, grind your amaranth and then measure to 1 cup and proceed. One cup rolled oats will yield about 1 cup oat flour. One cup amaranth will yield about 1 ¾ cups amaranth flour.

NOTES ON BAKING AND DESSERTS...

You will need to store all baked goods in the refrigerator after preparing because they don't contain any preservatives or white sugar used in typical baked goods. If you leave your muffins or your pie on the counter they will start to spoil!

Use fresh whole grain flours, baking soda, baking powder and spices. Whole grain flours do not have the long shelf life of refined and bleached flours. Old ingredients lose their flavor and nutritional value. Old baking powder also loses its ability to make baked goods rise. Buy in smaller quantities. Store whole grain flours in air-tight containers in a cool, dark place such as in your refrigerator or freezer. Use within one month. Baking soda, baking powder and spices last about 6 months when stored in a cool, dry, dark place, such as a pantry. As always, buy organic.

To clean a coffee grinder, place a tablespoon of uncooked rice (one way to use up any white rice you still have in your house) and grind it until pulverized. Unplug the grinder and throw away the ground rice. Carefully wipe clean with a damp towel. This will remove most of the coffee flavor and grounds. Repeat if necessary, adding a drop of white vinegar to the towel. Now it is ready to grind your nuts, seeds and spices.

Egg Free Options
Substitute one of the following for 1 egg

- ⅓ cup puréed silken tofu
- ½ mashed banana
- 1 TBS ground flax seeds mixed with ⅓ cup water, juice or non-dairy milk
- 1 ½ tsp Ener G egg replacer powder mixed with 2 TBS of water
- ⅓ cup fruit purée (prune puree, applesauce, etc.)
- Using baking soda and vinegar in a baking recipe

Make Your Own Date Syrup
Place 1 cup of **pitted** dates in a pan with 1 cup of water. Bring to a boil, then reduce heat and let simmer, covered, for 20-30 minutes, or until dates are very soft. Add more water if necessary. Let cool completely then add to a blender and blend until very smooth, adding more water if necessary. You want the mixture to resemble maple syrup. Store in a glass container in the refrigerator.

NOTES ON BAKING AND DESSERTS...

GF

Gluten-Free Flour Mix

2 cups brown rice or millet flour
⅔ cup potato starch
⅓ cup tapioca flour
1-2 tsp. of xanthan gum or guar gum*

Substitute 1 cup of this mixture for 1 cup all purpose flour, whole wheat or barley flour

***Guar gum** is derived from the seed of a legume and has many times the thickening power of cornstarch. Using too much can produce a heavy or stringy texture in baked goods, so measure carefully.

***Xanthan gum** is a corn-based fermented product used as a thickening agent, like guar gum. Using too much can produce a heavy or gummy texture, so measure carefully.

GF

Gluten-Free Baking Powder

⅓ cup baking soda
⅔ cup cream of tartar
⅔ cup arrowroot or potato starch

1½ teaspoons of this mixture = 1 teaspoon of regular baking power. Mix well. Store in an airtight container.

STEEL CUT OATMEAL WITH FRUIT AND NUTS

SERVES 4-6

I enjoy making this recipe the night before I plan on eating it so in the morning I only need to chop my fruit, grind my flax seeds and gently warm my portion of oatmeal.

1 cup steel cut oats
3-4 cups water, depending on how thick you like it
dried fruit, chopped if necessary
fresh fruit, chopped
chopped almonds, pumpkin seeds or walnuts
freshly ground flax seeds (may substitute freshly ground chia seeds)
unsweetened almond milk or other favorite non-dairy milk
dash of unrefined sea salt or Himalayan salt, optional
sweetener, optional (date syrup, agave nectar, molasses, brown rice syrup, or yacon syrup)

Dry toast the steel cut oats in a heavy bottomed pan over medium heat for 5 minutes, or until they smell nutty. Slowly and carefully pour in the water while stirring with a long wooden spoon (to avoid being splattered). Bring to a boil and let boil for 2 minutes. Cover tightly with a lid, turn off heat and let sit for 45 minutes or until all the water is absorbed and the oats are tender. When ready to serve, place just what you are going to be serving in a smaller pan with your favorite dried fruit, fresh fruit, nuts, seeds, milk and optional ingredients then heat gently over low heat until warm.

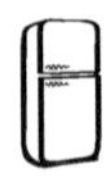

Store in a covered container in the refrigerator for up to 4 days.

CREAM OF AMARANTH OR TEFF

SERVES 4

This hearty alternative to oatmeal or wheat is creamy, delicious, and gluten-free!

1 cup amaranth or teff grain
3 cups water
your favorite non-dairy milk, for serving
optional ingredients: chopped almonds, walnuts, fruit, goji berries, or dried coconut, for serving

Recipe continues on next page...

CREAM OF AMARANTH OR TEFF...

Combine the grains and water in a saucepan and stir to combine. Bring to a boil, cover, and reduce heat to low. Let simmer, stirring occasionally, until water is absorbed, about 20 minutes. Serve with your favorite non-dairy milk and optional ingredients.

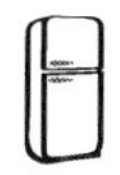

Store in a covered container in the refrigerator for up to 4 days.

LENTIL PORRIDGE

SERVES 4-6

The perfect marriage of easy to digest lentils and rolled oats gives you a hearty, warm breakfast full of fiber, protein and minerals.

1 cup red lentils, sorted through to remove stones, rinsed
1 cup rolled oats
8 cups water
unrefined sea salt or Himalayan salt, to taste
optional ingredients: green onions, miso slurry, or chopped fruit, for serving (see note)*

Simply cook red lentils and rolled oats in a pan with water over medium heat until very soft, about 25 minutes. Add more water if necessary. Add a pinch of salt, if desired. Then add optional ingredients.

This can also be cooked in a slow cooker.

This recipe is good savory (by adding green onions and miso slurry after cooking) or sweet (by adding chopped fruit after cooking). Try it both ways to decide your favorite.

Store in a covered container in the refrigerator for up to 4 days.

(GF)

INDIAN SPICED RICE PUDDING

SERVES 4-6

The most delicious scents in the world - all in one dish.

*3 cups **cooked** brown basmati rice* (see note)*
3 cups non-dairy milk (I like Eden brand soy-rice milk, sweetened with amasake)
⅛ tsp unrefined sea salt or Himalayan salt, optional
½ tsp cinnamon
¾ tsp freshly ground cardamom seeds (see note)*
1-2 tsp rose water, optional
⅓ cup green raisins (may substitute other dried fruit, like dried apricots, but use organic)
⅓ cup shredded, dried coconut, toasted (see note)*
⅓ cup chopped almonds

Place the rice, and milk and optional salt in a pan and simmer over low heat, stirring often, for about 20 minutes, or until thickened. Add the cinnamon, cardamom, rose water, and green raisins then let simmer a few minutes to soften fruit and blend flavors. Top with toasted coconut and chopped almonds.

If you can't find cardamom seeds, then buy cardamom pods and smash them open to get to the seeds. Grind the seeds and measure the ground seeds to ¾ tsp. You may only be able to find cardamom already ground - and that's ok to use too.

To cook the rice place 1 cup of rinsed and drained brown basmati rice into a pot with 2 cups of water (or use part rice or coconut milk). Bring to a boil, cover, reduce heat to low and cook for 40 minutes. Turn off heat and let sit another 10 minutes before lifting lid.

To toast the coconut, place coconut flakes in a dry skillet and toast, while stirring, over medium heat until they are lightly toasted. Move to a plate to cool and prevent burning.

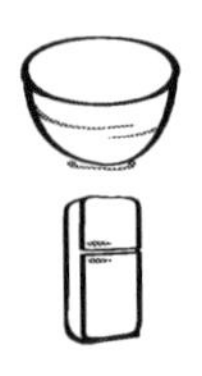

Serve hot or refrigerate and serve as dessert!

Store in a covered container in the refrigerator for up to 4 days.

LOVELY MORNING OAT PIE

SERVES 8-12

Thanks to my favorite cooking friend, Deb, for giving me the idea for this pie. This simple and delicious dish is great for serving a houseful of hungry guests! The trick is to make it the night before so in the morning all you have to do is reheat and serve.

2 cups steel cut oats
5 cups liquid (water, non-dairy milk or coconut milk)
½ cup chopped fine dried fruit (don't have to chop goji berries)
dash of unrefined sea salt or Himalayan salt
½ tsp cinnamon
1 tsp vanilla extract
date syrup, agave nectar, or brown rice syrup, optional
coconut oil for pie pan and skillet
Berry Compote, for serving (see next recipe)

Toast the dry steel cut oats in a large, heavy bottomed saucepan over medium heat until they begin to smell nutty, about 5 minutes. You will want to stir frequently so they don't burn. Then slowly and carefully add 5 cups of liquid while stirring with a long wooden spoon (to avoid being splattered). You can use any combination of water, non-dairy milk and coconut milk as long as it totals 5 cups. Also add the dried fruit. Bring to a boil, then reduce heat, cover and simmer for about 45 minutes. All the liquid should be absorbed and oats should be cooked through. It should be a thick porridge. Now add a dash of salt, cinnamon and vanilla, and stir to combine. Sweeten, if desired, and pour into a lightly oiled glass or ceramic pie dish.

Let the oats cool to room temperature and then place the dish into the refrigerator to cool and thicken. I do all of this at night and then in the morning, I finish it off by slicing the oats into pie shaped wedges and reheating them in a lightly oiled skillet until lightly browned on outside and warm in the center (you may need to cover your pan with a lid so the center will get warm). Once they've been lightly browned in the skillet you can keep these warm by placing them on a pan in a 300 F oven until ready to serve. Top with Berry Compote.

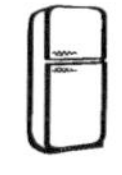

Store in a covered container in the refrigerator for up to 4 days.

BERRY COMPOTE

SERVES 6

All berries are good for your health. They contain fiber, vitamins, minerals and beneficial antioxidants that help protect against disease.

2 cups organic mixed berries, including blueberries, raspberries and dried goji berries
2 TBS ground kudzu (see note)*
1-2 TBS water
sweetener of choice (date syrup, agave nectar, yacon syrup, stevia, etc.)
cinnamon, optional

Rinse the berries and place in a medium saucepan. In a separate small bowl whisk together the kudzu and water to make a slurry. Add this to the saucepan and heat over medium heat, stirring occasionally, until berries are broken down and sauce is thickened. Sweeten if necessary, then sprinkle with cinnamon.

Kudzu root powder may sometimes need to be finely ground before using in a recipe. Do this with a mortar and pestle or in a clean coffee grinder.

Serve over french toast, pancakes, waffles or on top of oatmeal or other hot cereal.

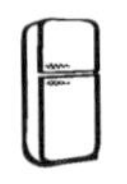

Store in a covered container in the refrigerator for up to 4 days.

GRANOLA

MAKES ABOUT 10 CUPS

Read through the entire recipe before starting. Having several baking sheets (the kind with rims) and a watchful eye will help make this recipe a success. And, as always, please use all organic ingredients, especially when it comes to dried fruits and nuts.

Mix together:

8 cups rolled oats
½ cup raw almonds (see note)*
¼ cup brown sesame seeds (see note)*
¼ cup raw pumpkin seeds (may substitute sunflower seeds) (see note)*

In separate bowl whisk together:

½ cup date syrup or agave nectar
½ cup brown rice syrup
2 TBS molasses
¼ cup macadamia nut oil (may substitute tea seed oil)
½ tsp unrefined sea salt or Himalayan salt

Add the wet ingredients to the dry ingredients and stir to evenly distribute. Spread granola onto the baking sheets. Bake in preheated 325 F oven for 30-40 minutes, stirring every 10 minutes to ensure even baking. Take care not to burn the oats or nuts/seeds. Let cool completely on a rack until room temperature, then place in a bowl and add:

1 cup goji berries
½ cup green raisins (may substitute diced dried apricot)
¼ cup each dried blueberries and strawberries

I like to use different nuts and seeds to add variation… pistachios and pecans are nice additions. If you are worried about burning the nuts (which WILL happen to you sooner or later) then just place them on a separate baking pan from the oats and monitor closely, checking every 5 minutes. Or better yet, don't bake the nuts and seeds at all and just add them in later.

Serve for breakfast with your favorite homemade non-dairy milk or add to trail mix. YUM!

Store in an airtight container in the refrigerator or in a cool, dark place for up to 5 days.

RASPBERRIES AND GRANOLA WITH LEMON CREAM

SERVES 4-6

Raspberries are high in antioxidants, and are said to help promote optimal health, protect against cancer, and against macular degeneration. Whatever you do, eat your berries.

1 ½ cups rolled oats (may substitute kamut or spelt flakes)
¼ cup date syrup or agave nectar
¼ tsp cinnamon
¼ tsp unrefined sea salt or Himalayan salt (optional)
½ cup raw walnuts (may substitute pecans)
4 cups fresh raspberries

Preheat oven to 325 F. In a bowl toss the oats with the sweetener, cinnamon and salt. Place oat mixture on a baking pan (one with rims). Bake the oats for 20-25 minutes or until lightly browned and crispy. Stir the oats every 5 minutes for even baking. Remove and let cool. Chop the nuts into small pieces. Toss the nuts with the toasted oat mixture and sprinkle over the raspberries.

GF

Lemon Cashew Cream

1 cup raw cashews, soaked in plenty of water for 1 hour or up to 24 hours in refrigerator
3 pitted dates (may substitute 3-4 TBS agave or brown rice syrup)
½ tsp lemon extract
½ tsp lemon rind
juice from 1 lemon
dash of unrefined sea salt or Himalayan salt
water, if necessary

Drain and rinse the cashews and place in a blender with the pitted dates, lemon extract, rind, juice, and a dash of salt. Turn on blender and slowly drizzle in water while blending until desired thickness is reached; stopping to scrape down the sides of the blender if needed. Taste for lemon and sweetness and adjust to your liking.

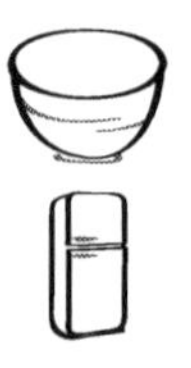

Serve in pretty bowls topped with lemon cashew cream.

Store in a covered container in the refrigerator for up to 5 days.

FRENCH TOAST

MAKES 6 SLICES

1 cup non-dairy milk (I like homemade cashew milk... Yum! (see pg. 92)
¼ cup of whole grain flour
1 TBS nutritional yeast
1 TBS date syrup, agave nectar or brown rice syrup
1 tsp vanilla extract
½ tsp cinnamon
a dash of unrefined sea salt or Himalayan salt, optional
6 slices of sprouted, whole grain bread
fresh fruit or berry compote (See pg. 382), for serving

Combine the milk, flour, nutritional yeast, sweetener, vanilla, cinnamon and salt in a blender. Blend until smooth then pour into a flat baking dish. Soak bread slices in this mixture until soft but not soggy. The amount of time this takes will vary from 5 seconds to 1 minute depending on the density of the bread used. When bread looks saturated, remove from soaking mixture and place in a lightly oiled, preheated skillet. Cook over medium heat for 3 minutes on each side or until lightly browned. Serve with fresh fruit or berry compote.

Store in a covered container in the refrigerator for up to 3 days.

THREE GRAIN PANCAKES

SERVES 4-6

Although buckwheat is technically a fruit seed from a plant in the rhubarb family I counted it as one of the grains here because "Two Grain Pancakes" just didn't sound as catchy.

½ cup rolled oats, partially ground (may substitute quinoa flakes)
¾ cup buckwheat flour
½ cup cornmeal
1 tsp baking powder
½ tsp cinnamon
½ tsp unrefined sea salt or Himalayan salt
2 TBS date syrup or agave nectar
1 banana
1 ½ cups almond milk
1 tsp vanilla extract
1-2 tsp coconut oil, to oil the pan
fresh fruit or berry compote (See pg. 382), for serving

Whisk dry ingredients in a bowl. Blend sweetener, banana, almond milk and vanilla in a blender until smooth. Add wet to dry and stir just to combine. Let batter rest for 5 minutes.

Meanwhile, warm a lightly oiled skillet over medium heat. Pour batter into pan and cook until bubbles appear. Flip and cook other side for 1-2 minutes. Serve with fresh fruit or berry compote.

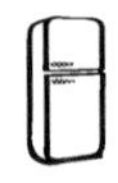

Store in a covered container in the refrigerator for up to 3 days.

CHESTNUT PANCAKES

SERVES 6

2 TBS coconut flakes
¾ cup non-dairy milk (almond, cashew, soy, oat or rice milk)
2 TBS flax seeds, ground (may substitute chia seeds, ground)
2 tsp baking powder
½ tsp unrefined sea salt or Himalayan salt
½ tsp cinnamon
1 cup chopped fresh chestnuts (may substitute jarred, peeled chestnuts)
1 medium banana, ripe
2 TBS flour (whole wheat, barley or amaranth)
1-2 tsp coconut oil, to oil the pan
fresh fruit or berry compote (See pg. 382), for serving

In a blender add the coconut flakes, almond milk, ground flax seeds, baking powder, salt, cinnamon, chopped chestnuts and banana and blend until smooth. Stir in the flour and pulse just a couple of times to combine. Heat a skillet over medium-low heat. Lightly brush with oil and then drop batter into desired shape and cook pancakes about 3 minutes on each side or until they are cooked through. Serve with fruit or berry compote.

Store in a covered container in the refrigerator for up to 3 days.

LEMON RICE PANCAKES WITH BLUEBERRIES

SERVES 8

1 cup non-dairy milk (almond, hemp, soy or rice)
1 TBS lemon juice
1 cup oat flour (made from blending about 1 cup rolled oats in a blender until flour-like)
1 tsp baking powder
1 tsp baking soda
½ tsp unrefined sea salt or Himalayan salt
1 TBS unrefined sesame oil (may substitute olive oil)
1 TBS date syrup or agave nectar
1 cup cooked brown rice, brown basmati is preferred, cooled
1 TBS lemon zest, finely chopped
¾ cup blueberries (fresh, frozen or dried)
1-2 tsp coconut oil, to oil the pan

Whisk the milk with the lemon juice and let sit for 10 minutes to become "buttermilk." Meanwhile, whisk together the oat flour, baking powder, baking soda and salt in a bowl. Whisk the oil and sweetener and add to the buttermilk. Add wet ingredients to dry ingredients and stir just to combine. Now fold in the cooled rice, lemon zest and blueberries. Pour batter onto a lightly oiled skillet and cook until bubbles appear. Flip and cook for another minute or two.

Store in a covered container in the refrigerator for up to 3 days.

PUMPKIN WAFFLES

SERVES 4-6

Thanks to Deb for perfecting this recipe!

2 cups kamut flour (may substitute barley flour)
2 TBS chickpea flour (a.k.a. garbanzo bean flour)
4 tsp baking powder
1 tsp each cinnamon, ground ginger, and unrefined sea salt or Himalayan salt
¼ tsp nutmeg, freshly ground on a microplane is best
⅛ tsp ground cloves
¾ c. pumpkin purée
1 ½ cups non-dairy milk (plus more, if needed)
½ cup chopped apple (approximately 1 small)
1 TBS macadamia nut oil
2 TBS date syrup or agave nectar
1 tsp vanilla extract
1-2 tsp coconut oil, to oil the pan (if necessary)

Preheat waffle iron according to manufacturer's instructions. Whisk together the flours, baking powder and spices in a large bowl and set aside. In a blender combine the pumpkin, non-dairy milk, apple, oil, sweetener and vanilla and blend until smooth. Add wet ingredients to dry and stir just until combined (do not over mix). You may need to add another 1-2 TBS of non-dairy milk if the batter is too thick.

Lightly oil the preheated waffle iron (if necessary). Add ¼-½ cup of the batter, depending on desired size, and follow manufacture's instructions for cooking time. Keep cooked waffles warming in a 250 F oven until all waffles are ready.

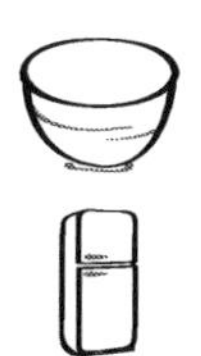

Serve with Berry Compote (see pg. 382) or fresh fruit.

Store in a covered container in the refrigerator for up to 3 days.

BREAKFAST POCKETS

SERVES 6

Fill your pockets with just about anything you like; a tasty way to use up leftovers. These are great to make ahead of time and take to work because they reheat perfectly in a little toaster oven.

Dough

1 ½ cup whole wheat pastry flour
2 cups barley flour, plus more for kneading (may substitute kamut flour)
1 tsp unrefined sea salt or Himalayan salt
½ tsp seasoning (cinnamon or ground ginger for sweet filling; cayenne or garlic powder for savory filling)
¼ cup macadamia nut oil
1 TBS date syrup or agave nectar
1 cup water
2 TBS non-dairy milk, for brushing dough

Filling

Use about 1 cup of leftover beans, grains, miso and steamed vegetables, or fruit compote and chopped seeds or nuts. Almost anything will work, as long as the filling is not watery.

Preheat oven to 400 F. Whisk together the flour, salt and seasonings (if using), then drizzle in the oil until flour looks like small crumbs. Stir sweetener into water and add to flour mixture gradually while stirring with a wooden spoon until a ball of dough starts to form (it helps to have a damp towel underneath the bowl to prevent slipping and sliding of bowl while stirring). Use hands and knead briefly to combine. Then roll out dough on a floured board until about ¼ inch thick, adding more flour if dough is too sticky. Cut into rounds, about 6 inches in diameter. Place 2 TBS of filling of choice onto bottom ½ of the circle. Moisten edges with water, then fold top of circle over the filling. Seal edge with fork. Make two small slits in the top of each pocket with a knife. Bake in a 400 F oven for 15-20 minutes on unbleached parchment paper. About halfway through the baking process, brush tops of dough with milk and return to oven to finish baking until lightly browned.

Serve warm.

Store in a covered container in the refrigerator for up to 5 days.

These can be frozen. Just prepare and bake as directed, then let cool completely on a rack. Once cooled, wrap each one tightly in waxed paper and place in a freezer bag and freeze for up to 2 months. Let thaw in refrigerator overnight. To reheat, remove wax paper and place pocket in a preheated 325 F oven for 15-20 minutes, or until heated through.

PUMPKIN BISCUITS

MAKES 2 DOZEN

Pumpkins are not just for carving on Halloween. Other varieties of pumpkin are grown and have wonderful flavor and are full of nutrition. Try roasting a whole kabacha squash (a.k.a. Japanese pumpkin) then mash or puree to use for this recipe. Kabocha squash is high in beta-carotene, and fiber and contains iron, vitamin C and potassium. Save the seeds and roast separately on a baking pan with a dash of salt for an amazing crunchy treat.

2 ¼ cups barley flour (may substitute kamut flour)
1 TBS baking powder
¾ tsp unrefined sea salt
or Himalayan salt
½ tsp cinnamon
½ tsp ground allspice
⅛ tsp ground cloves
¼ tsp freshly ground nutmeg
1 cup pumpkin purée (may substitute sweet potato purée)
½ cup almond milk
3 TBS macadamia nut oil
2 TBS date syrup or agave nectar
1 tsp vanilla extract

Preheat oven to 425 F. Line a sheet pan with unbleached parchment paper. Whisk together the dry ingredients in a large bowl. In a blender combine the pumpkin purée, almond milk, oil, sweetener and vanilla until smooth. Add wet ingredients to dry and stir gently, just to combine (over-stirring will produce tough biscuits). Roll dough out on a floured board until ½ inch thick. Use biscuit cutter to cut into 2 inch rounds. Place on baking sheet and bake for 15-20 minutes.

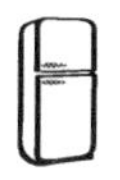

Store in a covered container in the refrigerator for up to 5 days.

GLUTEN-FREE PUMPKIN BISCUITS

MAKES ABOUT 2 DOZEN

2 cups gluten-free flour mix, plus more for rolling (see pg. 377)
1 TBS gluten-free baking powder (see pg. 377)
½ tsp unrefined sea salt or Himalayan salt
1 tsp pumpkin pie spice blend (may substitute1 tsp garam masala)
2 TBS unrefined sesame oil
⅓ cup coconut milk
1 ¾ cup pumpkin purée (may substitute sweet potato puree)
1 TBS date syrup or agave nectar
½ cup dried cranberries, optional (may substitute up to 1 cup fresh or frozen cranberries)

Preheat oven to 400 F. Line baking sheets with unbleached parchment paper and set aside. Mix the dry ingredients together in a large bowl. Add the oil, coconut milk, pumpkin purée and sweetener, then stir until combined well. Add optional cranberries. Roll dough out onto a floured board until ½ inch thick, adding more flour if necessary. Cut into biscuits and place on prepared pans. Bake at 400 F for 12-15 minutes.

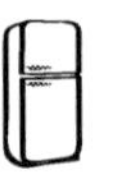

Store in a covered container in the refrigerator for up to 5 days.

RASPBERRY AND WALNUT SCONES

MAKES ABOUT 8-10 SCONES

Walnuts are prized for their Omega 3 content, an essential fatty acid helpful for improving heart health and decreasing inflammation in the body. A handful of walnuts a day helps keep the doctor away!

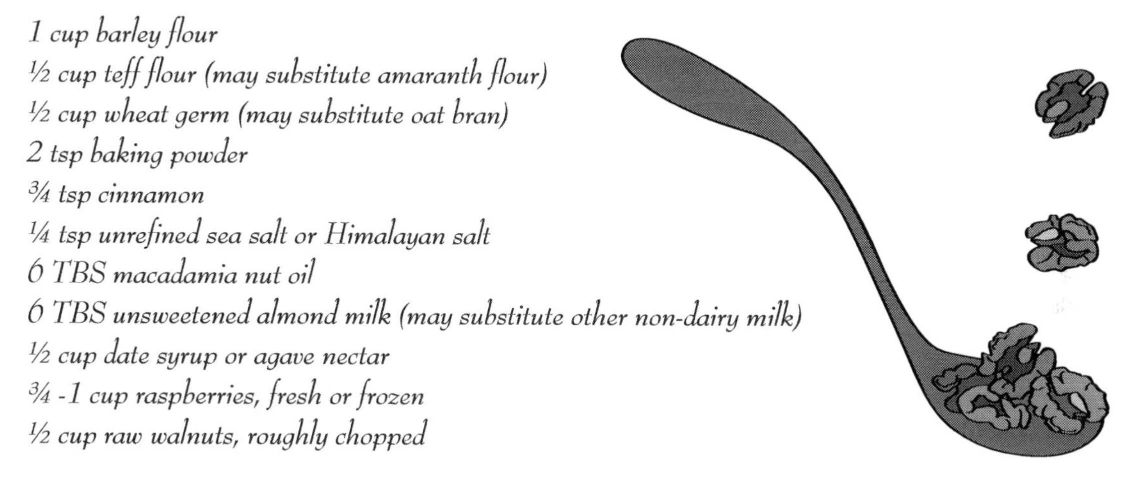

1 cup barley flour
½ cup teff flour (may substitute amaranth flour)
½ cup wheat germ (may substitute oat bran)
2 tsp baking powder
¾ tsp cinnamon
¼ tsp unrefined sea salt or Himalayan salt
6 TBS macadamia nut oil
6 TBS unsweetened almond milk (may substitute other non-dairy milk)
½ cup date syrup or agave nectar
¾ -1 cup raspberries, fresh or frozen
½ cup raw walnuts, roughly chopped

Preheat oven to 375 F. Line a baking sheet with unbleached parchment paper and set aside. In a medium bowl whisk together the flours, wheat germ, baking powder, cinnamon and salt. Drizzle in the oil and toss gently with a fork to combine. In a small bowl whisk together the milk and sweetener, then pour over the flour and stir just until combined. Gently fold in the raspberries and walnuts. Drop batter by the spoonful onto the parchment lined baking sheet, roughly 3-4 inches in diameter. You should end up with about 8-10 scones. Bake for about 12 to 14 minutes or until lightly browned. Let cool on a rack before serving.

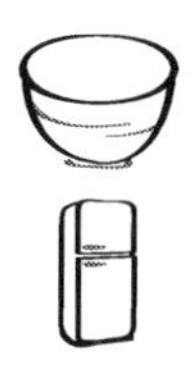

To serve, reheat in a 300 F toaster oven until warm.

Store in a covered container in the refrigerator for up to 5 days.

"A NIGHT IN TUNISIA" SCONES

MAKES 24 SMALL SCONES

Inspired by Dizzy and Ella.

2 cups barley flour (may substitute kamut flour)
½ cup rolled oats
1 TBS baking powder
¾ tsp cinnamon
¼ tsp ground ginger
¼ tsp ground allspice
¼ tsp ground cardamom
¼ tsp garam masala
¼ tsp unrefined sea salt or Himalayan salt
½ cup olive oil
1 cup thoroughly cooked and cooled red lentils (mashed potato consistency)
½ cup applesauce, unsweetened
2 TBS date syrup or agave nectar
1 TBS lemon juice
½ cup dried apricots, chopped small
¼ cup chopped raw pistachios (may substitute almonds)

Preheat oven to 375 F. Line 2 baking sheets with unbleached parchment paper and set aside. Whisk together the flour, oats, baking powder, spices and salt in a large bowl. Drizzle the oil over the flour mixture while stirring with a wooden spoon (it helps to place a damp towel underneath your bowl to prevent slipping and sliding while stirring and drizzling). In a small bowl whisk together the cooked lentils, applesauce, sweetener, and lemon juice, then add to the flour mixture and stir just until combined. Fold in the chopped apricots and pistachios. Drop dough onto baking sheets into approximately 2 inch mounds. Do not flatten or try to form too much. Bake for 15-18 minutes or until lightly browned. Transfer to a rack to cool for a few minutes.

Serve warm.

Store in a covered container in the refrigerator for up to 5 days. Reheat in a 300 F toaster oven until warm.

BREAKFAST LENTIL COOKIES

MAKES ABOUT 3 DOZEN

You might as well cook up a whole bunch of lentils
and use the extra lentils for soups or porridge.

⅔ cup red lentils, picked over to remove stones, and rinsed (see note)*
2 cups water
1 TBS flax seeds, freshly ground, mixed in 2 TBS water or orange juice
1 cup whole wheat pastry flour
1 cup barley flour
1 tsp baking powder
½ tsp unrefined sea salt or Himalayan salt
2 tsp cinnamon
½ tsp allspice
½ cup oil (macadamia nut, olive oil or unrefined sesame oil)
¾ cup date syrup or agave nectar
2 tsp vanilla extract
1 cup rolled oats (may substitute quinoa flakes)
½ cup goji berries, soaked for 10 minutes in water, then drained
½ cup dried cranberries
½ cup chopped raw nuts or seeds (I like sunflower or sesame seeds)

Preheat oven to 350 F. Line baking sheets with unbleached parchment paper and set aside. Cook lentils in water for 30 minutes over medium heat, covered. You want the lentils to be very soft and mushy, like mashed potatoes. Blend, if necessary, after cooking to reach creamy consistency. Measure lentils to equal 1 ½ cups. Set aside.

Meanwhile, grind the flax seeds and combine with water or orange juice and set aside. In a large bowl whisk together the flours, baking powder, salt, cinnamon and allspice. Add oil, sweetener, vanilla, the flax seed mixture and the lentils to the dry ingredients and stir to combine. Fold in the oats, berries and nuts or seeds. Form dough into tablespoon-size cookies on parchment lined baking sheet and bake for 20 minutes, or until golden brown. Cool on a rack.

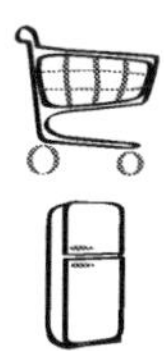

You must use the red lentils (actually orange in color) to achieve desired texture.

Store in a covered container in the refrigerator for up to 5 days.

BANANA SESAME MUFFINS
MAKES 18 MUFFINS

These are GOOD, and they make me happy.

2 TBS flax seeds, freshly ground, mixed with ¼ cup water (or chia seeds, ground)
4 TBS unrefined sesame oil (not toasted sesame oil)
½ cup date syrup or agave nectar
⅔ cup non-dairy milk
1 tsp vanilla extract
1 ½ cups diced, ripe banana (from about 3 medium bananas)
2 cups flour (barley, spelt, kamut, whole wheat or a combination)
2 tsp baking powder
½ tsp baking soda
½ tsp unrefined sea salt or Himalayan salt
⅛ tsp freshly ground nutmeg (This is key! Grate a nutmeg "nut" with a microplane.)
¾ cup sesame seeds (tan, not white)

Preheat oven to 375 F. Line your muffin pan with unbleached parchment paper cups. Combine the freshly ground seeds with the water in a small bowl and set aside. In a large bowl, whisk together the sesame oil, sweetener, milk and vanilla. Add the diced bananas and the flax seed mixture and fold to combine.

In a separate bowl, whisk together the flour, baking powder, baking soda, salt, and freshly ground nutmeg. Add the wet ingredients to the dry ingredients and stir just until combined, then fold in the sesame seeds. Be careful not to over mix the batter. Place batter into parchment paper muffin cups and bake for 20-25 minutes, or until lightly browned on top and cooked through. Let cool on a rack before serving.

Try not to open the oven door until they have been baking for at least 15 minutes or it may cause the muffins to deflate.

Store in a covered container in the refrigerator for up to 5 days.

CHOCOLATE BEET BANANA MUFFINS

MAKES 12 REGULAR MUFFINS

Fiber, minerals, antioxidants and liver cleansing properties - all in a muffin? Believe it and try it!

¾ cup millet flour (may substitute oat flour)
¾ cup teff flour (may substitute barley flour)
⅓ cup cornmeal, finely ground
¼ cup cocoa powder (may substitute raw cacao powder)
1 ½ tsp baking soda
¼ tsp unrefined sea salt or Himalayan salt
½ tsp cinnamon
¼ tsp freshly ground nutmeg
½ cup non-dairy milk
2 TBS macadamia oil
6 TBS date syrup or agave nectar
1 TBS apple cider vinegar
½ cup mashed ripe banana (use a potato masher)
1 cup packed, grated beets (from 1 medium beet, peeled first)

Preheat oven to 350 F and line muffin pan with unbleached parchment paper cups or lightly oil with coconut oil. Sift all dry ingredients together in a large bowl. In another bowl, combine the milk, oil, sweetener, vinegar and banana, then mix well. Pour wet into dry, stirring just until combined. Fold in the beets. Spoon into muffin tray and bake 20-25 minutes, until centers are firm to the touch. Remove from oven and let cool on a rack before serving.

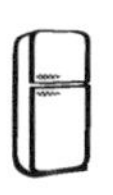

Store in a covered container in the refrigerator for up to 5 days.

ORANGE DATE MUFFINS

MAKES 16 MUFFINS

2 TBS whole flax seeds (may substitute chia seeds)
¼ cup water
1 cup barley flour (may substitute kamut or spelt flour)
2 tsp baking powder
½ tsp baking soda
¼ tsp unrefined sea salt or Himalayan salt
¼ tsp cinnamon
2 tsp orange zest
½ cup chopped, pitted dates (see note)*
¾ cup plain soy yogurt (may substitute rice or coconut yogurt)
½ cup orange juice
3 TBS macadamia nut oil
2 TBS date syrup or agave nectar
¼ cup goji berries, soaked in water for 15 minutes to soften, then drained
¼ cup raw walnuts, chopped

Preheat oven to 350 F. Line a muffin pan with unbleached parchment paper cups. Grind flax seeds or chia seeds in a coffee grinder, then remove and combine with water in a small bowl. Let sit until thickened (about 15 minutes). In a large bowl, whisk together the flour, baking powder, baking soda, salt, cinnamon and orange zest. In a blender or food processor combine the drained pitted dates, yogurt, orange juice, oil and sweetener until almost smooth, some little bits of dates are nice. Add wet ingredients, including the ground flax seeds, to the dry ingredients and stir just until combined. Fold in the drained goji berries and walnuts. Pour into muffin pan and bake for 35-40 minutes or until done.

You can substitute **figs** instead of the dates (but then you will have to call them "Orange Fig Muffins)." Instead of puréeing them just finely chop enough figs to equal ½ cup and fold them into the batter with the goji berries.

Unless you have a vita-mix blender you will need to soften the dates before adding them to your blender. Do this by removing the pits then placing dates in a pan and covering them with water. Simmer for 5-10 minutes or until softened. Drain and proceed.

Store in a covered container in the refrigerator for up to 5 days.

SWEET POTATO-CORN MUFFINS

MAKES 12 REGULAR MUFFINS

1 ¾ cup mashed sweet potato (or 1 can sweet potato puree)
⅓ cup macadamia nut oil
½ cup date syrup or agave nectar
¾ cup applesauce, unsweetened
2 cups barley flour
1 cup cornmeal
1 TBS baking powder
1 tsp cinnamon
½ tsp ground ginger
¼ tsp each ground cloves, freshly ground nutmeg and unrefined sea salt
¾ cup dried cranberries
¼ cup rolled oats

Preheat oven to 375 F. Line a muffin pan with unbleached parchment paper cups. Blend the sweet potatoes, oil, sweetener and applesauce until smooth. Whisk together the flour, cornmeal, baking powder and spices in a bowl. Add wet ingredients to dry. Fold in the dried cranberries and oats. Pour into muffin pan and bake for 30 minutes or until done. Let cool in pan on a rack for 10 minutes before removing from pan.

Store in a covered container in the refrigerator for up to 5 days.

APPLE OAT GOJI MUFFINS

MAKES ABOUT 12

1 large granny smith apple, peeled
½ cup plus 2 TBS almond milk
1 egg replacer of choice, equal to 1 egg (see pg. 376)
¾ tsp unrefined sea salt or Himalayan salt
½ cup applesauce, unsweetened
5 TBS date syrup or agave nectar
½ cup goji berries, softened (see note)*
3 TBS unrefined sesame oil
2 cups kamut flour
½ cup rolled oats
2 ½ tsp baking powder
¾ tsp ground cinnamon
¼ tsp allspice
¼ tsp ginger powder
¼ cup almond slivers
1 TBS rapadura (unrefined sugar)

Preheat oven to 400 F. Lightly oil a muffin pan with coconut oil or line with unbleached parchment paper cups. Grate the apple into a large bowl, avoiding the core of the apple. Add the almond milk, egg replacer, salt, apple sauce, sweetener, and softened and drained goji berries. Whisk until combined. In another bowl, whisk together the flour, oats, baking powder and spices. Add the wet to the dry ingredients and stir with a wooden spoon just until combined. Fill the muffin cups about ⅔ full. Top them with the almond slivers and sprinkle with rapadura. Bake for about 30 minutes, rotating the pan halfway through baking time. Let cool in pan for 5-10 minutes and then move to a rack to finish cooling.

To soften goji berries, place in a small glass bowl and pour a little boiling water over berries and let soften for 10 minutes. Scoop berries out of water and let drain before adding to recipe. Drink the reserved water or add to soups and teas.

Store in a covered container in the refrigerator for up to 5 days.

GRANOLA BARS

MAKES 12 BARS

These are nutrient dense and hearty. If they contained a cruciferous vegetable it would just about count as a complete meal.

1 cup rolled oats
1 cup whole grain cereal flakes, lightly crushed into smaller pieces
⅓ cup pumpkin seeds
¼ cup hemp seeds
½ cup dates, pitted and diced small (about 5 medjool dates)
½ cup goji berries, soaked for 10 minutes in water to soften, then drained
¼ cup chopped raw almonds (may substitute walnuts)
¼ cup quinoa flakes (may substitute raw quinoa, rinsed and drained)
1 TBS oil (olive, macadamia, unrefined sesame, tea seed or coconut oil)
½ cup date syrup or agave nectar
½ cup raw almond butter
½ tsp unrefined sea salt or Himalayan salt
¾ tsp cinnamon
½ tsp ground ginger
⅓ cup carob chips or chocolate chips, optional (place in freezer for 15 minutes)

Preheat oven to 350 F. Mix together the oats, cereal and pumpkin seeds and spread on a baking sheet. Toast in the oven for 10 minutes, stirring once or twice while baking. Transfer to a mixing bowl and add the hemp seeds, chopped dates, goji berries, almonds and quinoa. Use your hands to break up any clumps. Heat the oil and sweetener over medium heat. After 1 minute add the almond butter and spices and stir with a wooden spoon until smooth. Pour into dry ingredients and mix together quickly. Add the optional carob or chocolate chips now, being careful not to let them melt into the mixture (that's why you chill the chips before adding). Press mixture into a 9 x 13 inch pan with a spatula. Cover and refrigerate at least 4 hours before serving. Cut into small granola bar shapes and serve chilled.

Store in a covered container in the refrigerator for up to 5 days.

CHEWY BANANA BREAKFAST BARS

MAKES 9-12 BARS

2 cups oat flour (see note)*
1 cup rolled oats
1 tsp baking powder
½ tsp unrefined sea salt or Himalayan salt
¼ tsp cinnamon
1 medium banana, ripe, chopped
2 TBS macadamia nut oil (may substitute unrefined sesame oil or olive oil)
¼ cup puréed apricots, unsweetened (may substitute prune puree or applesauce)
1 TBS molasses
⅓ cup date syrup or agave nectar
¼ cup non-dairy milk
¼ cup dried fruit, chopped if necessary (apricots, dates, figs, cranberries or goji)
2 TBS raw pumpkin seeds, optional
2 TBS raw sunflower seeds, optional

Preheat oven to 350°F. Lightly oil a 9x13 inch baking dish. In a large bowl, combine the oat flour, rolled oats, baking powder, salt and cinnamon. In a blender combine the banana, oil, apricot purée, molasses, sweetener and milk, then blend until smooth. Add this mixture into the dry mixture and stir just until combined. Fold in the dried fruit and seeds, if using. Pour the batter into the prepared pan and spread to distribute evenly. Bake for 20-22 minutes, then remove and let the pan cool on a rack. Cut into bars and serve.

Oat flour can be made by placing about 2 cups of rolled oats in a blender or food processor and blending until the consistency is similar to coarse flour. Measure flour to 2 cups and proceed.

Store in a covered container in the refrigerator for up to 5 days.

ZUCCHINI POWER BREAD

MAKES A 9X13 INCH BREAD

The mesquite powder, seeds and goji berries are a great source of energy, healthy fats, protein and minerals.

1 TBS egg replacer powder mixed with 4 TBS water
2 cups whole wheat flour (may substitute spelt flour or barley flour)
½ cup mesquite powder
1 tsp baking soda
1 tsp baking powder
1 tsp cinnamon
½ tsp nutmeg, freshly ground is best
¼ tsp unrefined sea salt or Himalayan salt
½ cup non-dairy milk
1 cup grated apple
½ cup date syrup or agave nectar
2 TBS nut butter (I like raw almond or cashew butter, or tahini)
1 tsp vanilla extract
½ cup raw pumpkin seeds (may substitute sunflower seeds)
½ cup goji berries, soaked for 10 minutes to soften, if necessary, then drained
2 cups grated zucchini (from 3-4 small zucchinis)

Preheat oven to 350 F. Lightly oil the baking pan and set aside. Whisk together the egg replacer powder and water in a small bowl and set aside. In a large bowl, combine dry ingredients with a whisk. In another bowl, stir together the wet ingredients. Add wet ingredients, including the egg replacer mixture, to the dry ingredients until just blended. Then gently fold in the seeds, goji berries and grated zucchini. Pour into prepared pan and bake 40-50 minutes, or until done. Cool 10 minutes on a rack before slicing.

Store in a covered container in the refrigerator for up to 5 days.

CHERRY BREAD PUDDING

SERVES 4

I love cherries! Yet, I don't have a lot of recipes containing cherries because I usually just eat them fresh and never end up with enough leftovers to use in recipes. At any rate, find a way to get them into your diet (organic please!). I was once told by a Chinese Medicine Doctor that eating fruits and vegetables that are red are good for your heart and blood.

1 bag of frozen cherries, pitted
⅓ cup non-dairy milk
2 TBS date syrup or agave nectar
½ tsp ground ginger (see note)*
½ tsp cinnamon (see note)*
pinch of unrefined sea salt or Himalayan salt
½ tsp vanilla extract
⅓ cup goji berries
1 TBS ground kudzu (may substitute arrowroot) (see note)*
2 ½ cups whole grain bread cubes (from about 3 slices)

Preheat oven to 350 F. Lightly oil an 8 x 8 baking dish and set aside. Place the cherries and the milk in a medium saucepan and heat gently over low heat until cherries are thawed but still hold their shape. Then add sweetener, ginger, cinnamon, salt and vanilla. Toss gently to combine. Turn off heat and pour off any liquid into a medium bowl. Whisk in the ground kudzu root.

Meanwhile, add the goji berries to the pan with the cherries. Pour the cherries and goji berries into an 8 x 8 baking dish and then add the cubed bread. Next, pour the kudzu mixture over the cherries and bread and toss gently to combine. Bake 35 minutes. Remove from oven and let cool for 10 minutes.

Option: omit the cinnamon and ginger and add 2 TBS cocoa powder for a chocolate cherry bread pudding. Oh yeah!

Kudzu root powder may sometimes need to be finely ground before using in a recipe. Do this with a mortar and pestle or in a clean coffee grinder.

Serve warm with your favorite non-dairy vanilla "cream" (I like a frozen "rice cream" and cashew or coconut "ice cream").

Store in a covered container in the refrigerator for up to 5 days.

PUMPKIN BANANA CHIP BREAD

MAKES A 9X5 INCH LOAF

1 cup oat flour (grind about 1 cup rolled oats in blender until flour like)
1 cup barley flour
6 TBS quinoa flakes
2 tsp baking powder
1 tsp baking soda
½ tsp unrefined sea salt or Himalayan salt
2 tsp pumpkin pie spice mix (cinnamon, cloves cardamom and nutmeg)
1 TBS egg replacer powder mixed with 2 TBS warm water
½ cup date syrup or agave nectar
2 ripe medium bananas
2 TBS macadamia nut oil (may substitute olive oil)
1 can pumpkin purée (1 ¾ cups), unsweetened
1 tsp vanilla extract
1 tsp apple cider vinegar
½ cup chocolate chips (may substitute cacoa nibs)

Preheat oven to 350 F. Lightly oil a 9x5 inch loaf pan. Whisk together the dry ingredients (oat flour-spice mix) in a large bowl. Combine the egg replacer powder with the water in a small dish and set aside. Place the sweetener, bananas, oil, pumpkin purée, vanilla and apple cider vinegar in a blender and combine until smooth. Now add the egg replacer mixture and blend again to combine. Pour this into the bowl of dry ingredients and stir just until combined. Fold in the chocolate chips and pour batter into the prepared pan. Bake for 40-50 minutes, rotating pan halfway through to ensure even baking. Let cool on a rack before slicing.

Store in a covered container in the refrigerator for up to 5 days, but chances are it won't last that long!

LEMONY BREAKFAST BREAD

MAKES A 9X5 INCH LOAF

It's hard to decide which ingredient to acknowledge in this recipe because there are so many with impressive health benefits. I'll single out lemon this time because it adds an incredible flavor to this nutritious bread. Plus it provides you with vitamin C in the juice and anti-cancer compounds in the zest.

2 TBS whole flax seeds (may substitute chia seeds)
⅓ cup water
2 TBS macadamia nut oil (may substitute unrefined sesame oil or olive oil)
⅓ cup date syrup or agave nectar
⅔ cup unsweetened almond milk
Juice and zest of 2 medium lemons (please use organic)
2 cups barley flour
2 tsp baking powder
¾ tsp unrefined sea salt or Himalayan salt
½ cup raw sunflower seeds, chopped (may substitute pumpkin seeds)
½ cup dried blueberries (fresh or frozen works too)

Preheat oven to 350 F. Lightly oil a 9x5 loaf pan. Grind the flax seeds in a coffee grinder. Combine with water and let sit until thickened (about 15 minutes). Combine the oil, sweetener, almond milk, lemon juice and lemon zest in a large bowl. In a second bowl, whisk together the flour, baking powder and salt. Once the flax seed mixture is thickened, add it to the other wet ingredients and stir to combine. Now add dry ingredients to wet ingredients and stir just to combine. Gently fold in the chopped seeds and blueberries. Pour into pan and bake about 1 hour or until done. Let cool in the pan on a rack. Then slice and serve.

Store in a covered container in the refrigerator for up to 5 days.

HAPPY APPLE BREAD

MAKES A 9X5 INCH LOAF

Apples make me happy. Plus they help to keep your heart healthy and remove toxins from the liver so your body will be happy too.

1 TBS chia seeds, freshly ground (may substitute flax seeds, freshly ground)
½ cup non-dairy milk
1 cup whole wheat pastry flour (may substitute barley flour)
1 cup spelt flour
2 tsp baking powder
1 tsp baking soda
½ tsp unrefined sea salt or Himalayan salt
1 tsp cinnamon
½ tsp ground ginger
¼ tsp ground allspice
½ cup applesauce, unsweetened
¼ cup macadamia nut oil (may substitute unrefined sesame oil or olive oil)
¼ cup date syrup or agave nectar
2 cups grated apples tossed in 3 TBS lemon juice

Heat oven to 350 F. Lightly oil a bread pan and set aside. Grind your chia seeds and place in a bowl with ½ cup non-dairy milk. Whisk to combine and let rest for 10-15 minutes. Whisk together the flours, baking powder, soda, salt and spices in a large bowl. In a separate bowl mix the applesauce, oil and sweetener together until combined. Add wet ingredients (including ground seeds/milk mixture) to the dry ingredients and stir just until combined. Gently fold in the apple/lemon juice mixture, then place batter in the oiled pan. Bake for 45 minutes or until done all the way through. If the top is browned long before the center is finished baking, cover the top or the pan with foil or parchment paper and continue to bake until toothpick comes out clean. Let cool on a rack before slicing.

Store in a covered container in the refrigerator for up to 5 days.

BANANA BREAD

MAKES A 9X5 INCH LOAF

2 cups barley flour (may substitute kamut or spelt flour)
1 tsp baking soda
½ tsp unrefined sea salt or Himalayan salt
3-4 medium bananas, very ripe (2 cups chopped)
½ cup non-dairy milk (I like unsweetened almond milk)
¼ cup macadamia nut oil (may substitute olive oil or unrefined sesame oil)
½ cup date syrup or agave nectar
¼ cup applesauce, unsweetened
1 tsp vanilla extract
¼ cup raw cacao nibs
½ cup rolled oats
½ cup dark chocolate chips (may substitute carob chips), optional

Preheat oven to 350 F. Use coconut oil to grease a loaf pan (9x5). Whisk together the flour, soda and salt. In a blender combine bananas, milk, macadamia nut oil, sweetener, applesauce and vanilla until smooth. Add wet ingredients to dry. Gently fold in the cacao nibs and oats, and the optional chocolate/carob chips, if using. Pour into pan. Bake for 1 hour - 1 hour and 15 minutes, or until done. Let cool in pan for 10 minutes, then remove from pan and cool completely on a rack. Slice and serve.

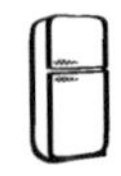

Store in a covered container in the refrigerator for up to 5 days.

BREAKFAST BURRITO

SERVES 6

Vegetable and Bean Filling
1 medium red onion, chopped
4 garlic cloves, pressed
6 medium shiitake mushrooms, cleaned and sliced
¼ cup vegetable broth

Recipe continues on next page...

BREAKFAST BURRITO...

½ red bell pepper, chopped
1 cup broccoli florets
½ tsp turmeric
2 tsp Indian curry powder or paste
1 tsp unrefined sea salt or Himalayan salt
*2 cups **cooked** and drained beans, cooked tempeh cubes or sliced seitan sausage*
1 carrot, scrubbed and grated
5 oz. arugula, cleaned and chopped

Additional Ingredients
1 cup medium salsa
2-3 cups cooked brown rice
2 TBS sesame seeds
1 TBS dulse flakes
1-2 TBS nutritional yeast
1 bunch of cilantro, chopped
6 sprouted tortillas

"Water sauté" the onion, garlic and mushrooms in the vegetable broth over medium heat until liquid is absorbed and vegetables are almost soft. Add the broccoli, red bell pepper, turmeric, curry powder/paste and salt and stir to coat. Add the cooked beans (tempeh or seitan) to the pan and stir to coat. Cook for a few minutes, or until vegetables are tender. Add the grated carrot and chopped arugula. Cook just until arugula is wilted. Remove from heat. Make your own burrito by placing a desired amount of the vegetable and bean filling in the center of each warmed tortilla and then topping with some salsa, brown rice, sesame seeds, seaweed flakes, nutritional yeast and cilantro, to taste. Fold up to make a burrito and serve.

Heat the sprouted wraps to make them easier to fill by steaming for a few minutes just prior to filling or by placing each wrap in a dry skillet and heating for a couple of minutes on each side until warm. Don't let the wraps overcook or they will be too crunchy to roll up into a burrito. In this case, just place toppings on top of the crispy wrap and call it a tostada!

You can store ready-made burritos by wrapping each one tightly in parchment paper and then placing in a covered container in the refrigerator for up to 5 days. To reheat, place the parchment paper wrapped burrito in a preheated 300 F oven for 15-20 minutes or until heated through.

TEMPEH BREAKFAST SAUSAGE

MAKES 16 2-INCH PATTIES

There is also a version under "Tempeh" (see pg. 298).

1 lb. of tempeh, cubed and boiled for 15 minutes
*2 TBS flax seeds or chia seeds, ground in a coffee grinder *(see note)*
¼ cup vegetable broth (may substitute water)
1 small onion, minced fine
2 garlic cloves, pressed
2 tsp dried sage
1 tsp dried oregano
¾ tsp red pepper flakes
½ tsp fennel seeds, ground
½ tsp unrefined sea salt or Himalayan salt
¼ cup nutritional yeast
oat flour (optional)

Preheat oven to 350 F. While tempeh is boiling, whisk together the ground flax seeds with the broth in a small bowl and let sit until thickened (about 15 minutes). In a separate bowl, stir together the minced onion, garlic and spices. Crumble the boiled tempeh into this and toss to combine. Now add the flax seed mixture and mix thoroughly. If mixture seems dry, sprinkle on more broth. If mixture is too wet, add a bit more nutritional yeast (or use oat flour). Using wet hands, shape into sausage patties, 2 inches in diameter and ½ inch thick. Place on a parchment lined baking sheet and bake for 25 minutes. Flip and bake another 10 minutes. Remove from oven and serve.

Always buy whole flax seeds and chia seeds and grind them yourself in a spice grinder or in a clean coffee grinder. This means buying the seeds whole, not already ground, and grinding only what you need as you need it. Once these seeds are ground they are exposed to air which causes the omega 3 oil in the seed to go rancid. Rancid food is not good for you!

Store in a covered container in the refrigerator for up to 5 days.

To clean a coffee grinder, place a tablespoon of uncooked rice (one way to use up any white rice you still have in your house) and grind it until pulverized. Unplug the grinder and throw away the ground rice. Carefully wipe clean with a damp towel. This will remove most of the coffee flavor and grounds, repeat if necessary, adding a drop of white vinegar to the towel.

Desserts

"You can have your cake and eat it too as long as it's a healthy cake."

~ Kristin Doyle

BERRY APPLESAUCE WITH GINGER

GF

SERVES 4-6

Berries are full of antioxidants and fiber which help boost the immune system and fight disease.

2 large granny smith apples, peeled and diced
1 bag of organic frozen mixed berries
1 inch piece of ginger, scrubbed well or peeled
cinnamon
¼ cup goji berries, to garnish
1 pint sized container of non-dairy ice cream (I like vanilla rice "cream")

Place the diced apples and frozen berries in a heavy bottomed pan and heat over medium heat for 20 minutes. Check a few times to make sure nothing is sticking or burning. The fruit should start to cook down. Now add the ginger by grating it with a microplane or small grater. Sprinkle on some cinnamon and top with goji berries. Serve over non-dairy ice cream.

Store applesauce in a covered container in the refrigerator for up to 5 days.

(GF) OATMEAL-GOJI BERRY BALLS

MAKES 3 DOZEN

The goji berry looks like a red raisin and is super high in antioxidants! It has been used for centuries in Tibet to promote a long, happy life free from illness. Goji berries help keep blood sugar levels stable, help protect vision, prevent cancer and heart disease and help to slow the aging process. Please buy organic to avoid pesticides.

2 cups rolled oats (use quinoa flakes for gluten-free), ground in a food processor until coarse crumbs
3 medium bananas, ripe
⅓ cup raw almonds or walnuts, ground in a food processor until coarse crumbs
1 cup chopped, pitted dates (chopped to same size as the goji berry)
1 cup goji berries, soaked for 15 minutes in warm water, then drained
¼ cup mesquite powder
½ tsp unrefined sea salt or Himalayan salt
1 TBS vanilla extract

Preheat oven to 325 F. Line a cookie sheet with unbleached parchment paper. In a medium bowl mash the bananas with a fork. Add the ground oats, nuts, chopped dates and goji berries. Mix well. Add mesquite powder, salt, vanilla and stir well to combine. Use wet hands to form 1 TBS sized balls onto sheet pan and bake for 25 minutes, rotating halfway through bake time.

You could also form these into balls and just refrigerate them without baking for an unbaked treat.

Store in a covered container in the refrigerator for up to 5 days.

SESAME LEMON COOKIES

MAKES ABOUT 2 DOZEN COOKIES

1 cup rolled oats
¾ cup sesame seeds, toasted
1 ½ cup barley flour
1 tsp baking soda
pinch of unrefined sea salt or Himalayan salt
2 TBS lemon zest, from about 2 organic lemons
6 TBS unrefined sesame oil (may substitute macadamia nut oil or melted coconut oil)
6 TBS date syrup or agave nectar
4 TBS lemon juice

Preheat oven to 375 F. Line a cookie sheet with unbleached parchment paper. Toast the sesame seeds in a dry skillet over medium-low heat until they smell nutty. If they start to pop out of the pan, lower the heat. Once they are lightly toasted remove immediately from the pan to a plate to cool. Process the rolled oats and toasted sesame seeds together in a food processor or blender. Add this to a bowl with the flour, baking soda, salt and lemon zest.

In a separate bowl mix the oil, sweetener and lemon juice. Add to the flour mixture and stir just to combine. Roll into 1 inch balls using wet hands and place on a parchment lined cookie sheet. Press to flatten slightly. Bake 12 minutes or until lightly browned. Cool on a rack.

Optional: Add 2 TBS goji berries to the batter (soak the berries first for 15 minutes in water, then drain)

Store in a covered container in the refrigerator for up to 5 days.

THUMBPRINT COOKIES

MAKES ABOUT 2 DOZEN COOKIES

These are gluten-free cookies with quinoa flakes for extra protein. Nutritious and delicious!

1 cup quinoa flakes, toasted (may substitute rolled oats, toasted) * *(see note)*
1 cup nuts (almonds, pecans or walnuts), toasted, cooled and ground in a food processor * *(see note)*
1 cup brown rice flour
1/8 tsp cinnamon
1/2 cup oil (macadamia, sesame or coconut)
1/2 cup date syrup, agave nectar or brown rice syrup
1 TBS vanilla extract
1/8 tsp unrefined sea salt or Himalayan salt
1/2 cup organic fruit preserves

Preheat oven to 350 F. Line a cookie sheet with unbleached parchment paper. Combine toasted flakes, ground nuts, flour and cinnamon in a large bowl. In a separate bowl combine the oil, sweetener, vanilla and salt. Add wet ingredients to the dry ingredients and stir to combine. Use wet hands to roll into small balls and place on a parchment lined cookie sheets. Press flat and use a thumb to make a well in the center of each cookie (a thumbprint). Fill with a teaspoon of fruit preserves. Bake for 12-15 minutes. Remove from oven and let cool on tray.

Toast the flakes by placing them on a sheet pan in a 300 F oven for 5-10 minutes or until lightly browned. The quinoa flakes will toast more quickly than the rolled oats.

Toast the nuts on a separate sheet pan from the quinoa flakes or rolled oats. Bake in a 300 F oven for about 10 minutes, until lightly toasted, checking often to prevent burning.

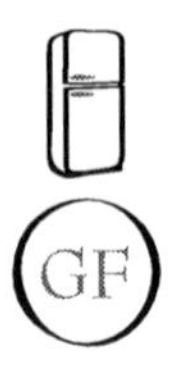

Store in a covered container in the refrigerator for up to 5 days.

Please note that the recipe will no longer be gluten-free if you use oats in this recipe.

CHOCOLATE CHIP COOKIES
MAKES ABOUT 2 DOZEN

2 ½ cups barley flour
1 cup oat flour (make by placing about 1 cup rolled oats in a blender until flour like)
1 tsp baking soda
½ tsp unrefined sea salt or Himalayan salt
½ cup oil (unrefined sesame oil, tea seed oil or macadamia oil)
½ cup date syrup or agave nectar
1 tsp vanilla extract
1 cup chocolate chips, (may substitute some carob chips or cacao nibs) (see note)*
a few TBS of water or non-dairy milk

Preheat oven to 350 F. Line a cookie sheet with unbleached parchment paper. Mix the flours, soda and salt with a whisk. In a separate bowl whisk the oil, sweetener, and vanilla. Combine the wet into the dry. Add the chocolate chips. Pour a little water or almond milk into a bowl. Use this to keep your hands wet so batter won't stick to hands when forming into balls. I usually take about 1-2 TBS and form into balls with wet hands (this will also make the outside of the cookie crispy). Place on a parchment lined sheet and bake at 350 F for about 12-15 minutes or until lightly browned. Let cool or not. Either way is Yummy!

You may add more or less chocolate chips depending on how much you like chocolate.

Store in a covered container in the refrigerator for up to 5 days.

GINGER COOKIES

MAKES ABOUT 2 DOZEN

2 cups spelt flour (may substitute a combination of spelt, barley and oat flours)
½ tsp baking soda
½ tsp cinnamon
¾ tsp ginger powder
¼ tsp unrefined sea salt or Himalayan salt
a dash or three of cayenne
¼ cup macadamia nut oil
6 TBS date syrup or agave nectar
2 TBS molasses

Heat oven to 350 F. Line a cookie sheet with unbleached parchment paper. Whisk together the dry ingredients in a large bowl. In a smaller bowl, whisk together the wet ingredients. Add wet to dry and mix well. Wrap dough tightly in parchment paper or waxed paper and let rest and chill in the refrigerator for 1 hour or more (just be sure it is wrapped tightly so that it doesn't dry out). Remove from fridge and discard paper. Use wet hands to form into small cookie shapes, about 1-2 inches in diameter and ¼-½ inch thick. Place on parchment lined sheets and bake in preheated oven for 8-10 minutes. Let cool on a rack before serving.

Store in a covered container in the refrigerator for up to 5 days.

GLUTEN-FREE GINGER COOKIES

MAKES ABOUT 1 ½ DOZEN

½ cup sorghum flour
¼ cup amaranth flour
¼ cup quinoa flour
1 tsp ground ginger powder
½ tsp baking soda
¼ tsp unrefined sea salt or Himalayan salt
dash of cayenne
1 TBS egg replacer powder
2 TBS water

Recipe continues on next page...

GLUTEN-FREE GINGER COOKIES...

2 TBS macadamia nut oil (may substitute tea seed oil or unrefined sesame oil)
2 TBS molasses
¼ cup date syrup or agave nectar

Follow same directions as indicated for ginger cookies.

COCOA-GINGER COOKIES

MAKES 1 ½ DOZEN

1 cup spelt flour (may substitute kamut, barley or whole wheat flour)
2 TBS cocoa powder (may substitute raw cacao powder)
1 tsp ground ginger powder
½ tsp baking soda
¼ tsp unrefined sea salt or Himalayan salt
dash of cayenne
1 TBS egg replacer powder
2 TBS warm water
2 TBS macadamia nut oil (may substitute tea seed oil or unrefined sesame oil)
2 TBS molasses
¼ cup date syrup or agave nectar

Whisk together the flour, ginger, baking soda, salt and cayenne in a medium bowl. In a small bowl whisk together the egg replacer powder with the water. Then add the oil, molasses and sweetener. Whisk to combine well, then pour into flour mixture and stir with a wooden spoon until combined. Cover dough and refrigerate for up to 30 minutes.

Meanwhile, preheat oven to 350 F. Line cookie sheets with unbleached parchment paper. Once dough is chilled shape into little balls (using wet hands), about 1 TBS each. Place on baking sheet about 2 inches apart then flatten lightly into cookie shape with the bottom of a measuring cup (dip bottom of cup in bowl of water to keep from sticking to dough). Bake for 10-12 minutes. Remove and cool on a rack.

Store in a covered container in the refrigerator for up to 5 days.

OAT AND FIG SQUARES

MAKES 16 SQUARES (2 INCHES BY 2 INCHES)

20 mission figs, dried (may substitute dates, remove pits) (see note)*
6 TBS unrefined sesame oil, plus extra for oiling pan (may substitute olive oil or macadamia oil)
¼ cup date syrup or agave nectar
6 TBS non-dairy milk
½ tsp vanilla extract
1 ¼ cup kamut flour (may substitute barley flour)
¾ cup quinoa flour (may substitute amaranth or brown rice flour)
¾ cup rolled oats
½ tsp baking soda
½ tsp unrefined sea salt or Himalayan salt

Preheat oven to 350 F. Coat an 8x8 pan with a little oil and set aside. Place dried figs in a saucepan and cover with water. Bring to a boil and then turn off heat and let soften. Meanwhile, in a bowl mix the oil, sweetener, milk and vanilla. In another bowl, combine the flours, oats, baking soda and salt. Once dried figs are re-hydrated, purée those in a blender or with a potato masher until smooth. You can use some of the re-hydrating water to make blending easier.

Add wet ingredients (**excluding figs**) to dry ingredients and mix well. Place half of the oat mixture into the prepared pan and spread evenly. Now spread the puréed figs on top, then the other half of the oat mixture on top of that. Bake for 20 minutes or until lightly browned. Let cool before cutting into squares.

If using fresh figs, no need to soak and soften figs, just mash figs in blender or with a potato masher with a little water until smooth.

Both fresh and dried figs will need to be trimmed to remove the hard stem that may still be intact. Just snip away with a small knife or a pair of kitchen shears.

Store in a covered container in the refrigerator for up to 5 days.

KRISTIN'S MINI TARTS

MAKES 10-12 TARTS

Use a regular sized muffin pan to make these mini tarts.

2 ½ cups rolled oats (may substitute kamut flakes)
½ cup barley flour (may substitute oat or kamut flour)
pinch of unrefined sea salt or Himalayan salt
7 TBS date syrup or agave nectar
2 TBS orange juice
3 cups chopped fresh fruit (peaches, berries, bananas, kiwi, mango, etc)
1 TBS lemon juice
1 TBS chopped mint leaves or parsley

Preheat oven to 350 F. Lightly oil a muffin tin or line with unbleached parchment paper cups. Combine the oats, flour and salt in a bowl and whisk to combine. Add the sweetener and juice and press into muffin pan (use wet hands when pressing). You want to make a mini pie/tart crust shape so be sure to press in where the sides meet the bottom edge so it is not too thick there. Bake for 12-15 minutes. Meanwhile, chop the fruit and place in a small bowl and toss with the lemon juice. Remove tarts from the oven and fill with chopped fresh fruit and serve sprinkled with mint.

Store in a covered container in the refrigerator for up to 5 days.

APPLE GOJI BERRY CRISP

SERVES 6-8

¼ cup macadamia nut oil
¼ cup date syrup or agave nectar
¾ cup rolled oats
¼ cup whole grain flour
½ cup raw almonds, chopped
1 tsp plus 1 tsp ground cinnamon, divided
pinch of unrefined sea salt or Himalayan salt
5 large apples (I like granny smith apples)
3 TBS lemon juice
1 cup goji berries, soaked in water for 15 minutes, then drained
2 tsp arrowroot powder

Preheat oven to 375 F. Place the oil, sweetener, oats, flour, almonds and 1 tsp of cinnamon in a bowl. Stir to combine. Peel and core the apples and slice them into ¼ inch slices. Place them in a bowl and toss with lemon juice and the other 1 tsp cinnamon. Add the drained goji berries. Sift the arrowroot over the apple mixture and toss to combine. Place the apple mixture in a baking dish (about 8 x 8 inch) and crumble the topping, with dampened fingers, over the apples evenly. Bake the crisp for about 40-45 minutes or until the topping is crisp and the apples are tender.

You may need to cover the top of the crisp with foil or parchment paper if it starts to brown before the inside is cooked and thickened.

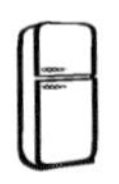

Store in a covered container in the refrigerator for up to 5 days.

BLUEBERRY CRISP

SERVES 6

Blueberries are high in antioxidants and anti-inflammatory compounds that have been shown to help protect the body against the chronic diseases associated with the aging process. Eat one cup of blueberries a day to help improve memory and protect the brain.

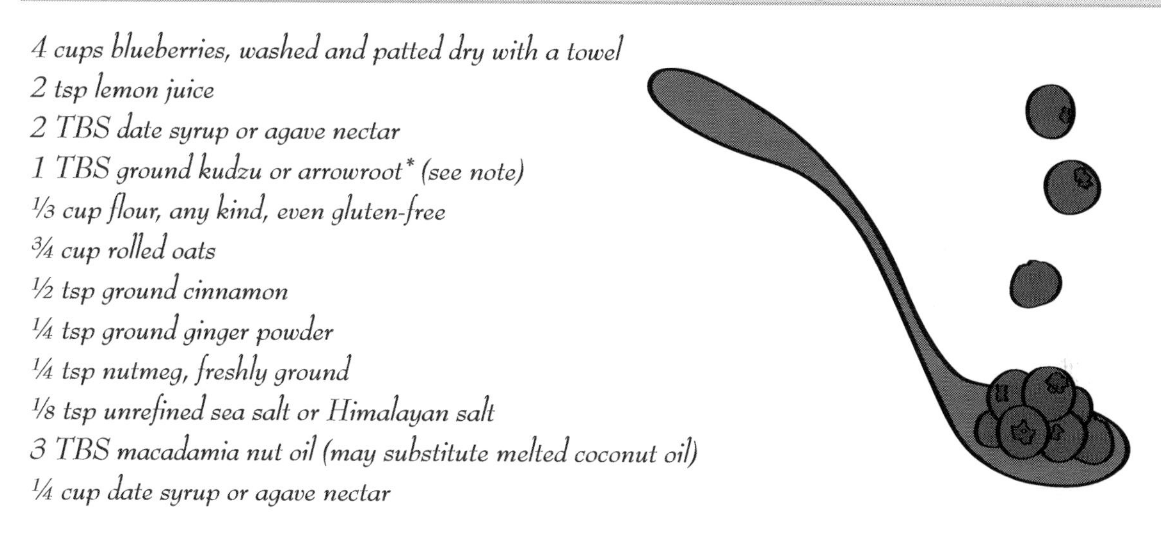

4 cups blueberries, washed and patted dry with a towel
2 tsp lemon juice
2 TBS date syrup or agave nectar
1 TBS ground kudzu or arrowroot (see note)*
1/3 cup flour, any kind, even gluten-free
3/4 cup rolled oats
1/2 tsp ground cinnamon
1/4 tsp ground ginger powder
1/4 tsp nutmeg, freshly ground
1/8 tsp unrefined sea salt or Himalayan salt
3 TBS macadamia nut oil (may substitute melted coconut oil)
1/4 cup date syrup or agave nectar

Preheat oven to 375 F. Lightly oil a medium baking dish (8 x 8). Gently mix berries with lemon juice and 2 TBS sweetener, then toss with the kudzu or arrowroot until evenly coated. Spread into the prepared pan. In a small bowl mix flour, oats, cinnamon, ginger, nutmeg and salt. Add oil and 1/4 cup sweetener and toss with fork until crumbly. Sprinkle over berries. Bake for 30 to 40 minutes or until topping is lightly browned and berries have thickened. Cool for at least 10 minutes before serving.

Kudzu root powder may sometimes need to be finely ground before using in a recipe. Do this with a mortar and pestle or in a clean coffee grinder.

Store in a covered container in the refrigerator for up to 5 days.

BASIC FRUIT CRISP

SERVES 6-8

4 cups of sliced or chopped fruit (apples, pears, blueberries, nectarines, etc)
1 TBS ground kudzu or arrowroot (see note)*
½ cup flour, any whole grain kind
½ cup rolled oats
1 tsp cinnamon
¼ tsp nutmeg, freshly ground is best
⅛ tsp unrefined sea salt or Himalayan salt
3 TBS macadamia nut oil (may substitute tea seed oil)
3 TBS date syrup or agave nectar

Heat oven to 375 F. Lightly oil an 8×8" baking dish. Gently toss sliced fruit with kudzu or arrowroot until evenly coated. Place in the prepared pan. In medium bowl, whisk together the flour, oats, spices and salt. Then drizzle in the oil and sweetener and stir with a fork to combine as best you can. Sprinkle this over fruit. Bake about 30-35 minutes or until topping is lightly browned and fruit is tender and thickened. Let cool for at least 10 minutes before serving.

Kudzu root powder may sometimes need to be finely ground before using in a recipe. Do this with a mortar and pestle or in a clean coffee grinder.

Store in a covered container in the refrigerator for up to 5 days.

SPELT CRUST

MAKES 1 9-INCH PIE CRUST

2 cups spelt flour
1 TBS ground kudzu (may substitute arrowroot) (see note)*
1 tsp baking powder
¼ tsp unrefined sea salt or Himalayan salt
⅓ cup macadamia nut oil (may substitute tea seed oil)
2 TBS date syrup or agave nectar
2-3 TBS water

Preheat oven to 350 F. Lightly oil your pie dish. Whisk together the flour, kudzu, baking powder and salt in a medium bowl. Keep stirring with one hand and drizzle in the oil with another hand (it helps to have a damp towel underneath the bowl to keep it in place, or better yet, recruit a helper for this part). Now switch to a wooden spoon and add the sweetener until combined. You may need to kind of spread it into the mixture. Lastly, add water gradually until the dough starts to hold together when pressed between your thumb and fingers. Press into your pie pan and bake at 350 F for 5-7 minutes. Then remove, let cool, fill with desired filling and bake or chill according to directions.

Kudzu root powder may sometimes need to be finely ground before using in a recipe. Do this with a mortar and pestle or in a clean coffee grinder.

(GF) RAW ALMOND PULP CRUST

MAKES 1 9-INCH PIE CRUST

1 cup almond pulp (leftover from making almond milk - see pg. 90)
½ cup walnuts, soaked for up to 24 hours, drained
1 cup brazil nuts, soaked for up to 24 hours, drained
10 small dates, pitted
½ tsp cinnamon
¼ tsp unrefined sea salt or Himalayan salt

Blend almond pulp, walnuts, brazil nuts, dates, cinnamon and salt in food processor until combined. Press into a lightly oiled pie dish, cover and refrigerate until ready to fill.

You don't need to bake this crust. Simply fill with a no-bake filling and chill.

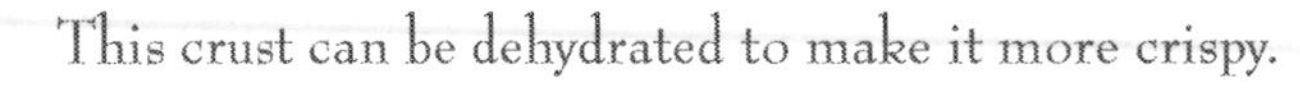
This crust can be dehydrated to make it more crispy.

SUNFLOWER-BRAZIL NUT CRUST

MAKES 1 9-INCH PIE CRUST

2 cups sunflower seeds, soaked 12-24 hours in water to cover in refrigerator
2 cups brazil nuts, soaked 12-24 hours in water to cover in refrigerator
10-12 pitted dates, soaked in hot water until soft (5 minutes to 1 hour)
dash of unrefined sea salt or Himalayan salt
dash of cinnamon

Drain the nuts and seeds, rinse and drain again. Place in a food processor with the drained, pitted dates and the salt and cinnamon and process until thoroughly blended. You may have to stop and scrape down the sides of the bowl and process again. Press into a lightly oiled 9-inch pie dish (or a spring-form pan).

You don't need to bake this crust. Simply fill with a no-bake filling and chill.

This crust can be dehydrated to make it more crispy.

CHOCO-NUT CRUST

GF

MAKES 1 9-INCH PIE CRUST

1 cup brazil nuts, chopped
1 cup shredded coconut
1-2 TBS raw cacao nibs
1 TBS raw cacao powder (may substitute cocoa powder)
Pinch of unrefined sea salt or Himalayan salt
¼ vanilla bean, cut open lengthwise to gather seeds
1-2 TBS raw agave nectar

Place the brazil nuts, shredded coconut, cacao nibs, cacao powder, salt, and vanilla bean seeds in a food processor and process until fine crumbs. Add 1 TBS of the agave and process until the mixture just starts to stick together, adding more if necessary. Press into the bottom of a lightly oiled pie dish or spring-form pan.

You don't need to bake this crust. Simply fill with a no-bake filling and chill.

This crust can be dehydrated to make it more crispy.

BEST EVER NECTARINE-BERRY PIE

SERVES 8

I must admit I think there's nothing better than a ripe nectarine.

1 whole grain pie crust to fit a 9-inch pie pan *(see pg. 425)*

Topping
¾ cup whole grain flour
½ cup rolled oats
1 tsp cinnamon
½ tsp unrefined sea salt or Himalayan salt
3 TBS macadamia nut oil
3 TBS date syrup or agave nectar

Filling
3 ripe nectarines, sliced ¼- ½ inch thick (no need to peel if organic)
2 cups berries (blueberries, raspberries, strawberries or gojis, picked through, rinsed)
1 TBS lemon juice
¼ cup date syrup or agave nectar
¼ cup ground kudzu root or arrowroot (see note)*

Preheat oven to 350 F. Have a pie crust neatly and evenly pressed into a pie pan. Make the topping by tossing together the flour, oats, cinnamon and salt in a small bowl. Whisk the oil and 3 TBS sweetener in a separate bowl and drizzle over the oats and toss to combine. Set aside.

Prepare the filling by placing the nectarines, berries, lemon juice and sweetener in a bowl and toss to combine. Evenly sprinkle on the kudzu and toss gently to coat the fruit. Pour the filling into the pie crust and use fingers to place little pieces of the topping on top of filling. Cover pie with foil and bake in oven for 30 minutes. Uncover and bake for another 20-30 minutes or until crust is lightly browned. Remove from oven and let cool thoroughly before slicing. This will allow the filling to set and remain thickened.

If necessary grind your kudzu root with a mortar and pestle or in a clean coffee grinder until perfectly smooth (no bits).

Store in a covered container in the refrigerator for up to 5 days.

NUTTY PUMPKIN PIE

MAKES A 9-INCH PIE

The holidays just got a little healthier!

1 ¾ cup pumpkin purée (plain, unsweetened)
½ cup raw almond butter
3 TBS non-dairy milk
6 TBS date syrup, agave nectar or brown rice syrup
2 TBS molasses
2 TBS ground kudzu (may substitute egg replacer powder) (see note)*
1 tsp vanilla extract
1 tsp cinnamon
¼ tsp unrefined sea salt or Himalayan salt
¼ tsp each ground cardamom, allspice and nutmeg
⅛ tsp ground cloves
1 crust recipe, your choice

Preheat oven to 350 F. Place all ingredients except crust in a blender and blend until smooth and creamy. Pour into partially baked crust and bake for 45 minutes to 1 hour, or until no longer jiggly. If it starts to burn on top, cover with foil or parchment paper and continue to bake until done.

I use a plunger style "adjust-a-cup" device that slides open and closed to measure and remove sticky items such as pumpkin puree, almond butter, syrups, agave nectar and molasses.

Kudzu root powder may sometimes need to be finely ground before using in a recipe. Do this with a mortar and pestle or in a clean coffee grinder.

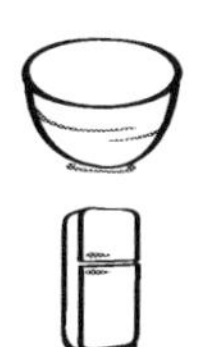

Serve with a side of cashew cream spiced with cinnamon.

Store in a covered container in the refrigerator for up to 5 days.

NECTARINE AND PLUOT GALETTE

SERVES 8-10

A Galette is a rustic free-form pie. Use almost any fruit you like or whatever's in season: peaches, plums, apples, pears, raspberries, blueberries, mango, persimmon, etc.

1 ½ cups barley flour, spelt or kamut flour, plus more for rolling
¼ tsp unrefined sea salt or Himalayan salt
5 TBS macadamia nut oil (may substitute olive oil or tea seed oil)
4 TBS water
cornmeal for dusting pan
3 ripe (but not soft) nectarines, sliced ⅓ inch thick wedges (do not peel)
3 ripe (but not soft) pluots, sliced like the nectarines
1 tsp grated ginger
½ tsp cinnamon
3 TBS ground kudzu (may substitute arrowroot) (see note)*
2 TBS date syrup, agave nectar or brown rice syrup
1 TBS non-dairy milk, for glazing crust

Place the flour and salt in a food processor and pulse to combine. Slowly pour in the oil through the top while machine is running until the mixture looks like coarse crumbs. Stop and scrape the sides of the bowl. Now slowly add the water while the machine is running just until the dough starts to come together (you may not need all of the water). Remove the dough and wrap in waxed paper and place in the freezer for 15 minutes.

Preheat oven to 375 F. Line a baking sheet with unbleached parchment paper and lightly dust with cornmeal. Unwrap the dough and place it on a lightly floured board to make a 12-inch circle. Carefully move the dough to the prepared baking sheet by folding it in half (very gently and lightly), then in half again so it is easier to move. Unfold it on the baking sheet (so it is a circle shape again).

In a medium bowl combine the fruit slices with the ginger, cinnamon and kudzu and toss gently to coat. Then toss with the sweetener. Place fruit mixture in the middle of the dough, leaving a border of 2 inches. You can arrange the fruit in alternating slices to make a spiral circle. Fold the bare edges of the dough over the fruit to make a rustic, open-faced, free-form pie. Bake for 20 minutes, then brush the crust with the milk and bake another 10 minutes, or until golden brown. Remove from oven and place pie on a rack to cool for at least 10 minutes before slicing.

Recipe continues on next page...

NECTARINE AND PLUOT GALETTE...

Kudzu root powder may sometimes need to be finely ground before using in a recipe. Do this with a mortar and pestle or in a clean coffee grinder.

Store in a covered container in the refrigerator for up to 5 days.

CHOCOLATE AVOCADO CREAM PIE WITH BERRIES (GF)

MAKES A 9 INCH PIE

2 cups of diced avocado, from 2-3 avocados (see note)*
½ cup ***pitted*** *dates, softened by soaking in hot water, if necessary, then drained*
¾ cup raw agave nectar (may substitute yacon syrup)
¾ cup raw cacao powder (may substitute cocoa powder or carob powder)
1 tsp vanilla extract
¼ tsp unrefined sea salt or Himalayan salt
1 cup fresh raspberries, blueberries or strawberries, for garnish
1 pie crust for a 9-inch pie pan, tart pan, or spring-form pan (see pg. 426)

Process the avocado, dates, agave, cacao powder, vanilla and salt in a food processor until creamy. Add a dash of water if necessary to get the blender going. You may need to stop and scrape down the sides of the blender and blend again until smooth. Taste for sweet, chocolate and salt. Adjust to meet needs. Pour into crust and place in refrigerator for at least 4 hours so it can set.

Serve chilled, garnished with fresh berries.

Store in a covered container in the refrigerator for up to 3 days.

Please be sure that your avocados are just ripe and not overripe. And, as always, discard any brown spots in the avocado - they won't taste good!

STRAWBERRY RHUBARB CAKE

MAKES 1 9-INCH ROUND CAKE (I USE A SPRING-FORM PAN)

Inspired by Susanne, because no one loves rhubarb more than she does!

2 cups barley flour (may substitute kamut flour)
2 tsp baking powder
1 tsp baking soda
¼ tsp unrefined sea salt or Himalayan salt
½ cup olive oil
1 TBS chia seeds, freshly ground (could also use flax seeds, freshly ground)
¾ cup date syrup or agave nectar
2 TBS almond milk
1 cup unsweetened soy or rice yogurt
1 tsp vanilla extract
1 TBS apple cider vinegar
1 ½ cups chopped strawberries
1 ½ cups chopped rhubarb
Garnish: 3 or 4 beautiful strawberries, 1 TBS lemon juice and 1 TBS brown rice syrup

Preheat oven to 350 F. Oil a 9-inch spring-form pan and set aside. Place the flour, baking powder, soda and salt in a large bowl and whisk to combine. In a separate bowl, whisk together the oil, ground chia seeds, sweetener, almond milk, yogurt and vanilla. Add this to the flour mixture and stir just until combined. Fold in the apple cider vinegar, and then fold in the chopped fruit. Pour batter into prepared pan and bake for 45 minutes or until done (check after 30 minutes). Let cool before serving.

Prepare the garnish by thinly slicing the strawberries across into heart-shaped pieces. Zest the lemon and then cut lemon in half. Place strawberries in a small bowl and toss with 1 TBS lemon juice and 1 TBS brown rice syrup (to make a glaze-sauce). Garnish the top of the cake with the glazed strawberries and sprinkle with lemon zest.

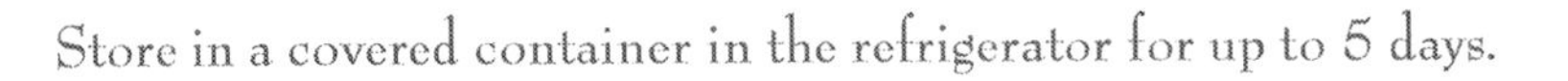

Store in a covered container in the refrigerator for up to 5 days.

Susanne says this cake is best if eaten with a spork.

CARROT DATE CAKE WITH CASHEW-CRANBERRY SAUCE

SERVES 9

2 cups grated carrots (340 grams or 12 oz. by weight)
1 cup barley flour (may substitute kamut flour)
1 cup whole wheat pastry flour
2 tsp baking powder
2 tsp baking soda
2 tsp cinnamon
¼ tsp freshly ground nutmeg
⅛ tsp ground cloves
½ cup macadamia nut oil
½ cup date syrup or agave nectar
¾ cup non-dairy milk
½ cup pitted, chopped dates
½ tsp unrefined sea salt or Himalayan salt
¾ cup rolled oats

Cashew Cranberry Sauce
1 cup cashews, raw
1 cup orange juice
2 pitted dates
¼ cup dried cranberries, softened in warm water, then drained (see note)*
1 TBS fresh lemon juice
½ tsp vanilla extract

Preheat oven to 350 F. Lightly oil a 9-inch spring-form pan and line with unbleached parchment paper. Grate the carrots and set aside. Whisk the flours, baking powder, soda and spices in a medium bowl. In a blender, blend the oil, sweetener, milk, dates and salt until emulsified. Add the wet ingredients to the dry and stir until flour is moistened. Fold in the oats and carrots. Pour batter into prepared pan and bake for 25-30 minutes or until done. Remove from oven and let cake cool completely on a rack.

Meanwhile, make the sauce by placing all sauce ingredients in a blender and blending until smooth. Add more orange juice or cashews depending on desired consistency. Serve cake drizzled with Cashew-Cranberry sauce.

Recipe continues on next page...

CARROT DATE CAKE WITH CASHEW-CRANBERRY SAUCE...

You can use ½ cup fresh or frozen cranberries in place of the dried cranberries.

It helps to have a powerful blender to reach the right consistency. I use a vita-mix. If you don't have one, try using soaked cashews or cashew butter for a smoother sauce.

Store in a covered container in the refrigerator for up to 5 days.

PLUM-BLUEBERRY CAKE WITH LEMON GLAZE

MAKES AN 8 X 8 CAKE OR A 9-INCH ROUND

2 TBS flax seeds (may substitute chia seeds)
¼ cup water
1 cup whole wheat pastry flour
½ cup barley flour
1 ½ tsp baking powder
¼ tsp unrefined sea salt or Himalayan salt
4 TBS macadamia nut oil
½ cup date syrup or agave nectar
½ cup unsweetened almond milk
2 TBS lemon juice
1 tsp vanilla extract
½ cup blueberries (fresh or frozen)
6 small plums (pears work too if plums aren't in season, but you'll only need 2)

Lemon Glaze
1 tsp lemon zest (organic, of course!)
3 TBS lemon juice
3 TBS brown rice syrup (may substitute yacon syrup), to taste (see note)*

Recipe continues on next page...

PLUM-BLUEBERRY CAKE WITH LEMON GLAZE...

Preheat oven to 350 F. Lightly oil your pan. Freshly grind the flax seeds or chia seeds in a clean coffee grinder. Remove and whisk ground seeds with ¼ cup of water in a small bowl and set aside to thicken.

Meanwhile, whisk together the flours, baking powder and salt in a medium bowl. In another bowl whisk together the oil, sweetener, almond milk, lemon juice and vanilla. Add the flax seed mixture to the wet ingredients and stir until well combined. Add all of the wet ingredients to the dry ingredients and stir just until combined. There will be some lumps and that's okay. Now gently fold in the blueberries and pour the batter into the prepared pan. Arrange plum slices on top in a decorative fashion. Place pan in oven and bake for 50 minutes or until done. Let cool before glazing.

Meanwhile, make the glaze by whisking together the lemon juice and syrup until desired sweetness is achieved. Drizzle this over cake when serving and then top with lemon zest.

I like using brown rice syrup in the glaze because it is thicker and has a richer flavor.

Store in a covered container in the refrigerator for up to 5 days.

FIGGY DIGGY CAKE

MAKES 9 SQUARES

This dense cake is a great breakfast food,
especially when topped with a little bit of almond butter. I dig it!

1 cup destemmed figs, dried
1 cup water
¼ cup macadamia nut oil
⅙ cup molasses
⅙ cup date syrup or agave nectar
⅓ cup applesauce, unsweetened
1 tsp vanilla extract
1 cup whole wheat pastry flour
1 cup barley flour (may substitute spelt flour)
2 tsp baking powder
½ tsp baking soda
¼ tsp unrefined sea salt or Himalayan salt
1 tsp cinnamon
½ tsp nutmeg
¼ tsp ground allspice

Lightly oil a 9x9 pan. Preheat oven to 350 F. Simmer figs in the water for 10 minutes. Remove figs with a slotted spoon, reserving the liquid in the pan, and let figs cool on a cutting board for a few minutes until cool enough to chop into smaller pieces (quartered, roughly). Whisk together the macadamia nut oil, molasses, sweetener, applesauce, vanilla and ⅓ cup of the reserved fig liquid. In a separate bowl whisk together the flours, baking powder, baking soda, salt and spices. Add the wet ingredients to the dry ingredients and stir just to combine. Gently fold in the figs and pour batter into the prepared pan. Bake for 35-40 minutes or until done. Let cool before cutting.

Store in a covered container in the refrigerator for up to 5 days.

GINGER-MOLASSES CAKE

MAKES 1 9X13 CAKE

Ginger is very helpful in aiding in digestion, relieving nausea, improving circulation, reducing inflammation and supporting the liver.

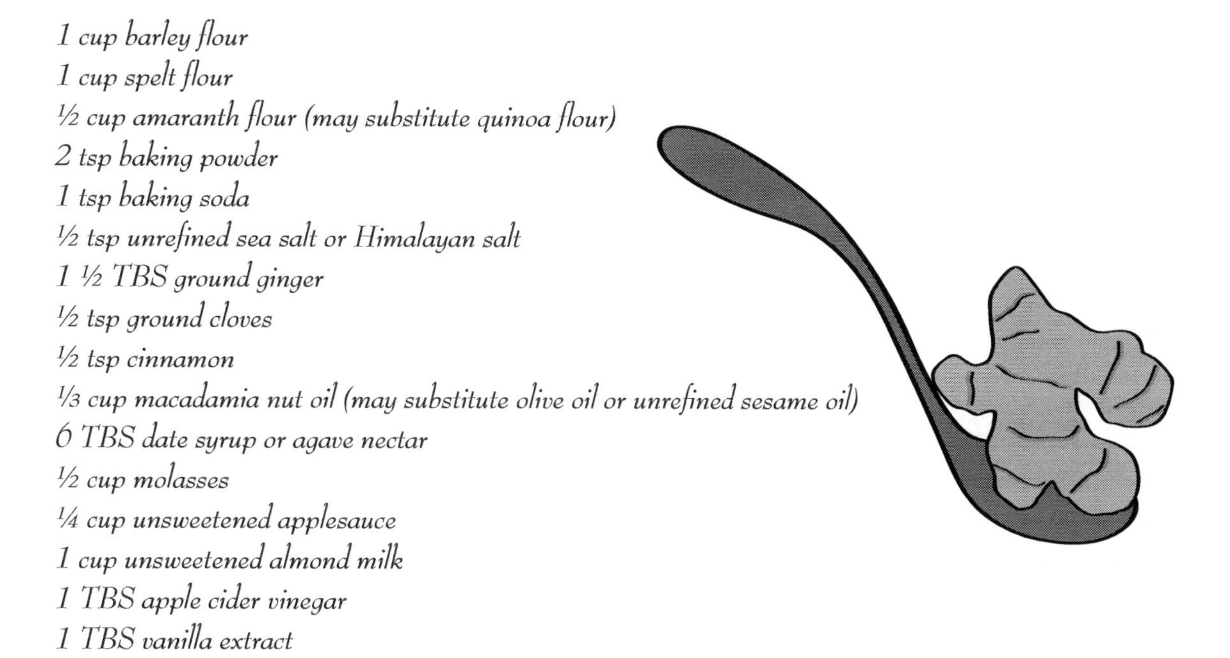

1 cup barley flour
1 cup spelt flour
½ cup amaranth flour (may substitute quinoa flour)
2 tsp baking powder
1 tsp baking soda
½ tsp unrefined sea salt or Himalayan salt
1 ½ TBS ground ginger
½ tsp ground cloves
½ tsp cinnamon
⅓ cup macadamia nut oil (may substitute olive oil or unrefined sesame oil)
6 TBS date syrup or agave nectar
½ cup molasses
¼ cup unsweetened applesauce
1 cup unsweetened almond milk
1 TBS apple cider vinegar
1 TBS vanilla extract

Preheat oven to 350 F. Lightly oil a 9 x 13 inch baking pan. Whisk together the flours, baking powder, baking soda, salt and spices. In a separate bowl whisk together the oil, sweetener, molasses, applesauce, milk, vinegar and vanilla extract until well combined. Add wet ingredients to dry, stirring gently with a wooden spoon, just until combined. **Don't over-stir the batter.** Immediately pour batter into prepared pan and bake for about 40-45 minutes or until done.

After the cake is baked if you'd like to top it with a "frosting," you could use homemade apple butter, pumpkin butter or a lemon cashew cream.

Store in a covered container in the refrigerator for up to 5 days.

GF

Gluten-Free Option

Use

2 ½ cups gluten-free flour mix (see pg. 377) instead of the barley flour
1 TBS gluten-free baking powder (see pg. 377) instead of regular baking powder

Then proceed as indicated above.

SWEETHEART CHOCOLATE BEET CAKE

MAKES 2 8-INCH ROUNDS OR 4 4-INCH ROUNDS * (SEE NOTE)

All my dreams came true with this cake. Named for the heart healthy properties of beets and the yummy sweetness of chocolate. Tell your sweethearts they can have their cake and eat it too.

1 ½ cup kamut flour (may substitute barley flour)
½ cup whole wheat pastry flour
½ cup cocoa powder, plus extra for dusting (see note)*
1 TBS baking soda
½ tsp unrefined sea salt or Himalayan salt
⅔ cup date syrup or agave nectar
⅔ cup water
*¼ cup olive oil or unrefined sesame oil (**not** toasted), plus extra for oiling pans*
2 TBS apple cider vinegar
1 tsp vanilla extract
1 ½ cups grated raw beets, packed (from 2 medium peeled beets) (see note)*
1 recipe of Pink Glaze (see pg. 439) or Chocolate Frosting (see pg. 441)

Preheat oven to 350 F. Prepare the cake pans by lightly oiling them then dusting with cocoa powder. Sift together the flours, cocoa powder, baking soda and salt in a large bowl. In another bowl, whisk the sweetener, water, oil, vinegar and vanilla together. Add wet ingredients to dry ingredients and stir to combine, but do not over stir the batter. Then gently fold in the beets. Pour batter into prepared pans and bake for 20-25 minutes or until done *(see notes on pan size and bake time). Let cool on a rack for 10 minutes then remove cakes from pans and let cool completely before frosting or glazing.

Please use a good quality dutch processed cocoa powder.

You could also substitute grated zucchini or carrot if you don't have beets. Chopped frozen spinach works too. But you'll have to think of a new name for the recipe.

Recipe continues on next page...

SWEETHEART CHOCOLATE BEET CAKE...

I sometimes like to make this in two pans, 8 inches round, then stack them between frosting. But they are pretty thin when made in the 8 inch pans so you may opt to use just one 8 or 9 inch pan and bake it a little longer to make one cake. If using the 4-inch dishes, bake for 13-18 minutes, and serve as individual cakes (no layers). Let cool then glaze (below) or frost (pg. 441).

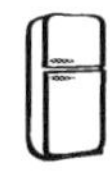

Store in a covered container in the refrigerator for up to 5 days.

Pink Glaze

1 cup **silken** *tofu, drained (try sprouted silken tofu if you can find it)*
¾ cup raw cashews, soaked for 4 -8 hours (to soften), then drained
½ cup date syrup, agave nectar, brown rice syrup or yacon syrup
2 TBS ground kudzu (see note)*
2 TBS beet juice (from taking grated raw beets and squeezing them over a bowl lined with a strainer)
⅛ tsp unrefined sea salt or Himalayan salt
1 tsp vanilla extract

Blend all glaze ingredients together in a blender until very smooth. Chill in the refrigerator for at least 1 hour before applying to cake.

If the glaze is thick you can spread it on the cake like a frosting; if it is thin you can drizzle it on like a glaze.

Kudzu root powder may sometimes need to be finely ground before using in a recipe. Do this with a mortar and pestle or in a clean coffee grinder.

Store in a covered container in the refrigerator for up to 5 days.

MEXICAN CHOCOLATE PUDDING CAKE

SERVES 6-8

I don't know if this qualifies as health food, but this a healthier option for those special occasions. Eat fruit as your everyday dessert.

1 cup kamut flour (may substitute barley flour)
1 TBS baking powder
¼ cup cocoa powder
½ tsp cinnamon
¼ tsp ground chile pepper powder (not chili powder)
¼ tsp unrefined sea salt or Himalayan salt
a dash of cayenne pepper
6 TBS date syrup or agave nectar
½ cup macadamia nut oil (may substitute olive oil)
6 TBS almond, soy or rice milk
1 tsp vanilla extract

Sauce
½ cup date syrup or agave nectar
¼ cup cocoa powder
dash of unrefined sea salt or Himalayan salt
1 ⅓ cups boiling water

Preheat oven to 350 F. Lightly oil an 8x5 inch loaf pan. Whisk together the flour, baking powder, cocoa, spices and salt. In a separate bowl, mix the sweetener, oil, milk and vanilla. Add the wet ingredients to the dry and stir until just mixed. Pour batter into the loaf pan. In another bowl, mix together the sweetener, cocoa powder and salt. Gently spread this on top of the batter mixture. Now carefully pour the boiling water over top. PLEASE: Do not attempt to mix this! Your patience will be rewarded. Place pan in oven and bake for 40 minutes.

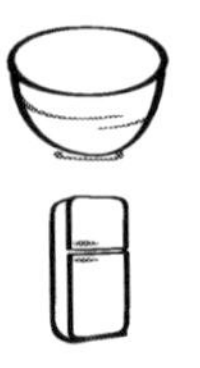

Serve warm.

Store in a covered container in the refrigerator for up to 5 days.

CHOCOLATE FILLED STRAWBERRIES

Gently hull out the center of the strawberries through the stem end with a small melon baller or paring knife. Fill with a teaspoon or so of dark chocolate bits/chips. Place strawberries in a muffin pan, cut side up, in a 400 F oven for just a few minutes until chocolate is melted. Then move to the refrigerator to let the chocolate set before serving.

Store in a covered container in the refrigerator for up to 2 days.

CHOCOLATE FROSTING OR SAUCE (GF)

MAKES ABOUT 1 ½ CUPS (ENOUGH TO FROST 1 CAKE)

Is this healthfood? Not necessarily but it's certainly better than most of the frostings out there which can be full of trans-fats, high fructose corn syrup and chemicals. I like this on the Sweetheart Chocolate Beet Cake.

1 cup cashew butter (may use half almond butter)
5 TBS date syrup, agave nectar, brown rice syrup or yacon syrup
7 TBS cocoa powder
2 tsp vanilla extract
⅛ tsp unrefined sea salt or Himalayan salt (to bring out the sweetness)
cashew or almond milk, about ½ cup

Place all ingredients except the milk in a blender and blend to combine. Stop and scrape down the sides of the blender and blend again while gradually adding milk through the top of the blender, one tablespoon at a time until the frosting comes together and appears spreadable.

The more liquid you add at the end the thinner it will become. Add slowly and if it ends up being too thin for a frosting then just call it a sauce. That works for me!

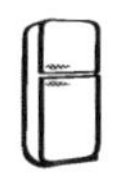

Store in a covered container in the refrigerator for up to 5 days.

PERSIMMON-GOJI "ICE CREAM"

SERVES 4

3 very ripe hachiya persimmons (see note)*
3 TBS goji berries, soaked in hot water to soften
4 TBS date syrup, agave nectar, brown rice syrup or yacon syrup
½ of a meyer lemon, juiced
⅛ tsp cinnamon, or to taste
⅔ cup unsweetened almond milk
mint leaves, for garnish

Freeze whole persimmons in freezer for at least 1 day. Remove from freezer 30 minutes before serving and let thaw on a cutting board for 30 minutes. Chop each persimmon into chunks, discarding the stems and seeds. Put the chunks into a blender with the goji berries (drain off the soaking water first), sweetener, lemon juice and cinnamon. Blend until chunks are broken up. Slowly add the almond milk while blending until smooth and creamy. Taste and add more sweetener if desired.

If you don't use very ripe hachiya persimmons it will not turn out. The hachiyas will be very, very soft when ripe. Under-ripe hachiyas are not sweet! Also, don't use fuju persimmons for this recipe because they are different and will not yield the same results.

Serve immediately in pretty bowls or champagne flutes. Garnish with mint leaves.

Store in a covered container in the freezer for up to two weeks. You may need to let thaw slightly to make scooping easier.

Appendix

THERAPEUTIC CHEF GUIDELINES FOR PREVENTING CANCER, HEART DISEASE AND DIABETES

Eat only foods that are nutrient dense, not nutrient negative. Processed foods are nutrient negative. Organic, whole plant foods are preferred.

Include a variety of colorful vegetables and fruits, preferably from your local, organic farmer's market or back yard. Eat a mixture of raw and lightly cooked produce.

Include green cruciferous vegetables at lunch and dinner to promote detoxification and prevent cancer and other diseases. Collard greens, kale, cabbage and chard are green, cruciferous and they provide healthy amounts of calcium and other minerals necessary for healthy bones.

Replace refined grains and flours with whole grains. No more enriched flour, white bread, bagels, white pasta or white rice.

Expand your horizons. Set aside wheat and try gluten-free whole grains such as brown rice, buckwheat, quinoa, amaranth and millet.

Eat beans and other legumes for protein. Beans are less expensive than meat and are a good source of fiber, protein and minerals. Plus they have no saturated fat or cholesterol.

Completely eliminate all dairy. Eat beans and greens for calcium and strong bones. Use unsweetened non-dairy milks when necessary.

Eliminate the bad fats (trans-fats, saturated fat from animals, and refined vegetable oils) and include small amounts of healthy fat at each meal (avocado, olives, nuts and seeds).

Avoid processed sugar, such as high fructose corn syrup, corn syrup and white sugar. Avoid artificial sweeteners. Enjoy foods in their natural state.

Avoid all processed soy foods (soy protein isolate, soy protein powder, TVP, MSG, etc.), and look for fermented whole soy foods such as miso, tempeh and natto.

Chew your food well; 50 times per mouthful.

POWERFOODS GLOSSARY

Eat Powerfoods for Prevention

Listed below is what I consider to be a short list of powerfoods, or superfoods; healing foods that should become common ingredients in your kitchen because of their nutrient dense profile and ability to boost immunity and fight illness. There are so many healthy foods out there, but I only had so much room in the book! I have favorites like broccoli, shiitakes, quinoa and sweet potatoes that I eat more often than others and you will too. Plus, you may discover additional powerfoods, like acai berries, freshly available to you if you live in Brazil. They would definitely make this list if they were more available to me in San Francisco. Anyway, this list is a good place to start if you want to increase the healing potential of your meals. If you aim to eat each of these foods in the course of a week (depending on the season) you should be doing pretty well in terms of staying well.

* Some of these may be new to you so this presents you with a reason to seek out something different. If you have trouble finding these ingredients at your local health food store please see the RESOURCES section for a list of websites from which you can order most of these foods.

Adzuki Beans (Aduki): Known as "the king of beans" in Japan, are small, oval-shaped red or brown, easy to digest beans. Like most beans, adzuki beans are rich in soluble fiber, which helps to eliminate cholesterol from the body. They are low in fat and a good source of magnesium, potassium, iron, zinc copper, manganese and vitamin B3.
Adzuki beans help reduce cholesterol, regulate blood pressure, and inhibit protease and other substances associated with tumor development. They help strengthen the kidney, bladder and reproductive functions. They also help detoxify the body and reduce swelling and edema. Use in salads, stews, spreads or as a main dish.

Agave Nectar: A syrup-like sweetener made from the agave cactus. It has a low glycemic index, which is important for people with diabetes. It can be used to sweeten any food or beverage by using 1/4 cup of agave in place of 1 cup of sugar or a 1:1 ratio in place of honey or maple syrup (which have a high glycemic index). **Yacon, Date** and **Brown Rice Syrups** may also be used in the same way as agave to sweeten foods without raising blood sugar levels. Please always buy **raw** and **organic** agave to avoid unhealthy imitations. Limit agave to 2 TBS/day (See pgs. 25, 374).

Asparagus: Is a great source of folate, which helps reduce heart disease. It is a very good source of potassium and has a diuretic effect that has been used historically to treat swelling, water retention and arthritis. Asparagus also has powerful anti-cancer properties. In the spring load up on flavor and nutrition by adding lightly steamed asparagus to any meal.

Astragalus: This traditional Chinese herb has been used for centuries to aid in the prevention of heart disease, cancer, colds and the flu, and can increase immune system functioning. Use in broths or as directed by your Traditional Chinese Medicine Doctor.

Barley: Choose hulled barley over pearled barley for increased fiber content and nutrition. Barley is beneficial in lowering blood sugar and insulin levels, and is used to lower total cholesterol. Use hulled barley to make grain dishes or mix with other grains, such as brown rice or kamut in your rice cooker. Use in stews and soups to add extra heartiness and nutty flavor. Look for barley flour to make wheat-free breads, pancakes, cookies and muffins.

Beans and Other Legumes: Beans, split peas and lentils are traditionally eaten around the world as an excellent source of protein, complex carbohydrates, and vitamins and minerals, especially calcium. Because they are low in fat and high in fiber they are associated with a lower incidence of heart disease, cancer and other degenerative diseases. They help lower cholesterol and keep blood sugar stable. Use as your protein source in any meal. **To increase the digestibility of beans**, soak 1 cup dried beans in plenty of filtered water for 4-8 hours (or up to 24 hours, if refrigerated). Drain and discard water and simmer beans in fresh, filtered water for the specified cooking time with a 5-inch piece of kombu seaweed. Skim away any foam that collects on top of the water and wait to add salt until the last few minutes of cooking. **Lentils**, my favorite legume, can be ready in as few as 20 minutes. No need to soak them, just rinse well, discarding any stones and simmer for 20 minutes. Use lentils to make dahl, stews, soups or mix with grains. Cooked lentils make a hearty "loaf" or "burger" and can also be used to make dips and spreads. Chilled lentils make great salads.

Beets: Beets are an amazing blood and liver purifier, good for treating anemia, good for improving blood and heart health, and good for maintaining proper bowel functioning. Use raw, steamed or roasted beets to add nutrition and color to any meal. Don't forget to use the beet greens too!

Blueberries: The blueberry has one of the highest concentrations of antioxidants found in a fruit. Blueberries have many health enhancing effects ranging from protection from heart disease, macular degeneration and gastrointestinal problems. Blueberries also help us fight against cancer, improve memory and slow the aging process. Please eat organic fresh (or frozen) berries daily as a snack, in a smoothie or add to just about any dish.

Broccoli: As a member of the cabbage family (Brassicaceae), this cruciferous vegetable has protective effects against heart disease and cancer. Broccoli is especially nourishing for the lungs and large intestine. Steam lightly to preserve the anti-cancer properties and to make it easier to digest.

Broccoli Sprouts: Made by sprouting the seeds of broccoli, broccoli sprouts contain 20-50 times the amount of sulforaphane glucosinolate, a powerful anti-cancer compound, than found in mature broccoli and other cruciferous vegetables. The sprouts look like alfalfa sprouts and can be used on sandwiches, in wraps and on salads. If you can't find a store that sells the sprouts order broccoli seeds, begin sprouting your own and eat daily as an easy way to help prevent cancer from forming in the body.

Buckwheat: Unrelated to wheat, and not actually a grain, buckwheat, is an edible fruit seed related to rhubarb, traditionally eaten in Russia, Eastern Europe and northern Asia. Roasted buckwheat is known as **kasha**. Buckwheat gives strong, warming energy and is a good blood-building food. This gluten-free 'grain' is beneficial for stabilizing the blood sugar and helps to reduce the risk of heart disease by improving cholesterol levels. Buckwheat is rich in B vitamins as well as phosphorus, magnesium, iron, zinc, copper and manganese. Buckwheat groats can be cooked as a hot breakfast cereal, prepared as a savory grain dish or used in soups. Look for soba noodles made from buckwheat and buckwheat flour to make hearty pancakes and other baked goods.

Burdock Root: Excellent for cleansing and purifying the blood, lungs, liver and kidneys. This root is used to treat arthritis, diabetes and liver disorders. Try this root in your next stew or stir-fry. Just scrub it well, no need to peel this funny looking vegetable, and cook it as you would carrots.

Cabbage: Part of the cruciferous family, one of the largest and most important vegetable families. Brassica or cruciferous vegetables, including cabbage, kale, broccoli, Brussels sprouts and cauliflower, are protective against cancer. Cabbage is particularly effective against lung, stomach and colon cancers. Cabbage is also beneficial for the stomach and can relieve ulcers and constipation. It is high in vitamin C and calcium and can be used for mental depression and irritability. It is the sulfur content of cabbage that is responsible for destroying intestinal parasites and purifying the blood. When applied as an external remedy, cabbage leaves will reduce fever, neutralize inflammation and relieve burns and bruises. Eat raw in salads and slaws or add to any grain or bean dish for some crunch. Cook gently for use in soups and grain dishes or stir-fries. Boiled or overcooked cabbage emits a sulfurous smell and can cause intestinal gas.

* Large amounts of the cruciferous family may need to be avoided in cases of thyroid deficiency (hypothyroidism) and low iodine. Check with your health care provider.

Chia Seeds: It was the third most important crop for the Aztecs, who recognized it as a "superfood" and prized it so highly that it was often used as currency. Chia seeds have more Omega-3 fatty acids than any other plant food including flax seeds. Chia seeds are about 20% protein. Use freshly ground chia seeds interchangeably with ground flax seeds in baking recipes in place of eggs to act like a binder.

Cilantro: This popular herb is great for aiding in digestion and soothing nausea, inflammation, arthritis, headaches, and stress. Mince the leaves and add at the end of cooking or add to spreads and purees.

Daikon: This pearly white root, similar in shape to a carrot but belonging to the cruciferous family, is used to strengthen the liver and lungs. It aids digestion and is effective against bacterial and fungal infections. It is also helpful in preventing cancer. Scrub and use as you would carrots.

Date Syrup: Made by blending boiled dates and water, this liquid sweetener is similar to agave and used to replace honey and maple syrup. It has a low glycemic index. (See pgs. 376 and 445)

Flax Seeds and Flax Seed Oil: A great source of Omega-3 essential fatty acid, which helps to maintain healthy blood, arteries, nerves and skin. It helps support brain, hormone and immune functions and helps break down cholesterol. The seeds are preferred over the oil because of their fiber, protein and healthy fat content. To use flax seeds you must buy them whole and grind them fresh immediately before consuming. Sprinkle ground flax seeds on oatmeal or other grains, beans and salads or whisk together with liquid and use as an egg replacement in low temperature baking. The flax seed oil can be used in salad dressing recipes or added to smoothies, but not as a cooking oil because heating will destroy the Omega 3 essential fatty acid. Keep both seeds and oil stored in the refrigerator to prevent rancidity.

Fermented Foods: Tempeh, miso, shoyu, natto, and traditionally made pickles, raw sauerkraut and kimchi offer many health benefits, such as better nutrient assimilation and contain the good bacteria (flora) necessary for healthy digestion. The good bacteria in these foods can inhibit the action of bad bacteria in the intestines. By reducing harmful bacteria in the digestive tract, fermented foods can reduce the risk of colon cancer and a variety of intestinal disorders. Not all fermented foods are created equal. Buy these foods at health food stores and keep refrigerated.

Garlic and Onions: Members of the allium family, they are beneficial in preventing cancer, lowering cholesterol and have antioxidant, antibiotic, antifungal and antiviral properties. To activate the medicinal properties you must press, smash or crush garlic before using. Smashed garlic and chopped onions **must** sit out on your cutting board for at least 10 minutes before cooking if you want the healing properties to remain active.

Ginger: This underground stem, or rhizome, is extremely beneficial in promoting digestion and is a remedy for nausea. It improves overall health, reduces inflammation, increases circulation, helps support the liver, and helps to relieve colds and the flu. Add fresh ginger to any dish, sweet or savory. Also great in smoothies or made into tea.

Goji Berries: (aka Wolf berries or Lycium berries) Tiny dried red berries used for centuries in the Himalayas to promote a long, vigorous, happy life free from disease. They are used to help prevent cancer, protect the liver, improve visual acuity, lower blood pressure and cholesterol, strengthen muscles and bones, and aid in the treatment of diabetes. They are a rich source of the antioxidant beta-carotene, a complete protein and high in iron. Add these at the end of cooking to any dish including grains, soups, oatmeal or in your trail mix!

Hato Mugi: (aka Job's tears) This barley-like grain is used to purify blood, to reduce inflammation, and to reduce the risk of cancer. It cooks similar to brown rice. Use alone or combine with other grains.

Hemp Seeds: These powerhouses contain all 20 known amino acids including all 9 essential amino acids, thus making them complete proteins. They are an excellent source of the essential fatty acids Omega 3, 6 and GLA in a perfectly balanced 3:1 ratio of omega 6 to omega 3. Plus, the seeds contain calcium, vitamin E, magnesium, potassium, iron and zinc. All of these nutrients help to lower bad LDL cholesterol, help lower blood pressure, improve cardiovascular function, help boost the immune system, increase energy and reduce inflammation and arthritis. The seeds can be purchased raw (not roasted) and shelled and stored in your freezer or refrigerator. You won't need to grind hemp seeds like you do with flax seeds and chia seeds. Use shelled hemp seeds to add healthy protein and fat to smoothies, dips, spreads or sprinkle on any salad, grain or bean dish. Whip up hempseed milk in a flash for an alternative to cow's milk in any recipe. Hemp seed oil is also available but the seeds are preferred because of their fiber, protein and mineral content. Cooking with or heating the seeds or the oil can alter the molecular structure of the oil and result in the production of unhealthy trans-fatty acids. This is also true of flax seeds and its oil. Keep seeds and oil refrigerated.

Himalayan Salt: This uncontaminated natural salt is over 250 million years old and contains all of the 84 elements necessary for optimal health, while being free of any toxins or pollutants found in other salts. Common table salt has been stripped of beneficial minerals, refined and processed with chemicals that pollute your body and wreak havoc on your health. **Unrefined sea salt** may also be used in place of common table salt if you can't find Himalayan salt. Although these salts are better for you than the refined stuff you should stay in the habit of not over-salting your food.

Kimchee/Kimchi: A naturally fermented or pickled cabbage that is used to aid digestion. It is a rich source of enzymes and healthy bacteria/flora as long as it is **raw** and not heated or pasteurized.

Kale: A dark, green leafy vegetable in the cruciferous family, with tight, curly leaves and a hard, fibrous stalk. It is best in the fall and winter months when it is more tender and sweet. Kale is most noted for its calcium content and bioavailability of calcium. Researchers reported that the calcium in kale is absorbed more efficiently by the body than the calcium contained in milk from cows. Healthy calcium consumption from kale and other green leafy vegetables is linked to healthy bones and teeth and a decreased risk for osteoporosis. Kale is rich in anti-oxidants and phytochemicals, which help protect against macular degeneration and colon cancer. Young kale leaves can be used in salad. Mature dinosaur, curly or Russian kale is best steamed or lightly sautéed with a squeeze of lemon at the end of cooking for added flavor. You can also add raw kale leaves to smoothies.

Kombu: a large, thick sea vegetable of the kelp family with a mild taste and firm texture. It strengthens the blood and eliminates toxic wastes (including radioactivity) from the body. Kombu also has anti-tumor properties. Always add a 5-inch piece to every pot of beans (and grains) to help aid in the digestion of beans. After cooking, mince the kombu and add to any dish.

Millet: Millet is the only true alkaline-forming grain and is traditionally eaten in China, India, Africa and other parts of the world. This gluten-free grain has a rich amino-acid content, is high in iron and is easy to digest. Its mild, sweet taste gives balanced energy that is helpful for regulating blood sugar levels.

Miso: Miso is a thick paste made from fermented soybeans and a grain, such as rice or barley. Miso comes in many flavors depending on the aging process and other ingredients added. Light-colored misos (mellow, white or sweet) are more delicate with less sodium, while darker-colored misos are stronger and more pungent. There is also a chickpea miso, which is soy-free. Miso is an anti-carcinogen and body detoxifier used to clean and rejuvenate the body as a whole. In addition to helping to fight cancer it is beneficial in preventing heart disease and reducing the effects of radiation, chemotherapy and pollution. As a fermented food, miso contains live cultures and enzymes. Lactobacillus and other "good bacteria" help to restore the flora in our intestines, aid in the digestion and assimilation of all foods, and have been shown to ward off and destroy harmful microorganisms, thereby creating a healthy digestive system. Boiling miso destroys the beneficial bacteria and digestive enzymes so **add at the end of cooking**. Keep miso refrigerated. Use to season soups, dressings, sauces and spreads.

Parsley: Use this popular herb to purify the blood, aid in digestion, treat ear infections and to freshen breath. It is loaded with vitamin A and C, and iron. Add fresh parsley to any vegetable dish or in dressings and dips.

Pomegranate: High in Vitamin C, iron, calcium, antioxidants and fiber. Research suggests that pomegranates may help fight heart disease, diabetes and cancer; improve eyesight; and treat diarrhea and urinary tract infections. The arils (seed casings) are used to add a texture and sweetness to salads and grain dishes. As always, choose the whole fruit over bottled juice.

Quinoa: This grain-like crop is the only 'grain' that is a complete protein, aka "The Mother Grain", discovered by the Incas. It is ideal food for athletes due to its rich and balanced nutrient profile. It contains more protein than any other grain; healthy amounts of fiber; all the essential amino acids; and iron, calcium, phosphorus, and vitamins B and E. It is easy to digest and easy to prepare. Rinse well to remove the bitter saponin coating and then cook just as you would white rice.

Shiitake Mushroom: Used to help strengthen, detoxify and boost the immune system. These mushrooms have antiviral and antitumor qualities and help lower cholesterol. They are used to help fight AIDS, cancer and candida; increase energy; eliminate worms and cure the common cold. They are rich in vitamins D, B2, and B12. Shiitakes contain an anti-cancer compound called lentinan, which helps stimulate the immune system to clear the body of tumor cells.

Sweet Potatoes: Also known as the 'protector of the children' in eastern Africa, it is one of the most nutritious vegetables around. Sweet potatoes boast an impressive amount of the anti-oxidant beta carotene, as well as vitamin C, vitamin B6, fiber and many other nutrients, which help to boost immunity, decrease inflammation and help fight cancer. They are easy to digest and soothing to the stomach and intestines. Sweet potatoes come in many varieties and colors such as cream, yellow, orange and purple. The orange colored root vegetable labeled as a 'yam' at your grocery store is actually a type of sweet potato. Neither is in the same family as white potatoes and even though sweet potatoes are sweet they have a lower glycemic index than the russet potato, which means they are beneficial for maintaining steady blood sugar levels even for people with diabetes.

Tempeh: Tempeh, a food native to Indonesia, is made from cooked whole soybeans that have been inoculated with Rhizopus oligosporus or Rgizopus oryzae spores and incubated to achieve a controlled fermentation. Because it is a fermented, whole soy food, it has many health benefits compared to unfermented and refined soy foods, which have little to no medicinal value. High in isoflavones and phytoestrogens, tempeh helps protect against heart disease, cancer and other serious diseases. Depending on the spores used to ferment tempeh, it may contain vitamin B12, an important vitamin that can be difficult to obtain from foods if eating a strict plant-based diet. Tempeh also contains the essential fatty acid, Omega 3. Tempeh is not to be eaten raw. It must be boiled for 15 minutes in order for it to be digested. Once boiled, tempeh can be marinated, baked, grated, simmered, sautéed and grilled. It is used in place of meat in many recipes and contains more protein per serving than hamburger but no harmful saturated fat and cholesterol.

Turmeric: Turmeric (aka curcumin) has long been used in both Chinese and Ayurvedic medicine to relieve arthritis pain by reducing inflammation. It also enhances digestion and liver function and is helpful in relieving heartburn, ulcers and gallstones. Turmeric may also be applied directly to the skin for eczema, cold sores and to speed wound healing.

Umeboshi Plum: Technically a Japanese apricot, the umeboshi plum is one of the most important foods in macrobiotics. Sour, unripe plums are sun dried and then fermented in salt with shiso (perilla) leaves, until pickled. The shiso acts as a natural preservative and turns the plums a pink color. Umeboshi plums are used to treat acidic conditions helping to keep the body in a healthy alkaline state. Eat one plum to help allieviate symptoms of colds, flu, fatigue, muscle soreness, migraines, heartburn, indigestion, morning sickness and hangovers. They are also useful in treating many chronic illnesses, such as cancer, because many illnesses are due to an acidic body. Umeboshi plums are used in cooking to add salty tart flavors to foods. The plums must be pitted before using. Then puree and add to any dressing recipe or sauce in place of salt, lemon and vinegar. Spread umeboshi plum paste on corn on the cob instead of butter. The liquid produced from aging the salted plums is bottled as "umeboshi vinegar." Although it is not a true vinegar, it can be used in place of other vinegars to add a sour, salty flavor to dishes. Please buy umeboshi plums at a health food store in the macrobiotic section to avoid cheap imitations.

Walnuts: Full of protein, healthy Omega 3 fatty acid, fiber and antioxidants such as vitamin E, this nut should be included in your whole plant-foods diet to help reduce the risk of cancer and heart disease and to lower blood pressure and bad LDL cholesterol. Omega 3 EFA also promotes better cognitive functioning and reduces inflammation in the body (arthritis, asthma and eczema). One quarter cup of raw walnuts is all you need in a day to get your dose of Omega 3 essential fatty acid. For those allergic to nuts try substituting hemp or pumpkin seeds for similar health benefits.

RESOURCES

Books, DVD's and Websites where you can find additional information on the topic of food and how it relates to health, the environment, the farmers and the animals.

Books and DVD's

The China Study, T. Colin Campbell, PhD
Reversing Heart Disease, Dr. Esselstyn
Neal Barnard's Program for Reversing Diabetes, Neal Barnard, M.D.
Breaking the Food Seduction, Neal Barnard, M.D.
Building Bone Vitality, Amy Lanou, Ph.D and Michael Castleman
The Food Revolution, John Robbins
Healthy at 100, John Robbins
Diet for a New America, John Robbins
Fast Food Nation, Eric Schlosser
In Defense of Food, Michael Pollan
Omnivore's Dilemma, Michael Pollan
Cancer Prevention Diet, Michio Kushi
Uncertain Peril, Claire Hope Cummings on GMO's
Seeds of Deception, Jeffrey M. smith
Food Politics: How the Food Industry Influences Nutrition and Health, Marion Nestle
Any book by Michio and Aveline Kushi (Macrobiotics)
Thrive, Brendan Brazier (Plant-based nutrition for athletes)
World Peace Diet, Will Tuttle, Ph. D
Skinny Bitch, Rory Freedman and Kim Barnouin
Dr. McDougall's Money Saving Medical Advice (DVD)
Super Size Me (DVD)
Sustainable Table: What's on your plate? (DVD)
Food Inc. (DVD)
Processed People (DVD)
Healing Cancer from Inside Out (DVD)
The Rave Diet (DVD)
The Future of Food, by Deborah Koons Garcia (DVD) on the controversy over genetically modified foods.

Websites for More Information, Recipes and for Ordering Products

www.cancerproject.org (Information about nutrition for cancer prevention and survival)
www.pcrm.org (Physician's Committee for Responsible Medicine)
www.foodforlifeTV.org (Interactive webcasts on diabetes and diet)
www.drmcdougall.com (order his books, attend his workshops and sign up for newsletter)
www.organicconsumers.org (sign up for free e-newsletter)
www.nutritionMD.org (find diet and nutrition information for any illness)
www.edenfoods.com (great website for recipes and ordering macrobiotic ingredients)
www.happycow.net (to find plant-based restaurants in almost any city)
www.organicconsumers.org (for the latest information on organic foods, products, GMO foods, food safety and health).
www.ucusa.org (Union of Concerned Scientists)
www.peta.org (People for the Ethical Treatment of Animals)
www.saynotogmos.org (reasons why you should avoid GMO foods)
www.communitygarden.org (to locate a community garden near you)
www.informedeating.org (Center for Informed Food Choices)
www.localharvest.com (Directory of CSA's, farmer's markets)
www.sunfood.com (order superfoods such as goji berries, mesquite meal, yacon syrup)
www.znaturalfoods.com (order superfoods, green powders, teas, spices, oils, etc.)
www.bearwallowherbs.com (for herbal first aid kit, tinctures and glycerites)
www.republicoftea.com for buying tea seed oil
www.arrowheadmills.elsstore.com for buying whole grain flours

Index

EASY RECIPES FOR THE BEGINNER COOK

Maybe you're not a novice in the kitchen, perhaps you just don't have a lot of time to cook, or maybe you don't live close to a health food store. Below is a list of recipes that are quick and easy using ingredients that you should be able to find at most supermarkets.

And here's another tip...you don't always have to use a recipe to eat healthy meals. One week, while writing this book, I was so busy that I had no time to think about cooking (ironic, isn't it). I put 1 cup of millet and 1 cup of red lentils (both rinsed and drained) in my rice cooker with 4 cups of water and a strip of kombu seaweed. Pressed the button and went back to my computer. When I came back into the kitchen later the millet and lentils were perfectly cooked with hardly any work on my part. I used this whole grain and legume mixture for the next few days as the center of my meal. In the mornings it could be reheated as a porridge and topped with dried fruit and nuts and non-dairy milk. For lunches and dinners I heated the mixture and served it over a bed of arugula and topped it with sliced tomatoes, avocado and fresh lemon juice. One day I used it as a base in a burrito and added black beans, salsa, salad greens and a little avocado. No recipe required. Eating healthy can be as easy or as complicated as you want it to be.

Don't be intimidated if you are not familiar with some of the ingredients used in this book. You'll get there eventually. Start with these easy recipes listed below and add a new ingredient to your shopping cart each week. If you have trouble finding certain ingredients ask your local health food store if they can start carrying them, or find a place on-line where you can order them (see resources on pg. 453). So, don't delay! Start eating healthy today!

EASY RECIPES FOR THE BEGINNER COOK...

FOOD REMEDIES FOR ILLNESS PREVENTION

Arthritis

Cancer

FOOD REMEDIES FOR ILLNESS PREVENTION...

Diabetes

Adzuki Beans: To Spread…or Not 293
Apple Cider Vinegar Water 89
Black Bean Soup with Sweet Potato and Greens 115
Fava Bean and Dandelion Greens Over Barley 271
Green Tea 85
Kitchari 103
Lentil Porridge 379
Lentil Vegetable Soup 131
Louisiana Black-Eyed Peas 292
Nettle Soup 106
Nettle Tea 81
Quinoa with Saffron, Lemon and Asparagus 275
Rice with Yellow Split Peas and Garlic 354
Simple Curried Beans and Broccoli 290
Simple Lentil and Herb Salad 283
Spinach Onion "Quesadillas" 329
Tempeh Breakfast Sausage 410
Turkish Lentil Balls 336
Tuscan Beans and Greens 291
White Bean Soup with Rosemary and Lemon 117
Yellow Split Pea-Yam Stew 125

Digestion

Adzuki Beans: To Spread…or Not 293
Apple Cider Vinegar Water 89
Barley Lemonade 87
Chai Tea 81
Cleansing Ginger Ale 89
Daikon Digestion Dish 220
Happy Tummy Tea 80
Kimchi or Kimchee 215
Kitchari 103
Lemon Verbena-Mint Tea 82
Marrakesh Spice Blend 198
Rosemary-Ginger-Lemonade with Berries and Mint 86
Simple Lentil and Herb Salad 283
Simple Rice Congee (Jook) 101
Sweet Sesame Ginger Miso Sauce 167
Ume-Shoyu-Kudzu Tea: The Macrobiotic "Cure All" 84

Heart Disease

Ancient Grains Over Mixed Greens 266
Apple Cider Vinegar Water 89
Beets in Umeboshi Vinegar 222

Immune System

GLUTEN-FREE RECIPES

GLUTEN-FREE RECIPES...

Breakfast & Baking

Desserts

Dips & Spreads

Dressings, Sauces & Condiments

GLUTEN-FREE RECIPES...

GLUTEN-FREE RECIPES...

GLUTEN-FREE RECIPES...

Whole Grains

RECIPE INDEX BY TITLE

Beans & Other Legumes

Beverages

RECIPE INDEX BY TITLE...

Desserts

Dips & Spreads

Salads

Vegetables

Whole Grains

RECIPE INDEX BY TITLE...

GENERAL INDEX

11640747R0028

Made in the USA
Lexington, KY
21 October 2011